MEMORIES, DREAMS, REFLECTIONS

by C. G. Jung

RECORDED AND EDITED BY

Aniela Jaffé

TRANSLATED FROM THE GERMAN BY

Richard and Clara Winston

REVISED EDITION

VINTAGE BOOKS

A Division of Random House, Inc.

NEW YORK

VINTAGE BOOKS EDITION, APRIL 1989

Copyright © 1961, 1962, 1963 by Random House, Inc.

All rights reserved under International and Pan-American Copyright
Conventions. Published in the United States by Random House, Inc.,
New York. Distributed in Canada by Random House of Canada
Limited, Toronto. Originally published by Pantheon Books, a division
of Random House, Inc., in 1963. Final revised edition in hardcover
published by Pantheon Books, February 1973.

Originally published under the title "Erinnerungen
Träume Gedanken."

Library of Congress Cataloging-in-Publication Data
Jung, C. G. (Carl Gustav), 1875-1961.
   [Erinnerungen, Träume, Gedanken. English]
   Memories, dreams, reflections / by C.G. Jung; recorded and edited
by Aniela Jaffé; translated from the German by Richard and Clara
Winston.—Rev. ed.
   p.   cm.
   Originally published under title: Erinnerungen Träume
Gedanken.
   Bibliography: p.
   Includes index.
   ISBN 0-679-72395-1
   1. Jung, C. G. (Carl Gustav), 1856-1939.   2. Psychoanalysts—
Switzerland—Biography.   I. Jaffé, Aniela.   II. Title.
BF109.J8A3   1989
150.19'54—dc19
[B]   88-37040
                                                           CIP

Manufactured in the United States of America
3579F864

Introduction

> He looked at his own Soul
> with a Telescope. What seemed
> all irregular, he saw and
> shewed to be beautiful
> Constellations; and he added
> to the Consciousness hidden
> worlds within worlds.
>
> COLERIDGE, *Notebooks*

THIS BOOK had its inception during the Eranos Conference held in Ascona in the summer of 1956. There the publisher Kurt Wolff, in conversation with friends from Zürich, spoke of his wish to have Pantheon Books of New York publish a biography of Carl Gustav Jung. Dr. Jolande Jacobi, one of C. G. Jung's associates, proposed that the office of biographer be entrusted to me.

All of us were well aware that the task would by no means be an easy one. Jung's distaste for exposing his personal life to the public eye was well known. Indeed, he gave his consent only after a long period of doubt and hesitation. But once he had done so, he allotted to me an entire afternoon once a week for our work together. Considering the press of his regular program of work, and how easily he tired—for even then he was past eighty—that was a great deal of time.

We began in the spring of 1957. It had been proposed that

the book be written not as a "biography," but in the form of an "autobiography," with Jung himself as the narrator. This plan determined the form of the book, and my first task consisted solely in asking questions and noting down Jung's replies. Although he was rather reticent at the beginning, he soon warmed to the work. He began telling about himself, his development, his dreams, and his thoughts with growing interest.

By the end of the year Jung's affirmative attitude toward our joint efforts led to a decisive step. After a period of inner turbulence, long-submerged images out of his childhood rose to the surface of his mind. He sensed their connection with ideas in the works he had written in his old age, but could not grasp it clearly. One morning he informed me that he wanted to set down his recollections of his childhood directly. By this time he had already told me a good many of his earliest memories, but there were still great gaps in the story.

This decision was as gratifying as it was unexpected, for I knew how great a strain writing was for Jung. At his advanced age he would not undertake anything of the sort unless he felt it was a "task" imposed on him from within. Here was evidence that the "autobiography" was justified in terms of Jung's own inner life.

Some time after this new development, I noted down a remark of his: "A book of mine is always a matter of fate. There is something unpredictable about the process of writing, and I cannot prescribe for myself any predetermined course. Thus this 'autobiography' is now taking a direction quite different from what I had imagined at the beginning. It has become a necessity for me to write down my early memories. If I neglect to do so for a single day, unpleasant physical symptoms immediately follow. As soon as I set to work they vanish and my head feels perfectly clear."

In April 1958 Jung finished the three chapters on his childhood, school days, and years at the university. At first he called them, "On the Early Events of My Life." These chapters ended with the completion of his medical studies in 1900.

This, however, was not the sole direct contribution that Jung made to the book. In January 1959 he was at his country house in Bollingen. He devoted every morning to reading chosen chapters of our book, which had meanwhile been hammered into shape. When he returned the chapter, "On Life after Death," he said to me, "Something within me has been touched. A gradient has formed, and I must write." Such was the origin of "Late Thoughts," in which he voiced his deepest and perhaps his most far-reaching convictions.

In the summer of that same year of 1959, likewise in Bollingen, Jung wrote the chapter on Kenya and Uganda. The section on the Pueblo Indians is taken from an unpublished and unfinished manuscript that deals with general questions of the psychology of primitives.

In order to complete the chapters "Sigmund Freud" and "Confrontation with the Unconscious," I incorporated a number of passages from a seminar delivered in 1925, in which Jung spoke for the first time of his inner development.

The chapter "Psychiatric Activities" is based on conversations between Jung and the young assistant doctors of the Zürich mental hospital of Burghölzli in 1956. At that time one of his grandsons was working as a psychiatrist there. The conversations took place in Jung's house in Küsnacht.

Jung read through the manuscript of this book and approved it. Occasionally he corrected passages or added new material. In turn, I have used the records of our conversations to supplement the chapters he wrote himself, have expanded his sometimes terse allusions, and have eliminated repetitions. The further the book progressed, the closer became the fusion between his work and mine.

The genesis of the book to some extent determined its contents. Conversation or spontaneous narration is inevitably casual, and that tone has carried over to the entire "autobiography." The chapters are rapidly moving beams of light that only fleetingly illuminate the outward events of Jung's life and work. In recompense, they transmit the atmosphere of his intellectual world and the experience of a man to whom the psyche was a profound reality. I often asked Jung for specific data on outward happenings, but I asked in vain. Only the spiritual essence of his life's experience remained in his memory, and this alone seemed to him worth the effort of telling.

Far more significant than the difficulties of formal organization of the text were those prior obstacles, of a more personal kind, to which Jung refers in a letter to a friend of his student days. Replying to a request, in the latter part of 1957, to set down the memories of his youth, he wrote:

". . . You are quite right. When we are old, we are drawn back, both from within and from without, to memories of youth. Once before, some thirty years ago, my pupils asked me for an account of how I arrived at my conceptions of the unconscious. I fulfilled this request by giving a seminar.[1] During the last years the suggestion has come to me from various quarters that I should do something akin to an autobiography. I have been unable to conceive of my doing anything of the sort. I know too many autobiographies, with their self-deceptions and downright lies, and I know too much about the impossibility of self-portrayal, to want to venture on any such attempt.

"Recently I was asked for autobiographical information, and in the course of answering some questions I discovered hidden in my memories certain objective problems which seem to call for closer examination. I have therefore weighed the matter and come to the conclusion that I shall fend off other obligations long enough to take up the very first beginnings of my life and consider them in an objective fashion. This task has proved so difficult and singular that in order to go ahead with it, I have had to promise myself that the results would not be published in my lifetime. Such a promise seemed to me essential in order to assure for myself the necessary detachment and calm. It became clear that all the memories which have remained vivid to me had to do with emotional experiences that arouse uneasiness and passion in the mind—scarcely the best condition for an objective account! Your letter 'naturally' came at the very moment when I had virtually resolved to take the plunge.

"Fate will have it—and this has always been the case with

[1] The 1925 seminar mentioned earlier.

me—that all the 'outer' aspects of my life should be accidental. Only what is interior has proved to have substance and a determining value. As a result, all memory of outer events has faded, and perhaps these 'outer' experiences were never so very essential anyhow, or were so only in that they coincided with phases of my inner development. An enormous part of these 'outer' manifestations of my life has vanished from my memory —for the very reason, so it has seemed to me, that I participated in them with all my energies. Yet these are the very things that make up a sensible biography: persons one has met, travels, adventures, entanglements, blows of destiny, and so on. But with few exceptions all these things have become for me phantasms which I barely recollect and which my mind has no desire to reconstruct, for they no longer stir my imagination.

"On the other hand, my recollection of 'inner' experiences has grown all the more vivid and colorful. This poses a problem of description which I scarcely feel able to cope with, at least for the present. Unfortunately, I cannot, for these reasons, fulfill your request, greatly as I regret my inability to do so. . . ."

This letter characterizes Jung's attitude. Although he had already "resolved to take the plunge," the letter ends with a refusal. To the day of his death the conflict between affirmation and rejection was never entirely settled. There always remained a residue of skepticism, a shying away from his future readers. He did not regard these memoirs as a scientific work, nor even as a book by himself. Rather, he always spoke and wrote of it as "Aniela Jaffé's project," to which he had made contributions. At his specific request it is not to be included in his *Collected Works*.

Jung has been particularly reticent in speaking of his encounters with people, both public figures and close friends and relatives. "I have spoken with many famous men of my time, the great ones in science and politics, with explorers, artists and writers, princes and financial magnates; but if I am to be honest I must say that only a few such encounters have been significant experiences for me. Our meetings were like those of ships on the high seas, when they dip their flags to one another. Usually, too, these persons had something to ask of me which I am not at liberty to divulge. Thus I have retained no memories of them, however important these persons may be in the eyes of the world. Our meetings were without portent; they soon faded away and bore no deeper consequences. But of those relationships which were vital to me, and which came to me like memories of far-off times, I cannot speak, for they pertain not only to my innermost life but also to that of others. It is not for me to fling open to the public eye doors that are closed forever."

The paucity of outward events is, however, amply compensated by the account of Jung's inner experiences, and by a rich harvest of thoughts which, as he himself says, are an integral part of his biography. This is true first and foremost of his religious ideas, for this book contains Jung's religious testament.

Jung was led to a confrontation with religious questions by a number of different routes. There were his childhood visions, which brought him face to face with the reality of religious experience and remained with him to the end of his life. There was his insuppressible curiosity concerning everything that had to do with the contents of the psyche and its manifestations—the urge to know which characterized his scientific work. And, last but not least, there was his conscience as a physician. Jung regarded himself primarily as a doctor, a psychiatrist. He was well aware that the patient's religious attitude plays a crucial part in the therapy of psychic illnesses. This observation coincided with his discovery that the psyche spontaneously produces images with a religious content, that it is "by nature religious." It also became apparent to him that numerous neuroses spring from a disregard for this fundamental characteristic of the psyche, especially during the second half of life.

Jung's concept of religion differed in many respects from traditional Christianity—above all in his answer to the problem of evil and his conception of a God who is not entirely good or kind. From the viewpoint of dogmatic Christianity, Jung was distinctly an "outsider." For all his world-wide fame, this verdict was forcibly borne in upon him by the reactions to his writings. This grieved him, and here and there in this book he expresses the disappointment of an investigator who felt that his religious ideas were not properly understood. More than once he said grimly, "They would have burned me as a heretic in the Middle Ages!" Only since his death have theologians in increasing numbers begun to say that Jung was indubitably an outstanding figure in the religious history of our century.

Jung explicitly declared his allegiance to Christianity, and the most important of his works deal with the religious problems of the Christian. He looked at these questions from the standpoint of psychology, deliberately setting a bound between it and the theological approach. In so doing he stressed the necessity of understanding and reflecting, as against the Christian demand for faith. He took this necessity for granted, as one of the essential features of life. "I find that all my thoughts circle around God like the planets around the sun, and are as irresistibly attracted by Him. I would feel it to be the grossest sin if I were to oppose any resistance to this force," he wrote in 1952 to a young clergyman.

This book is the only place in his extensive writings in which Jung speaks of God and his personal experience of God. While he was writing of his youthful rebellion against the church, he once said, "At that time I realized that God—for me, at least— was one of the most immediate experiences." In his scientific works Jung seldom speaks of God; there he is at pains to use the term "the God-image in the human psyche." This is no contradiction. In the one case his language is subjective, based upon inner experience; in the other it is the objective language of scientific inquiry. In the first case he is speaking as an individual, whose thoughts are influenced by passionate, powerful feelings, intuitions, and experiences of a long and unusually rich life; in the second, he is speaking as the scientist who consciously restricts himself to what may be demonstrated and supported by evidence. As a scientist, Jung is an empiricist. When Jung speaks of his religious experiences in this book, he is assuming that his readers are willing to enter into his point of view. His subjective statements will be acceptable only to those who have had similar experiences—or, to put it another way, to those in whose psyche the God-image bears the same or similar features.

Although Jung was active and affirmative in the making of the "autobiography," for a long time his attitude toward the prospect of its publication remained—quite understandably—highly critical and negative. He rather dreaded the reaction of the public, for one thing because of the candor with which he had revealed his religious experiences and ideas, and for another because the hostility aroused by his book, *Answer to Job*, was still too close, and the incomprehension or misunderstanding of the world in general too painful. "I have guarded this material all my life, and have never wanted it exposed to the world; for if it is assailed, I shall be affected even more than in the case of my other books. I do not know whether I shall be so far removed from this world that the arrows of criticism will no longer reach me and that I shall be able to bear the adverse reactions. I have suffered enough from incomprehension and from the isolation one falls into when one says things that people do not understand. If the Job book met with so much misunderstanding, my 'memoirs' will have an even more unfortunate fate. The 'autobiography' is my life, viewed in the light of the knowledge I have gained from my scientific endeavors. Both are one, and therefore this book makes great demands on people who do not know or cannot understand my scientific ideas. My life has been in a sense the quintessence of what I have written, not the other way around. The way I am and the way I write are a unity. All my ideas and all my endeavors are myself. Thus the 'autobiography' is merely the dot on the i."

During the years in which the book was taking shape a process of transformation and objectivization was also taking place in Jung. With each succeeding chapter he moved, as it were, farther away from himself, until at last he was able to see himself as well as the significance of his life and work from a distance. "If I ask the value of my life, I can only measure myself against the centuries and then I must say, Yes, it means something. Measured by the ideas of today, it means nothing." The impersonality, the feeling of historical continuity expressed in these words, emerges ever more strongly in the course of the book, as the reader will see.

The chapter entitled "The Work," with its brief survey of the genesis of Jung's most important writings, is fragmentary. How could this be otherwise, when his collected works comprise nearly twenty volumes? Moreover, Jung never felt any disposition to offer a summary of his ideas—either in conversation or in writing. When he was asked to do so, he replied in his characteristic, rather drastic fashion, "That sort of thing lies totally outside my range. I see no sense in publishing a condensation of papers in which I went to so much trouble to discuss the subject in detail. I should have to omit all my evidence and rely on a type of categorical statement which would not make my results any easier to understand. The characteristic ruminant activity of ungulate animals, which consists in the regurgitation of what has already been chewed over, is anything but stimulating to my appetite. . . ."

The reader should therefore regard this chapter as a retrospective sketch written in response to a special occasion, and not expect it to be comprehensive.

The short glossary which I have included at the end of the book, at the publisher's request, will, I hope, be of help to the reader who is not familiar with Jung's work and terminology. I have taken a small number of the definitions from the *Wörterbuch der Psychologie und ihrer Grenzgebiete,* with the kind permission of its editor, Kurt von Sury, M.D. Wherever possible I have elucidated the concepts of Jungian psychology by quotations from Jung's works, and have supplemented the dictionary's definitions in the same way. These quotations must, however, be regarded as no more than suggestive hints. Jung was constantly defining his concepts in new and different ways, for an ultimate definition, he felt, was not possible. He thought it wise to let the inexplicable elements that always cling to psychic realities remain as riddles or mysteries.

A great many persons have helped me with this inspiring and difficult task, have shown unfailing interest during the slow growth of the book, and have furthered its progress by stimulating suggestions and criticism. To all of them I offer heartfelt thanks. Here I shall mention by name only Helen and Kurt

Introduction

Wolff, of Locarno, who conceived the idea of the book and helped to bring that idea to fruition; Marianne and Walther Niehus-Jung, of Küsnacht-Zürich, who throughout the years in which it was taking shape aided me by word and deed; and R. F. C. Hull, of Palma de Mallorca, who gave me advice and help with unflagging patience.

ANIELA JAFFÉ

December 1961

Contents

MEMORIES,
DREAMS,
REFLECTIONS

Prologue

M Y LIFE is a story of the self-realization of the unconscious. Everything in the unconscious seeks outward manifestation, and the personality too desires to evolve out of its unconscious conditions and to experience itself as a whole. I cannot employ the language of science to trace this process of growth in myself, for I cannot experience myself as a scientific problem.

What we are to our inward vision, and what man appears to be *sub specie aeternitatis*, can only be expressed by way of myth. Myth is more individual and expresses life more precisely than does science. Science works with concepts of averages which are far too general to do justice to the subjective variety of an individual life.

Thus it is that I have now undertaken, in my eighty-third year, to tell my personal myth. I can only make direct statements, only "tell stories." Whether or not the stories are "true" is not the problem. The only question is whether what I tell is *my* fable, *my* truth.

An autobiography is so difficult to write because we possess no standards, no objective foundation, from which to judge ourselves. There are really no proper bases for comparison. I know

3

that in many things I am not like others, but I do not know what I really am like. Man cannot compare himself with any other creature; he is not a monkey, not a cow, not a tree. I am a man. But what is it to be that? Like every other being, I am a splinter of the infinite deity, but I cannot contrast myself with any animal, any plant or any stone. Only a mythical being has a range greater than man's. How then can a man form any definite opinions about himself?

We are a psychic process which we do not control, or only partly direct. Consequently, we cannot have any final judgment about ourselves or our lives. If we had, we would know everything—but at most that is only a pretense. At bottom we never know how it has all come about. The story of a life begins somewhere, at some particular point we happen to remember; and even then it was already highly complex. We do not know how life is going to turn out. Therefore the story has no beginning, and the end can only be vaguely hinted at.

The life of man is a dubious experiment. It is a tremendous phenomenon only in numerical terms. Individually, it is so fleeting, so insufficient, that it is literally a miracle that anything can exist and develop at all. I was impressed by that fact long ago, as a young medical student, and it seemed to me miraculous that I should not have been prematurely annihilated.

Life has always seemed to me like a plant that lives on its rhizome. Its true life is invisible, hidden in the rhizome. The part that appears above ground lasts only a single summer. Then it withers away—an ephemeral apparition. When we think of the unending growth and decay of life and civilizations, we cannot escape the impression of absolute nullity. Yet I have never lost a sense of something that lives and endures underneath the eternal flux. What we see is the blossom, which passes. The rhizome remains.

In the end the only events in my life worth telling are those when the imperishable world irrupted into this transitory one. That is why I speak chiefly of inner experiences, amongst which I include my dreams and visions. These form the *prima materia* of my scientific work. They were the fiery magma out of which the stone that had to be worked was crystallized.

4

All other memories of travels, people and my surroundings have paled beside these interior happenings. Many people have participated in the story of our times and written about it; if the reader wants an account of that, let him turn to them or get somebody to tell it to him. Recollection of the outward events of my life has largely faded or disappeared. But my encounters with the "other" reality, my bouts with the unconscious, are indelibly engraved upon my memory. In that realm there has always been wealth in abundance, and everything else has lost importance by comparison.

Similarly, other people are established inalienably in my memories only if their names were entered in the scrolls of my destiny from the beginning, so that encountering them was at the same time a kind of recollection.

Inner experiences also set their seal on the outward events that came my way and assumed importance for me in youth or later on. I early arrived at the insight that when no answer comes from within to the problems and complexities of life, they ultimately mean very little. Outward circumstances are no substitute for inner experience. Therefore my life has been singularly poor in outward happenings. I cannot tell much about them, for it would strike me as hollow and insubstantial. I can understand myself only in the light of inner happenings. It is these that make up the singularity of my life, and with these my autobiography deals.

· I ·

First Years

Wᴜᴇɴ I was six months old, my parents moved from
Kesswil on Lake Constance to Laufen, the castle and
vicarage above the Falls of the Rhine. This was in 1875.
My memories begin with my second or third year. I recall the
vicarage, the garden, the laundry house, the church, the castle,
the Falls, the small castle of Worth, and the sexton's farm. These
are nothing but islands of memory afloat in a sea of vagueness,
each by itself, apparently with no connection between them.

One memory comes up which is perhaps the earliest of my life,
and is indeed only a rather hazy impression. I am lying in a
pram, in the shadow of a tree. It is a fine, warm summer day, the
sky blue, and golden sunlight darting through green leaves. The
hood of the pram has been left up. I have just awakened to the
glorious beauty of the day, and have a sense of indescribable
well-being. I see the sun glittering through the leaves and
blossoms of the bushes. Everything is wholly wonderful, colorful, and splendid.

Another memory: I am sitting in our dining room, on the
west side of the house, perched in a high chair and spooning up
warm milk with bits of broken bread in it. The milk has a

pleasant taste and a characteristic smell. This was the first time I became aware of the smell of milk. It was the moment when, so to speak, I became conscious of smelling. This memory, too, goes very far back.

Still another: a lovely summer evening. An aunt said to me, "Now I am going to show you something." She took me out in front of the house, on the road to Dachsen. On the far horizon the chain of the Alps lay bathed in glowing sunset reds. The Alps could be seen very clearly that evening. "Now look over there"—I can hear her saying to me in Swiss dialect—"the mountains are all red." For the first time I consciously saw the Alps. Then I was told that the next day the village children would be going on a school outing to the Uetliberg, near Zürich. I wanted so much to go too. To my sorrow, I was informed that children as small as I could not go along, there was nothing to be done about it. From then on the Uetliberg and Zürich became an unattainable land of dreams, near to the glowing, snow-covered mountains.

From a somewhat later period comes another memory. My mother took me to the Thurgau to visit friends, who had a castle on Lake Constance. I could not be dragged away from the water. The waves from the steamer washed up to the shore, the sun glistened on the water, and the sand under the water had been curled into little ridges by the waves. The lake stretched away and away into the distance. This expanse of water was an inconceivable pleasure to me, an incomparable splendor. At that time the idea became fixed in my mind that I must live near a lake; without water, I thought, nobody could live at all.

Still another memory comes up: strangers, bustle, excitement. The maid comes running and exclaims, "The fishermen have found a corpse—came down the Falls—they want to put it in the washhouse!" My father says, "Yes, yes." I want to see the dead body at once. My mother holds me back and sternly forbids me to go into the garden. When all the men had left, I quickly stole into the garden to the washhouse. But the door was locked. I went around the house; at the back there was an open drain running down the slope, and I saw blood and water trickling out. I found this extraordinarily interesting. At that time I was not yet four years old.

Yet another image: I am restive, feverish, unable to sleep. My father carries me in his arms, paces up and down, singing his old student songs. I particularly remember one I was especially fond of and which always used to soothe me, *"Alles schweige, jeder neige . . ."* The beginning went something like that. To this day I can remember my father's voice, singing over me in the stillness of the night.

I was suffering, so my mother told me afterward, from general eczema. Dim intimations of trouble in my parents' marriage hovered around me. My illness, in 1878, must have been connected with a temporary separation of my parents. My mother spent several months in a hospital in Basel, and presumably her illness had something to do with the difficulty in the marriage. An aunt of mine, who was a spinster and some twenty years older than my mother, took care of me. I was deeply troubled by my mother's being away. From then on, I always felt mistrustful when the word "love" was spoken. The feeling I associated with "woman" was for a long time that of innate unreliability. "Father," on the other hand, meant reliability and—powerlessness. That is the handicap I started off with. Later, these early impressions were revised: I have trusted men friends and been disappointed by them, and I have mistrusted women and was not disappointed.

While my mother was away, our maid, too, looked after me. I still remember her picking me up and laying my head against her shoulder. She had black hair and an olive complexion, and was quite different from my mother. I can see, even now, her hairline, her throat, with its darkly pigmented skin, and her ear. All this seemed to me very strange and yet strangely familiar. It was as though she belonged not to my family but only to me, as though she were connected in some way with other mysterious things I could not understand. This type of girl later became a component of my anima.[1] The feeling of strangeness which she

[1] For this and other technical terms which are commonly used by Jung but may be unfamiliar to the reader or no longer fresh in his mind, see the glossary at the end of the book.

conveyed, and yet of having known her always, was a characteristic of that figure which later came to symbolize for me the whole essence of womanhood.

From the period of my parents' separation I have another memory image: a young, very pretty and charming girl with blue eyes and fair hair is leading me, on a blue autumn day, under golden maple and chestnut trees along the Rhine below the Falls, near Wörth castle. The sun is shining through the foliage, and yellow leaves lie on the ground. This girl later became my mother-in-law. She admired my father. I did not see her again until I was twenty-one years old.

These are my outward memories. What follow now are more powerful, indeed overwhelming images, some of which I recall only dimly. There was a fall downstairs, for example, and another fall against the angle of a stove leg. I remember pain and blood, a doctor sewing a wound in my head—the scar remained visible until my senior year at the Gymnasium. My mother told me, too, of the time when I was crossing the bridge over the Rhine Falls to Neuhausen. The maid caught me just in time—I already had one leg under the railing and was about to slip through. These things point to an unconscious suicidal urge or, it may be, to a fatal resistance to life in this world.

At that time I also had vague fears at night. I would hear things walking about in the house. The muted roar of the Rhine Falls was always audible, and all around lay a danger zone. People drowned, bodies were swept over the rocks. In the cemetery nearby, the sexton would dig a hole—heaps of brown, upturned earth. Black, solemn men in long frock coats with unusually tall hats and shiny black boots would bring a black box. My father would be there in his clerical gown, speaking in a resounding voice. Women wept. I was told that someone was being buried in this hole in the ground. Certain persons who had been around previously would suddenly no longer be there. Then I would hear that they had been buried, and that Lord Jesus had taken them to himself.

My mother had taught me a prayer which I had to say every evening. I gladly did so because it gave me a sense of comfort in face of the vague uncertainties of the night:

Spread out thy wings, Lord Jesus mild,
And take to thee thy chick, thy child.
"If Satan would devour it,
No harm shall overpower it,"
So let the angels sing! [2]

Lord Jesus was comforting, a nice, benevolent gentleman like Herr Wegenstein up at the castle, rich, powerful, respected, and mindful of little children at night. Why he should be winged like a bird was a conundrum that did not worry me any further. Far more significant and thought-provoking was the fact that little children were compared to chicks which Lord Jesus evidently "took" reluctantly, like bitter medicine. This was difficult to understand. But I understood at once that Satan liked chicks and had to be prevented from eating them. So, although Lord Jesus did not like the taste, he ate them anyway, so that Satan would not get them. As far as that went, my argument was comforting. But now I was hearing that Lord Jesus "took" other people to himself as well, and that this "taking" was the same as putting them in a hole in the ground.

This sinister analogy had unfortunate consequences. I began to distrust Lord Jesus. He lost the aspect of a big, comforting, benevolent bird and became associated with the gloomy black men in frock coats, top hats, and shiny black boots who busied themselves with the black box.

These ruminations of mine led to my first conscious trauma. One hot summer day I was sitting alone, as usual, on the road in front of the house, playing in the sand. The road led past the house up a hill, then disappeared in the wood on the hilltop. So from the house you could see a stretch of the road. Looking up, I saw a figure in a strangely broad hat and a long black garment coming down from the wood. It looked like a man wearing women's clothes. Slowly the figure drew nearer, and I could now

[2] *Breit' aus die Flüglein beide,*
O Jesu meine Freude
Und nimm dein Küchlein ein.
Will Satan es verschlingen,
Dann lass die Engel singen:
Dies Kind soll unverletzet sein.

see that it really was a man wearing a kind of black robe that
reached to his feet. At the sight of him I was overcome with
fear, which rapidly grew into deadly terror as the frightful
recognition shot through my mind: "That is a Jesuit." Shortly
before, I had overheard a conversation between my father and a
visiting colleague concerning the nefarious activities of the
Jesuits. From the half-irritated, half-fearful tone of my father's
remarks I gathered that "Jesuits" meant something specially
dangerous, even for my father. Actually I had no idea what
Jesuits were, but I was familiar with the word "Jesus" from my
little prayer.

The man coming down the road must be in disguise, I
thought; that was why he wore women's clothes. Probably he
had evil intentions. Terrified, I ran helter-skelter into the house,
rushed up the stairs, and hid under a beam in the darkest corner
of the attic. I don't know how long I remained there, but it must
have been a fairly long time, because, when I ventured down
again to the first floor and cautiously stuck my head out of the
window, far and wide there was not a trace of the black figure to
be seen. For days afterward the hellish fright clung to my limbs
and kept me in the house. And even when I began to play in the
road again, the wooded hilltop was still the object of my uneasy
vigilance. Later I realized, of course, that the black figure was
a harmless Catholic priest.

At about the same time—I could not say with absolute certainty whether it preceded this experience or not—I had the
earliest dream I can remember, a dream which was to pre-
occupy me all my life. I was then between three and four years
old.

The vicarage stood quite alone near Laufen castle, and there
was a big meadow stretching back from the sexton's farm. In the
dream I was in this meadow. Suddenly I discovered a dark,
rectangular, stone-lined hole in the ground. I had never seen it
before. I ran forward curiously and peered down into it. Then I
saw a stone stairway leading down. Hesitantly and fearfully, I
descended. At the bottom was a doorway with a round arch,
closed off by a green curtain. It was a big, heavy curtain of
worked stuff like brocade, and it looked very sumptuous. Curi-

ous to see what might be hidden behind, I pushed it aside. I saw before me in the dim light a rectangular chamber about thirty feet long. The ceiling was arched and of hewn stone. The floor was laid with flagstones, and in the center a red carpet ran from the entrance to a low platform. On this platform stood a wonderfully rich golden throne. I am not certain, but perhaps a red cushion lay on the seat. It was a magnificent throne, a real king's throne in a fairy tale. Something was standing on it which I thought at first was a tree trunk twelve to fifteen feet high and about one and a half to two feet thick. It was a huge thing, reaching almost to the ceiling. But it was of a curious composition: it was made of skin and naked flesh, and on top there was something like a rounded head with no face and no hair. On the very top of the head was a single eye, gazing motionlessly upward.

It was fairly light in the room, although there were no windows and no apparent source of light. Above the head, however, was an aura of brightness. The thing did not move, yet I had the feeling that it might at any moment crawl off the throne like a worm and creep toward me. I was paralyzed with terror. At that moment I heard from outside and above me my mother's voice. She called out, "Yes, just look at him. That is the man-eater!" That intensified my terror still more, and I awoke sweating and scared to death. For many nights afterward I was afraid to go to sleep, because I feared I might have another dream like that.

This dream haunted me for years. Only much later did I realize that what I had seen was a phallus, and it was decades before I understood that it was a ritual phallus. I could never make out whether my mother meant, "*That* is the man-eater," or, "That is the *man-eater*." In the first case she would have meant that not Lord Jesus or the Jesuit was the devourer of little children, but the phallus; in the second case that the "man-eater" in general was symbolized by the phallus, so that the dark Lord Jesus, the Jesuit, and the phallus were identical.

The abstract significance of the phallus is shown by the fact that it was enthroned by itself, "ithyphallically" (ιθύς, "upright"). The hole in the meadow probably represented a grave.

The grave itself was an underground temple whose green curtain symbolized the *meadow,* in other words the mystery of Earth with her covering of green vegetation. The carpet was *blood-red.* What about the vault? Perhaps I had already been to the Munôt, the citadel of Schaffhausen? This is not likely, since no one would take a three-year-old child up there. So it cannot be a memory-trace. Equally, I do not know where the anatomically correct phallus can have come from. The interpretation of the *orificium urethrae* as an eye, with the source of light apparently above it, points to the etymology of the word phallus (φαλόs, shining, bright).[3]

At all events, the phallus of this dream seems to be a subterranean God "not to be named," and such it remained throughout my youth, reappearing whenever anyone spoke too emphatically about Lord Jesus. Lord Jesus never became quite real for me, never quite acceptable, never quite lovable, for again and again I would think of his underground counterpart, a frightful revelation which had been accorded me without my seeking it. The Jesuit's "disguise" cast its shadow over the Christian doctrine I had been taught. Often it seemed to me a solemn masquerade, a kind of funeral at which the mourners put on serious or mournful faces but the next moment were secretly laughing and not really sad at all. Lord Jesus seemed to me in some ways a god of death, helpful, it is true, in that he scared away the terrors of the night, but himself uncanny, a crucified and bloody corpse. Secretly, his love and kindness, which I always heard praised, appeared doubtful to me, chiefly because the people who talked most about "dear Lord Jesus" wore black frock coats and shiny black boots which reminded me of burials. They were my father's colleagues as well as eight of my uncles—all parsons. For many years they inspired fear in me—not to speak of occasional Catholic priests who reminded me of the terrifying Jesuit who had irritated and even alarmed my father. In later years and until my confirmation, I made

---

[3] Cf. *Symbols of Transformation* (CW 5), p. 220. CW refers to the Collected Works of C. G. Jung, published by Princeton University Press. For a list of these works, see pp. 403–410.

every effort to force myself to take the required positive attitude to Christ. But I could never succeed in overcoming my secret distrust.

The fear of the "black man," which is felt by every child, was not the essential thing in that experience; it was, rather, the recognition that stabbed through my childish brain: "That is a Jesuit." So the important thing in the dream was its remarkable symbolic setting and the astounding interpretation: "That is the man-eater." Not the child's ogre of a man-eater, but the fact that *this* was the man-eater, and that *it* was sitting on a golden throne beneath the earth. For my childish imagination it was first of all the king who sat on a golden throne; then, on a much more beautiful and much higher and much more golden throne far, far away in the blue sky, sat God and Lord Jesus, with golden crowns and white robes. Yet from this same Lord Jesus came the "Jesuit," in black women's garb, with a broad black hat, down from the wooded hill. I had to glance up there every so often to see whether another danger might not be approaching. In the dream I went down into the hole in the earth and found something very different on a golden throne, something non-human and underworldly, which gazed fixedly upward and fed on human flesh. It was only fifty years later that a passage in a study of religious ritual burned into my eyes, concerning the motif of cannibalism that underlies the symbolism of the Mass. Only then did it become clear to me how exceedingly unchildlike, how sophisticated and oversophisticated was the thought that had begun to break through into consciousness in those two experiences. Who was it speaking in me? Whose mind had devised them? What kind of superior intelligence was at work? I know every numbskull will babble on about "black man," "man-eater," "chance," and "retrospective interpretation," in order to banish something terribly inconvenient that might sully the familiar picture of childhood innocence. Ah, these good, efficient, healthy-minded people, they always remind me of those optimistic tadpoles who bask in a puddle in the sun, in the shallowest of waters, crowding together and amiably wriggling their tails, totally unaware that the next morning the puddle will have dried up and left them stranded.

Who spoke to me then? Who talked of problems far beyond my knowledge? Who brought the Above and Below together, and laid the foundation for everything that was to fill the second half of my life with stormiest passion? Who but that alien guest who came both from above and from below?

Through this childhood dream I was initiated into the secrets of the earth. What happened then was a kind of burial in the earth, and many years were to pass before I came out again. Today I know that it happened in order to bring the greatest possible amount of light into the darkness. It was an initiation into the realm of darkness. My intellectual life had its unconscious beginnings at that time.

I no longer remember our move to Klein-Hüningen, near Basel, in 1879. But I do have a memory of something that happened several years later. One evening my father took me out of bed and carried me in his arms to our porch, which faced west. He showed me the evening sky, shimmering in the most glorious green. That was after the eruption of Krakatoa, in 1883.

Another time my father took me outside and showed me a large comet on the eastern horizon.

And once there was a great flood. The river Wiese, which flowed through the village, had broken its dam, and in its upper reaches a bridge had collapsed. Fourteen people were drowned and were carried down by the yellow flood water to the Rhine. When the water retreated, some of the corpses got stuck in the sand. When I was told about it, there was no holding me. I actually found the body of a middle-aged man, in a black frock coat; apparently he had just come from church. He lay half covered by sand, his arm over his eyes. Similarly, I was fascinated to watch a pig being slaughtered. To the horror of my mother, I watched the whole procedure. She thought it terrible, but the slaughtering and the dead man were simply matters of interest to me.

My earliest memories of art go back to those years at Klein-Hüningen. The house where my parents lived was the eighteenth-century parsonage, and in it there was a dark room.

Here all the furniture was good, and old paintings hung on the walls. I particularly remember an Italian painting of David and Goliath. It was a mirror copy from the workshop of Guido Reni; the original hangs in the Louvre. How it came into our family I do not know. There was another old painting in that room which now hangs in my son's house: a landscape of Basel dating from the early nineteenth century. Often I would steal into that dark, sequestered room and sit for hours in front of the pictures, gazing at all this beauty. It was the only beautiful thing I knew.

About that time—I must still have been a very little fellow, no more than six years old—an aunt took me to Basel and showed me the stuffed animals in the museum. We stayed a long time, because I wanted to look at everything very carefully. At four o'clock the bell rang, a sign that the museum was about to close. My aunt nagged at me, but I could not tear myself away from the showcases. In the meantime the room had been locked, and we had to go by another way to the staircase, through the gallery of antiquities. Suddenly I was standing before these marvelous figures! Utterly overwhelmed, I opened my eyes wide, for I had never seen anything so beautiful. I could not look at them long enough. My aunt pulled me by the hand to the exit —I trailing always a step behind her—crying out, "Disgusting boy, shut your eyes; disgusting boy, shut your eyes!" Only then did I see that the figures were naked and wore fig leaves. I hadn't noticed it at all before. Such was my first encounter with the fine arts. My aunt was simmering with indignation, as though she had been dragged through a pornographic institute.

When I was six years old, my parents took me on an excursion to Arlesheim. On this occasion my mother wore a dress I have never forgotten, and it is the only dress of hers that I can recall: it was of some black stuff printed all over with little green crescents. My earliest recollection of my mother is of a slender young woman wearing this dress. In all my other memories she is older and corpulent.

We came to a church, and my mother said, "That is a Catholic church." My curiosity, mingled with fear, prompted me to slip away from my mother and peer through the open door into the interior. I just had time to glimpse the big candles on a richly adorned altar (it was around Easter) when I suddenly stumbled on a step and struck my chin on a piece of iron. I remember that I had a gash that was bleeding badly when my parents picked me up. My state of mind was curious: on the one hand I was ashamed because my screams were attracting the attention of the churchgoers, and on the other hand I felt that I had done something forbidden. "Jesuits—green curtain—secret of the man-eater. . . . So that is the Catholic Church which has to do with Jesuits. It is their fault that I stumbled and screamed."

For years afterward I was unable to set foot inside a Catholic church without a secret fear of blood and falling and Jesuits. That was the aura or atmosphere that hung about it, but at the same time it always fascinated me. The proximity of a Catholic priest made me even more uneasy, if that were possible. Not until I was in my thirties was I able to confront Mater Ecclesia without this sense of oppression. The first time was in St. Stephen's Cathedral in Vienna.

Soon after I was six my father began giving me Latin lessons, and I also went to school. I did not mind school; it was easy for me, since I was always ahead of the others and had learned to read before I went there. However, I remember a time when I could not yet read, but pestered my mother to read aloud to me out of the *Orbis Pictus,* an old, richly illustrated children's book, which contained an account of exotic religions, especially that of the Hindus. There were illustrations of Brahma, Vishnu, and Shiva which I found an inexhaustible source of interest. My mother later told me that I always returned to these pictures. Whenever I did so, I had an obscure feeling of their affinity with my "original revelation"—which I never spoke of to anyone. It was a secret I must never betray. Indirectly, my mother confirmed this feeling, for the faint tone of contempt with which she spoke of "heathens" did not escape me. I knew that she would reject my "revelation" with horror, and I did not want to expose myself to any such injury.

This unchildlike behavior was connected on the one hand with an intense sensitivity and vulnerability, on the other hand —and this especially—with the loneliness of my early youth. (My sister was born nine years after me.) I played alone, and in my own way. Unfortunately I cannot remember what I played; I recall only that I did not want to be disturbed. I was deeply absorbed in my games and could not endure being watched or judged while I played them. My first concrete memory of games dates from my seventh or eighth year. I was passionately fond of playing with bricks, and built towers which I then rapturously destroyed by an "earthquake." Between my eighth and eleventh years I drew endlessly—battle pictures, sieges, bombardments, naval engagements. Then I filled a whole exercise book with ink blots and amused myself giving them fantastic interpretations. One of my reasons for liking school was that there I found at last the playmates I had lacked for so long.

At school, I also discovered something else. But before I go into this I should first mention that the nocturnal atmosphere had begun to thicken. All sorts of things were happening at night, things incomprehensible and alarming. My parents were sleeping apart. I slept in my father's room. From the door to my mother's room came frightening influences. At night Mother was strange and mysterious. One night I saw coming from her door a faintly luminous, indefinite figure whose head detached itself from the neck and floated along in front of it, in the air, like a little moon. Immediately another head was produced and again detached itself. This process was repeated six or seven times. I had anxiety dreams of things that were now small, now large. For instance, I saw a tiny ball at a great distance; gradually it approached, growing steadily into a monstrous and suffocating object. Or I saw telegraph wires with birds sitting on them, and the wires grew thicker and thicker and my fear greater until the terror awoke me.

Although these dreams were overtures to the physiological changes of puberty, they had in their turn a prelude which occurred about my seventh year. At that time I was sick with pseudo-croup, accompanied by choking fits. One night during an attack I stood at the foot of the bed, my head bent back over the bed rail, while my father held me under the arms. Above me I saw a glowing blue circle about the size of the full moon, and inside it moved golden figures which I thought were angels. This vision was repeated, and each time it allayed my fear of suffocation. But the suffocation returned in the anxiety dreams. I see in this a psychogenic factor: the atmosphere of the house was beginning to be unbreathable.

I hated going to church. The one exception was Christmas Day. The Christmas carol "This Is the Day That God Has Made" pleased me enormously. And then in the evening, of course, came the Christmas tree. Christmas was the only Christian festival I could celebrate with fervor. All others left me cold. New Year's Eve alone had something of the attractiveness of Christmas, but definitely took second place; Advent had a quality about it that somehow did not fit in with the coming Christmas. It had to do with night, storms, and wind, and also with the darkness of the house. There was something whispering, something queer going on.

I return now to the discovery I made in the course of associating with my rustic schoolmates. I found that they alienated me from myself. When I was with them I became different from the way I was at home. I joined in their pranks, or invented ones which at home would never have occurred to me, so it seemed; although, as I knew only too well, I could hatch up all sorts of things when I was alone. It seemed to me that the change in myself was due to the influence of my schoolfellows, who somehow misled me or compelled me to be different from what I thought I was. The influence of this wider world, this world which contained others besides my parents, seemed to me dubious if not altogether suspect and, in some obscure way, hostile. Though I became increasingly aware of the beauty of the bright daylight world where "golden sunlight filters through green leaves," at the same time I had a premonition of an inescapable world of shadows filled with frightening, unanswerable questions which had me at their mercy. My nightly prayer did, of course, grant me a ritual protection since it concluded the day properly and just as properly ushered in night and sleep. But the new peril lurked by day. It was as if I sensed a splitting of myself, and feared it. My inner security was threatened.

I also recall from this period (seven to nine) that I was fond of playing with fire. In our garden there was an old wall built of large blocks of stone, the interstices of which made interesting caves. I used to tend a little fire in one of these caves, with other children helping me; a fire that had to burn forever and therefore had to be constantly maintained by our united efforts, which consisted in gathering the necessary wood. No one but myself was allowed to tend this fire. Others could light other fires in other caves, but these fires were profane and did not concern me. My fire alone was living and had an unmistakable aura of sanctity.

In front of this wall was a slope in which was embedded a stone that jutted out—my stone. Often, when I was alone, I sat down on this stone, and then began an imaginary game that went something like this: "I am sitting on top of this stone and it is underneath." But the stone also could say "I" and think: "I am lying here on this slope and he is sitting on top of me." The question then arose: "Am I the one who is sitting on the stone, or am I the stone on which *he* is sitting?" This question always perplexed me, and I would stand up, wondering who was what now. The answer remained totally unclear, and my uncertainty was accompanied by a feeling of curious and fascinating darkness. But there was no doubt whatsoever that this stone stood in some secret relationship to me. I could sit on it for hours, fascinated by the puzzle it set me.

Thirty years later I again stood on that slope. I was a married man, had children, a house, a place in the world, and a head full of ideas and plans, and suddenly I was again the child who had kindled a fire full of secret significance and sat down on a stone without knowing whether it was I or I was it. I thought suddenly of my life in Zürich, and it seemed alien to me, like news from some remote world and time. This was frightening, for the world of my childhood in which I had just become absorbed was *eternal*, and I had been wrenched away from it and had fallen into a time that continued to roll onward, moving farther and farther away. The pull of that other world was so strong that I had to tear myself violently from the spot in order not to lose hold of my future.

I have never forgotten that moment, for it illuminated in a

flash of lightning the quality of eternity in my childhood. What this meant was revealed soon afterward, in my tenth year. My disunion with myself and uncertainty in the world at large led me to an action which at the time was quite incomprehensible to me. I had in those days a yellow, varnished pencil case of the kind commonly used by primary-school pupils, with a little lock and the customary ruler. At the end of this ruler I now carved a little manikin, about two inches long, with frock coat, top hat, and shiny black boots. I colored him black with ink, sawed him off the ruler, and put him in the pencil case, where I made him a little bed. I even made a coat for him out of a bit of wool. In the case I also placed a smooth, oblong blackish stone from the Rhine, which I had painted with water colors to look as though it were divided into an upper and lower half, and had long carried around in my trouser pocket. This was *his* stone. All this was a great secret. Secretly I took the case to the forbidden attic at the top of the house (forbidden because the floorboards were worm-eaten and rotten) and hid it with great satisfaction on one of the beams under the roof—for no one must ever see it! I knew that not a soul would ever find it there. No one could discover my secret and destroy it. I felt safe, and the tormenting sense of being at odds with myself was gone. In all difficult situations, whenever I had done something wrong or my feelings had been hurt, or when my father's irritability or my mother's invalidism oppressed me, I thought of my carefully bedded-down and wrapped-up manikin and his smooth, prettily colored stone. From time to time—often at intervals of weeks—I secretly stole up to the attic when I could be certain that no one would see me. Then I clambered up on the beam, opened the case, and looked at my manikin and his stone. Each time I did this I placed in the case a little scroll of paper on which I had previously written something during school hours in a secret language of my own invention. The addition of a new scroll always had the character of a solemn ceremonial act. Unfortunately I cannot remember what I wanted to communicate to the manikin. I only know that my "letters" constituted a kind of library for him. I fancy, though I cannot be certain, that they may have consisted of sayings that particularly pleased me.

The meaning of these actions, or how I might explain them, never worried me. I contented myself with the feeling of newly won security, and was satisfied to possess something that no one knew and no one could get at. It was an inviolable secret which must never be betrayed, for the safety of my life depended on it. Why that was so I did not ask myself. It simply was so.

This possession of a secret had a very powerful formative influence on my character; I consider it the essential factor of my boyhood. Similarly, I never told anyone about the dream of the phallus; and the Jesuit, too, belonged to that mysterious realm which I knew I must not talk about. The little wooden figure with the stone was a first attempt, still unconscious and childish, to give shape to the secret. I was always absorbed by it and had the feeling I ought to fathom it; and yet I did not know what it was I was trying to express. I always hoped I might be able to find something—perhaps in nature—that would give me the clue and show me where or what the secret was. At that time my interest in plants, animals, and stones grew. I was constantly on the lookout for something mysterious. Consciously, I was religious in the Christian sense, though always with the reservation: "But it is not so certain as all that!" or, "What about that thing under the ground?" And when religious teachings were pumped into me and I was told, "This is beautiful and this is good," I would think to myself: "Yes, but there is something else, something very secret that people don't know about."

The episode with the carved manikin formed the climax and the conclusion of my childhood. It lasted about a year. Thereafter I completely forgot the whole affair until I was thirty-five. Then this fragment of memory rose up again from the mists of childhood with pristine clarity. While I was engaged on the preliminary studies for my book *Wandlungen und Symbole der Libido*,[4] I read about the cache of soul-stones near Arlesheim, and the Australian *churingas*. I suddenly discovered that I had a quite definite image of such a stone, though I had never seen any reproductions. It was oblong, blackish, and painted into an upper and lower half. This image was joined by that of the

---

[4] Translated as *Psychology of the Unconscious*, 1917; revised edition, retitled *Symbols of Transformation* (CW 5), 1956.

pencil box and the manikin. The manikin was a little cloaked god of the ancient world, a Telesphoros such as stands on the monuments of Asklepios and reads to him from a scroll. Along with this recollection there came to me, for the first time, the conviction that there are archaic psychic components which have entered the individual psyche without any direct line of tradition. My father's library—which I examined only very much later—contained not a single book which might have transmitted any such information. Moreover, my father demonstrably knew nothing about these things.

When I was in England in 1920, I carved out of wood two similar figures without having the slightest recollection of that childhood experience. One of them I had reproduced on a larger scale in stone, and this figure now stands in my garden in Küsnacht. Only while I was doing this work did the unconscious supply me with a name. It called the figure Atmavictu—the "breath of life." It was a further development of that fearful tree of my childhood dream, which was now revealed as the "breath of life," the creative impulse. Ultimately, the manikin was a *kabir*, wrapped in his little cloak, hidden in the *kista*, and provided with a supply of life-force, the oblong black stone. But these are connections which became clear to me only much later in life. When I was a child I performed the ritual just as I have seen it done by the natives of Africa; they act first and do not know what they are doing. Only long afterward do they reflect on what they have done.

· I I ·

School Years

MY ELEVENTH YEAR was significant for me in another way, as I was then sent to the Gymnasium in Basel. Thus I was taken away from my rustic playmates, and truly entered the "great world," where powerful personages, far more powerful than my father, lived in big, splendid houses, drove about in expensive carriages drawn by magnificent horses, and talked a refined German and French. Their sons, well dressed, equipped with fine manners and plenty of pocket money, were now my classmates. With great astonishment and a horrible secret envy I heard them tell about their vacations in the Alps. They had been among those glowing snowy peaks near Zürich, had even been to the sea—this last absolutely flabbergasted me. I gazed upon them as if they were beings from another world, from that unattainable glory of flaming, snow-covered mountains and from the remote, unimaginable sea. Then, for the first time, I became aware how poor we were, that my father was a poor country parson and I a still poorer parson's son who had holes in his shoes and had to sit for six hours in school with wet socks. I began to see my parents with different eyes, and to understand their cares and worries. For my father in particular I felt compassion—less, curiously enough, for my mother. She always seemed to me the stronger of the two. Nevertheless I always felt on her side when my father gave vent to his moody irritability. This necessity for taking sides was not exactly favorable to the formation of my character. In order to liberate myself from these conflicts I fell into the role of the superior arbitrator who willy-nilly had to judge his parents. That caused a certain inflatedness in me; my unstable self-assurance was increased and diminished at the same time.

When I was nine years old my mother had had a little girl. My father was excited and pleased. "Tonight you've been given a little sister," he said to me, and I was utterly surprised, for I hadn't noticed anything. I had thought nothing of my mother's lying in bed more frequently than usual, for I considered her taking to her bed an inexcusable weakness in any case. My father brought me to my mother's bedside, and she held out a little creature that looked dreadfully disappointing: a red, shrunken face like an old man's, the eyes closed, and probably as blind as a young puppy, I thought. On its back the thing had a few single long red hairs which were shown to me—had it been intended for a monkey? I was shocked and did not know what to feel. Was this how newborn babies looked? They mumbled something about the stork which was supposed to have brought the baby. But then what about a litter of puppies or kittens? How many times would the stork have to fly back and forth before the litter was complete? And what about cows? I could not imagine how the stork could manage to carry a whole calf in its bill. Besides, the farmers said the cow calved, not that the stork brought the calf. This story was obviously another of those humbugs which were always being imposed on me. I felt sure that my mother had once again done something I was supposed not to know about.

This sudden appearance of my sister left me with a vague sense of distrust which sharpened my curiosity and observation. Subsequent odd reactions on the part of my mother confirmed my suspicions that something regrettable was connected with this birth. Otherwise this event did not bother me very much, though it probably contributed to intensifying an experience I had when I was twelve.

My mother had the unpleasant habit of calling after me all sorts of good advice when I was setting out for some place to which I had been invited. On these occasions I not only wore my best clothes and polished shoes, but felt the dignity of my purpose and of my appearance in public, so that it was a humiliation for me to have people on the street hear all the ignominious things my mother called out after me, "And don't forget to give them regards from Papa and Mama, and wipe your nose—do you have a handkerchief? Have you washed your hands?" And so on. It struck me as definitely unfair that the inferiority feelings which accompanied my self-importance should thus be exposed to the world when I had taken every care, out of *amour-propre* and vanity, to present as irreproachable an appearance as possible. For these occasions meant a very great deal to me. On the way to the house to which I was invited I felt important and dignified, as I always did when I wore my Sunday clothes on a weekday. The picture changed radically, however, as soon as I came in sight of the house I was visiting. Then a sense of the grandeur and power of those people overcame me. I was afraid of them, and in my smallness wished I might sink fathoms deep into the ground. That was how I felt when I rang the bell. The tinkling sound from inside rang like the toll of doom in my ears. I felt as timid and craven as a stray dog. It was ever so much worse when my mother had prepared me properly beforehand. Then the bell would ring in my ears: "My shoes are filthy, and so are my hands; I have no handkerchief and my neck is black with dirt." Out of defiance I would then not convey my parents' regards, or I would act with unnecessary shyness and stubbornness. If things became too bad I would think of my secret treasure in the attic, and that helped me regain my poise. For in my forlorn state I remembered that I was also the "Other," the person who possessed that inviolable secret, the black stone and the little man in frock coat and top hat.

I cannot recall in my boyhood ever having thought of the possibility of a connection between Lord Jesus—or the Jesuit in the black robe—the men in frock coats and top hats standing by the grave, the gravelike hole in the meadow, the underground temple of the phallus, and my little man in the pencil case. The dream of the ithyphallic god was my first great secret; the manikin was the second. It does seem to me, however, that I had a vague sense of relationship between the "soul-stone" and the stone which was also myself.

To this day, writing down my memories at the age of eighty-three, I have never fully unwound the tangle of my earliest memories. They are like individual shoots of a single underground rhizome, like stations on a road of unconscious development. While it became increasingly impossible for me to adopt a positive attitude to Lord Jesus, I remember that from the time I was eleven the idea of God began to interest me. I took to praying to God, and this somehow satisfied me because it was a prayer without contradictions. God was not complicated by my distrust. Moreover, he was not a person in a black robe, and not Lord Jesus of the pictures, draped with brightly colored clothes, with whom people behaved so familiarly. Rather he was a unique being of whom, so I heard, it was impossible to form any correct conception. He was, to be sure, something like a very powerful old man. But to my great satisfaction there was a commandment to the effect that "Thou shalt not make unto thee any graven image or any likeness of anything." Therefore one could not deal with him as familiarly as with Lord Jesus, who was no "secret." A certain analogy with my secret in the attic began to dawn on me.

School came to bore me. It took up far too much time which I would rather have spent drawing battles and playing with fire. Divinity classes were unspeakably dull, and I felt a downright fear of the mathematics class. The teacher pretended that algebra was a perfectly natural affair, to be taken for granted, whereas I didn't even know what numbers really were. They were not flowers, not animals, not fossils; they were nothing that could be imagined, mere quantities that resulted from counting. To my confusion these quantities were now represented by letters, which signified sounds, so that it became possible to hear them, so to speak. Oddly enough, my classmates could handle these things and found them self-evident. No one could tell me what numbers were, and I was unable even to formulate the question. To my horror I found that no one understood my difficulty. The teacher, I must admit, went to great lengths to explain to me the purpose of this curious operation of translating understandable quantities into sounds. I finally grasped that what was aimed at was a kind of system of abbreviation, with the help of which many quantities could be put in a short formula. But this did not interest me in the least. I thought the whole business was entirely arbitrary. Why should numbers be expressed by sounds? One might just as well express a by apple tree, b by box, and x by a question mark. a, b, c, x, y, z were not concrete and did not explain to me anything about the essence of numbers, any more than an apple tree did. But the thing that exasperated me most of all was the proposition: If $a = b$ and $b = c$, then $a = c$, even though by definition a meant something other than b, and, being different, could therefore not be equated with b, let alone with c. Whenever it was a question of an equivalence, then it was said that $a = a$, $b = b$, and so on. This I could accept, whereas $a = b$ seemed to me a downright lie or a fraud. I was equally outraged when the teacher stated in the teeth of his own definition of parallel lines that they met at infinity. This seemed to me no better than a stupid trick to catch peasants with, and I could not and would not have anything to do with it. My intellectual morality fought against these whimsical inconsistencies, which have forever debarred me from understanding mathematics. Right into old age I have had the incorrigible feeling that if, like my schoolmates, I could have accepted without a struggle the proposition that $a = b$, or that sun = moon, dog = cat, then mathematics might have fooled me endlessly—just *how* much I only began to realize at the age of eighty-four. All my life it remained a puzzle to me why it was that I never managed to get my bearings in mathematics when there was no doubt whatever that I could calculate properly. Least of all did I understand my own *moral* doubts concerning mathematics.

Equations I could comprehend only by inserting specific numerical values in place of the letters and verifying the meaning of the operation by actual calculation. As we went on in mathematics I was able to get along, more or less, by copying out algebraic formulas whose meaning I did not understand, and by memorizing where a particular combination of letters had stood on the blackboard. I could no longer make headway by substituting numbers, for from time to time the teacher would say, "Here we put the expression so-and-so," and then he would scribble a few letters on the blackboard. I had no idea where he got them and why he did it—the only reason I could see was that it enabled him to bring the procedure to what he felt was a satisfactory conclusion. I was so intimidated by my incomprehension that I did not dare to ask any questions.

Mathematics classes became sheer terror and torture to me. Other subjects I found easy; and as, thanks to my good visual memory, I contrived for a long while to swindle my way through mathematics, I usually had good marks. But my fear of failure and my sense of smallness in face of the vast world around me created in me not only a dislike but a kind of silent despair which completely ruined school for me. In addition, I was exempted from drawing classes on grounds of utter incapacity. This in a way was welcome to me, since it gave me more free time; but on the other hand it was a fresh defeat, since I had some facility in drawing, although I did not realize that it depended essentially on the way I was feeling. I could draw only what stirred my imagination. But I was forced to copy prints of Greek gods with sightless eyes, and when that wouldn't go properly the teacher obviously thought I needed something more naturalistic and set before me the picture of a goat's head. This assignment I failed completely, and that was the end of my drawing classes.

To my defeats in mathematics and drawing there was now added a third: from the very first I hated gymnastics. I could not endure having others tell me how to move. I was going to school in order to learn something, not to practice useless and senseless acrobatics. Moreover, as a result of my earlier accidents, I had a certain physical timidity which I was not able to overcome until much later on. This timidity was in turn linked with a distrust of the world and its potentialities. To be sure, the world seemed to me beautiful and desirable, but it was also

29

filled with vague and incomprehensible perils. Therefore I always wanted to know at the start to what and to whom I was entrusting myself. Was this perhaps connected with my mother, who had abandoned me for several months? When, as I shall describe later, my neurotic fainting spells began, the doctor forbade me to engage in gymnastics, much to my satisfaction. I was rid of that burden—and had swallowed another defeat.

The time thus gained was not spent solely on play. It permitted me to indulge somewhat more freely the absolute craving I had developed to read every scrap of printed matter that fell into my hands.

My twelfth year was indeed a fateful one for me. One day in the early summer of 1887 I was standing in the cathedral square, waiting for a classmate who went home by the same route as myself. It was twelve o'clock, and the morning classes were over. Suddenly another boy gave me a shove that knocked me off my feet. I fell, striking my head against the curbstone so hard that I almost lost consciousness. For about half an hour afterward I was a little dazed. At the moment I felt the blow the thought flashed through my mind: "Now you won't have to go to school any more." I was only half unconscious, but I remained lying there a few moments longer than was strictly necessary, chiefly in order to avenge myself on my assailant. Then people picked me up and took me to a house nearby, where two elderly spinster aunts lived.

From then on I began to have fainting spells whenever I had to return to school, and whenever my parents set me to doing my homework. For more than six months I stayed away from school, and for me that was a picnic. I was free, could dream for hours, be anywhere I liked, in the woods or by the water, or draw. I resumed my battle pictures and furious scenes of war, of old castles that were being assaulted or burned, or drew page upon page of caricatures. Similar caricatures sometimes appear to me before falling asleep to this day, grinning masks that constantly move and change, among them familiar faces of people who soon afterward died.

Above all, I was able to plunge into the world of the mysterious. To that realm belonged trees, a pool, the swamp, stones and animals, and my father's library. But I was growing more and more away from the world, and had all the while faint pangs of conscience. I frittered away my time with loafing, collecting, reading, and playing. But I did not feel any happier for it; I had the obscure feeling that I was fleeing from myself.

I forgot completely how all this had come about, but I pitied my parents' worries. They consulted various doctors, who scratched their heads and packed me off to spend the holidays with relatives in Winterthur. This city had a railroad station that proved a source of endless delight to me. But when I returned home everything was as before. One doctor thought I had epilepsy. I knew what epileptic fits were like and I inwardly laughed at such nonsense. My parents became more worried than ever. Then one day a friend called on my father. They were sitting in the garden and I hid behind a shrub, for I was possessed of an insatiable curiosity. I heard the visitor saying to my father, "And how is your son?" "Ah, that's a sad business," my father replied. "The doctors no longer know what is wrong with him. They think it may be epilepsy. It would be dreadful if he were incurable. I have lost what little I had, and what will become of the boy if he cannot earn his own living?"

I was thunderstruck. This was the collision with reality. "Why, then, I must get to work!" I thought suddenly.

From that moment on I became a serious child. I crept away, went to my father's study, took out my Latin grammar, and began to cram with intense concentration. After ten minutes of this I had the finest of fainting fits. I almost fell off the chair, but after a few minutes I felt better and went on working. "Devil take it, I'm not going to faint," I told myself, and persisted in my purpose. This time it took about fifteen minutes before the second attack came. That, too, passed like the first. "And now you must really get to work!" I stuck it out, and after an hour came the third attack. Still I did not give up, and worked for another hour, until I had the feeling that I had overcome the attacks. Suddenly I felt better than I had in all the months before. And in fact the attacks did not recur. From that day on I worked over my grammar and other schoolbooks every day. A few weeks later I returned to school, and never suffered another attack, even there. The whole bag of tricks was over and done with! That was when I learned what a neurosis is.

Gradually the recollection of how it had all come about returned to me, and I saw clearly that I myself had arranged this whole disgraceful situation. That was why I had never been seriously angry with the schoolmate who pushed me over. I knew that he had been put up to it, so to speak, and that the whole affair was a diabolical plot on my part. I knew, too, that this was never going to happen to me again. I had a feeling of rage against myself, and at the same time was ashamed of myself. For I knew that I had wronged myself and made a fool of myself in my own eyes. Nobody else was to blame; I was the cursed renegade! From then on I could no longer endure my parents' worrying about me or speaking of me in a pitying tone.

The neurosis became another of my secrets, but it was a shameful secret, a defeat. Nevertheless it induced in me a studied punctiliousness and an unusual diligence. Those days saw the beginnings of my conscientiousness, practiced not for the sake of appearances, so that I would amount to something, but for my own sake. Regularly I would get up at five o'clock in order to study, and sometimes I worked from three in the morning till seven, before going to school.

What had led me astray during the crisis was my passion for being alone, my delight in solitude. Nature seemed to me full of wonders, and I wanted to steep myself in them. Every stone, every plant, every single thing seemed alive and indescribably marvelous. I immersed myself in nature, crawled, as it were, into the very essence of nature and away from the whole human world.

I had another important experience at about this time. I was taking the long road to school from Klein-Hüningen, where we lived, to Basel, when suddenly for a single moment I had the overwhelming impression of having just emerged from a dense cloud. I knew all at once: now I am *myself!* It was as if a wall of mist were at my back, and behind that wall there was not yet an "I." But at this moment *I came upon myself.* Previously I had existed, too, but everything had merely happened to me.

Now I happened to myself. Now I knew: I am myself now, now I exist. Previously I had been willed to do this and that; now *I* willed. This experience seemed to me tremendously important and new: there was "authority" in me. Curiously enough, at this time and also during the months of my fainting neurosis I had lost all memory of the treasure in the attic. Otherwise I would probably have realized even then the analogy between my feeling of authority and the feeling of value which the treasure inspired in me. But that was not so; all memory of the pencil case had vanished.

Around this time I was invited to spend the holidays with friends of the family who had a house on Lake Lucerne. To my delight the house was situated right on the lake, and there was a boathouse and a rowboat. My host allowed his son and me to use the boat, although we were sternly warned not to be reckless. Unfortunately I also knew how to steer a *Waidling* (a boat of the gondola type)—that is to say, standing. At home we had such a punt, in which we had tried out every imaginable trick. The first thing I did, therefore, was to take my stand on the stern seat and with one oar push off into the lake. That was too much for the anxious master of the house. He whistled us back and gave me a first-class dressing-down. I was thoroughly crestfallen but had to admit that I had done exactly what he had said not to, and that his lecture was quite justified. At the same time I was seized with rage that this fat, ignorant boor should dare to insult ME. This ME was not only grown up, but important, an authority, a person with office and dignity, an old man, an object of respect and awe. Yet the contrast with reality was so grotesque that in the midst of my fury I suddenly stopped myself, for the question rose to my lips: "Who in the world are you, anyway? You are reacting as though you were the devil only knows how important! And yet you know he is perfectly right. You are barely twelve years old, a schoolboy, and he is a father and a rich, powerful man besides, who owns two houses and several splendid horses."

Then, to my intense confusion, it occurred to me that I was actually two different persons. One of them was the schoolboy who could not grasp algebra and was far from sure of himself;

the other was important, a high authority, a man not to be trifled with, as powerful and influential as this manufacturer. This "other" was an old man who lived in the eighteenth century, wore buckled shoes and a white wig and went driving in a fly with high, concave rear wheels between which the box was suspended on springs and leather straps.

This notion sprang from a curious experience I had had. When we were living in Klein-Hüningen an ancient green carriage from the Black Forest drove past our house one day. It was truly an antique, looking exactly as if it had come straight out of the eighteenth century. When I saw it, I felt with great excitement: "That's it! Sure enough, that comes from *my* times." It was as though I had recognized it because it was the same type as the one I had driven in myself. Then came a curious *sentiment écoeurant,* as though someone had stolen something from me, or as though I had been cheated—cheated out of my beloved past. The carriage was a relic of those times! I cannot describe what was happening in me or what it was that affected me so strongly: a longing, a nostalgia, or a recognition that kept saying, "Yes, that's how it was! Yes, that's how it was!"

I had still another experience that harked back to the eighteenth century. At the home of one of my aunts I had seen an eighteenth-century statuette, an old terra-cotta piece consisting of two painted figures. One of them was old Dr. Stückelberger, a well-known personality in the city of Basel toward the end of the eighteenth century. The other figure was a patient of his; she was depicted with closed eyes, sticking out her tongue. The story went that old Stückelberger was one day crossing the Rhine bridge when this annoying patient suddenly came up to him out of nowhere and babbled out a complaint. Old Stückelberger said testily, "Yes, yes, there must be something wrong with you. Put out your tongue and shut your eyes." The woman did so, and Stückelberger instantly ran off, and she remained standing there with her tongue stuck out, while the people laughed. This statuette of the old doctor had buckled shoes which in a strange way I recognized as my own. I was convinced that these were shoes I had worn. The conviction drove me wild with excitement. "Why, those must be my shoes!" I could still feel those shoes on my feet, and yet I could not explain where this crazy feeling came from. I could not understand this identity I felt with the eighteenth century. Often in those days I would write the date 1786 instead of 1886, and each time this happened I was overcome by an inexplicable nostalgia.

After my escapade with the boat, and my well-merited punishment, I began pondering these isolated impressions, and they coalesced into a coherent picture: of myself living in two ages simultaneously, and being two different persons. I felt confused, and was full to the brim with heavy reflections. At last I reached the disappointing realization that now, at any rate, I was nothing but the little schoolboy who had deserved his punishment, and who had to behave according to his age. The other person must be sheer nonsense. I suspected that he was somehow connected with the many tales I had heard from my parents and relatives about my grandfather. Yet that was not quite right either, for he had been born in 1795 and had therefore lived in the nineteenth century; moreover he had died long before I was born. It could not be that I was identical with him. At the time these considerations were, I should say, mostly in the form of vague glimmerings and dreams. I can no longer remember whether at that time I knew anything about my legendary kinship with Goethe. I think not, however, for I know that I first heard this tale from strangers. I should add that there is an annoying tradition that my grandfather was a natural son of Goethe.[1]

---

[1] In regard to the legend, twice alluded to in this book, that Jung was a descendant of Goethe, he related: "The wife of my great-grandfather (Franz Ignaz Jung, d. 1831), Sophie Ziegler, and her sister were associated with the Mannheim Theater and were friends of many writers. The story goes that Sophie Ziegler had an illegitimate child by Goethe, and that this child was my grandfather, Carl Gustav Jung. This was considered virtually an established fact. My grandfather says not a word about it in his diaries, however. He mentions only that he once saw Goethe in Weimar, and then merely from behind! Sophie Ziegler Jung was later friendly with Lotte Kestner, a niece of Goethe's "Lottchen." This Lotte frequently came to see my grandfather—as, incidentally, did Franz Liszt. In later years Lotte Kestner settled in Basel, no doubt because of these close ties with the Jung family."

No proof of this item of family tradition has been found in the available sources,

One fine summer day that same year I came out of school at noon and went to the cathedral square. The sky was gloriously blue, the day one of radiant sunshine. The roof of the cathedral glittered, the sun sparkling from the new, brightly glazed tiles. I was overwhelmed by the beauty of the sight, and thought: "The world is beautiful and the church is beautiful, and God made all this and sits above it far away in the blue sky on a golden throne and . . ." Here came a great hole in my thoughts, and a choking sensation. I felt numbed, and knew only: "Don't go on thinking now! Something terrible is coming, something I do not want to think, something I dare not even approach. Why not? Because I would be committing the most frightful of sins. What is the most terrible sin? Murder? No, it can't be that. The most terrible sin is the sin against the Holy Ghost, which cannot be forgiven. Anyone who commits that sin is damned to hell for all eternity. That would be very sad for my parents, if their only son, to whom they are so attached, should be doomed to eternal damnation. I cannot do that to my parents. All I need do is not go on thinking."

That was easier said than done. On my long walk home I tried to think all sorts of other things, but I found my thoughts returning again and again to the beautiful cathedral which I loved so much, and to God sitting on the throne—and then my thoughts would fly off again as if they had received a powerful electric shock. I kept repeating to myself: "Don't think of it, just don't think of it!" I reached home in a pretty worked-up state. My mother noticed that something was wrong, and asked,

---

the archives of the Goethehaus in Frankfurt am Main and the baptismal register in the Jesuitenkirche in Mannheim. Goethe was not in Mannheim at the period in question, and there is no record of Sophie Ziegler's staying in Weimar or anywhere in Goethe's vicinity.

Jung used to speak of this stubbornly persistent legend with a certain gratified amusement, for it might serve to explain one subtle aspect of his fascination with Goethe's *Faust;* it belonged to an inner reality, as it were. On the other hand he would also call the story "annoying." He thought it "in bad taste" and maintained that the world was already full of "too many fools who tell such tales of the 'unknown father.'" Above all, he felt that the legitimate line of descent, in particular from the learned Catholic doctor and jurist Carl Jung (d. 1645)—discussed at the end of Chapter VIII—was equally significant.—A. J.

"What is the matter with you? Has something happened at school?" I was able to assure her, without lying, that nothing had happened at school. I did have the thought that it might help me if I could confess to my mother the real reason for my turmoil. But to do so I would have to do the very thing that seemed impossible: think my thought right to the end. The poor dear was utterly unsuspecting and could not possibly know that I was in terrible danger of committing the unforgivable sin and plunging myself into hell. I rejected the idea of confessing and tried to efface myself as much as possible.

That night I slept badly; again and again the forbidden thought, which I did not yet know, tried to break out, and I struggled desperately to fend it off. The next two days were sheer torture, and my mother was convinced that I was ill. But I resisted the temptation to confess, aided by the thought that it would cause my parents intense sorrow.

On the third night, however, the torment became so unbearable that I no longer knew what to do. I awoke from a restless sleep just in time to catch myself thinking again about the cathedral and God. I had almost continued the thought! I felt my resistance weakening. Sweating with fear, I sat up in bed to shake off sleep. "Now it is coming, now it's serious! *I must think.* It must be thought out beforehand. *Why* should I think something I do not know? I don't want to, by God, that's sure. But *who* wants me to? Who wants to force me to think something I don't know and don't want to know? Where does this terrible will come from? And why should I be the one to be subjected to it? I was thinking praises of the Creator of this beautiful world, I was grateful to him for this immeasurable gift, so why should *I* have to think something inconceivably wicked? I don't know what it is, I really don't, for I cannot and must not come anywhere near this thought, for that would be to risk thinking it at once. *I* haven't done this or wanted this, it has come on me like a bad dream. Where do such things come from? This has happened to me without my doing. Why? After all, I didn't create myself, I came into the world the way God made me— that is, the way I was shaped by my parents. Or can it have been that my parents wanted something of this sort? But my good

37

parents would never have had any thoughts like that. Nothing so atrocious would ever have occurred to them."

I found this idea utterly absurd. Then I thought of my grandparents, whom I knew only from their portraits. They looked benevolent and dignified enough to repulse any idea that they might possibly be to blame. I mentally ran through the long procession of unknown ancestors until finally I arrived at Adam and Eve. And with them came the decisive thought: Adam and Eve were the first people; they had no parents, but were created directly by God, who intentionally made them as they were. They had no choice but to be exactly the way God had created them. Therefore they did not know how they could possibly be different. They were perfect creatures of God, for He creates only perfection, and yet they committed the first sin by doing what God did not want them to do. How was that possible? They could not have done it if God had not placed in them the possibility of doing it. That was clear, too, from the serpent, whom God had created before them, obviously so that it could induce Adam and Eve to sin. God in His omniscience had arranged everything so that the first parents would have to sin. *Therefore it was God's intention that they should sin.*

This thought liberated me instantly from my worst torment, since I now knew that God Himself had placed me in this situation. At first I did not know whether He intended me to commit my sin or not. I no longer thought of praying for illumination, since God had landed me in this fix without my willing it and had left me without any help. I was certain that I must search out His intention myself, and seek the way out alone. At this point another argument began.

"What does God want? To act or not to act? I must find out what God wants with me, and I must find out right away." I was aware, of course, that according to conventional morality there was no question but that sin must be avoided. That was what I had been doing up to now, but I knew I could not go on doing it. My broken sleep and my spiritual distress had worn me out to such a point that fending off the thought was tying me into unbearable knots. This could not go on. At the same time, I could not yield before I understood what God's will was and what He intended. For I was now certain that He was the author of this desperate problem. Oddly enough, I did not think for a moment that the devil might be playing a trick on me. The devil played little part in my mental world at that time, and in any case I regarded him as powerless compared with God. But from the moment I emerged from the mist and became conscious of myself, the unity, the greatness, and the superhuman majesty of God began to haunt my imagination. Hence there was no question in my mind but that God Himself was arranging a decisive test for me, and that everything depended on my understanding Him correctly. I knew, beyond a doubt, that I would ultimately be compelled to break down, to give way, but I did not want it to happen without my understanding it, since the salvation of my eternal soul was at stake.

"God knows that I cannot resist much longer, and He does not help me, although I am on the point of having to commit the unforgivable sin. In His omnipotence He could easily lift this compulsion from me, but evidently He is not going to. Can it be that He wishes to test my obedience by imposing on me the unusual task of doing something against my own moral judgment and against the teachings of my religion, and even against His own commandment, something I am resisting with all my strength because I fear eternal damnation? Is it possible that God wishes to see whether I am capable of obeying His will even though my faith and my reason raise before me the specters of death and hell? That might really be the answer! But these are merely my own thoughts. I may be mistaken. I dare not trust my own reasoning as far as that. I must think it all through once more."

I thought it over again and arrived at the same conclusion. "Obviously God also desires me to show courage," I thought. "If that is so and I go through with it, then He will give me His grace and illumination."

I gathered all my courage, as though I were about to leap forthwith into hell-fire, and let the thought come. I saw before me the cathedral, the blue sky. God sits on His golden throne, high above the world—and from under the throne an enormous turd falls upon the sparkling new roof, shatters it, and breaks the walls of the cathedral asunder.

So that was it! I felt an enormous, an indescribable relief. Instead of the expected damnation, grace had come upon me, and with it an unutterable bliss such as I had never known. I wept for happiness and gratitude. The wisdom and goodness of God had been revealed to me now that I had yielded to His inexorable command. It was as though I had experienced an illumination. A great many things I had not previously understood became clear to me. That was what my father had not understood, I thought; he had failed to experience the will of God, had opposed it for the best reasons and out of the deepest faith. And that was why he had never experienced the miracle of grace which heals all and makes all comprehensible. He had taken the Bible's commandments as his guide; he believed in God as the Bible prescribed and as his forefathers had taught him. But he did not know the immediate living God who stands, omnipotent and free, above His Bible and His Church, who calls upon man to partake of His freedom, and can force him to renounce his own views and convictions in order to fulfill without reserve the command of God. In His trial of human courage God refuses to abide by traditions, no matter how sacred. In His omnipotence He will see to it that nothing really evil comes of such tests of courage. If one fulfills the will of God one can be sure of going the right way.

God had also created Adam and Eve in such a way that they had to think what they did not at all want to think. He had done that in order to find out whether they were obedient. And He could also demand something of me that I would have had to reject on traditional religious grounds. It was obedience which brought me grace, and after that experience I knew what God's grace was. One must be utterly abandoned to God; nothing matters but fulfilling His will. Otherwise all is folly and meaninglessness. From that moment on, when I experienced grace, my true responsibility began. Why did God befoul His cathedral? That, for me, was a terrible thought. But then came the dim understanding that God could be something terrible. I had experienced a dark and terrible secret. It overshadowed my whole life, and I became deeply pensive.

The experience also had the effect of increasing my sense of inferiority. I am a devil or a swine, I thought; I am infinitely depraved. But then I began searching through the New Testament and read, with a certain satisfaction, about the Pharisee and the publican, and that reprobates are the chosen ones. It made a lasting impression on me that the unjust steward was praised, and that Peter, the waverer, was appointed the rock upon which the Church was built.

The greater my inferiority feelings became, the more incomprehensible did God's grace appear to me. After all, I had never been sure of myself. When my mother once said to me, "You have always been a good boy," I simply could not grasp it. I a good boy? That was quite new to me. I often thought of myself as a corrupt and inferior person.

With the experience of God and the cathedral I at last had something tangible that was part of the great secret—as if I had always talked of stones falling from heaven and now had one in my pocket. But actually, it was a shaming experience. I had fallen into something bad, something evil and sinister, though at the same time it was a kind of distinction. Sometimes I had an overwhelming urge to speak, not about that, but only to hint that there were some curious things about me which no one knew of. I wanted to find out whether other people had undergone similar experiences. I never succeeded in discovering so much as a trace of them in others. As a result, I had the feeling that I was either outlawed or elect, accursed or blessed.

It would never have occurred to me to speak of my experience openly, nor of my dream of the phallus in the underground temple, nor of my carved manikin. As a matter of fact, I did not say anything about the phallus dream until I was sixty-five. I may have spoken about the other experiences to my wife, but only in later years. A strict taboo hung over all these matters, inherited from my childhood. I could never have talked about them with friends.

My entire youth can be understood in terms of this secret. It induced in me an almost unendurable loneliness. My one great achievement during those years was that I resisted the temptation to talk about it with anyone. Thus the pattern of my relationship to the world was already prefigured: today as then I am a solitary, because I know things and must hint at things which other people do not know, and usually do not even want to know.

In my mother's family there were six parsons, and on my father's side not only was my father a parson but two of my uncles also. Thus I heard many religious conversations, theological discussions, and sermons. Whenever I listened to them I had the feeling: "Yes, yes, that is all very well. But what about the secret? The secret is also the secret of grace. None of you know anything about that. You don't know that God wants to force me to do wrong, that He forces me to think abominations in order to experience His grace." Everything the others said was completely beside the point. I thought, "For Heaven's sake, there must be someone who knows something about it; somewhere there must be the truth." I rummaged through my father's library, reading whatever I could on God, the Trinity, spirit, consciousness. I devoured the books, but came away none the wiser. I always found myself thinking, "They don't know either." I even searched about in my father's Luther Bible. Unfortunately, the conventional "edifying" interpretation of Job prevented me from taking a deeper interest in this book. I would have found consolation in it, especially in chapter 9, verses 30 ff.: "Though I wash myself with snow water . . . yet shalt thou plunge me in the mire."

Later my mother told me that in those days I was often depressed. It was not really that; rather, I was brooding on the secret. At such times it was strangely reassuring and calming to sit on my stone. Somehow it would free me of all my doubts. Whenever I thought that I was the stone, the conflict ceased. "The stone has no uncertainties, no urge to communicate, and is eternally the same for thousands of years," I would think, "while I am only a passing phenomenon which bursts into all kinds of emotions, like a flame that flares up quickly and then goes out." I was but the sum of my emotions, and the Other in me was the timeless, imperishable stone.

At that time, too, there arose in me profound doubts about everything my father said. When I heard him preaching about

42

grace, I always thought of my own experience. What he said sounded stale and hollow, like a tale told by someone who knows it only by hearsay and cannot quite believe it himself. I wanted to help him, but I did not know how. Moreover, I was too shy to tell him of my experience, or to meddle in his personal preoccupations. I felt myself to be on the one hand too little, and on the other hand I was afraid to wield that authority which my "second personality" inspired in me.

Later, when I was eighteen years old, I had many discussions with my father, always with the secret hope of being able to let him know about the miracle of grace, and thereby help to mitigate his pangs of conscience. I was convinced that if he fulfilled the will of God everything would turn out for the best. But our discussions invariably came to an unsatisfactory end. They irritated him, and saddened him. "Oh nonsense," he was in the habit of saying, "you always want to think. One ought not to think, but believe." I would think, "No, one must experience and know," but I would say, "Give me this belief," whereupon he would shrug and turn resignedly away.

I began making friendships, mostly with shy boys of simple origins. My marks in school improved. During the following years I even succeeded in reaching the top of the class. However, I observed that below me were schoolmates who envied me and tried at every opportunity to catch up with me. That spoiled my pleasure. I hated all competition, and if someone played a game too competitively I turned my back on the game. Thereafter I remained second in the class, and found this considerably more enjoyable. Schoolwork was a nuisance enough anyway without my wanting to make it harder by competitiveness. A very few teachers, whom I remember with gratitude, showed particular confidence in me. The one I recall with the greatest pleasure was the Latin teacher. He was a university professor and a very clever fellow. As it happened, I had known Latin since I was six, because my father had given me lessons in it. So, instead of making me sit in class, this teacher would often send me to the university library to fetch books for him, and I would joyfully dip into them while prolonging the walk back as much as possible.

Most of the teachers thought me stupid and crafty. Whenever anything went wrong in school I was the first on whom suspicion rested. If there was a row somewhere, I was thought to be the instigator. In reality I was involved in such a brawl only once, and it was then that I discovered that a number of my schoolmates were hostile to me. Seven of them lay in ambush for me and suddenly attacked me. I was big and strong by then— it was when I was fifteen—and inclined to violent rages. I suddenly saw red, seized one of the boys by both arms, swung him around me and with his legs knocked several of the others to the ground. The teachers found out about the affair, but I only dimly remember some sort of punishment which seemed to me unjust. From then on I was let alone. No one dared to attack me again.

To have enemies and be accused unjustly was not what I had expected, but somehow I did not find it incomprehensible. Everything I was reproached for irritated me, but I could not deny these reproaches to myself. I knew so little about myself, and the little was so contradictory that I could not with a good conscience reject any accusations. As a matter of fact I always had a guilty conscience and was aware of both actual and potential faults. For that reason I was particularly sensitive to reproofs, since all of them more or less struck home. Although I had not in reality done what I was accused of, I felt that I might have done it. I would even draw up a list of alibis in case I should be accused of something. I felt positively relieved when I had actually done something wrong. Then at least I knew what my guilty conscience was for.

Naturally I compensated my inner insecurity by an outward show of security, or—to put it better—the defect compensated itself without the intervention of my will. That is, I found myself being guilty and at the same time wishing to be innocent. Somewhere deep in the background I always knew that I was two persons. One was the son of my parents, who went to school and was less intelligent, attentive, hard-working, decent, and clean than many other boys. The other was grown up—old, in fact—skeptical, mistrustful, remote from the world of men, but close to nature, the earth, the sun, the moon, the weather, all living creatures, and above all close to the night, to dreams, and to whatever "God" worked directly in him. I put "God" in quotation marks here. For nature seemed, like myself, to have been set aside by God as non-divine, although created by Him as an expression of Himself. Nothing could persuade me that "in the image of God" applied only to man. In fact it seemed to me that the high mountains, the rivers, lakes, trees, flowers, and animals far better exemplified the essence of God than men with their ridiculous clothes, their meanness, vanity, mendacity, and abhorrent egotism—all qualities with which I was only too familiar from myself, that is, from personality No. 1, the schoolboy of 1890. Besides his world there existed another realm, like a temple in which anyone who entered was transformed and suddenly overpowered by a vision of the whole cosmos, so that he could only marvel and admire, forgetful of himself. Here lived the "Other," who knew God as a hidden, personal, and at the same time suprapersonal secret. Here nothing separated man from God; indeed, it was as though the human mind looked down upon Creation simultaneously with God.

What I am here unfolding, sentence by sentence, is something I was then not conscious of in any articulate way, though I sensed it with an overpowering premonition and intensity of feeling. At such times I *knew* I was worthy of myself, that I was my true self. As soon as I was alone, I could pass over into this state. I therefore sought the peace and solitude of this "Other," personality No. 2.

The play and counterplay between personalities No. 1 and No. 2, which has run through my whole life, has nothing to do with a "split" or dissociation in the ordinary medical sense. On the contrary, it is played out in every individual. In my life No. 2 has been of prime importance, and I have always tried to make room for anything that wanted to come to me from within. He is a typical figure, but he is perceived only by the very few. Most people's conscious understanding is not sufficient to realize that he is also what they are.

Church gradually became a place of torment to me. For there men dared to preach aloud—I am tempted to say, shamelessly—

about God, about His intentions and actions. There people were exhorted to have those feelings and to *believe* that secret which I *knew* to be the deepest, innermost certainty, a certainty not to be betrayed by a single word. I could only conclude that apparently no one knew about this secret, not even the parson, for otherwise no one would have dared to expose the mystery of God in public and to profane those inexpressible feelings with stale sentimentalities. Moreover, I was certain that this was the wrong way to reach God, for I knew, knew from experience, that this grace was accorded only to one who fulfilled the will of God without reservation. This was preached from the pulpit, too, but always on the assumption that revelation had made the will of God plain. To me, on the other hand, it seemed the most obscure and unknown thing of all. To me it seemed that one's duty was to explore daily the will of God. I did not do that, but I felt sure that I would do it as soon as an urgent reason for so doing presented itself. Personality No. 1 preoccupied me too much of the time. It often seemed to me that religious precepts were being put in place of the will of God—which could be so unexpected and so alarming—for the sole purpose of sparing people the necessity for understanding God's will. I grew more and more skeptical, and my father's sermons and those of other parsons became acutely embarrassing to me. All the people about me seemed to take the jargon for granted, and the dense obscurity that emanated from it; thoughtlessly they swallowed all the contradictions, such as that God is omniscient and therefore foresaw all human history, and that he actually created human beings so that they would have to sin, and nevertheless forbids them to sin and even punishes them by eternal damnation in hell-fire.

For a long time the devil had played no part in my thinking, curiously enough. The devil appeared to me no worse than a powerful man's vicious watchdog, chained up. Nobody had any responsibility for the world except God, and, as I knew only too well, He could be terrible. My doubts and uneasiness increased whenever I heard my father in his emotional sermons speak of the "good" God, praising God's love for man and exhorting man to love God in return. "Does he really know what he is talking about?" I wondered. "Could he have me, his son, put to the knife as a human sacrifice, like Isaac, or deliver him to an unjust court which would have him crucified like Jesus? No, he could not do that. Therefore in some cases he could not do the will of God, which can be absolutely terrible, as the Bible itself shows." It became clear to me that when people are exhorted, among other things, to obey God rather than man, this is said just casually and thoughtlessly. Obviously we do not know the will of God at all, for if we did we would treat this central problem with awe, if only out of sheer fear of the overpowering God who can work His terrifying will on helpless human beings, as He had done to me. Could anyone who pretended to know the will of God have foreseen what He had caused me to do? In the New Testament, at any rate, there was nothing comparable. The Old Testament, and especially the Book of Job, might have opened my eyes in this respect, but at that time I was not familiar enough with it. Nor had I heard anything of the sort in the instruction for confirmation, which I was then receiving. The fear of God, which was of course mentioned, was considered antiquated, "Jewish," and long since superseded by the Christian message of God's love and goodness.

The symbolism of my childhood experiences and the violence of the imagery upset me terribly. I asked myself: "*Who* talks like that? Who has the impudence to exhibit a phallus so nakedly, and in a shrine? Who makes me think that God destroys His Church in this abominable manner?" At last I asked myself whether it was not the devil's doing. For that it must have been God or the devil who spoke and acted in this way was something I never doubted. I felt absolutely sure that it was not myself who had invented these thoughts and images.

These were the crucial experiences of my life. It was then that it dawned on me: I must take the responsibility, it is up to me how my fate turns out. I had been confronted with a problem to which I had to find the answer. And who posed the problem? Nobody ever answered me that. I knew that I had to find the answer out of my deepest self, that I was alone before God, and that God alone asked me these terrible things.

From the beginning I had a sense of destiny, as though my life was assigned to me by fate and had to be fulfilled. This gave me an inner security, and, though I could never prove it to myself, it proved itself to me. *I* did not have this certainty, *it* had me. Nobody could rob me of the conviction that it was enjoined upon me to do what God wanted and not what I wanted. That gave me the strength to go my own way. Often I had the feeling that in all decisive matters I was no longer among men, but was alone with God. And when I was "there," where I was no longer alone, I was outside time; I belonged to the centuries; and He who then gave answer was He who had always been, who had been before my birth. He who always is was there. These talks with the "Other" were my profoundest experiences: on the one hand a bloody struggle, on the other supreme ecstasy.

Naturally, I could not talk with anyone about these things. I knew of no one to whom I might have communicated them except, possibly, my mother. She seemed to think along somewhat similar lines as myself. But I soon noticed that in conversation she was not adequate for me. Her attitude toward me was above all one of admiration, and that was not good for me. And so I remained alone with my thoughts. On the whole, I liked that best. I played alone, daydreamed or strolled in the woods alone, and had a secret world of my own.

My mother was a very good mother to me. She had a hearty animal warmth, cooked wonderfully, and was most companionable and pleasant. She was very stout, and a ready listener. She also liked to talk, and her chatter was like the gay plashing of a fountain. She had a decided literary gift, as well as taste and depth. But this quality never properly emerged; it remained hidden beneath the semblance of a kindly, fat old woman, extremely hospitable, and possessor of a great sense of humor. She held all the conventional opinions a person was obliged to have, but then her unconscious personality would suddenly put in an appearance. That personality was unexpectedly powerful: a somber, imposing figure possessed of unassailable authority— and no bones about it. I was sure that she consisted of two personalities, one innocuous and human, the other uncanny.

This other emerged only now and then, but each time it was unexpected and frightening. She would then speak as if talking to herself, but what she said was aimed at me and usually struck to the core of my being, so that I was stunned into silence.

The first time I remember this happening was when I was about six years old. At that time we had neighbors who were fairly well off. They had three children, the eldest a boy of about my own age, and two younger sisters. They were city folk who, especially on Sundays, dressed their children in a manner that seemed ridiculous to me—patent-leather shoes, white frills, little white gloves. Even on weekdays the children were scrubbed and combed. They had fancy manners and anxiously kept their distance from the tough, rude boy with tattered trousers, holes in his shoes, and dirty hands. My mother annoyed me no end with her comparisons and admonishments: "Now look at those nice children, so well brought up and polite, but you behave like a little lout." Such exhortations humiliated me, and I decided to give the boy a hiding—which I did. His mother was furious, hastened to mine and made a great to-do over my act of violence. My mother was properly horrified and gave me a lecture, spiced with tears, longer and more passionate than anything I had ever heard from her before. I had not been conscious of any fault; on the contrary, I was feeling pretty pleased with myself, for it seemed to me that I had somehow made amends for the incongruous presence of this stranger in our village. Deeply awed by my mother's excitement, I withdrew penitently to my table behind our old spinet and began playing with my bricks. For some time there was silence in the room. My mother had taken her usual seat by the window, and was knitting. Then I heard her muttering to herself, and from occasional words that I picked up I gathered that she was thinking about the incident, but was now taking another view of it. Suddenly she said aloud, "Of course one should never have kept a litter like that!" I realized at once that she was talking about those "dressed-up monkeys." Her favorite brother was a hunter who kept dogs and was always talking about dog breeding, mongrels, purebreds, and litters. To my relief I realized that she too regarded those odious children as inferior whelps, and that her scolding therefore need not be taken at face value. But I also knew, even at that age, that I must keep perfectly still and not come out triumphantly with: "You see, you think as I do!" She would have repudiated the idea indignantly: "You horrid boy, how dare you pretend such a thing about your mother!" I conclude from this that I must already have had earlier experiences of a similar nature which I have forgotten.

I tell this story because at the time of my growing religious skepticism there was another instance which threw light on my mother's twofold nature. At table one day the talk turned on the dullness of the tunes of certain hymns. A possible revision of the hymnal was mentioned. At that my mother murmured, *"O du Liebe meiner Liebe, du verwünschte* [2] *Seligkeit"* (O thou love of my love, thou accursed bliss). As in the past I pretended that I had not heard and was careful not to cry out in glee, in spite of my feeling of triumph.

There was an enormous difference between my mother's two personalities. That was why as a child I often had anxiety dreams about her. By day she was a loving mother, but at night she seemed uncanny. Then she was like one of those seers who is at the same time a strange animal, like a priestess in a bear's cave. Archaic and ruthless; ruthless as truth and nature. At such moments she was the embodiment of what I have called the "natural mind." [3]

I too have this archaic nature, and in me it is linked with the gift—not always pleasant—of seeing people and things as they are. I can let myself be deceived from here to Tipperary when I don't want to recognize something, and yet at bottom I know quite well how matters really stand. In this I am like a dog— he can be tricked, but he always smells it out in the end. This "insight" is based on instinct, or on a *"participation mystique"* with others. It is as if the "eyes of the background" do the seeing in an impersonal act of perception.

[2] Slip of the tongue for *erwünscht* (longed for).

[3] The "natural mind" is the "mind which says absolutely straight and ruthless things." (Seminar on *Interpretation of Visions* [Zürich, privately printed, 1940], V, p. iv.) "That is the sort of mind which springs from natural sources, and not from opinions taken from books; it wells up from the earth like a natural spring, and brings with it the peculiar wisdom of nature." (*Ibid.*, VI, p. 34.)

This was something I did not realize until much later, when some very strange things happened to me. For instance, there was the time when I recounted the life story of a man without knowing him. It was at the wedding of a friend of my wife's; the bride and her family were all entirely unknown to me. During the meal I was sitting opposite a middle-aged gentleman with a long, handsome beard, who had been introduced to me as a barrister. We were having an animated conversation about criminal psychology. In order to answer a particular question of his, I made up a story to illustrate it, embellishing it with all sorts of details. While I was telling my story, I noticed that a quite different expression came over the man's face, and a silence fell on the table. Very much abashed, I stopped speaking. Thank heavens we were already at the dessert, so I soon stood up and went into the lounge of the hotel. There I withdrew into a corner, lit a cigar, and tried to think over the situation. At this moment one of the other guests who had been sitting at my table came over and asked reproachfully, "How did you ever come to commit such a frightful indiscretion?" "Indiscretion?" "Why yes, that story you told." "But I made it all up!"

To my amazement and horror it turned out that I had told the story of the man opposite me, exactly and in all its details. I also discovered, at this moment, that I could no longer remember a single word of the story—even to this day I have been unable to recall it. In his *Selbstschau,* Zschokke [4] describes a similar incident: how once, in an inn, he was able to unmask an unknown young man as a thief, because he had seen the theft being committed before his inner eye.

In the course of my life it has often happened to me that I suddenly knew something which I really could not know at all. The knowledge came to me as though it were my own idea. It was the same with my mother. She did not know what she was saying; it was like a voice wielding absolute authority, which said exactly what fitted the situation.

My mother usually assumed that I was mentally far beyond

[4] Johann Heinrich Daniel Zschokke (1771–1848), Swiss author of historical novels and studies in Swiss and Bavarian history. Cf. *Civilization in Transition* (CW 10, par. 850).

my age, and she would talk to me as to a grown-up. It was plain
that she was telling me everything she could not say to my
father, for she early made me her confidant and confided her
troubles to me. Thus, I was about eleven years old when she
informed me of a matter that concerned my father and alarmed
me greatly. I racked my brains, and at last came to the conclusion that I must consult a certain friend of my father's whom I
knew by hearsay to be an influential person. Without saying a
word to my mother, I went into town one afternoon after school
and called at this man's house. The maid who opened the door
told me that he was out. Depressed and disappointed, I returned
home. But it was by the mercy of providence that he was not
there. Soon afterward my mother again referred to this matter,
and this time gave me a very different and far milder picture
of the situation, so that the whole thing went up in smoke. That
struck me to the quick, and I thought: "What an ass you were to
believe it, and you nearly caused a disaster with your stupid
seriousness." From then on I decided to divide everything my
mother said by two. My confidence in her was strictly limited,
and that was what prevented me from ever telling her about
my deeper preoccupations.

But then came the moments when her second personality
burst forth, and what she said on those occasions was so true
and to the point that I trembled before it. If my mother could
then have been pinned down, I would have had a wonderful
interlocutor.

With my father it was quite different. I would have liked to
lay my religious difficulties before him and ask him for advice, but I did not do so because it seemed to me that I knew in
advance what he would be obliged to reply out of respect for his
office. How right I was in this assumption was demonstrated to
me soon afterward. My father personally gave me my instruction
for confirmation. It bored me to death. One day I was leafing
through the catechism, hoping to find something besides the
sentimental-sounding and usually incomprehensible as well as
uninteresting expatiations on Lord Jesus. I came across the
paragraph on the Trinity. Here was something that challenged
my interest: a oneness which was simultaneously a threeness.

This was a problem that fascinated me because of its inner contradiction. I waited longingly for the moment when we would reach this question. But when we got that far, my father said, "We now come to the Trinity, but we'll skip that, for I really understand nothing of it myself." I admired my father's honesty, but on the other hand I was profoundly disappointed and said to myself, "There we have it; they know nothing about it and don't give it a thought. Then how can I talk about my secret?"

I made vain, tentative attempts with certain of my schoolfellows who struck me as reflective. I awakened no response, but, on the contrary, a stupefaction that warned me off.

In spite of the boredom, I made every effort to believe without understanding—an attitude which seemed to correspond with my father's—and prepared myself for Communion, on which I had set my last hopes. This was, I thought, merely a memorial meal, a kind of anniversary celebration for Lord Jesus who had died $1890 - 30 = 1860$ years ago. But still, he had let fall certain hints such as, "Take, eat, this is my body," meaning that we should eat the Communion bread as if it were his body, which after all had originally been flesh. Likewise we were to drink the wine which had originally been blood. It was clear to me that in this fashion we were to incorporate him into ourselves. This seemed to me so preposterous an impossibility that I was sure some great mystery must lie behind it, and that I would participate in this mystery in the course of Communion, on which my father seemed to place so high a value.

As was customary, a member of the church committee stood godfather to me. He was a nice, taciturn old man, a wheelwright in whose workshop I had often stood, watching his skill with lathe and adze. Now he came, solemnly transformed by frock coat and top hat, and took me to church, where my father in his familiar robes stood behind the altar and read prayers from the liturgy. On the white cloth covering the altar lay large trays filled with small pieces of bread. I could see that the bread came from our baker, whose baked goods were generally poor and flat in taste. From a pewter jug, wine was poured into a pewter cup. My father ate a piece of the bread, took a swallow of the wine—I knew the tavern from which it had come—and passed the cup to one of the old men. All were stiff, solemn, and, it seemed to me, uninterested. I looked on in suspense, but could not see or guess whether anything unusual was going on inside the old men. The atmosphere was the same as that of all other performances in church—baptisms, funerals, and so on. I had the impression that something was being performed here in the traditionally correct manner. My father, too, seemed to be chiefly concerned with going through it all according to rule, and it was part of this rule that the appropriate words were read or spoken with emphasis. There was no mention of the fact that it was now 1860 years since Jesus had died, whereas in all other memorial services the date was stressed. I saw no sadness and no joy, and felt that the feast was meager in every respect, considering the extraordinary importance of the person whose memory was being celebrated. It did not compare at all with secular festivals.

Suddenly my turn came. I ate the bread; it tasted flat, as I had expected. The wine, of which I took only the smallest sip, was thin and rather sour, plainly not of the best. Then came the final prayer, and the people went out, neither depressed nor illumined with joy, but with faces that said, "So that's that."

I walked home with my father, intensely conscious that I was wearing a new black felt hat and a new black suit which was already beginning to turn into a frock coat. It was a kind of lengthened jacket that spread out into two little wings over the seat, and between these was a slit with a pocket into which I could tuck a handkerchief—which seemed to me a grown-up, manly gesture. I felt socially elevated and by implication accepted into the society of men. That day, too, Sunday dinner was an unusually good one. I would be able to stroll about in my new suit all day. But otherwise I was empty and did not know what I was feeling.

Only gradually, in the course of the following days, did it dawn on me that nothing had happened. I had reached the pinnacle of religious initiation, had expected something—I knew not what—to happen, and nothing at all had happened. I knew that God could do stupendous things to me, things of fire and unearthly light; but this ceremony contained no trace of God—not for me, at any rate. To be sure, there had been talk about Him, but it had all amounted to no more than words. Among the others I had noticed nothing of the vast despair, the overpowering elation and outpouring of grace which for me constituted the essence of God. I had observed no sign of "communion," of "union, becoming one with . . ." With whom? With Jesus? Yet he was only a man who had died 1860 years ago. Why should a person become one with him? He was called the "Son of God"—a demigod, therefore, like the Greek heroes: how then could an ordinary person become one with him? This was called the "Christian religion," but none of it had anything to do with God as I had experienced Him. On the other hand it was quite clear that Jesus, the man, did have to do with God; he had despaired in Gethsemane and on the cross, after having taught that God was a kind and loving father. He too, then, must have seen the fearfulness of God. That I could understand, but what was the purpose of this wretched memorial service with the flat bread and the sour wine? Slowly I came to understand that this communion had been a fatal experience for me. It had proved hollow; more than that, it had proved to be a total loss. I knew that I would never again be able to participate in this ceremony. "Why, that is not religion at all," I thought. "It is an absence of God; the church is a place I should not go to. It is not life which is there, but death."

I was seized with the most vehement pity for my father. All at once I understood the tragedy of his profession and his life. He was struggling with a death whose existence he could not admit. An abyss had opened between him and me, and I saw no possibility of ever bridging it, for it was infinite in extent. I could not plunge my dear and generous father, who in so many matters left me to myself and had never tyrannized over me, into that despair and sacrilege which were necessary for an experience of divine grace. Only God could do that. I had no right to; it would be inhuman. God is not human, I thought; that is His greatness, that nothing human impinges on Him. He is kind and terrible—both at once—and is therefore a great peril from which everyone naturally tries to save himself. People cling one-sidedly to His love and goodness, for fear they will fall victim to the tempter and destroyer. Jesus, too, had noticed that, and had therefore taught: "Lead us not into temptation."

My sense of union with the Church and with the human world, so far as I knew it, was shattered. I had, so it seemed to me, suffered the greatest defeat of my life. The religious outlook which I imagined constituted my sole meaningful relation with the universe had disintegrated; I could no longer participate in the general faith, but found myself involved in something inexpressible, in my secret, which I could share with no one. It was terrible and—this was the worst of it—vulgar and ridiculous also, a diabolical mockery.

I began to ponder: What must one think of God? I had not invented that thought about God and the cathedral, still less the dream that had befallen me at the age of three. A stronger will than mine had imposed both on me. Had nature been responsible? But nature was nothing other than the will of the Creator. Nor did it help to accuse the devil, for he too was a creature of God. God alone was real—an annihilating fire and an indescribable grace.

What about the failure of Communion to affect me? Was that my own failure? I had prepared for it in all earnestness, had hoped for an experience of grace and illumination, and nothing had happened. God had been absent. For God's sake I now found myself cut off from the Church and from my father's and everybody else's faith. Insofar as they all represented the Christian religion, I was an outsider. This knowledge filled me with a sadness which was to overshadow all the years until the time I entered the university.

I began looking in my father's relatively modest library—which in those days seemed impressive to me—for books that would tell me what was known about God. At first I found only the traditional conceptions, but not what I was seeking—a writer who thought independently. At last I hit upon Biedermann's *Christliche Dogmatik*, published in 1869. Here, apparently, was a man who thought for himself, who worked out his own views. I learned from him that religion was "a spiritual act

consisting in man's establishing his own relationship to God."
I disagreed with that, for I understood religion as something
that God did to me; it was an act on His part, to which I must
simply yield, for He was the stronger. My "religion" recognized
no human relationship to God, for how could anyone relate to
something so little known as God? I must know more about God
in order to establish a relationship to him. In Biedermann's
chapter on "The Nature of God" I found that God showed Himself to be a "personality to be conceived after the analogy of
the human ego: the unique, utterly supramundane ego who
embraces the entire cosmos."

As far as I knew the Bible, this definition seemed to fit. God
has a personality and is the ego of the universe, just as I myself
am the ego of my psychic and physical being. But here I encountered a formidable obstacle. Personality, after all, surely
signifies character. Now, character is one thing and not another;
that is to say, it involves certain specific attributes. But if God is
everything, how can He still possess a distinguishable character?
On the other hand, if He does have a character, He can only be
the ego of a subjective, limited world. Moreover, what kind of
character or what kind of personality does He have? Everything
depends on that, for unless one knows the answer one cannot
establish a relationship to Him.

I felt the strongest resistances to imagining God by analogy
with my own ego. That seemed to me boundlessly arrogant, if
not downright blasphemous. My ego was, in any case, difficult
enough for me to grasp. In the first place, I was aware that it
consisted of two contradictory aspects: No. 1 and No. 2. Second,
in both its aspects my ego was extremely limited, subject to all
possible self-deceptions and errors, moods, emotions, passions,
and sins. It suffered far more defeats than triumphs, was childish, vain, self-seeking, defiant, in need of love, covetous, unjust,
sensitive, lazy, irresponsible, and so on. To my sorrow it lacked
many of the virtues and talents I admired and envied in others.
How could this be the analogy according to which we were to
imagine the nature of God?

Eagerly I looked up the other characteristics of God, and
found them all listed in the way familiar to me from my instruc-

tion for confirmation. I found that according to Article 172 "the most immediate expression of the supramundane nature of God is 1) *negative:* His invisibility to men," etc., "and 2) *positive:* His dwelling in Heaven," etc. This was disastrous, for at once there rushed to my mind the blasphemous vision which God directly or indirectly (i.e., via the devil) had imposed on my will.

Article 183 informed me that "God's supramundane nature with regard to the moral world" consists in His "justice," which is not merely "judicial" but is also "an expression of His holy being." I had hoped that this paragraph would say something about God's dark aspects which were giving me so much trouble: His vindictiveness, His dangerous wrathfulness, His incomprehensible conduct toward the creatures His omnipotence had made, whose inadequacies He must know by virtue of that same omnipotence, and whom moreover it pleased Him to lead astray, or at least to test, even though He knew in advance the outcome of His experiments. What, indeed, was God's character? What would we say of a human personality who behaved in this manner? I did not dare to think this question out to its conclusion. And then I read that God, "although sufficient unto Himself and needing nothing outside Himself," had created the world "out of His satisfaction," and "as a natural world has filled it with His goodness and as a moral world desires to fill it with His love."

At first I pondered over the perplexing word "satisfaction." Satisfaction with what or with whom? Obviously with the world, for He had looked upon His work and called it good. But it was just this that I had never understood. Certainly the world is immeasurably beautiful, but it is quite as horrible. In a small village in the country, where there are few people and nothing much happens, "old age, disease, and death" are experienced more intensely, in greater detail, and more nakedly than elsewhere. Although I was not yet sixteen years old I had seen a great deal of the reality of the life of man and beast, and in church and school I had heard enough of the sufferings and corruption of the world. God could at most have felt "satisfaction" with paradise, but then He Himself had taken good care that the glory of paradise should not last too long by planting in it that poisonous serpent, the devil. Had He taken satisfaction in that too? I felt certain that Biedermann did not mean this, but was simply babbling on in that mindless way that characterized religious instruction, not even aware that he was writing nonsense. As I saw it, it was not at all unreasonable to suppose that God, for all that He probably did not feel any such cruel satisfaction in the unmerited sufferings of man and beast, had nevertheless intended to create a world of contradictions in which one creature devoured another and life meant simply being born to die. The "wonderful harmonies" of natural law looked to me more like a chaos tamed by fearful effort, and the "eternal" starry firmament with its predetermined orbits seemed plainly an accumulation of random bodies without order or meaning. For no one could really see the constellations people spoke about. They were mere arbitrary configurations.

I either did not see or gravely doubted that God filled the natural world with His goodness. This, apparently, was another of those points which must not be reasoned about but must be believed. In fact, if God is the highest good, why is the world, His creation, so imperfect, so corrupt, so pitiable? "Obviously it has been infected and thrown into confusion by the devil," I thought. But the devil, too, was a creature of God. I had to read up on the devil. He seemed to be highly important after all. I again opened Biedermann's book on Christian dogmatics and looked for the answer to this burning question. What were the reasons for suffering, imperfection, and evil? I could find nothing.

That finished it for me. This weighty tome on dogmatics was nothing but fancy drivel; worse still, it was a fraud or a specimen of uncommon stupidity whose sole aim was to obscure the truth. I was disillusioned and even indignant, and once more seized with pity for my father, who had fallen victim to this mumbo-jumbo.

But somewhere and at some time there must have been people who sought the truth as I was doing, who thought rationally and did not wish to deceive themselves and others and deny the sorrowful reality of the world. It was about this time that my mother, or rather, her No. 2 personality, suddenly and without preamble said, "You must read Goethe's *Faust* one of these days." We had a handsome edition of Goethe, and I picked out *Faust*. It poured into my soul like a miraculous balm. "Here at last," I thought, "is someone who takes the devil seriously and even concludes a blood pact with him—with the adversary who has the power to frustrate God's plan to make a perfect world." I regretted Faust's behavior, for to my mind he should not have been so one-sided and so easily tricked. He should have been cleverer and also more moral. How childish he was to gamble away his soul so frivolously! Faust was plainly a bit of a windbag. I had the impression that the weight of the drama and its significance lay chiefly on the side of Mephistopheles. It would not have grieved me if Faust's soul had gone to hell. He deserved it. I did not like the idea of the "cheated devil" at the end, for after all Mephistopheles had been anything but a stupid devil, and it was contrary to logic for him to be tricked by silly little angels. Mephistopheles seemed to me cheated in quite a different sense: he had not received his promised rights because Faust, that somewhat characterless fellow, had carried his swindle through right into the Hereafter. There, admittedly, his puerility came to light, but, as I saw it, he did not deserve the initiation into the great mysteries. I would have given him a taste of purgatorial fires. The real problem, it seemed to me, lay with Mephistopheles, whose whole figure made the deepest impression on me, and who, I vaguely sensed, had a relationship to the mystery of the Mothers.[5] At any rate Mephistopheles and the great initiation at the end remained for me a wonderful and mysterious experience on the fringes of my conscious world.

At last I had found confirmation that there were or had been people who saw evil and its universal power, and—more important—the mysterious role it played in delivering man from darkness and suffering. To that extent Goethe became, in my eyes, a prophet. But I could not forgive him for having dismissed Mephistopheles by a mere trick, by a bit of jiggery-pokery. For

[5] *Faust,* Part Two, trans. by Philip Wayne (Harmondsworth, England, Penguin Books Ltd, 1959), pp. 76 ff.

me that was too theological, too frivolous and irresponsible, and I was deeply sorry that Goethe too had fallen for those cunning devices by which evil is rendered innocuous.

In reading the drama I had discovered that Faust had been a philosopher of sorts, and although he turned away from philosophy, he had obviously learned from it a certain receptivity to the truth. Hitherto I had heard virtually nothing of philosophy, and now a new hope dawned. Perhaps, I thought, there were philosophers who had grappled with these questions and could shed light on them for me.

Since there were no philosophers in my father's library—they were suspect because they thought—I had to content myself with Krug's *General Dictionary of the Philosophical Sciences*, second edition, 1832. I plunged forthwith into the article on God. To my discontent it began with the etymology of the word "God," which, it said, "incontestably" derived from "good" and signified the *ens summum* or *perfectissimum*. The existence of God could not be proved, it continued, nor the innateness of the idea of God. The latter, however, could exist a priori in man, if not in actuality at any rate potentially. In any case our "intellectual powers" must "already be developed to a certain degree before they are capable of engendering so sublime an idea."

This explanation astounded me beyond measure. What is wrong with these "philosophers"? I wondered. Evidently they know of God only by hearsay. The theologians are different in this respect, at any rate; at least they are sure that God exists, even though they make contradictory statements about Him. This lexicographer Krug expresses himself in so involved a manner that it is easy to see he would like to assert that he is already sufficiently convinced of God's existence. Then why doesn't he say so outright? Why does he pretend—as if he really thought that we "engender" the idea of God, and to do so must first have reached a certain level of development? So far as I knew, even the savages wandering naked in their jungles had such ideas. And they were certainly not "philosophers" who sat down to "engender an idea of God." I never engendered any idea of God, either. Of course God cannot be proved, for how could, say, a clothes moth that eats Australian wool prove to other moths that

Australia exists? God's existence does not depend on our proofs. How had I arrived at my certainty about God? I was told all sorts of things about Him, yet I could believe nothing. None of it convinced me. That was not where my idea came from. In fact it was not an idea at all—that is, not something thought out. It was not like imagining something and thinking it out and afterward believing it. For example, all that about Lord Jesus was always suspect to me and I never really believed it, although it was impressed upon me far more than God, who was usually only hinted at in the background. Why have I come to take God for granted? Why do these philosophers pretend that God is an idea, a kind of arbitrary assumption which they can engender or not, when it is perfectly plain that He exists, as plain as a brick that falls on your head?

Suddenly I understood that God was, for me at least, one of the most certain and immediate of experiences. After all, I didn't invent that horrible image about the cathedral. On the contrary, it was forced on me and I was compelled, with the utmost cruelty, to think it, and afterward that inexpressible feeling of grace came to me. I had no control over these things. I came to the conclusion that there must be something the matter with these philosophers, for they had the curious notion that God was a kind of hypothesis that could be discussed. I also found it extremely unsatisfying that the philosophers offered no opinions or explanations about the dark deeds of God. These, it seemed to me, merited special attention and consideration from philosophy, since they constituted a problem which, I gathered, was rather a hard one for the theologians. All the greater was my disappointment to discover that the philosophers had apparently never even heard of it.

I therefore passed on to the next topic that interested me, the article on the devil. If, I read, we conceived of the devil as originally evil, we would become entangled in patent contradictions, that is to say, we would fall into dualism. Therefore we would do better to assume that the devil was originally created a good being but had been corrupted by his pride. However, as the author of the article pointed out—and I was glad to see this point made —this hypothesis presupposed the evil it was attempting to explain—namely, pride. For the rest, he continued, the origin of evil was "unexplained and inexplicable"—which meant to me: Like the theologians, he does not want to think about it. The article on evil and its origin proved equally unilluminating.

The account I have given here summarizes trains of thought and developments of ideas which, broken by long intervals, extended over several years. They went on exclusively in my No. 2 personality, and were strictly private. I used my father's library for these researches, secretly and without asking his permission. In the intervals, personality No. 1 openly read all the novels of Gerstäcker, and German translations of the classic English novels. I also began reading German literature, concentrating on those classics which school, with its needlessly laborious explanations of the obvious, had not spoiled for me. I read vastly and planlessly, drama, poetry, history, and later natural science. Reading was not only interesting but provided a welcome and beneficial distraction from the preoccupations of personality No. 2, which in increasing measure were leading me to depressions. For everywhere in the realm of religious questions I encountered only locked doors, and if ever one door should chance to open I was disappointed by what lay behind it. Other people all seemed to have totally different concerns. I felt completely alone with my certainties. More than ever I wanted someone to talk with, but nowhere did I find a point of contact; on the contrary, I sensed in others an estrangement, a distrust, an apprehension which robbed me of speech. That, too, depressed me. I did not know what to make of it. Why has no one had experiences similar to mine? I wondered. Why is there nothing about it in scholarly books? Am I the only one who has had such experiences? Why should I be the only one? It never occurred to me that I might be crazy, for the light and darkness of God seemed to me facts that could be understood even though they oppressed my feelings.

I felt the singularity into which I was being forced as something threatening, for it meant isolation, and that seemed all the more unpleasant to me as I was unjustly taken for a scapegoat a good deal more often than I liked. Moreover, something had happened in school to increase my isolation. In the German class

I was rather mediocre, for the subject matter, especially German grammar and syntax, did not interest me at all. I was lazy and bored. The subjects for composition usually seemed to me shallow or silly, and my essays turned out accordingly: either careless or labored. I slipped through with average marks, and this suited me very well, as it fitted in with my general tendency not to be conspicuous. On the whole I sympathized with boys from poor families who, like myself, had come from nowhere, and I had a liking for those who were none too bright, though I tended to become excessively irritated by their stupidity and ignorance. For the fact of the matter was that they had something to offer which I craved deeply: in their simplicity they noticed nothing unusual about me. My "unusualness" was gradually beginning to give me the disagreeable, rather uncanny feeling that I must possess repulsive traits, of which I was not aware, that caused my teachers and schoolmates to shun me.

In the midst of these preoccupations the following incident burst on me like a thunderclap. We had been assigned a subject for composition which for once interested me. Consequently I set to work with a will and produced what seemed to me a carefully written and successful paper. I hoped to receive at least one of the highest marks for it—not the highest, of course, for that would have made me conspicuous, but one close to the top.

Our teacher was in the habit of discussing the compositions in order of merit. The first one he turned to was by the boy at the head of the class. That was all right. Then followed the compositions of the others, and I waited and waited in vain for my name. Still it did not come. "It just can't be," I thought, "that mine is so bad that it is even below these poor ones he has come to. What can be the matter?" Was I simply *hors concours*—which would mean being isolated and attracting attention in the most dreadful way of all?

When all the essays had been read, the teacher paused. Then he said, "Now I have one more composition—Jung's. It is by far the best, and I ought to have given it first place. But unfortunately it is a fraud. Where did you copy it from? Confess the truth!"

I shot to my feet, as horrified as I was furious, and cried, "I did not copy it! I went to a lot of trouble to write a good composition." But the teacher shouted at me, "You're lying! You could never write a composition like this. No one is going to believe that. Now—where did you copy it from?"

Vainly I swore to my innocence. The teacher clung to his theory. He became threatening. "I can tell you this: if I knew where you had copied it from, you would be chucked out of the school." And he turned away. My classmates threw odd glances at me, and I realized with horror that they were thinking, "A-ha, so that's the way it is." My protestations fell on deaf ears.

I felt that from now on I was branded, and that all the paths which might have led me out of unusualness had been cut off. Profoundly disheartened and dishonored, I swore vengeance on the teacher, and if I had had an opportunity something straight out of the law of the jungle would have resulted. How in the world could I possibly prove that I had not copied the essay?

For days I turned this incident over in my thoughts, and again and again came to the conclusion that I was powerless, the sport of a blind and stupid fate that had marked me as a liar and a cheat. Now I realized many things I had not previously understood—for example, how it was that one of the teachers could say to my father, who had inquired about my conduct in school, "Oh, he's just average, but he works commendably hard." I was thought to be relatively stupid and superficial. That did not annoy me really. But what made me furious was that they should think me capable of cheating, and thus morally destroy me.

My grief and rage threatened to get out of control. And then something happened that I had already observed in myself several times before: there was a sudden inner silence, as though a soundproof door had been closed on a noisy room. It was as if a mood of cool curiosity came over me, and I asked myself, "What is really going on here? All right, you are excited. Of course the teacher is an idiot who doesn't understand your nature—that is, doesn't understand it any more than you do. Therefore he is as mistrustful as you are. You distrust yourself and others, and that is why you side with those who are naïve, simple, and easily seen through. One gets excited when one doesn't understand things."

In the light of these considerations *sine ira et studio,* I was struck by the analogy with that other train of ideas which had impressed itself on me so forcefully when I did not want to think the forbidden thought. Although at that time I doubtless saw no difference as yet between personalities No. 1 and No. 2, and still claimed the world of No. 2 as my own personal world, there was always, deep in the background, the feeling that something other than myself was involved. It was as though a breath of the great world of stars and endless space had touched me, or as if a spirit had invisibly entered the room—the spirit of one who had long been dead and yet was perpetually present in timelessness until far into the future. Denouements of this sort were wreathed with the halo of a numen.

At that time, of course, I could never have expressed myself in this fashion, nor am I now attributing to my state of consciousness something that was not there at the time. I am only trying to express the feelings I had then, and to shed light on that twilight world with the help of what I know now.

It was some months after the incident just described that my schoolmates hung the nickname "Father Abraham" on me. No. 1 could not understand why, and thought it silly and ridiculous. Yet somewhere in the background I felt that the name had hit the mark. All allusions to this background were painful to me, for the more I read and the more familiar I became with city life, the stronger grew my impression that what I was now getting to know as reality belonged to an order of things different from the view of the world I had grown up with in the country, among rivers and woods, among men and animals in a small village bathed in sunlight, with the winds and the clouds moving over it, and encompassed by dark night in which uncertain things happened. It was no mere locality on the map, but "God's world," so ordered by Him and filled with secret meaning. But apparently men did not know this, and even the animals had somehow lost the senses to perceive it. That was evident, for example, in the sorrowful, lost look of the cows, and in the resigned eyes of horses, in the devotion of dogs, who clung so desperately to human beings, and even in the self-assured step of the cats who had chosen house and barn as their residence and hunting ground. People were like the animals, and seemed as unconscious as they. They looked down upon the ground or up into the trees in order to see what could be put to use, and for what purpose; like animals they herded, paired, and fought, but did not see that they dwelt in a unified cosmos, in God's world, in an eternity where everything is already born and everything has already died.

Because they are so closely akin to us and share our unknowingness, I loved all warm-blooded animals who have souls like ourselves and with whom, so I thought, we have an instinctive understanding. We experience joy and sorrow, love and hate, hunger and thirst, fear and trust in common—all the essential features of existence with the exception of speech, sharpened consciousness, and science. And although I admired science in the conventional way, I also saw it giving rise to alienation and aberration from God's world, as leading to a degeneration which animals were not capable of. Animals were dear and faithful, unchanging and trustworthy. People I now distrusted more than ever.

Insects I did not regard as proper animals, and I took cold-blooded vertebrates to be a rather lowly intermediate stage on the way down to the insects. Creatures in this category were objects for observation and collection, curiosities merely, alien and extra-human; they were manifestations of impersonal life and more akin to plants than to human beings.

The earthly manifestations of "God's world" began with the realm of plants, as a kind of direct communication from it. It was as though one were peering over the shoulder of the Creator, who, thinking Himself unobserved, was making toys and decorations. Man and the proper animals, on the other hand, were bits of God that had become independent. That was why they could move about on their own and choose their abodes. Plants were bound for good or ill to their places. They expressed not only the beauty but also the thoughts of God's world, with no intent of their own and without deviation. Trees in particular were mysterious and seemed to me direct embodiments of the incomprehensible meaning of life. For that reason the woods were the place where I felt closest to its deepest meaning and to its awe-inspiring workings.

This impression was reinforced when I became acquainted with Gothic cathedrals. But there the infinity of the cosmos, the chaos of meaning and meaninglessness, of impersonal purpose and mechanical law, were wrapped in stone. This contained and at the same time *was* the bottomless mystery of being, the embodiment of spirit. What I dimly felt to be my kinship with stone was the divine nature in both, in the dead and the living matter.

At that time it would, as I have said, have been beyond my powers to formulate my feelings and intuitions in any graphic way, for they all occurred in No. 2 personality, while my active and comprehending ego remained passive and was absorbed into the sphere of the "old man," who belonged to the centuries. I experienced him and his influence in a curiously unreflective manner; when he was present, No. 1 personality paled to the point of nonexistence, and when the ego that became increasingly identical with No. 1 personality dominated the scene, the old man, if remembered at all, seemed a remote and unreal dream.

Between my sixteenth and nineteenth years the fog of my dilemma slowly lifted, and my depressive states of mind improved. No. 1 personality emerged more and more distinctly. School and city life took up my time, and my increased knowledge gradually permeated or repressed the world of intuitive premonitions. I began systematically pursuing questions I had consciously framed. I read a brief introduction to the history of philosophy and in this way gained a bird's-eye view of everything that had been thought in this field. I found to my gratification that many of my intuitions had historical analogues. Above all I was attracted to the thought of Pythagoras, Heraclitus, Empedocles, and Plato, despite the long-windedness of Socratic argumentation. Their ideas were beautiful and academic, like pictures in a gallery, but somewhat remote. Only in Meister Eckhart did I feel the breath of life—not that I understood him. The Schoolmen left me cold, and the Aristotelian intellectualism of St. Thomas appeared to me more lifeless than a desert. I thought, "They all want to force something to come out by tricks of logic, something they have not been granted and do not really know about. They want to prove a belief to themselves, whereas actually it is a matter of experience." They seemed to me like people who knew by hearsay that elephants existed, but had never seen one, and were now trying to prove by arguments that on logical grounds such animals must exist and must be constituted as in fact they are. For obvious reasons, the critical philosophy of the eighteenth century at first did not appeal to me at all. Of the nineteenth-century philosophers, Hegel put me off by his language, as arrogant as it was laborious; I regarded him with downright mistrust. He seemed to me like a man who was caged in the edifice of his own words and was pompously gesticulating in his prison.

But the great find resulting from my researches was Schopenhauer. He was the first to speak of the suffering of the world, which visibly and glaringly surrounds us, and of confusion, passion, evil—all those things which the others hardly seemed to notice and always tried to resolve into all-embracing harmony and comprehensibility. Here at last was a philosopher who had the courage to see that all was not for the best in the fundaments of the universe. He spoke neither of the all-good and all-wise providence of a Creator, nor of the harmony of the cosmos, but stated bluntly that a fundamental flaw underlay the sorrowful course of human history and the cruelty of nature: the blindness of the world-creating Will. This was confirmed not only by the early observations I had made of diseased and dying fishes, of mangy foxes, frozen or starved birds, of the pitiless tragedies concealed in a flowery meadow: earthworms tormented to death by ants, insects that tore each other apart piece by piece, and so on. My experiences with human beings, too, had taught me anything rather than a belief in man's original goodness and decency. I knew myself well enough to know that I was only gradually, as it were, distinguishing myself from an animal.

Schopenhauer's somber picture of the world had my undivided approval, but not his solution of the problem. I felt sure that by "Will" he really meant God, the Creator, and that he was saying that God was blind. Since I knew from experience that God was not offended by any blasphemy, that on the contrary He could even encourage it because He wished to evoke not only man's bright and positive side but also his darkness and ungodliness, Schopenhauer's view did not distress me. I considered it a verdict justified by the facts. But I was all the more disappointed by his theory that the intellect need only confront the blind Will with its image in order to cause it to reverse itself. How could the Will see this image at all, since it was blind? And why should it, even if it could see, thereby be persuaded to reverse itself, since the image would show it precisely what it willed? And what was the intellect? It was a function of the human soul, not a mirror but an infinitesimal fragment of a mirror such as a child might hold up to the sun, expecting the sun to be dazzled by it. I was puzzled that Schopenhauer should ever have been satisfied with such an inadequate answer.

Because of this I was impelled to study him more thoroughly, and I became increasingly impressed by his relation to Kant. I therefore began reading the works of this philosopher, above all his *Critique of Pure Reason,* which put me to some hard thinking. My efforts were rewarded, for I discovered the fundamental flaw, so I thought, in Schopenhauer's system. He had committed the deadly sin of hypostatizing a metaphysical assertion, and of endowing a mere noumenon, a *Ding an sich,* with special qualities. I got this from Kant's theory of knowledge, and it afforded me an even greater illumination, if that were possible, than Schopenhauer's "pessimistic" view of the world.

This philosophical development extended from my seventeenth year until well into the period of my medical studies. It brought about a revolutionary alteration of my attitude to the world and to life. Whereas formerly I had been shy, timid, mistrustful, pallid, thin, and apparently unstable in health, I now began to display a tremendous appetite on all fronts. I knew what I wanted and went after it. I also became noticeably more accessible and more communicative. I discovered that poverty was no handicap and was far from being the principal reason for suffering; that the sons of the rich really did not enjoy any advantages over the poor and ill-clad boys. There were far deeper reasons for happiness and unhappiness than one's allotment of pocket money. I made more and better friends than before. I felt firmer ground under my feet and even summoned up courage to speak openly of my ideas. But that, as I discovered all too soon, was a misunderstanding which I had cause to regret. For I met not only with embarrassment or mockery, but with hostile rejection. To my consternation and discomfiture, I found that certain people considered me a braggart, a poseur, and a humbug. The old charge of cheat was revived, even though in a somewhat milder form. Once again it had to do with a subject for composition that had aroused my interest. I had worked out my paper with particular care, taking the greatest pains to polish my style. The result was crushing. "Here is an essay by Jung," said the teacher. "It is downright brilliant, but tossed off so carelessly that it is easy to see how little serious effort went into it. I can tell you this, Jung, you won't get through life with that slapdash attitude. Life calls for earnestness and conscientiousness, work and effort. Look at D.'s paper. He has none of your brilliance, but he is honest, conscientious, and hard-working. That is the way to success in life."

My feelings were not as hurt as on the first occasion, for in spite of himself the teacher had been impressed by my essay, and had at least not accused me of stealing it. I protested against his reproaches, but was dismissed with the comment: "The *Ars Poetica* maintains that the best poem is the one which conceals the effort of creation. But you cannot make me believe that about your essay, for it was tossed off frivolously and without any effort." There were, I knew, a few good ideas in it, but the teacher did not even bother to discuss them.

I felt some bitterness over this incident, but the suspicions of my schoolmates were a far more serious matter, for they threatened to throw me back into my former isolation and depression. I racked my brains, trying to understand what I could have done to deserve their slanders. By cautious inquiries I discovered that they looked askance at me because I often made remarks, or dropped hints, about things which I could not possibly know. For instance, I pretended to know something about Kant and

Schopenhauer, or about paleontology, which we had not even had in school as yet. These astonishing discoveries showed me that practically all the burning questions had nothing to do with everyday life, but belonged, like my ultimate secret, to "God's world," which it was better not to speak of.

Henceforth I took care not to mention these esoteric matters among my schoolmates, and among the adults of my acquaintance I knew no one with whom I might have talked without risk of being thought a boaster and impostor. The most painful thing of all was the frustration of my attempts to overcome the inner split in myself, my division into two worlds. Again and again events occurred which forced me out of my ordinary, everyday existence into the boundlessness of "God's world."

This expression, "God's world," may sound sentimental to some ears. For me it did not have this character at all. To "God's world" belonged everything superhuman—dazzling light, the darkness of the abyss, the cold impassivity of infinite space and time, and the uncanny grotesqueness of the irrational world of chance. "God," for me, was everything—and anything but "edifying."

The older I grew, the more frequently I was asked by my parents and others what I wanted to be. I had no clear notions on that score. My interests drew me in different directions. On the one hand I was powerfully attracted by science, with its truths based on facts; on the other hand I was fascinated by everything to do with comparative religion. In the sciences I was drawn principally to zoology, paleontology, and geology; in the humanities to Greco-Roman, Egyptian, and prehistoric archaeology. At that time, of course, I did not realize how very much this choice of the most varied subjects corresponded to the nature of my inner dichotomy. What appealed to me in science were the concrete facts and their historical background, and in comparative religion the spiritual problems, into which philosophy also entered. In science I missed the factor of meaning; and in religion, that of empiricism. Science met, to a very large extent, the needs of No. 1 personality, whereas the humane or historical studies provided beneficial instruction for No. 2.

Torn between these two poles, I was for a long time unable to settle on anything. I noticed that my uncle, the head of my mother's family, who was pastor of St. Alban's in Basel, was gently pushing me in the direction of theology. The unusual attentiveness with which I had followed a conversation at table, when he was discussing a point of religion with one of his sons, all of whom were theologians, had not escaped him. I wondered whether there might possibly be theologians who were in close touch with the dizzy heights of the university and therefore knew more than my father. Such conversations never gave me the impression that they were concerned with real experiences, and certainly not with experiences like mine. They dealt exclusively with doctrinal opinions on the Biblical narratives, all of which made me feel distinctly uncomfortable, because of the numerous and barely credible accounts of miracles.

While I was attending the Gymnasium I was allowed to lunch at this uncle's house every Thursday. I was grateful to him not only for the lunch but for the unique opportunity of occasionally hearing at his table an adult, intelligent, and intellectual conversation. It was a marvelous experience for me to discover that anything of this sort existed at all, for in my home surroundings I had never heard anyone discussing learned topics. I did sometimes attempt to talk seriously with my father, but encountered an impatience and anxious defensiveness which puzzled me. Not until several years later did I come to understand that my poor father did not dare to think, because he was consumed by inward doubts. He was taking refuge from himself and therefore insisted on blind faith. He could not receive it as a grace because he wanted to "win it by struggle," forcing it to come with convulsive efforts.

My uncle and my cousins could calmly discuss the dogmas and doctrines of the Church Fathers and the opinions of modern theologians. They seemed safely ensconced in a self-evident world order, in which the name of Nietzsche did not occur at all and Jakob Burckhardt was paid only a grudging compliment. Burckhardt was "liberal," "rather too much of a freethinker"; I gathered that he stood somewhat askew in the eternal order of things. My uncle, I knew, never suspected how remote I was from theology, and I was deeply sorry to have to disappoint him. I would never have dared to lay my problems before him, since I knew only too well how disastrously this would turn out for me. I had nothing to say in my defense. On the contrary, No. 1 personality was fast taking the lead, and my scientific knowledge, though still meager, was thoroughly saturated with the scientific materialism of the time. It was only painfully held in check by the evidence of history and by Kant's *Critique of Pure Reason*, which apparently nobody in my environment understood. For although Kant was mentioned by my theologian uncle and cousins in tones of praise, his principles were used only to discredit opposing views but were never applied to their own. About this, too, I said nothing.

Consequently, I began to feel more and more uncomfortable when I sat down to table with my uncle and his family. Given my habitually guilty conscience, these Thursdays became black days for me. In this world of social and spiritual security and ease I felt less and less at home, although I thirsted for the drops of intellectual stimulation which occasionally trickled forth. I felt dishonest and ashamed. I had to admit to myself: "Yes, you are a cheat; you lie and deceive people who mean well by you. It's not their fault that they live in a world of social and intellectual certitudes, that they know nothing of poverty, that their religion is also their paid profession, that they are totally unconscious of the fact that God Himself can wrench a person out of his orderly spiritual world and condemn him to blaspheme. I have no way of explaining this to them. I must take the odium on myself and learn to bear it." Unfortunately, I had so far been singularly unsuccessful in this endeavor.

As the tensions of this moral conflict increased, No. 2 personality became more and more doubtful and distasteful to me, and I could no longer hide this fact from myself. I tried to extinguish No. 2, but could not succeed in that either. At school and in the presence of my friends I could forget him, and he also disappeared when I was studying science. But as soon as I was by myself, at home or out in the country, Schopenhauer and Kant returned in full force, and with them the grandeur of "God's world." My scientific knowledge also formed a part of it, and filled the great canvas with vivid colors and figures. Then No. 1 and his worries about the choice of a profession sank below the horizon, a tiny episode in the last decade of the nineteenth century. But when I returned from my expedition into the centuries, I brought with me a kind of hangover. I, or rather No. 1, lived in the here and now, and sooner or later would have to form a definite idea of what profession he wished to pursue.

Several times my father had a serious talk with me. I was free to study anything I liked, he said, but if I wanted his advice I should keep away from theology. "Be anything you like except a theologian," he said emphatically. By this time there was a tacit agreement between us that certain things could be said or done without comment. He had never taken me to task for cutting church as often as possible and for not going to Communion any more. The farther away I was from church, the better I felt. The only things I missed were the organ and the choral music, but certainly not the "religious community." The phrase meant nothing to me at all, for the habitual churchgoers struck me as being far less of a community than the "worldly" folk. The latter may have been less virtuous, but on the other hand they were much nicer people, with natural emotions, more sociable and cheerful, warmer-hearted and more sincere.

I was able to reassure my father that I had not the slightest desire to be a theologian. But I continued to waver between science and the humanities. Both powerfully attracted me. I was beginning to realize that No. 2 had no *pied-à-terre*. In him I was lifted beyond the here and now; in him I felt myself a single eye in a thousand-eyed universe, but incapable of moving so much as a pebble upon the earth. No. 1 rebelled against this passivity; he wanted to be up and doing, but for the present he was caught in an insoluble conflict. Obviously I had to wait and see what would happen. If anyone asked me what I wanted to be I was in the habit of replying: a philologist, by which I secretly meant Assyrian and Egyptian archaeology. In reality, however, I continued to study science and philosophy in my leisure hours, and particularly during the holidays, which I spent at home with my mother and sister. The days were long past when I ran to my mother, lamenting, "I'm bored, I don't know what to do." Holidays were now the best time of the year, when I could amuse myself alone. Moreover, during the summer vacations at least, my father was away, as he used regularly to spend his holidays in Sachseln.

Only once did it happen that I too went on a vacation trip. I was fourteen when, on our doctor's orders, I was sent to Entlebuch for a cure, in the hope that my fitful appetite and my then unstable health would be improved. For the first time I was alone among adult strangers. I was quartered in the Catholic priest's house. For me this was an eerie and at the same time fascinating adventure. I seldom got a glimpse of the priest himself, and his housekeeper was scarcely an alarming person, though prone to be curt. Nothing in the least menacing happened to me. I was under the supervision of an old country doctor who ran a kind of hotel-sanatorium for convalescents of all types. It was a very mixed group: farm people, minor officials, merchants, and a few cultivated people from Basel, among them a chemist who had attained that pinnacle of glory, the doctorate. My father, too, was a Ph.D., but he was merely a philologist and linguist. This chemist was a fascinating novelty to me: here was a scientist, perhaps one of those who understood the secrets of stones. He was still a young man and taught me to play croquet, but he imparted to me none of his presumably vast learning. And I was too shy, too awkward, and far too ignorant to ask him. I revered him as the first person I had ever met in the flesh who was initiated into the secrets of nature, or some of them, at least. He sat at the same table with me, ate the same food as I did, and occasionally even exchanged a few words with me. I felt transported into the sublimer sphere of adulthood. This elevation in my status was confirmed when I was permitted to go on the outings arranged for the boarders. On one of these occasions we visited a distillery, and were invited to sample the wares. In literal fulfillment of the verse:

> *But now there comes a kicker,*
> *This stuff, you see, is liquor* [6]

I found the various little glasses so inspiring that I was wafted

[6] Wilhelm Busch, *Die Jobsiade*.

into an entirely new and unexpected state of consciousness. There was no longer any inside or outside, no longer an "I" and the "others," No. 1 and No. 2 were no more; caution and timidity were gone, and the earth and sky, the universe and everything in it that creeps and flies, revolves, rises, or falls, had all become one. I was shamefully, gloriously, triumphantly drunk. It was as if I were drowned in a sea of blissful musings, but, because of the violent heaving of the waves, had to cling with eyes, hands, and feet to all solid objects in order to keep my balance on the swaying streets and between the rocking houses and trees. "Marvelous," I thought, "only unfortunately just a little too much." The experience came to a rather woeful end, but it nevertheless remained a discovery, a premonition of beauty and meaning which I had spoiled only by my stupidity.

At the end of my stay my father came to fetch me, and we traveled together to Lucerne, where—what happiness!—we went aboard a steamship. I had never seen anything like it. I could not see enough of the action of the steam engine, and then suddenly I was told we had arrived in Vitznau. Above the village towered a high mountain, and my father now explained to me that this was the Rigi, and that a cogwheel railway ran up it. We went to a small station building, and there stood the strangest locomotive in the world, with the boiler upright but tilted at a queer angle. Even the seats in the carriage were tilted. My father pressed a ticket into my hand and said, "You can ride up to the peak alone. I'll stay here, it's too expensive for the two of us. Be careful not to fall down anywhere."

I was speechless with joy. Here I was at the foot of this mighty mountain, higher than any I had ever seen, and quite close to the fiery peaks of my faraway childhood. I was, indeed, almost a man by now. For this trip I had bought myself a bamboo cane and an English jockey cap—the proper articles of dress for a world traveler. And now I was to ascend this enormous mountain! I no longer knew which was bigger, I or the mountain. With a tremendous puffing, the wonderful locomotive shook and rattled me up to the dizzy heights where ever-new abysses and panoramas opened out before my gaze, until at last I stood on the peak in the strange thin air, looking into unimaginable distances. "Yes," I thought, "this is it, my world, the real world, the secret, where there are no teachers, no schools, no unanswerable questions, where one can *be* without having to ask anything." I kept carefully to the paths, for there were tremendous precipices all around. It was all very solemn, and I felt one had to be polite and silent up here, for one was in God's world. Here it was physically present. This was the best and most precious gift my father had ever given me.

So profound was the impression this made upon me that my memories of everything that happened afterward in "God's world" were completely blotted out. But No. 1 also came into his own on this trip, and his impressions remained with me for the rest of my life. I still see myself, grown up and independent, wearing a stiff black hat and with an expensive cane, sitting on the terrace of one of the overwhelmingly elegant palatial hotels beside Lake Lucerne, or in the beautiful gardens of Vitznau, having my morning coffee at a small, white-covered table under a striped awning spangled with sunlight, eating croissants with golden butter and various kinds of jam, and considering plans for outings that would fill the whole long summer day. After the coffee I would stroll calmly, without excitement and at a deliberate pace, to a steamship, which would carry me toward the Gotthard and the foot of those giant mountains whose tops were covered with gleaming glaciers.

For many decades this image rose up whenever I was wearied from overwork and sought a point of rest. In real life I have promised myself this splendor again and again, but I have never kept my promise.

This, my first conscious journey, was followed by a second a year or two later. I had been allowed to visit my father, who was on holiday in Sachseln. From him I learned the impressive news that he had become friendly with the Catholic priest there. This seemed to me an act of extraordinary boldness, and secretly I admired my father's courage. While there, I paid a visit to the hermitage of Flüeli and the relics of Brother Klaus, who by then had been beatified. I wondered how the Catholics knew that he was in a beatific state. Perhaps he was still wandering about and had told people so? I was powerfully impressed by the genius loci, and was able not only to imagine the possibility of a life so entirely dedicated to God but even to understand it. But I did so with an inward shudder and a question to which I knew no answer: How could his wife and children have borne having a saint for a husband and father, when it was precisely my father's faults and inadequacies that made him particularly lovable to me? "Yes," I thought, "how could anyone live with a saint?" Obviously he saw that it was impossible, and therefore he had to become a hermit. Still, it was not so very far from his cell to his house. This wasn't a bad idea, I thought, to have the family in one house, while I would live some distance away, in a hut with a pile of books and a writing table, and an open fire where I would roast chestnuts and cook my soup on a tripod. As a holy hermit I wouldn't have to go to church any more, but would have my own private chapel instead.

From the hermitage I strolled on up the hill, lost in my thoughts, and was just turning to descend when from the left the slender figure of a young girl appeared. She wore the local costume, had a pretty face, and greeted me with friendly blue eyes. As though it were the most natural thing in the world we descended into the valley together. She was about my own age. Since I knew no other girls except my cousins, I felt rather embarrassed and did not know how to talk to her. So I began hesitantly explaining that I was here for a couple of days on holiday, that I was at the Gymnasium in Basel and later wanted to study at the university. While I was talking, a strange feeling of fatefulness crept over me. "She has appeared just at this moment," I thought to myself, "and she walks along with me as naturally as if we belonged together." I glanced sideways at her and saw an expression of mingled shyness and admiration in her face, which embarrassed me and somehow pierced me. Can it be possible, I wondered, that this is fate? Is my meeting her mere chance? A peasant girl—could it possibly be? She is a Catholic, but perhaps her priest is the very one with whom my father has made friends? She has no idea who I am. I certainly couldn't talk to her about Schopenhauer and the negation of the Will, could I? Yet she doesn't seem in any way sinister. Perhaps her priest is not one of those Jesuits skulking about in black robes.

But I cannot tell her, either, that my father is a Protestant clergyman. That might frighten or offend her. And to talk about philosophy, or about the devil, who is more important than Faust even though Goethe made such a simpleton of him—that is quite out of the question. She still dwells in the distant land of innocence, but I have plunged into reality, into the splendor and cruelty of creation. How can she endure to hear about that? An impenetrable wall stands between us. There is not and cannot be any relationship.

Sad at heart, I retreated into myself and turned the conversation to less dangerous topics. Was she going to Sachseln, wasn't the weather lovely, and what a view, and so on.

Outwardly this encounter was completely meaningless. But, seen from within, it was so weighty that it not only occupied my thoughts for days but has remained forever in my memory, like a shrine by the wayside. At that time I was still in that childlike state where life consists of single, unrelated experiences. For who could discover the threads of fate which led from Brother Klaus to the pretty girl?

This period of my life was filled with conflicting thoughts. Schopenhauer and Christianity would not square with one another, for one thing; and for another, No. 1 wanted to free himself from the pressure or melancholy of No. 2. It was not No. 2 who was depressed, but No. 1 when he remembered No. 2. It was just at this time that, out of the clash of opposites, the first systematic fantasy of my life was born. It made its appearance piece by piece, and it had its origin, so far as I can remember, in an experience which stirred me profoundly.

One day a northwest wind was lashing the Rhine into foaming waves. My way to school led along the river. Suddenly I saw approaching from the north a ship with a great mainsail running up the Rhine before the storm. Here was something completely new in my experience—a sailing vessel on the Rhine! My imagination took wings. If, instead of this swiftly flowing river, all of Alsace were a lake, we would have sailing boats and great steamers. Then Basel would be a port; it would be almost as good as living by the sea. Then everything would be different, and we would live in another time and another world. There would be no Gymnasium, no long walk to school, and I would be grown up and able to arrange my life as I wished. There would be a hill of rock rising out of the lake, connected by a narrow isthmus to the mainland, cut through by a broad canal with a wooden bridge over it, leading to a gate flanked by towers and opening into a little medieval city built on the surrounding slopes. On the rock stood a well-fortified castle with a tall keep, a watchtower. This was my house. In it there were no fine halls or any signs of magnificence. The rooms were simple, paneled, and rather small. There was an uncommonly attractive library where you could find everything worth knowing. There was also a collection of weapons, and the bastions were mounted with heavy cannon. Besides that, there was a garrison of fifty men-at-arms in the castle. The little town had several hundred inhabitants and was governed by a mayor and a town council of old men. I myself was justice of the peace, arbitrator, and adviser, who appeared only now and then to hold court. On the landward side the town had a port in which lay my two-masted schooner, armed with several small cannon.

The nerve center and *raison d'être* of this whole arrangement was the secret of the keep, which I alone knew. The thought had come to me like a shock. For, inside the tower, extending from the battlements to the vaulted cellar, was a copper column or heavy wire cable as thick as a man's arm, which ramified at the top into the finest branches, like the crown of a tree or —better still—like a taproot with all its tiny rootlets turned upside down and reaching into the air. From the air they drew a certain inconceivable something which was conducted down the copper column into the cellar. Here I had an equally inconceivable apparatus, a kind of laboratory in which I made gold out of the mysterious substance which the copper roots drew from the air. This was really an arcanum, of whose nature I neither had nor wished to form any conception. Nor did my imagination concern itself with the nature of the transformation process. Tactfully and with a certain nervousness it skirted around what actually went on in this laboratory. There was a kind of inner prohibition: one was not supposed to look into it too closely, nor ask what kind of substance was extracted from the air. As Goethe says of the Mothers, "Even to speak of them dismays the bold." [7]

"Spirit," of course, meant for me something ineffable, but at bottom I did not regard it as essentially different from very rarefied air. What the roots absorbed and transmitted to the copper trunk was a kind of spiritual essence which became visible down in the cellar as finished gold coins. This was certainly no mere conjuring trick, but a venerable and vitally important secret of nature which had come to me I know not how and which I had to conceal not only from the council of elders but, in a sense, also from myself.

My long, boring walk to and from school began to shorten most delightfully. Scarcely was I out of the schoolhouse than I was already in the castle, where structural alterations were in progress, council sessions were being held, evildoers sentenced, disputes arbitrated, cannon fired. The schooner's decks were cleared, the sails rigged, and the vessel steered carefully out of the harbor before a gentle breeze, and then, as it emerged from behind the rock, tacked into a stiff nor'wester. Suddenly I found myself on my doorstep, as though only a few minutes had passed. I stepped out of my fantasy as out of a carriage which had effortlessly driven me home. This highly enjoyable occupation lasted for several months before I got sick of it. Then I found the fantasy silly and ridiculous. Instead of daydreaming I began building castles and artfully fortified emplacements out of small stones, using mud as mortar—the fortress of Hüningen, which at that time was still intact, serving me as a model. I studied all the available fortification plans of Vauban, and was soon familiar with all the technicalities. From Vauban I turned to modern methods of fortification, and tried with my limited means to build models of all the different types. This preoccupied me in my leisure hours for more than two years, during which time my leanings toward nature study and concrete things steadily increased, at the cost of No. 2.

As long as I knew so little about real things, there was no point, I thought, in thinking about them. Anyone could have fantasies, but real knowledge was another matter. My parents

[7] *Faust*, Part Two, p. 76.

allowed me to take out a subscription for a scientific periodical, which I read with passionate interest. I hunted and collected all the fossils to be found in our Jura mountains, and all the obtainable minerals, also insects and the bones of mammoths and men—mammoth bones from gravel pits in the Rhineland plain, human bones from a mass grave near Hüningen, dating from 1811. Plants interested me too, but not in a scientific sense. I was attracted to them for a reason I could not understand, and with a strong feeling that they ought not to be pulled up and dried. They were living beings which had meaning only so long as they were growing and flowering—a hidden, secret meaning, one of God's thoughts. They were to be regarded with awe and contemplated with philosophical wonderment. What the biologist had to say about them was interesting, but it was not the essential thing. Yet I could not explain to myself what this essential thing was. How were plants related to the Christian religion or to the negation of the Will, for example? This was something I could not fathom. They obviously partook of the divine state of innocence which it was better not to disturb. By way of contrast, insects were denatured plants—flowers and fruits which had presumed to crawl about on legs or stilts and to fly around with wings like the petals of blossoms, and busied themselves preying on plants. Because of this unlawful activity they were condemned to mass executions, June bugs and caterpillars being the especial targets of such punitive expeditions. My "sympathy with all creatures" was strictly limited to warm-blooded animals. The only exceptions among the cold-blooded vertebrates were frogs and toads, because of their resemblance to human beings.

· III ·

Student Years

IN SPITE OF my growing scientific interests, I turned back from time to time to my philosophical books. The question of my choice of a profession was drawing alarmingly close. I looked forward with longing to the end of my school days. Then I would go to the university and study—natural science, of course. Then I would know something real. But no sooner had I made myself this promise than my doubts began. Was not my bent rather toward history and philosophy? Then again, I was intensely interested in everything Egyptian and Babylonian, and would have liked best to be an archaeologist. But I had no money to study anywhere except in Basel, and in Basel there was no teacher for this subject. So this plan very soon came to an end. For a long time I could not make up my mind and constantly postponed the decision. My father was very worried. He said once, "The boy is interested in everything imaginable, but he does not know what he wants." I could only admit that he was right. As matriculation approached and we had to decide what faculty to register for, I abruptly decided on science, but I left my schoolfellows in doubt as to whether I intended to go in definitely for science or the humanities.

This apparently sudden decision had a background of its own. Some weeks previously, just at the time when No. 1 and No. 2 were wrestling for a decision, I had two dreams. In the first dream I was in a dark wood that stretched along the Rhine. I came to a little hill, a burial mound, and began to dig. After a while I turned up, to my astonishment, some bones of prehistoric animals. This interested me enormously, and at that moment I knew: I must get to know nature, the world in which we live, and the things around us.

Then came a second dream. Again I was in a wood; it was threaded with watercourses, and in the darkest place I saw a circular pool, surrounded by dense undergrowth. Half immersed in the water lay the strangest and most wonderful creature: a round animal, shimmering in opalescent hues, and consisting of innumerable little cells, or of organs shaped like tentacles. It was a giant radiolarian, measuring about three feet across. It seemed to me indescribably wonderful that this magnificent creature should be lying there undisturbed, in the hidden place, in the clear, deep water. It aroused in me an intense desire for knowledge, so that I awoke with a beating heart. These two dreams decided me overwhelmingly in favor of science, and removed all my doubts.

It became clear to me that I was living in a time and a place where a person had to earn his living. To do so, one had to be this or that, and it made a deep impression on me that all my schoolfellows were imbued with this necessity and thought about nothing else. I felt I was in some way odd. Why could I not make up my mind and commit myself to something definite? Even that plodding fellow D. who had been held up to me by my German teacher as a model of diligence and conscientiousness was certain that he would study theology. I saw that I would have to settle down and think the matter through. If I took up zoology, for instance, I could be only a schoolmaster, or at best an employee in a zoological garden. There was no future in that, even if one's demands were modest—though I would certainly have preferred working in a zoo to the life of a schoolteacher.

In this blind alley the inspiration suddenly came to me that I could study medicine. Strangely enough, this had never occurred to me before, although my paternal grandfather, of whom I had heard so much, had been a doctor. Indeed, for that very reason I had a certain resistance to this profession. "Only don't imitate," was my motto. But now I told myself that the study of medicine at least began with scientific subjects. To that extent I would be doing what I wanted. Moreover, the field of medicine was so broad that there was always the possibility of specializing later. I had definitely opted for science, and the only question was: How? I had to earn my living, and as I had no money I could not attend a university abroad and obtain the kind of training that would give me hopes of a scientific career. At best I could become only a dilettante in science. Nor, since I possessed a personality that made me disliked by many of my schoolfellows and of the people who counted (i.e., the teachers), was there any hope of finding a patron who would support my wish. When, therefore, I finally decided on medicine, it was with the rather disagreeable feeling that it was not a good thing to start life with such a compromise. Nevertheless, I felt considerably relieved now that this irrevocable decision had been made.

The painful question then presented itself: Where was the money to come from? My father could raise only part of it. He applied to the University of Basel for a stipend for me, and to my shame it was granted. I was ashamed, not so much because our poverty was laid bare for all the world to see, but because I had secretly been convinced that all the "top" people, the people who "counted," were ill disposed toward me. I had never expected any such kindness from them. I had obviously profited by the reputation of my father, who was a good and uncomplicated person. Yet I felt myself totally different from him. I had, in fact, two different conceptions of myself. Through No. 1's eyes I saw myself as a rather disagreeable and moderately gifted young man with vaulting ambitions, an undisciplined temperament, and dubious manners, alternating between naïve enthusiasm and fits of childish disappointment, in his innnermost essence a hermit and obscurantist. On the other hand, No. 2 regarded No. 1 as a difficult and thankless moral task, a lesson that had to be got through somehow, complicated by a variety of faults such as spells of laziness, despondency, depression, inept enthusiasm for ideas and things that nobody valued, liable to imaginary friendships, limited, prejudiced, stupid (mathematics!), with a lack of understanding for other people, vague and confused in philosophical matters, neither an honest Christian nor anything else. No. 2 had no definable character at all; he was a *vita peracta,* born, living, dead, everything in one; a total vision of life. Though pitilessly clear about himself, he was unable to express himself through the dense, dark medium of No. 1, though he longed to do so. When No. 2 predominated, No. 1 was contained and obliterated in him, just as, conversely, No. 1 regarded No. 2 as a region of inner darkness. No. 2 felt that any conceivable expression of himself would be like a stone thrown over the edge of the world, dropping soundlessly into infinite night. But in him (No. 2) light reigned, as in the spacious halls of a royal palace whose high casements open upon a landscape flooded with sunlight. Here were meaning and historical continuity, in strong contrast to the incoherent fortuitousness of No. 1's life, which had no real points of contact with its environment. No. 2, on the other hand, felt himself in secret accord with the Middle Ages, as personified by *Faust,* with the legacy of a past which had obviously stirred Goethe to the depths. For Goethe too, therefore—and this was my great consolation—No. 2 was a reality. *Faust,* as I now realized with something of a shock, meant more to me than my beloved Gospel according to St. John. There was something in *Faust* that worked directly on my feelings. John's Christ was strange to me, but still stranger was the Savior of the other gospels. *Faust,* on the other hand, was the living equivalent of No. 2, and I was convinced that *he* was the answer which Goethe had given to his times. This insight was not only comforting to me, it also gave me an increased feeling of inner security and a sense of belonging to the human community. I was no longer isolated and a mere curiosity, a sport of cruel nature. My godfather and authority was the great Goethe himself.

About this time I had a dream which both frightened and encouraged me. It was night in some unknown place, and I was making slow and painful headway against a mighty wind. Dense fog was flying along everywhere. I had my hands cupped around a tiny light which threatened to go out at any moment. Everything depended on my keeping this little light alive. Suddenly I had the feeling that something was coming up behind me. I looked back, and saw a gigantic black figure following me. But at the same moment I was conscious, in spite of my terror, that I must keep my little light going through night and wind, regardless of all dangers. When I awoke I realized at once that the figure was a "specter of the Brocken," my own shadow on the swirling mists, brought into being by the little light I was carrying. I knew, too, that this little light was my consciousness, the only light I have. My own understanding is the sole treasure I possess, and the greatest. Though infinitely small and fragile in comparison with the powers of darkness, it is still a light, my only light.

This dream was a great illumination for me. Now I knew that No. 1 was the bearer of the light, and that No. 2 followed him like a shadow. My task was to shield the light and not look back at the *vita peracta;* this was evidently a forbidden realm of light of a different sort. I must go forward against the storm, which sought to thrust me back into the immeasurable darkness of a world where one is aware of nothing except the surfaces of things in the background. In the role of No. 1, I had to go forward—into study, moneymaking, responsibilities, entanglements, confusions, errors, submissions, defeats. The storm pushing against me was time, ceaselessly flowing into the past, which just as ceaselessly dogs our heels. It exerts a mighty suction which greedily draws everything living into itself; we can only escape from it—for a while—by pressing forward. The past is terribly real and present, and it catches everyone who cannot save his skin with a satisfactory answer.

My view of the world spun around another ninety degrees; I recognized clearly that my path led irrevocably outward, into the limitations and darkness of three-dimensionality. It seemed to me that Adam must once have left Paradise in this manner; Eden had become a specter for him, and light was where a stony field had to be tilled in the sweat of his brow.

I asked myself: "Whence comes such a dream?" Till then I had taken it for granted that such dreams were sent directly by God. But now I had imbibed so much epistemology that doubts assailed me. One might say, for instance, that my insight had been slowly ripening for a long time and had then suddenly broken through in a dream. And that, indeed, is what had happened. But this explanation is merely a description. The real question was why this process took place and why it broke through into consciousness. Consciously I had done nothing to promote any such development; on the contrary, my sympathies were on the other side. Something must therefore have been at work behind the scenes, some intelligence, at any rate something more intelligent than myself. For the extraordinary idea that in the light of consciousness the inner realm of light appears as a gigantic shadow was not something I would have hit on of my own accord. Now all at once I understood many things that had been inexplicable to me before—in particular that cold shadow of embarrassment and estrangement which passed over people's faces whenever I alluded to anything reminiscent of the inner realm.

I must leave No. 2 behind me, that was clear. But under no circumstances ought I to deny him to myself or declare him invalid. That would have been a self-mutilation, and would moreover have deprived me of any possibility of explaining the origin of the dreams. For there was no doubt in my mind that No. 2 had something to do with the creation of dreams, and I could easily credit him with the necessary superior intelligence. But I felt myself to be increasingly identical with No. 1, and this state proved in turn to be merely a part of the far more comprehensive No. 2, with whom for that very reason I could no longer feel myself identical. He was indeed a specter, a spirit who could hold his own against the world of darkness. This was something I had not known before the dream, and even at the time—I am sure of this in retrospect—I was conscious of it only vaguely, although I knew it emotionally beyond a doubt.

At any rate, a schism had taken place between me and No. 2, with the result that "I" was assigned to No. 1 and was separated from No. 2 in the same degree, who thereby acquired, as it were, an autonomous personality. I did not connect this with the idea of any definite individuality, such as a revenant might have, although with my rustic origins this possibility would not have seemed strange to me. In the country people believe in these things according to the circumstances: they are and they are not. The only distinct feature about this spirit was his historical character, his extension in time, or rather, his timelessness. Of course I did not tell myself this in so many words, nor did I form any conception of his spatial existence. He played the role of a factor in the background of my No. 1 existence, never clearly defined but yet definitely present.

Children react much less to what grown-ups say than to the imponderables in the surrounding atmosphere. The child unconsciously adapts himself to them, and this produces in him correlations of a compensatory nature. The peculiar "religious" ideas that came to me even in my earliest childhood were spontaneous products which can be understood only as reactions to my parental environment and to the spirit of the age. The religious doubts to which my father was later to succumb naturally had to pass through a long period of incubation. Such a revolution of one's world, and of the world in general, threw its shadows ahead, and the shadows were all the longer, the more desperately my father's conscious mind resisted their power. It is not surprising that my father's forebodings put him in a state of unrest, which then communicated itself to me.

I never had the impression that these influences emanated from my mother, for she was somehow rooted in deep, invisible ground, though it never appeared to me as confidence in her Christian faith. For me it was somehow connected with animals, trees, mountains, meadows, and running water, all of which contrasted most strangely with her Christian surface and her conventional assertions of faith. This background corresponded so well to my own attitude that it caused me no uneasiness; on the contrary, it gave me a sense of security and the conviction that here was solid ground on which one could stand. It never occurred to me how "pagan" this foundation was. My mother's "No. 2" offered me the strongest support in the conflict then beginning between paternal tradition and the strange, compensatory products which my unconscious had been stimulated to create.

Looking back, I now see how very much my development as a child anticipated future events and paved the way for modes of adaptation to my father's religious collapse as well as to the shattering revelation of the world as we see it today—a revelation which had not taken shape from one day to the next, but had cast its shadows long in advance. Although we human beings have our own personal life, we are yet in large measure the representatives, the victims and promoters of a collective spirit whose years are counted in centuries. We can well think all our lives long that we are following our own noses, and may never discover that we are, for the most part, supernumeraries on the stage of the world theater. There are factors which, although we do not know them, nevertheless influence our lives, the more so if they are unconscious. Thus at least a part of our being lives in the centuries—that part which, for my private use, I have designated "No. 2." That it is not an individual curiosity is proved by the religion of the West, which expressly applies itself to this inner man and for two thousand years has earnestly tried to bring him to the knowledge of our surface consciousness with its personalistic preoccupations: *"Non foras ire, in interiore homine habitat veritas"* (Go not outside; truth dwells in the inner man).

During the years 1892–94 I had a number of rather vehement discussions with my father. He had studied Oriental languages in Göttingen and had done his dissertation on the Arabic version of the Song of Songs. His days of glory had ended with his final examination. Thereafter he forgot his linguistic talent. As a country parson he lapsed into a sort of sentimental idealism and into reminiscences of his golden student days, continued to smoke a long student's pipe, and discovered that his marriage was not all he had imagined it to be. He did a great deal of good —far too much—and as a result was usually irritable. Both parents made great efforts to live devout lives, with the result that there were angry scenes between them only too frequently.

These difficulties, understandably enough, later shattered my father's faith.

At that time his irritability and discontent had increased, and his condition filled me with concern. My mother avoided everything that might excite him and refused to engage in disputes. Though I realized that this was the wisest course to take, often I could not keep my own temper in check. I would remain passive during his outbursts of rage, but when he seemed to be in a more accessible mood I sometimes tried to strike up a conversation with him, hoping to learn something about his inner thoughts and his understanding of himself. It was clear to me that something quite specific was tormenting him, and I suspected that it had to do with his faith. From a number of hints he let fall I was convinced that he suffered from religious doubts. This, it seemed to me, was bound to be the case if the necessary experience had not come to him. From my attempts at discussion I learned in fact that something of the sort was amiss, for all my questions were met with the same old lifeless theological answers, or with a resigned shrug which aroused the spirit of contradiction in me. I could not understand why he did not seize on these opportunities pugnaciously and come to terms with his situation. I saw that my critical questions made him sad, but I nevertheless hoped for a constructive talk, since it appeared almost inconceivable to me that he should not have had experience of God, the most evident of all experiences. I knew enough about epistemology to realize that knowledge of this sort could not be proved, but it was equally clear to me that it stood in no more need of proof than the beauty of a sunset or the terrors of the night. I tried, no doubt very clumsily, to convey these obvious truths to him, with the hopeful intention of helping him to bear the fate which had inevitably befallen him. He had to quarrel with somebody, so he did it with his family and himself. Why didn't he do it with God, the dark author of all created things, who alone was responsible for the sufferings of the world? God would assuredly have sent him by way of an answer one of those magical, infinitely profound dreams which He had sent to me even without being asked, and which had sealed my fate. I did not know why, it simply was so. Yes, He had even allowed me a glimpse into His own being. This was a great secret which I dared not and could not reveal to my father. I might have been able to reveal it had he been capable of understanding the direct experience of God. But in my talks with him I never got that far, never even came within sight of the problem, because I always set about it in a very unpsychological and intellectual way, and did everything possible to avoid the emotional aspects. Each time this approach was like a red rag to a bull and led to irritable reactions which were incomprehensible to me. I was unable to understand how a perfectly rational argument could meet with such emotional resistance.

These fruitless discussions exasperated my father and me, and in the end we abandoned them, each burdened with his own specific feeling of inferiority. Theology had alienated my father and me from one another. I felt that I had once again suffered a fatal defeat, though I sensed I was not alone. I had a dim premonition that he was inescapably succumbing to his fate. He was lonely and had no friend to talk with. At least I knew no one among our acquaintances whom I would have trusted to say the saving word. Once I heard him praying. He struggled desperately to keep his faith. I was shaken and outraged at once, because I saw how hopelessly he was entrapped by the Church and its theological thinking. They had blocked all avenues by which he might have reached God directly, and then faithlessly abandoned him. Now I understood the deepest meaning of my earlier experience: God Himself had disavowed theology and the Church founded upon it. On the other hand God condoned this theology, as He condoned so much else. It seemed ridiculous to me to suppose that men were responsible for such developments. What were men, anyway? "They are born dumb and blind as puppies," I thought, "and like all God's creatures are furnished with the dimmest light, never enough to illuminate the darkness in which they grope." I was equally sure that none of the theologians I knew had ever seen "the light that shineth in the darkness" with his own eyes, for if they had they would not have been able to teach a "theological religion," which seemed quite inadequate to me, since there was nothing to do with it but believe it without hope. This was what my father had tried valiantly to do, and had run aground. He could not even defend himself against the ridiculous materialism of the psychiatrists. This, too, was something that one had to believe, just like theology, only in the opposite sense. I felt more certain than ever that both of them lacked epistemological criticism as well as experience.

My father was obviously under the impression that psychiatrists had discovered something in the brain which proved that in the place where mind should have been there was only matter, and nothing "spiritual." This was borne out by his admonitions that if I studied medicine I should in Heaven's name not become a materialist. To me this warning meant that I ought to believe nothing at all, for I knew that materialists believed in their definitions just as the theologians did in theirs, and that my poor father had simply jumped out of the frying pan into the fire. I recognized that this celebrated faith of his had played this deadly trick on him, and not only on him but on most of the cultivated and serious people I knew. The arch sin of faith, it seemed to me, was that it forestalled experience. How did the theologians know that God had deliberately arranged certain things and "permitted" certain others, and how did the psychiatrists know that matter was endowed with the qualities of the human mind? I was in no danger of succumbing to materialism, but my father certainly was. Apparently someone had whispered something about "suggestion," for I discovered that he was reading Bernheim's book on suggestion in Sigmund Freud's translation.[1] This was a new and significant departure, for I had never before seen my father reading anything but novels or an occasional travel book. All "clever" and interesting books were taboo. But his psychiatric reading made him no happier. His depressive moods increased in frequency and intensity, and so did his hypochondria. For a number of years he had complained of all sorts of abdominal symptoms, though his doctor had been unable to find anything definite wrong with him. Now he complained of the sensation of having "stones in

[1] *Die Suggestion und ihre Heilwirkung* (Leipzig and Vienna, 1888).

the abdomen." For a long time we did not take this seriously, but at last the doctor became suspicious. This was toward the end of the summer of 1895.

In the spring of that year I had begun my studies at the University of Basel. The only time in my life that I have ever been bored—my school days at the Gymnasium—was over at last and the golden gates to the *universitas litterarum* and to academic freedom were opening wide for me. Now I would hear the truth about nature, at least its most essential aspects. I would learn all there was to know about the anatomy and physiology of man, and would acquire knowledge of the diseases. In addition to all this, I was admitted into a color-wearing fraternity to which my father had belonged. Early in my freshman year he came along on a fraternity outing to a wine-growing village in the Markgrafen country and there delivered a whimsical speech in which, to my delight, the gay spirit of his own student days came back again. I realized in a flash that his life had come to a standstill at his graduation, and the verse of a student song echoed in my ears:

> *Sie zogen mit gesenktem Blick*
> *In das Philisterland zurück.*
> *O jerum, jerum, jerum,*
> *O quae mutatio rerum!* [2]

The words fell heavily on my soul. Once upon a time he too had been an enthusiastic student in his first year, as I was now; the world had opened out for him, as it was doing for me; the infinite treasures of knowledge had spread before him, as now before me. How can it have happened that everything was blighted for him, had turned to sourness and bitterness? I found no answer, or too many. The speech he delivered that summer evening over the wine was the last chance he had to live out his memories of the time when he was what he should have been. Soon afterward his condition deteriorated. In the late autumn of 1895 he became bedridden, and early in 1896 he died.

I had come home after lectures, and asked how he was. "Oh,

[2] "With downcast eyes they marched back to the land of the Philistines. O dear, O dear, O dear, how things have changed!"

still the same. He's very weak," my mother said. He whispered something to her, which she repeated to me, warning me with her eyes of his delirious condition: "He wants to know whether you have passed the state examination." I saw that I must lie. "Yes, it went very well." He sighed with relief, and closed his eyes. A little later I went in to see him again. He was alone; my mother was doing something in the adjoining room. There was a rattling in his throat, and I could see that he was in the death agony. I stood by his bed, fascinated. I had never seen anyone die before. Suddenly he stopped breathing. I waited and waited for the next breath. It did not come. Then I remembered my mother and went into the next room, where she sat by the window, knitting. "He is dying," I said. She came with me to the bed, and saw that he was dead. She said as if in wonderment: "How quickly it has all passed."

The following days were gloomy and painful, and little of them has remained in my memory. Once my mother spoke to me or to the surrounding air in her "second" voice, and remarked, "He died in time for you." Which appeared to mean: "You did not understand each other and he might have become a hindrance to you." This view seemed to me to fit in with my mother's No. 2 personality.

The words "for you" hit me terribly hard, and I felt that a bit of the old days had now come irrevocably to an end. At the same time, a bit of manliness and freedom awoke in me. After my father's death I moved into his room, and took his place inside the family. For instance, I had to hand out the housekeeping money to my mother every week, because she was unable to economize and could not manage money.

Six weeks after his death my father appeared to me in a dream. Suddenly he stood before me and said that he was coming back from his holiday. He had made a good recovery and was now coming home. I thought he would be annoyed with me for having moved into his room. But not a bit of it! Nevertheless, I felt ashamed because I had imagined he was dead. Two days later the dream was repeated. My father had recovered and was coming home, and again I reproached myself because I had thought he was dead. Later I kept asking myself: "What does it mean that my father returns in dreams and that he seems so real?" It was an unforgettable experience, and it forced me for the first time to think about life after death.

With the death of my father difficult problems arose concerning the continuation of my studies. Some of my mother's relations took the view that I ought to look for a clerk's job in a business house, so as to earn money as quickly as possible. My mother's youngest brother offered to help her, since her resources were not nearly sufficient to live on. An uncle on my father's side helped me. At the end of my studies I owed him three thousand francs. The rest I earned by working as a junior assistant and by helping an aged aunt dispose of her small collection of antiques. I sold them piece by piece at good prices, and received a very welcome percentage.

I would not have missed this time of poverty. One learns to value simple things. I still remember the time when I was given a box of cigars as a present. It seemed to me princely. They lasted a whole year, for I allowed myself one only on Sundays.

My student days were a good time for me. Everything was intellectually alive, and it was also a time of friendships. In the fraternity meetings I gave several lectures on theological and psychological subjects. We had many animated discussions, and not always about medical questions only. We argued over Schopenhauer and Kant, we knew all about the stylistic niceties of Cicero, and were interested in theology and philosophy.

During my student days I received much stimulation in regard to religious questions. At home I had the welcome opportunity to talk with a theologian who had been my father's vicar. He was distinguished not only by his phenomenal appetite, which put mine quite in the shade, but by his remarkable erudition. From him I learned a great deal about the Church Fathers and the history of dogma. He also introduced me to new aspects of Protestant theology. Ritschl's theology was much in fashion in those days. Its historicism irritated me, especially the comparison with a railway train.[3] The theological students with whom I had discussions in the fraternity all seemed quite

---

[3] Albrecht Ritschl (1822–89) compared Christ's coming to the shunting of a railroad train. The engine gives a push from behind, the motion passes through the entire train, and the foremost car begins to move. Thus the impulse given by Christ is transmitted down the centuries.—A. J.

content with the theory of the historical effect produced by Christ's life. This view seemed to me not only soft-witted but altogether lifeless. Neither could I subscribe to the tendency to move Christ into the foreground and make him the sole decisive figure in the drama of God and man. To me this absolutely belied Christ's own view that the Holy Ghost, who had begotten him, would take his place among men after his death.

For me the Holy Ghost was a manifestation of the inconceivable God. The workings of the Holy Ghost were not only sublime but also partook of that strange and even questionable quality which characterized the deeds of Yahweh, whom I naïvely identified with the Christian image of God, as I had been taught in my instruction for confirmation. (I was also not aware at this time that the devil, properly speaking, had been born with Christianity.) Lord Jesus was to me unquestionably a man and therefore a fallible figure, or else a mere mouthpiece of the Holy Ghost. This highly unorthodox view, a far cry from the theological one, naturally ran up against utter incomprehension. The disappointment I felt about this gradually led me to a kind of resigned indifference, and confirmed my conviction that in religious matters only experience counted.

During my first years at the university I made the discovery that while science opened the door to enormous quantities of knowledge, it provided genuine insights very sparingly, and these in the main were of a specialized nature. I knew from my philosophical reading that the existence of the psyche was responsible for this situation. Without the psyche there would be neither knowledge nor insight. Yet nothing was ever said about the psyche. Everywhere it was tacitly taken for granted, and even when someone mentioned it—as did C. G. Carus, for example—there was no real knowledge of it but only philosophical speculation which might just as easily take one turn as another. I could make neither head nor tail of this curious observation.

At the end of my second semester, however, I made another discovery, which was to have great consequences. In the library of a classmate's father I came upon a small book on spiritualistic phenomena, dating from the seventies. It was an account of the beginnings of spiritualism, and was written by a theologian. My initial doubts were quickly dissipated, for I could not help seeing that the phenomena described in the book were in principle much the same as the stories I had heard again and again in the country since my earliest childhood. The material, without a doubt, was authentic. But the great question of whether these stories were physically true was not answered to my satisfaction. Nevertheless, it could be established that at all times and all over the world the same stories had been reported again and again. There must be some reason for this, and it could not possibly have been the predominance of the same religious conceptions everywhere, for that was obviously not the case. Rather it must be connected with the objective behavior of the human psyche. But with regard to this cardinal question—the objective nature of the psyche—I could find out absolutely nothing, except what the philosophers said.

The observations of the spiritualists, weird and questionable as they seemed to me, were the first accounts I had seen of objective psychic phenomena. Names like Zoellner and Crookes impressed themselves on me, and I read virtually the whole of the literature available to me at the time. Naturally I also spoke of these matters to my comrades, who to my great astonishment reacted with derision and disbelief or with anxious defensiveness. I wondered at the sureness with which they could assert that things like ghosts and table-turning were impossible and therefore fraudulent, and on the other hand at the evidently anxious nature of their defensiveness. I, too, was not certain of the absolute reliability of the reports, but why, after all, should there not be ghosts? How did we know that something was "impossible"? And, above all, what did the anxiety signify? For myself I found such possibilities extremely interesting and attractive. They added another dimension to my life; the world gained depth and background. Could, for example, dreams have anything to do with ghosts? Kant's *Dreams of a Spirit Seer* came just at the right moment, and soon I also discovered Karl Duprel, who had evaluated these ideas philosophically and psychologically. I dug up Eschenmayer, Passavant, Justinus Kerner, and Görres, and read seven volumes of Swedenborg.

My mother's No. 2 sympathized wholeheartedly with my enthusiasm, but everyone else I knew was distinctly discouraging. Hitherto I had encountered only the brick wall of traditional views, but now I came up against the steel of people's prejudice and their utter incapacity to admit unconventional possibilities. I found this even with my closest friends. To them all this was far worse than my preoccupation with theology. I had the feeling that I had pushed to the brink of the world; what was of burning interest to me was null and void for others, and even a cause for dread.

Dread of what? I could find no explanation for this. After all, there was nothing preposterous or world-shaking in the idea that there might be events which overstepped the limited categories of space, time, and causality. Animals were known to sense beforehand storms and earthquakes. There were dreams which foresaw the death of certain persons, clocks which stopped at the moment of death, glasses which shattered at the critical moment. All these things had been taken for granted in the world of my childhood. And now I was apparently the only person who had ever heard of them. In all earnestness I asked myself what kind of world I had stumbled into. Plainly the urban world knew nothing about the country world, the real world of mountains, woods, and rivers, of animals and "God's thoughts" (plants and crystals). I found this explanation comforting. At all events, it bolstered my self-esteem, for I realized that for all its wealth of learning the urban world was mentally rather limited. This insight proved dangerous, because it tricked me into fits of superiority, misplaced criticism, and aggressiveness, which got me deservedly disliked. This eventually brought back all the old doubts, inferiority feelings, and depressions—a vicious circle I was resolved to break at all costs. No longer would I stand outside the world, enjoying the dubious reputation of a freak.

After my first introductory course I became junior assistant in anatomy, and the following semester the demonstrator placed me in charge of the course in histology—to my intense satisfaction, naturally. I interested myself primarily in evolutionary theory and comparative anatomy, and I also became acquainted with neo-vitalistic doctrines. What fascinated me most of all was the morphological point of view in the broadest sense. With physiology it was just the opposite. I found the subject thoroughly repellent because of vivisection, which was practiced merely for purposes of demonstration. I could never free myself from the feeling that warm-blooded creatures were akin to us and not just cerebral automata. Consequently I cut demonstration classes whenever I could. I realized that one had to experiment on animals, but the demonstration of such experiments nevertheless seemed to me horrible, barbarous, and above all unnecessary. I had imagination enough to picture the demonstrated procedures from a mere description of them. My compassion for animals did not derive from the Buddhistic trimmings of Schopenhauer's philosophy, but rested on the deeper foundation of a primitive attitude of mind—on an unconscious identity with animals. At the time, of course, I was wholly ignorant of this important psychological fact. My repugnance for physiology was so great that my examination results in this subject were correspondingly poor. Nevertheless, I scraped through.

The clinical semesters that followed kept me so busy that scarcely any time remained for my forays into outlying fields. I was able to study Kant only on Sundays. I also read Eduard von Hartmann assiduously. Nietzsche had been on my program for some time, but I hesitated to begin reading him because I felt I was insufficiently prepared. At that time he was much discussed, mostly in adverse terms, by the allegedly competent philosophy students, from which I was able to deduce the hostility he aroused in the higher echelons. The supreme authority, of course, was Jakob Burckhardt, whose various critical comments on Nietzsche were bandied about. Moreover, there were some persons at the university who had known Nietzsche personally and were able to retail all sorts of unflattering tidbits about him. Most of them had not read a word of Nietzsche and therefore dwelt at length on his outward foibles, for example, his putting on airs as a gentleman, his manner of playing the piano, his stylistic exaggerations—idiosyncrasies which got on the nerves of the good people of Basel in those days. Such things would certainly not have caused me to postpone the reading of Nietzsche—on the contrary, they acted as the strongest incentive. But I was held back by a secret fear that I might perhaps be like him, at least in regard to the "secret" which had isolated him from his environment. Perhaps—who knows?—he had had inner experiences, insights which he had unfortunately attempted to talk about, and had found that no one understood him. Obviously he was, or at least was considered to be, an eccentric, a sport of nature, which I did not want to be under any circumstances. I feared I might be forced to recognize that I too was another such strange bird. Of course, he was a professor, had written whole long books and so had attained unimaginable heights, but, like me, he was a clergyman's son. He, however, had been born in the great land of Germany, which reached as far as the sea, while I was only a Swiss and sprang from a modest parsonage in a small border village. He spoke a polished High German, knew Latin and Greek, possibly French, Italian, and Spanish as well, whereas the only language I commanded with any certainty was the Waggis-Basel dialect. He, possessed of all these splendors, could well afford to be something of an eccentric, but I must not let myself find out how far I might be like him.

In spite of these trepidations I was curious, and finally resolved to read him. *Thoughts Out of Season* was the first volume that fell into my hands. I was carried away by enthusiasm, and soon afterward read *Thus Spake Zarathustra*. This, like Goethe's *Faust*, was a tremendous experience for me. *Zarathustra* was Nietzsche's *Faust*, his No. 2, and my No. 2 now corresponded to *Zarathustra*—though this was rather like comparing a molehill with Mount Blanc. And *Zarathustra*—there could be no doubt about that—was morbid. Was my No. 2 also morbid? This possibility filled me with a terror which for a long time I refused to admit, but the idea cropped up again and again at inopportune moments, throwing me into a cold sweat, so that in the end I was forced to reflect on myself. Nietzsche had discovered his No. 2 only late in life, when he was already past middle age, whereas I had known mine ever since boyhood. Nietzsche had spoken naïvely and incautiously about this *arrhe-*

ton, this thing not to be named, as though it were quite in order. But I had noticed in time that this only leads to trouble. He was so brilliant that he was able to come to Basel as a professor when still a young man, not suspecting what lay ahead of him. Because of his very brilliance he should have noticed in time that something was amiss. That, I thought, was his morbid misunderstanding: that he fearlessly and unsuspectingly let his No. 2 loose upon a world that knew and understood nothing about such things. He was moved by the childish hope of finding people who would be able to share his ecstasies and could grasp his "transvaluation of all values." But he found only educated Philistines—tragi-comically, he was one himself. Like the rest of them, he did not understand himself when he fell head first into the unutterable mystery and wanted to sing its praises to the dull, godforsaken masses. That was the reason for the bombastic language, the piling up of metaphors, the hymnlike raptures—all a vain attempt to catch the ear of a world which had sold its soul for a mass of disconnected facts. And he fell—tightrope-walker that he proclaimed himself to be —into depths far beyond himself. He did not know his way about in this world and was like a man possessed, one who could be handled only with the utmost caution. Among my friends and acquaintances I knew of only two who openly declared themselves adherents of Nietzsche. Both were homosexual; one of them ended by committing suicide, the other ran to seed as a misunderstood genius. The rest of my friends were not so much dumfounded by the phenomenon of *Zarathustra* as simply immune to its appeal.

Just as *Faust* had opened a door for me, *Zarathustra* slammed one shut, and it remained shut for a long time to come. I felt like the old peasant who discovered that two of his cows had evidently been bewitched and had got their heads in the same halter. "How did that happen?" asked his small son. "Boy, one doesn't talk about such things," replied his father.

I realized that one gets nowhere unless one talks to people about the things they know. The naïve person does not appreciate what an insult it is to talk to one's fellows about anything that is unknown to them. They pardon such ruthless behavior only in a writer, journalist, or poet. I came to see that a new idea, or even just an unusual aspect of an old one, can be communicated only by facts. Facts remain and cannot be brushed aside; sooner or later someone will come upon them and know what he has found. I realized that I talked only for want of something better, that I ought to be offering facts, and these I lacked entirely. I had nothing concrete in my hands. More than ever I found myself driven toward empiricism. I began to blame the philosophers for rattling away when experience was lacking, and holding their tongues when they ought to have been answering with facts. In this respect they all seemed like watered-down theologians. I felt that at some time or other I had passed through the valley of diamonds, but I could convince no one—not even myself, when I looked at them more closely—that the specimens I had brought back were not mere pieces of gravel.

This was in 1898, when I began to think more seriously about my career as a medical man. I soon came to the conclusion that I would have to specialize. The choice seemed to lie between surgery and internal medicine. I inclined toward the former because of my special training in anatomy and my preference for pathology, and would very probably have made surgery my profession if I had possessed the necessary financial means. All along, it had been extremely painful to me to have to go into debt in order to study at all. I knew that after the final examination I would have to begin earning my living as soon as possible. I imagined a career as assistant at some cantonal hospital, where there was more hope of obtaining a paid position than in a clinic. Moreover, a post in a clinic depended to a large extent on the backing or personal interest of the chief. With my questionable popularity and estrangement from others—experienced all too often—I dared not think of any such stroke of luck, and therefore contented myself with the modest prospect of a post in one of the local hospitals. The rest depended on hard work and on my capability and application.

During the summer holidays, however, something happened that was destined to influence me profoundly. One day I was sitting in my room, studying my textbooks. In the adjoining room, the door to which stood ajar, my mother was knitting. That was our dining room, where the round walnut dining table stood. The table had come from the dowry of my paternal grandmother, and was at this time about seventy years old. My mother was sitting by the window, about a yard away from the table. My sister was at school and our maid in the kitchen. Suddenly there sounded a report like a pistol shot. I jumped up and rushed into the room from which the noise of the explosion had come. My mother was sitting flabbergasted in her armchair, the knitting fallen from her hands. She stammered out, "W-w-what's happened? It was right beside me!" and stared at the table. Following her eyes, I saw what had happened. The table top had split from the rim to beyond the center, and not along any joint; the split ran right through the solid wood. I was thunderstruck. How could such a thing happen? A table of solid walnut that had dried out for seventy years—how could it split on a summer day in the relatively high degree of humidity characteristic of our climate? If it had stood next to a heated stove on a cold, dry winter day, then it might have been conceivable. What in the world could have caused such an explosion? "There certainly are curious accidents," I thought. My mother nodded darkly. "Yes, yes," she said in her No. 2 voice, "that means something." Against my will I was impressed and annoyed with myself for not finding anything to say.

Some two weeks later I came home at six o'clock in the evening and found the household—my mother, my fourteen-year-old sister, and the maid—in a great state of agitation. About an hour earlier there had been another deafening report. This time it was not the already damaged table; the noise had come from the direction of the sideboard, a heavy piece of furniture dating from the early nineteenth century. They had already looked all over it, but had found no trace of a split. I immediately began examining the sideboard and the entire surrounding area, but just as fruitlessly. Then I began on the interior of the sideboard. In the cupboard containing the bread basket I found a loaf of bread, and, beside it, the bread knife. The greater part of the blade had snapped off in several pieces. The handle lay in one corner of the rectangular basket, and in each of the other corners lay a piece of the blade. The knife had been used shortly before, at four-o'clock tea, and afterward put away. Since then no one had gone to the sideboard.

The next day I took the shattered knife to one of the best cutlers in the town. He examined the fractures with a magnifying glass, and shook his head. "This knife is perfectly sound," he said. "There is no fault in the steel. Someone must have deliberately broken it piece by piece. It could be done, for instance, by sticking the blade into the crack of the drawer and breaking off a piece at a time. Or else it might have been dropped on stone from a great height. But good steel can't explode. Someone has been pulling your leg." I have carefully kept the pieces of the knife to this day.

My mother and my sister had been in the room when the sudden report made them jump. My mother's No. 2 looked at me meaningfully, but I could find nothing to say. I was completely at a loss and could offer no explanation of what had happened, and this was all the more annoying as I had to admit that I was profoundly impressed. Why and how had the table split and the knife shattered? The hypothesis that it was just a coincidence went much too far. It seemed highly improbable to me that the Rhine would flow backward just once, by mere chance—and all other possible explanations were automatically ruled out. So what was it?

A few weeks later I heard of certain relatives who had been engaged for some time in table-turning, and also had a medium, a young girl of fifteen and a half. The group had been thinking of having me meet the medium, who produced somnambulistic states and spiritualistic phenomena. When I heard this, I immediately thought of the strange manifestations in our house, and I conjectured that they might be somehow connected with this medium. I therefore began attending the regular séances which my relatives held every Saturday evening. We had results in the form of communications and tapping noises from the walls and the table. Movements of the table independently of the medium were questionable, and I soon found out that limiting conditions imposed on the experiment generally had an obstructive effect. I therefore accepted the obvious autonomy of the tapping noises and turned my attention to the content of the communications. I set forth the results of these observations in my doctoral thesis. After about two years of experimentation we all became rather weary of it. I caught the medium trying to produce phenomena by trickery, and this made me break off the experiments—very much to my regret, for I had learned from this example how a No. 2 personality is formed, how it enters into a child's consciousness and finally integrates it into itself. She was one of these precociously matured personalities, and she died of tuberculosis at the age of twenty-six. I saw her once again, when she was twenty-four, and received a lasting impression of the independence and maturity of her personality. After her death I learned from her family that during the last months of her life her character disintegrated bit by bit, and that ultimately she returned to the state of a two-year-old child, in which condition she fell into her last sleep.

All in all, this was the one great experience which wiped out all my earlier philosophy and made it possible for me to achieve a psychological point of view. I had discovered some objective facts about the human psyche. Yet the nature of the experience was such that once again I was unable to speak of it. I knew no one to whom I could have told the whole story. Once more I had to lay aside an unfinished problem. It was not until two years later that my dissertation appeared.[4]

At the medical clinic Friedrich von Müller had taken the place of old Immermann. In Müller I encountered a mind that appealed to me. I saw how a keen intelligence grasped the problem and formulated questions which in themselves were half the solution. He, for his part, seemed to see something in me, for toward the end of my studies he proposed that I should go with him, as his assistant, to Munich, where he had received an appointment. This invitation almost persuaded me to devote myself to internal medicine. I might have done so had not something happened in the meantime which removed all my doubts concerning my future career.

[4] *Zur Psychologie und Pathologie sogenannter occulter Phänomene: eine psychiatrische Studie* (1902); English trans.: "On the Psychology and Pathology of So-called Occult Phenomena," in *Psychiatric Studies* (CW 1).

Though I had attended psychiatric lectures and clinics, the current instructor in psychiatry was not exactly stimulating, and when I recalled the effects which the experience of asylums had had on my father, this was not calculated to prepossess me in favor of psychiatry. In preparing myself for the state examination, therefore, the textbook on psychiatry was the last I attacked. I expected nothing of it, and I still remember that as I opened the book by Krafft-Ebing [5] the thought came to me: "Well, now let's see what a psychiatrist has to say for himself." The lectures and clinical demonstrations had not made the slightest impression on me. I could not remember a single one of the cases I had seen in the clinic, but only my boredom and disgust.

I began with the preface, intending to find out how a psychiatrist introduced his subject or, indeed, justified his reason for existing at all. By way of excuse for this high and mighty attitude I must make it clear that in the medical world at that time psychiatry was quite generally held in contempt. No one really knew anything about it, and there was no psychology which regarded man as a whole and included his pathological variations in the total picture. The director was locked up in the same institution with his patients, and the institution was equally cut off, isolated on the outskirts of the city like an ancient lazaret with its lepers. No one liked looking in that direction. The doctors knew almost as little as the layman and therefore shared his feelings. Mental disease was a hopeless and fatal affair which cast its shadow over psychiatry as well. The psychiatrist was a strange figure in those days, as I was soon to learn from personal experience.

Beginning with the preface, I read: "It is probably due to the peculiarity of the subject and its incomplete state of development that psychiatric textbooks are stamped with a more or less subjective character." A few lines further on, the author called the psychoses "diseases of the personality." My heart suddenly began to pound. I had to stand up and draw a deep breath. My excitement was intense, for it had become clear to me, in a flash of illumination, that for me the only possible goal

[5] *Lehrbuch der Psychiatrie,* 4th edn. (1890).

was psychiatry. Here alone the two currents of my interest could flow together and in a united stream dig their own bed. Here was the empirical field common to biological and spiritual facts, which I had everywhere sought and nowhere found. Here at last was the place where the collision of nature and spirit became a reality.

My violent reaction set in when Krafft-Ebing spoke of the "subjective character" of psychiatric textbooks. So, I thought, the textbook is in part the subjective confession of the author. With his specific prejudice, with the totality of his being, he stands behind the objectivity of his experiences and responds to the "disease of the personality" with the whole of his own personality. Never had I heard anything of this sort from my teacher at the clinic. In spite of the fact that Krafft-Ebing's textbook did not differ essentially from other books of the kind, these few hints cast such a transfiguring light on psychiatry that I was irretrievably drawn under its spell.

The decision was taken. When I informed my teacher in internal medicine of my intention, I could read in his face his amazement and disappointment. My old wound, the feeling of being an outsider and of alienating others, began to ache again. But now I understood why. No one, not even I myself, had ever imagined I could become interested in this obscure bypath. My friends were astounded and put out, thinking me a fool for throwing up the enviable chance of a sensible career in internal medicine, which dangled so temptingly before my nose, in favor of this psychiatric nonsense.

I saw that once again I had obviously got myself into a side alley where no one could or would follow me. But I knew—and nothing and nobody could have deflected me from my purpose —that my decision stood, and that it was fate. It was as though two rivers had united and in one grand torrent were bearing me inexorably toward distant goals. This confident feeling that I was a "united double nature" carried me as if on a magical wave through the examination, in which I came out at the top. Characteristically, the stumbling block that lurks in the path of all miracles that turn out too well tripped me up in the very subject in which I really excelled, pathological anatomy. By a ridiculous error, in a slide which apart from all sorts of debris seemed to contain only epithelial cells, I overlooked some molds hiding in a corner. In the other subjects, I had even guessed what questions I would be asked. Thanks to this, I cleared several dangerous reefs with flying colors. In revenge, I was then fooled in the most grotesque way just where I felt most certain of myself. Had it not been for this I would have had the highest mark in the examination.

As it was, another candidate received the same number of points as I did. He was a lone wolf, with a personality quite opaque to me and suspiciously banal. It was impossible to talk to him about anything except "shop." He reacted to everything with an enigmatic smile, which reminded me of the Greek statues at Aegina. He had an air of superiority, and yet underneath it he seemed embarrassed and never quite fitted into any situation. Or was it a kind of stupidity? I could never make him out. The only definite thing about him was the impression he gave of almost monomaniacal ambition which precluded interest in anything but sheer facts. A few years afterward he became schizophrenic. I mention this as a characteristic example of the parallelism of events. My first book was on the psychology of dementia praecox (schizophrenia), and in it my personality with its bias or "personal equation" responded to this "disease of the personality." I maintained that psychiatry, in the broadest sense, is a dialogue between the sick psyche and the psyche of the doctor, which is presumed to be "normal." It is a coming to terms between the sick personality and that of the therapist, both in principle equally subjective. My aim was to show that delusions and hallucinations were not just specific symptoms of mental disease but also had a human meaning.

The evening after my last examination I treated myself—for the first time in my life—to the longed-for luxury of going to the theater. Until then my finances had not permitted any such extravagance. But I still had some money left from the sale of the antiques, and this allowed me not only a visit to the opera but even a trip to Munich and Stuttgart.

Bizet intoxicated and overwhelmed me, rocked me on the waves of an infinite sea. And next day, when the train carried

me over the border into a wider world, the melodies of *Carmen*
accompanied me. In Munich I saw real classical art for the first
time, and this in conjunction with Bizet's music put me in a
springlike, nuptial mood, whose depth and meaning I could
only dimly grasp. Outwardly, however, it was a dismal week
between the first and the ninth of December, 1900.

In Stuttgart I paid a farewell visit to my aunt, Frau Reimer-
Jung, whose husband was a psychiatrist. She was the daughter
of my paternal grandfather's first marriage to Virginia de Las-
saulx. She was an enchanting old lady with sparkling blue eyes
and a vivacious temperament. She seemed to me immersed in a
world of impalpable fantasies and of memories that refused to
go home—the last breath of a vanishing, irrevocable past. This
visit was a final farewell to the nostalgias of my childhood.

On December 10, 1900, I took up my post as assistant at
Burghölzli Mental Hospital, Zürich. I was glad to be in Zürich,
for in the course of the years Basel had become too stuffy for me.
For the Baslers no town exists but their own: only Basel is
"civilized," and north of the river Birs the land of the barbarians
begins. My friends could not understand my going away, and
reckoned I would be back in no time. But that was out of the
question, for in Basel I was stamped for all time as the son of the
Reverend Paul Jung and the grandson of Professor Carl Gustav
Jung. I was an intellectual and belonged to a definite social set.
I felt resistances against this, for I could not and would not let
myself be classified. The intellectual atmosphere of Basel
seemed to me enviably cosmopolitan, but the pressure of tradition was too much for me. When I came to Zürich I felt the
difference at once. Zürich relates to the world not by the intellect
but by commerce. Yet here the air was free, and I had always
valued that. Here you were not weighed down by the brown
fog of the centuries, even though one missed the rich background of culture. For Basel I have to this day a nostalgic
weakness, despite the fact that I know it no longer is as it was. I
still remember the days when Bachofen and Burckhardt walked
in the streets, and behind the cathedral stood the old chapter
house, and the old bridge over the Rhine, half made of wood.

For my mother it was hard that I was leaving Basel. But I knew that I could not spare her this pain, and she bore it bravely. She lived together with my sister, a delicate and rather sickly nature, in every respect different from me. She was as though born to live the life of a spinster, and she never married. But she developed a remarkable personality, and I admired her attitude. She had to undergo an operation that was considered harmless, but she did not survive it. I was deeply impressed when I discovered that she had put all her affairs in order beforehand, down to the last detail. At bottom she was always a stranger to me, but I had great respect for her. I was rather emotional, whereas she was always composed, though very sensitive deep down. I could imagine her spending her days in a Home for Gentlewomen, just as the only sister of my grandfather had done.

With my work at Burghölzli, life took on an undivided reality—all intention, consciousness, duty, and responsibility. It was an entry into the monastery of the world, a submission to the vow to believe only in what was probable, average, commonplace, barren of meaning, to renounce everything strange and significant, and reduce anything extraordinary to the banal. Henceforth there were only surfaces that hid nothing, only beginnings without continuations, accidents without coherence, knowledge that shrank to ever smaller circles, failures that claimed to be problems, oppressively narrow horizons, and the unending desert of routine. For six months I locked myself within the monastic walls in order to get accustomed to the life and spirit of the asylum, and I read through the fifty volumes of the *Allgemeine Zeitschrift für Psychiatrie* from its very beginnings, in order to acquaint myself with the psychiatric mentality. I wanted to know how the human mind reacted to the sight of its own destruction, for psychiatry seemed to me an articulate expression of that biological reaction which seizes upon the so-called healthy mind in the presence of mental illness. My professional colleagues seemed to me no less interesting than the patients. In the years that followed I secretly compiled statistics on the hereditary background of my Swiss colleagues, and gained much instruction. I did this for my personal edification as well as for the sake of understanding the psychiatric mentality.

I need scarcely mention that my concentration and self-imposed confinement alienated me from my colleagues. They did not know, of course, how strange psychiatry seemed to me, and how intent I was on penetrating into its spirit. At that time my interest in therapy had not awakened, but the pathological variants of so-called normality fascinated me, because they offered me the longed-for opportunity to obtain a deeper insight into the psyche in general.

These, then, were the conditions under which my career in psychiatry began—the subjective experiment out of which my objective life emerged. I have neither the desire nor the capacity to stand outside myself and observe my fate in a truly objective way. I would commit the familiar autobiographical mistake either of weaving an illusion about how it ought to have been, or of writing an *apologia pro vita sua*. In the end, man is an event which cannot judge itself, but, for better or worse, is left to the judgment of others.

·IV·

Psychiatric Activities

T HE YEARS at Burghölzli were my years of apprentice-
ship. Dominating my interests and research was the burning question: "What actually takes place inside the
mentally ill?" That was something which I did not understand
then, nor had any of my colleagues concerned themselves with
such problems. Psychiatry teachers were not interested in what
the patient had to say, but rather in how to make a diagnosis or
how to describe symptoms and to compile statistics. From the
clinical point of view which then prevailed, the human personality of the patient, his individuality, did not matter at all.
Rather, the doctor was confronted with Patient X, with a long
list of cut-and-dried diagnoses and a detailing of symptoms.
Patients were labeled, rubber-stamped with a diagnosis, and,
for the most part, that settled the matter. The psychology of the
mental patient played no role whatsoever.

At this point Freud became vitally important to me, especially
because of his fundamental researches into the psychology of
hysteria and of dreams. For me his ideas pointed the way to a
closer investigation and understanding of individual cases.
Freud introduced psychology into psychiatry, although he himself was a neurologist.

I still recollect very well a case which greatly interested me at the time. A young woman had been admitted to the hospital, suffering from "melancholia." The examination was conducted with the usual care: anamnesis, tests, physical check-ups, and so on. The diagnosis was schizophrenia, or "dementia praecox," in the phrase of those days. The prognosis: poor.

This woman happened to be in my section. At first I did not dare to question the diagnosis. I was still a young man then, a beginner, and would not have had the temerity to suggest another one. And yet the case struck me as strange. I had the feeling that it was not a matter of schizophrenia but of ordinary depression, and resolved to apply my own method. At the time I was much occupied with diagnostic association studies, and so I undertook an association experiment with the patient. In addition, I discussed her dreams with her. In this way I succeeded in uncovering her past, which the anamnesis had not clarified. I obtained information directly from the unconscious, and this information revealed a dark and tragic story.

Before the woman married she had known a man, the son of a wealthy industrialist, in whom all the girls of the neighborhood were interested. Since she was very pretty, she thought her chances of catching him were fairly good. But apparently he did not care for her, and so she married another man.

Five years later an old friend visited her. They were talking over old times, and he said to her, "When you got married it was quite a shock to someone—your Mr. X" (the wealthy industrialist's son). That was the moment! Her depression dated from this period, and several weeks later led to a catastrophe. She was bathing her children, first her four-year-old girl and then her two-year-old son. She lived in a country where the water supply was not perfectly hygienic; there was pure spring water for drinking, and tainted water from the river for bathing and washing. While she was bathing the little girl, she saw the child sucking at the sponge, but did not stop her. She even gave her little son a glass of the impure water to drink. Naturally, she did this unconsciously, or only half consciously, for her mind was already under the shadow of the incipient depression.

A short time later, after the incubation period had passed,

the girl came down with typhoid fever and died. The girl had been her favorite. The boy was not infected. At that moment the depression reached its acute stage, and the woman was sent to the institution.

From the association test I had seen that she was a murderess, and I had learned many of the details of her secret. It was at once apparent that this was a sufficient reason for her depression. Essentially it was a psychogenic disturbance and not a case of schizophrenia.

Now what could be done in the way of therapy? Up to then the woman had been given narcotics to combat her insomnia and had been under guard to prevent attempts at suicide. But otherwise nothing had been done. Physically, she was in good condition.

I was confronted with the problem: Should I speak openly with her or not? Should I undertake the major operation? I was faced with a conflict of duties altogether without precedent in my experience. I had a difficult question of conscience to answer, and had to settle the matter with myself alone. If I had asked my colleagues, they would probably have warned me, "For heaven's sake, don't tell the woman any such thing. That will only make her still crazier." To my mind, the effect might well be the reverse. In general it may be said that unequivocal rules scarcely exist in psychology. A question can be answered one way or another, depending on whether or not we take the unconscious factors into account. Of course I knew very well the personal risk I was running: if the patient got worse, I would be in the soup too!

Nevertheless, I decided to take a chance on a therapy whose outcome was uncertain. I told her everything I had discovered through the association test. It can easily be imagined how difficult it was for me to do this. To accuse a person point-blank of murder is no small matter. And it was tragic for the patient to have to listen to it and accept it. But the result was that in two weeks it proved possible to discharge her, and she was never again institutionalized.

There were other reasons that caused me to say nothing to my colleagues about this case. I was afraid of their discussing it and possibly raising legal questions. Nothing could be proved against the patient, of course, and yet such a discussion might have had disastrous consequences for her. Fate had punished her enough! It seemed to me more meaningful that she should return to life in order to atone in life for her crime. When she was discharged, she departed bearing her heavy burden. She *had* to bear this burden. The loss of the child had been frightful for her, and her expiation had already begun with the depression and her confinement to the institution.

In many cases in psychiatry, the patient who comes to us has a story that is not told, and which as a rule no one knows of. To my mind, therapy only really begins after the investigation of that wholly personal story. It is the patient's secret, the rock against which he is shattered. If I know his secret story, I have a key to the treatment. The doctor's task is to find out how to gain that knowledge. In most cases exploration of the conscious material is insufficient. Sometimes an association test can open the way; so can the interpretation of dreams, or long and patient human contact with the individual. In therapy the problem is always the whole person, never the symptom alone. We must ask questions which challenge the whole personality.

In 1905 I became lecturer in psychiatry at the University of Zürich, and that same year I became senior physician at the Psychiatric Clinic. I held this position for four years. Then in 1909 I had to resign because by this time I was simply over my head in work. In the course of the years I had acquired so large a private practice that I could no longer keep up with my tasks. However, I continued my professorship until the year 1913. I lectured on psychopathology, and, naturally, also on the foundations of Freudian psychoanalysis, as well as on the psychology of primitives. These were my principal subjects. During the first semesters my lectures dealt chiefly with hypnosis, also with Janet and Flournoy. Later the problem of Freudian psychoanalysis moved into the foreground.

In my courses on hypnosis I used to inquire into the personal history of the patients whom I presented to the students. One case I still remember very well.

A middle-aged woman, apparently with a strong religious bent, appeared one day. She was fifty-eight years old, and came on crutches, led by her maid. For seventeen years she had been suffering from a painful paralysis of the left leg. I placed her in a comfortable chair and asked her for her story. She began to tell it to me, and how terrible it all was—the whole long tale of her illness came out with the greatest circumstantiality. Finally I interrupted her and said, "Well now, we have no more time for so much talk. I am now going to hypnotize you."

I had scarcely said the words when she closed her eyes and fell into a profound trance—without any hypnosis at all! I wondered at this, but did not disturb her. She went on talking without pause, and related the most remarkable dreams—dreams that represented a fairly deep experience of the unconscious. This, however, I did not understand until years later. At the time I assumed she was in a kind of delirium. The situation was gradually growing rather uncomfortable for me. Here were twenty students present, to whom I was going to demonstrate hypnosis!

After half an hour of this, I wanted to awaken the patient again. She would not wake up. I became alarmed; it occurred to me that I might inadvertently have probed into a latent psychosis. It took some ten minutes before I succeeded in waking her. All the while I dared not let the students observe my nervousness. When the woman came to, she was giddy and confused. I said to her, "I am the doctor, and everything is all right." Whereupon she cried out, "But I am cured!" threw away her crutches, and was able to walk. Flushed with embarrassment, I said to the students, "Now you've seen what can be done with hypnosis!" In fact I had not the slightest idea what had happened.

That was one of the experiences that prompted me to abandon hypnosis. I could not understand what had really happened, but the woman was in fact cured, and departed in the best of spirits. I asked her to let me hear from her, since I counted on a relapse in twenty-four hours at the latest. But her pains did not recur; in spite of my skepticism, I had to accept the fact of her cure. At the first lecture of the summer semester next year, she reappeared. This time she complained of violent pains in the back which had, she said, begun only recently. Naturally I asked myself whether there was some connection with the resumption of my lectures. Perhaps she had read the announcement of the lecture in the newspaper. I asked her when the pain had started, and what had caused it. She could not recall that anything had happened to her at any specific time nor could she offer the slightest explanation. Finally I elicited the fact that the pains had actually begun on the day and at the very hour she saw the announcement in the newspaper. That confirmed my guess, but I still did not see how the miraculous cure had come about. I hypnotized her once more—that is to say, she again fell spontaneously into a trance—and afterward the pain was gone.

This time I kept her after the lecture in order to find out more about her life. It turned out that she had a feeble-minded son who was in my department in the hospital. I knew nothing about this because she bore her second husband's name and the son was a child of her first marriage. He was her only child. Naturally, she had hoped for a talented and successful son, and it had been a terrible blow when he became mentally ill at an early age. At that time I was still a young doctor, and represented everything she had hoped her son might become. Her ambitious longing to be the mother of a hero therefore fastened upon me. She adopted me as her son, and proclaimed her miraculous cure far and wide.

In actual fact she was responsible for my local fame as a wizard, and since the story soon got around, I was indebted to her for my first private patients. My psychotherapeutic practice began with a mother's putting me in the place of her mentally ill son! Naturally I explained the whole matter to her, in all its ramifications. She took it very well, and did not again suffer a relapse.

That was my first real therapeutic experience—I might say: my first analysis. I distinctly recall my talk with the old lady. She was intelligent, and exceedingly grateful that I had taken her seriously and displayed concern for her fate and that of her son. This had helped her.

In the beginning I employed hypnosis in my private practice

also, but I soon gave it up because in using it one is only groping in the dark. One never knows how long an improvement or a cure will last, and I always had compunctions about working in such uncertainty. Nor was I fond of deciding on my own what the patient ought to do. I was much more concerned to learn from the patient himself where his natural bent would lead him. In order to find that out, careful analysis of dreams and of other manifestations of the unconscious was necessary.

During the years 1904–5 I set up a laboratory for experimental psychopathology at the Psychiatric Clinic. I had a number of students there with whom I investigated psychic reactions (i.e., associations). Franz Riklin, Sr., was my collaborator. Ludwig Binswanger was currently writing his doctoral dissertation on the association experiment in connection with the psychogalvanic effect,[1] and I wrote my paper "On the Psychological Diagnosis of Facts." [2] There were also a number of Americans among our associates, including Frederick Peterson and Charles Ricksher. Their papers were published in American journals. It was these association studies which later, in 1909, procured me my invitation to Clark University; I was asked to lecture on my work. Simultaneously, and independently of me, Freud was invited. The degree of Doctor of Laws *honoris causa* was bestowed on both of us.

The association experiment and the psychogalvanic experiment were chiefly responsible for my reputation in America. Very soon many patients from that country were coming to me. I remember well one of the first cases. An American colleague sent me a patient. The accompanying diagnosis read "alcoholic neurasthenia." The prognosis called him "incurable." My colleague had therefore taken the precaution of advising the patient to see also a certain neurological authority in Berlin, for he expected that my attempt at therapy would lead to noth-

[1] The psychogalvanic reflex is a momentary decrease in the apparent electrical resistance of the skin, resulting from activity of the sweat glands in response to mental excitement.—A. J.

[2] "Zur psychologischen Tatbestandsdiagnostik," *Zentralblatt für Nervenheilkunde und Psychiatrie,* XXVIII (1905), 813–15; English trans.: "On the Psychological Diagnosis of Facts," in *Psychiatric Studies* (CW 1).

ing. The patient came for consultation, and after I had talked a little with him I saw that the man had an ordinary neurosis, of whose psychic origins he had no inkling. I made an association test and discovered that he was suffering from the effects of a formidable mother complex. He came from a rich and respected family, had a likeable wife and no cares—externally speaking. Only he drank too much. The drinking was a desperate attempt to narcotize himself, to forget his oppressive situation. Naturally, it did not help.

His mother was the owner of a large company, and the unusually talented son occupied a leading post in the firm. He really should long since have escaped from his oppressive subordination to his mother, but he could not summon up the resolution to throw up his excellent position. Thus he remained chained to his mother, who had installed him in the business. Whenever he was with her, or had to submit to her interference with his work, he would start drinking in order to stupefy or discharge his emotions. A part of him did not really want to leave the comfortably warm nest, and against his own instincts he was allowing himself to be seduced by wealth and comfort.

After brief treatment he stopped drinking, and considered himself cured. But I told him, "I do not guarantee that you will not relapse into the same state if you return to your former situation." He did not believe me, and returned home to America in fine fettle.

As soon as he was back under his mother's influence, the drinking began again. Thereupon I was called by her to a consultation during her stay in Switzerland. She was an intelligent woman, but was a real "power devil." I saw what the son had to contend with, and realized that he did not have the strength to resist. Physically, too, he was rather delicate and no match for his mother. I therefore decided upon an act of *force majeure*. Behind his back I gave his mother a medical certificate to the effect that her son's alcoholism rendered him incapable of fulfilling the requirements of his job. I recommended his discharge. This advice was followed—and the son, of course, was furious with me.

Here I had done something which normally would be considered unethical for a medical man. But I knew that for the patient's sake I had had to take this step.

His further development? Separated from his mother, his own personality was able to unfold. He made a brilliant career—in spite of, or rather just because of the strong horse pill I had given him. His wife was grateful to me, for her husband had not only overcome his alcoholism, but had also struck out on his own individual path with the greatest success.

Nevertheless, for years I had a guilty conscience about this patient because I had made out that certificate behind his back, though I was certain that only such an act could free him. And indeed, once his liberation was accomplished, the neurosis disappeared.

In my practice I was constantly impressed by the way the human psyche reacts to a crime committed unconsciously. After all, that young woman was initially not aware that she had killed her child. And yet she had fallen into a condition that appeared to be the expression of extreme consciousness of guilt.

I once had a similar case which I have never forgotten. A lady came to my office. She refused to give her name, said it did not matter, since she wished to have only the one consultation. It was apparent that she belonged to the upper levels of society. She had been a doctor, she said. What she had to communicate to me was a confession; some twenty years ago she had committed a murder out of jealousy. She had poisoned her best friend because she wanted to marry the friend's husband. She had thought that if the murder was not discovered, it would not disturb her. She wanted to marry the husband, and the simplest way was to eliminate her friend. Moral considerations were of no importance to her, she thought.

The consequences? She had in fact married the man, but he died soon afterward, relatively young. During the following years a number of strange things happened. The daughter of this marriage endeavored to get away from her as soon as she was grown up. She married young and vanished from view, drew farther and farther away, and ultimately the mother lost all contact with her.

This lady was a passionate horsewoman and owned several riding horses of which she was extremely fond. One day she discovered that the horses were beginning to grow nervous under her. Even her favorite shied and threw her. Finally she had to give up riding. Thereafter she clung to her dogs. She owned an unusually beautiful wolfhound to which she was greatly attached. As chance would have it, this very dog was stricken with paralysis. With that, her cup was full; she felt that she was morally done for. She had to confess, and for this purpose she came to me. She was a murderess, but on top of that she had also murdered herself. For one who commits such a crime destroys his own soul. The murderer has already passed sentence on himself. If someone has committed a crime and is caught, he suffers judicial punishment. If he has done it secretly, without moral consciousness of it, and remains undiscovered, the punishment can nevertheless be visited upon him, as our case shows. It comes out in the end. Sometimes it seems as if even animals and plants "know" it.

As a result of the murder, the woman was plunged into unbearable loneliness. She had even become alienated from animals. And in order to shake off this loneliness, she had made me share her knowledge. She had to have someone who was not a murderer to share the secret. She wanted to find a person who could accept her confession without prejudice, for by so doing she would achieve once more something resembling a relationship to humanity. And the person would have to be a doctor rather than a professional confessor. She would have suspected a priest of listening to her because of his office, and of not accepting the facts for their own sake but for the purpose of moral judgment. She had seen people and animals turn away from her, and had been so struck by this silent verdict that she could not have endured any further condemnation.

I never found out who she was, nor do I have any proof that her story was true. Sometimes I have asked myself what might have become of her. For that was by no means the end of her journey. Perhaps she was driven ultimately to suicide. I cannot imagine how she could have gone on living in that utter loneliness.

Clinical diagnoses are important, since they give the doctor a certain orientation; but they do not help the patient. The crucial thing is the story. For it alone shows the human background and the human suffering, and only at that point can the doctor's therapy begin to operate. A case demonstrated this to me most cogently.[3]

The case concerned an old patient in the women's ward. She was about seventy-five, and had been bedridden for forty years. Almost fifty years ago she had entered the institution, but there was no one left who could recall her admittance; everyone who had been there had since died. Only one head nurse, who had been working at the institution for thirty-five years, still remembered something of the patient's story. The old woman could not speak, and could only take fluid or semifluid nourishment. She ate with her fingers, letting the food drip off them into her mouth. Sometimes it would take her almost two hours to consume a cup of milk. When not eating, she made curious rhythmic motions with her hands and arms. I did not understand what they meant. I was profoundly impressed by the degree of destruction that can be wrought by mental disease, but saw no possible explanation. At the clinical lectures she used to be presented as a catatonic form of dementia praecox, but that meant nothing to me, for these words did not contribute in the slightest to an understanding of the significance and origin of those curious gestures.

The impression this case made upon me typifies my reaction to the psychiatry of the period. When I became an assistant, I had the feeling that I understood nothing whatsoever about what psychiatry purported to be. I felt extremely uncomfortable beside my chief and my colleagues, who assumed such airs of certainty while I was groping perplexedly in the dark. For I regarded the main task of psychiatry as understanding the things that were taking place within the sick mind, and as yet I knew nothing about these things. Here I was engaged in a profession in which I did not know my way about!

Late one evening, as I was walking through the ward, I saw the old woman still making her mysterious movements, and

[3] Cf. *The Psychogenesis of Mental Disease* (CW 3), pp. 171–72.

again asked myself, "Why must this be?" Thereupon I went to our old head nurse and asked whether the patient had always been that way. "Yes," she replied. "But my predecessor told me she used to make shoes." I then checked through her yellowing case history once more, and sure enough, there was a note to the effect that she was in the habit of making cobbler's motions. In the past shoemakers used to hold shoes between their knees and draw the threads through the leather with precisely such movements. (Village cobblers can still be seen doing this today.) When the patient died shortly afterward, her elder brother came to the funeral. "Why did your sister lose her sanity?" I asked him. He told me that she had been in love with a shoemaker who for some reason had not wanted to marry her, and that when he finally rejected her she had "gone off." The shoemaker movements indicated an identification with her sweetheart which had lasted until her death. That case gave me my first inkling of the psychic origins of dementia praecox. Henceforth I devoted all my attention to the meaningful connections in a psychosis.

Another patient's story revealed to me the psychological background of psychosis and, above all, of the "senseless" delusions. From this case I was able for the first time to understand the language of schizophrenics, which had hitherto been regarded as meaningless. The patient was Babette S., whose story I have published elsewhere.[4] In 1908 I delivered a lecture on her in the town hall of Zürich.

She came out of the Old Town of Zürich, out of narrow, dirty streets where she had been born in poverty-stricken circumstances and had grown up in a mean environment. Her sister was a prostitute, her father a drunkard. At the age of thirty-nine she succumbed to a paranoid form of dementia praecox, with characteristic megalomania. When I saw her, she had been in the institution for twenty years. She had served as an object lesson to hundreds of medical students. In her they had seen the uncanny process of psychic disintegration; she was a classic

[4] Cf. "The Psychology of Dementia Praecox" and "The Content of the Psychoses," in *The Psychogenesis of Mental Disease* (CW 3).

case. Babette was completely demented and given to saying the craziest things which made no sense at all. I tried with all my might to understand the content of her abstruse utterances. For example, she would say, "I am the Lorelei"; the reason for that was that the doctors, when trying to understand her case, would always say, *"Ich weiss nicht, was soll es bedeuten."* [5] Or she would wail, "I am Socrates' deputy." That, as I discovered, was intended to mean: "I am unjustly accused like Socrates." Absurd outbursts like: "I am the double polytechnic irreplaceable," or, "I am plum cake on a corn-meal bottom," "I am Germania and Helvetia of exclusively sweet butter," "Naples and I must supply the world with noodles," signified an increase in her self-valuation, that is to say, a compensation for inferiority feelings.

My preoccupation with Babette and other such cases convinced me that much of what we had hitherto regarded as senseless was not as crazy as it seemed. More than once I have seen that even with such patients there remains in the background a personality which must be called normal. It stands looking on, so to speak. Occasionally, too, this personality—usually by way of voices or dreams—can make altogether sensible remarks and objections. It can even, when physical illness ensues, move into the foreground again and make the patient seem almost normal.

I once had to treat a schizophrenic old woman who showed me very distinctly the "normal" personality in the background. This was a case which could not be cured, only cared for. Every physician, after all, has patients whom he cannot hope to cure, for whom he can only smooth the path to death. She heard voices which were distributed throughout her entire body, and a voice in the middle of the thorax was "God's voice."

"We must rely on that voice," I said to her, and was astonished at my own courage. As a rule this voice made very sensible remarks, and with its aid I managed very well with the patient. Once the voice said, "Let him test you on the Bible!" She brought along an old, tattered, much-read Bible, and at each visit I had to assign her a chapter to read. The next time I had to test her on it. I did this for about seven years, once every two

[5] "I know not what it means": the first line of Heine's famous poem "Die Lorelei."

weeks. At first I felt very odd in this role, but after a while I realized what the lessons signified. In this way her attention was kept alert, so that she did not sink deeper into the disintegrating dream. The result was that after some six years the voices which had formerly been everywhere had retired to the left half of her body, while the right half was completely free of them. Nor had the intensity of the phenomena been doubled on the left side; it was much the same as in the past. Hence it must be concluded that the patient was cured—at least halfway. That was an unexpected success, for I would not have imagined that these memory exercises could have a therapeutic effect.

Through my work with the patients I realized that paranoid ideas and hallucinations contain a germ of meaning. A personality, a life history, a pattern of hopes and desires lie behind the psychosis. The fault is ours if we do not understand them. It dawned upon me then for the first time that a general psychology of the personality lies concealed within psychosis, and that even here we come upon the old human conflicts. Although patients may appear dull and apathetic, or totally imbecilic, there is more going on in their minds, and more that is meaningful, than there seems to be. At bottom we discover nothing new and unknown in the mentally ill; rather, we encounter the substratum of our own natures.

It was always astounding to me that psychiatry should have taken so long to look into the content of the psychoses. No one concerned himself with the meaning of fantasies, or thought to ask why this patient had one kind of fantasy, another an altogether different one; or what it signified when, for instance, a patient had the fantasy of being persecuted by the Jesuits, or when another imagined that the Jews wanted to poison him, or a third was convinced that the police were after him. Such questions seemed altogether uninteresting to doctors of those days. The fantasies were simply lumped together under some generic name as, for instance, "ideas of persecution." It seems equally odd to me that my investigations of that time are almost forgotten today. Already at the beginning of the century I treated schizophrenia psychotherapeutically. That method, therefore, is not something that has only just been discovered. It did, however, take a long time before people began to introduce psychology into psychiatry.

While I was still at the clinic, I had to be most circumspect about treating my schizophrenic patients, or I would have been accused of woolgathering. Schizophrenia was considered incurable. If one did achieve some improvement with a case of schizophrenia, the answer was that it had not been real schizophrenia.

When Freud visited me in Zürich in 1908, I demonstrated the case of Babette to him. Afterward he said to me, "You know, Jung, what you have found out about this patient is certainly interesting. But how in the world were you able to bear spending hours and days with this phenomenally ugly female?" I must have given him a rather dashed look, for this idea had never occurred to me. In a way I regarded the woman as a pleasant old creature because she had such lovely delusions and said such interesting things. And after all, even in her insanity, the human being emerged from a cloud of grotesque nonsense. Therapeutically, nothing was accomplished with Babette; she had been sick for too long. But I have seen other cases in which this kind of attentive entering into the personality of the patient produced a lasting therapeutic effect.

Regarding them from the outside, all we see of the mentally ill is their tragic destruction, rarely the life of that side of the psyche which is turned away from us. Outward appearances are frequently deceptive, as I discovered to my astonishment in the case of a young catatonic patient. She was eighteen years old, and came from a cultivated family. At the age of fifteen she had been seduced by her brother and abused by a schoolmate. From her sixteenth year on, she retreated into isolation. She concealed herself from people, and ultimately the only emotional relationship left to her was one with a vicious watchdog which belonged to another family, and which she tried to win over. She grew steadily odder, and at seventeen was taken to the mental hospital, where she spent a year and a half. She heard voices, refused food, and was completely mutistic (i.e., no longer spoke). When I first saw her she was in a typical catatonic state.

In the course of many weeks I succeeded, very gradually, in persuading her to speak. After overcoming many resistances, she told me that she had lived on the moon. The moon, it seemed, was inhabited, but at first she had seen only men. They had at once taken her with them and deposited her in a sublunar dwelling where their children and wives were kept. For on the high mountains of the moon there lived a vampire who kidnaped and killed the women and children, so that the moon people were threatened with extinction. That was the reason for the sublunar existence of the feminine half of the population.

My patient made up her mind to do something for the moon people, and planned to destroy the vampire. After long preparations, she waited for the vampire on the platform of a tower which had been erected for this purpose. After a number of nights she at last saw the monster approaching from afar, winging his way toward her like a great black bird. She took her long sacrificial knife, concealed it in her gown, and waited for the vampire's arrival. Suddenly he stood before her. He had several pairs of wings. His face and entire figure were covered by them, so that she could see nothing but his feathers. Wonder-struck, she was seized by curiosity to find out what he really looked like. She approached, hand on the knife. Suddenly the wings opened and a man of unearthly beauty stood before her. He enclosed her in his winged arms with an iron grip, so that she could no longer wield the knife. In any case she was so spellbound by the vampire's look that she would not have been capable of striking. He raised her from the platform and flew off with her.

After this revelation she was once again able to speak without inhibition, and now her resistances emerged. It seemed that I had stopped her return to the moon; she could no longer escape from the earth. This world was not beautiful, she said, but the moon was beautiful, and life there was rich in meaning. Sometime later she suffered a relapse into her catatonia, and I had to have her taken to a sanatorium. For a while she was violently insane.

When she was discharged after some two months, it was once again possible to talk with her. Gradually she came to see that life on earth was unavoidable. Desperately, she fought against this conclusion and its consequences, and had to be sent back to the sanatorium. Once I visited her in her cell and said to her, "All this won't do you any good; you cannot return to the moon!" She took this in silence and with an appearance of utter apathy. This time she was released after a short stay and resigned herself to her fate.

For a while she took a job as nurse in a sanatorium. There was an assistant doctor there who made a somewhat rash approach to her. She responded with a revolver shot. Luckily, the man was only slightly wounded. But the incident revealed that she went about with a revolver all the time. Once before, she had turned up with a loaded gun. During the last interview, at the end of the treatment, she gave it to me. When I asked in amazement what she was doing with it, she replied, "I would have shot you down if you had failed me!"

When the excitement over the shooting had subsided, she returned to her native town. She married, had several children, and survived two world wars in the East, without ever again suffering a relapse.

What can be said by way of interpretation of these fantasies? As a result of the incest to which she had been subjected as a girl, she felt humiliated in the eyes of the world, but elevated in the realm of fantasy. She had been transported into a mythic realm; for incest is traditionally a prerogative of royalty and divinities. The consequence was complete alienation from the world, a state of psychosis. She became "extramundane," as it were, and lost contact with humanity. She plunged into cosmic distances, into outer space, where she met with the winged demon. As is the rule with such things, she projected his figure onto me during the treatment. Thus I was automatically threatened with death, as was everyone who might have persuaded her to return to normal human life. By telling me her story she had in a sense betrayed the demon and attached herself to an earthly human being. Hence she was able to return to life and even to marry.

Thereafter I regarded the sufferings of the mentally ill in a different light. For I had gained insight into the richness and importance of their inner experience.

I am often asked about my psychotherapeutic or analytic method. I cannot reply unequivocally to the question. Therapy is different in every case. When a doctor tells me that he adheres strictly to this or that method, I have my doubts about his therapeutic effect. So much is said in the literature about the resistance of the patient that it would almost seem as if the doctor were trying to put something over on him, whereas the cure ought to grow naturally out of the patient himself. Psychotherapy and analysis are as varied as are human individuals. I treat every patient as individually as possible, because the solution of the problem is always an individual one. Universal rules can be postulated only with a grain of salt. A psychological truth is valid only if it can be reversed. A solution which would be out of the question for me may be just the right one for someone else.

Naturally, a doctor must be familiar with the so-called "methods." But he must guard against falling into any specific, routine approach. In general one must guard against theoretical assumptions. Today they may be valid, tomorrow it may be the turn of other assumptions. In my analyses they play no part. I am unsystematic very much by intention. To my mind, in dealing with individuals, only individual understanding will do. We need a different language for every patient. In one analysis I can be heard talking the Adlerian dialect, in another the Freudian.

The crucial point is that I confront the patient as one human being to another. Analysis is a dialogue demanding two partners. Analyst and patient sit facing one another, eye to eye; the doctor has something to say, but so has the patient.

Since the essence of psychotherapy is not the application of a method, psychiatric study alone does not suffice. I myself had to work for a very long time before I possessed the equipment for psychotherapy. As early as 1909 I realized that I could not treat latent psychoses if I did not understand their symbolism. It was then that I began to study mythology.

With cultivated and intelligent patients the psychiatrist needs more than merely professional knowledge. He must understand, aside from all theoretical assumptions, what really motivates the patient. Otherwise he stirs up unnecessary resistances. What counts, after all, is not whether a theory is corroborated, but whether the patient grasps himself as an individual. This, however, is not possible without reference to the collective views, concerning which the doctor ought to be informed. For that, mere medical training does not suffice, for the horizon of the human psyche embraces infinitely more than the limited purview of the doctor's consulting room.

The psyche is distinctly more complicated and inaccessible than the body. It is, so to speak, the half of the world which comes into existence only when we become conscious of it. For that reason the psyche is not only a personal but a world problem, and the psychiatrist has to deal with an entire world.

Nowadays we can see as never before that the peril which threatens all of us comes not from nature, but from man, from the psyches of the individual and the mass. The psychic aberration of man is the danger. Everything depends upon whether or not our psyche functions properly. If certain persons lose their heads nowadays, a hydrogen bomb will go off.

The psychotherapist, however, must understand not only the patient; it is equally important that he should understand himself. For that reason the *sine qua non* is the analysis of the analyst, what is called the training analysis. The patient's treatment begins with the doctor, so to speak. Only if the doctor knows how to cope with himself and his own problems will he be able to teach the patient to do the same. Only then. In the training analysis the doctor must learn to know his own psyche and to take it seriously. If he cannot do that, the patient will not learn either. He will lose a portion of his psyche, just as the doctor has lost that portion of his psyche which he has not learned to understand. It is not enough, therefore, for the training analysis to consist in acquiring a system of concepts. The analysand must realize that it concerns himself, that the training analysis is a bit of real life and is not a method which can be learned by rote. The student who does not grasp that fact in his own training analysis will have to pay dearly for the failure later on.

Though there is treatment known as "minor psychotherapy," in any thoroughgoing analysis the whole personality of both patient and doctor is called into play. There are many cases which the doctor cannot cure without committing himself. When important matters are at stake, it makes all the difference whether the doctor sees himself as a part of the drama, or cloaks himself in his authority. In the great crises of life, in the supreme moments when to be or not to be is the question, little tricks of suggestion do not help. Then the doctor's whole being is challenged.

The therapist must at all times keep watch over himself, over the way he is reacting to his patient. For we do not react only with our consciousness. Also we must always be asking ourselves: How is our unconscious experiencing this situation? We must therefore observe our dreams, pay the closest attention and study ourselves just as carefully as we do the patient. Otherwise the entire treatment may go off the rails. I shall give a single example of this.

I once had a patient, a highly intelligent woman, who for various reasons aroused my doubts. At first the analysis went very well, but after a while I began to feel that I was no longer getting at the correct interpretation of her dreams, and I thought I also noticed an increasing shallowness in our dialogue. I therefore decided to talk with my patient about this, since it had of course not escaped her that something was going wrong. The night before I was to speak with her, I had the following dream.

I was walking down a highway through a valley in late-afternoon sunlight. To my right was a steep hill. At its top stood a castle, and on the highest tower there was a woman sitting on a kind of balustrade. In order to see her properly, I had to bend my head far back. I awoke with a crick in the back of my neck. Even in the dream I had recognized the woman as my patient.

The interpretation was immediately apparent to me. If in the dream I had to look up at the patient in this fashion, in reality I had probably been looking down on her. Dreams are, after all, compensations for the conscious attitude. I told her of the dream and my interpretation. This produced an immediate change in the situation, and the treatment once more began to move forward.

As a doctor I constantly have to ask myself what kind of message the patient is bringing me. What does he mean to me? If he means nothing, I have no point of attack. The doctor is effective only when he himself is affected. "Only the wounded physician heals." But when the doctor wears his personality like a coat of armor, he has no effect. I take my patients seriously. Perhaps I am confronted with a problem just as much as they. It often happens that the patient is exactly the right plaster for the doctor's sore spot. Because this is so, difficult situations can arise for the doctor too—or rather, especially for the doctor.

Every therapist ought to have a control by some third person, so that he remains open to another point of view. Even the pope has a confessor. I always advise analysts: "Have a father confessor, or a mother confessor!" Women are particularly gifted for playing such a part. They often have excellent intuition and a trenchant critical insight, and can see what men have up their sleeves, at times see also into men's anima intrigues. They see aspects that the man does not see. That is why no woman has ever been convinced that her husband is a superman!

It is understandable that a person should undergo analysis if he has a neurosis; but if he feels he is normal, he is under no compulsion to do so. Yet I can assure you, I have had some astonishing experiences with so-called "normality." Once I encountered an entirely "normal" pupil. He was a doctor, and came to me with the best recommendations from an old colleague. He had been his assistant and had later taken over his practice. Now he had a normal practice, normal success, a normal wife, normal children, lived in a normal little house in a normal little town, had a normal income and probably a normal diet. He wanted to be an analyst. I said to him, "Do you know what that means? It means that you must first learn to know yourself. You yourself are the instrument. If you are not right, how can the patient be made right? If you are not convinced, how can you convince him? You yourself must be the real stuff. If you are not, God help you! Then you will lead patients astray. Therefore you must first accept an analysis of yourself."

That was all right, the man said, but almost at once followed this with: "I have no problems to tell you about." That should have been a warning to me. I said, "Very well, then we can examine your dreams." "I have no dreams," he said. "You will soon have some," I responded. Anyone else would probably have dreamt that very night. But he was unable to recall any dreams. So it went on for about two weeks, and I began to feel rather uneasy about the whole affair.

At last an impressive dream turned up. I am going to tell it because it shows how important it is, in practical psychiatry, to understand dreams. He dreamt that he was traveling by railroad. The train had a two-hour stop in a certain city. Since he did not know the city and wanted to see something of it, he set out toward the city center. There he found a medieval building, probably the town hall, and went into it. He wandered down long corridors and came upon handsome rooms, their walls lined with old paintings and fine tapestries. Precious old objects stood about. Suddenly he saw that it had grown darker, and the sun had set. He thought, I must get back to the railroad station. At this moment he discovered that he was lost, and no longer knew where the exit was. He started in alarm, and simultaneously realized that he had not met a single person in this building. He began to feel uneasy, and quickened his pace, hoping to run into someone. But he met no one. Then he came to a large door, and thought with relief: That is the exit. He opened the door and discovered that he had stumbled upon a gigantic room. It was so huge and dark that he could not even see the opposite wall. Profoundly alarmed, the dreamer ran across the great, empty room, hoping to find the exit on the other side. Then he saw—precisely in the middle of the room—something white on the floor. As he approached he discovered that it was an idiot child of about two years old. It was sitting on a chamber pot and had smeared itself with feces. At that moment he awoke with a cry, in a state of panic.

I knew all I needed to know—here was a latent psychosis! I must say I sweated as I tried to lead him out of that dream. I had to represent it to him as something quite innocuous, and gloss over all the perilous details.

What the dream says is approximately this: the trip on which he sets out is the trip to Zürich. He remains there, however, for only a short time. The child in the center of the room is himself as a two-year-old child. In small children, such uncouth behavior is somewhat unusual, but still possible. They may be intrigued by their feces, which are colored and have an odd smell. Raised in a city environment, and possibly along strict lines, a child might easily be guilty of such a failing.

But the dreamer, the doctor, was no child; he was a grown man. And therefore the dream image in the center of the room is a sinister symbol. When he told me the dream, I realized that his normality was a compensation. I had caught him in the nick of time, for the latent psychosis was within a hair's breadth of breaking out and becoming manifest. This had to be prevented. Finally, with the aid of one of his other dreams, I succeeded in finding an acceptable pretext for ending the training analysis. We were both of us very glad to stop. I had not informed him of my diagnosis, but he had probably become aware that he was on the verge of a fatal panic, for he had a dream in which he was being pursued by a dangerous maniac. Immediately afterward he returned home. He never again stirred up the unconscious. His emphatic normality reflected a personality which would not have been developed but simply shattered by a confrontation with the unconscious. These latent psychoses are the *bêtes noires* of psychotherapists, since they are often very difficult to recognize.

With this, we come to the question of lay analysis. I am in favor of non-medical men studying psychotherapy and practicing it; but in dealing with latent psychoses there is the risk of their making dangerous mistakes. Therefore I favor laymen working as analysts, but under the guidance of a professional physician. As soon as a lay analyst feels the slightest bit uncertain, he ought to consult his mentor. Even for doctors it is difficult to recognize and treat a latent schizophrenia; all the more so for laymen. But I have repeatedly found that laymen who have practiced psychotherapy for years, and who have themselves been in analysis, are shrewd and capable. Moreover, there are not enough doctors practicing psychotherapy. For such practice, long and thorough training is necessary, and a wide culture which very few possess.

The relationship between doctor and patient, especially when a transference on the part of the patient occurs, or a more or less unconscious identification of doctor and patient, can lead to parapsychological phenomena. I have frequently run into this. One such case which was particularly impressive was that of a patient whom I had pulled out of a psychogenic depression. He went back home and married; but I did not care for his wife. The first time I saw her, I had an uneasy feeling. Her husband was grateful to me, and I observed that I was a thorn in her side because of my influence over him. It frequently happens that women who do not really love their husbands are jealous and destroy their friendships. They want the husband to belong entirely to them because they themselves do not belong to him. The kernel of all jealousy is lack of love.

The wife's attitude placed a tremendous burden on the patient which he was incapable of coping with. Under its pressure he relapsed, after a year of marriage, into a new depression. Foreseeing this possibility, I had arranged with him that he was to get in touch with me at once if he observed his spirits sinking. He neglected to do so, partly because of his wife, who scoffed at his moods. I heard not a word from him.

At that time I had to deliver a lecture in B. I returned to my hotel around midnight. I sat with some friends for a while after the lecture, then went to bed, but I lay awake for a long time. At about two o'clock—I must have just fallen asleep—I awoke with a start, and had the feeling that someone had come into the room; I even had the impression that the door had been hastily opened. I instantly turned on the light, but there was nothing. Someone might have mistaken the door, I thought, and I looked into the corridor. But it was still as death. "Odd," I thought, "someone did come into the room!" Then I tried to recall exactly what had happened, and it occurred to me that I had been awakened by a feeling of dull pain, as though something had struck my forehead and then the back of my skull. The following day I received a telegram saying that my patient had committed suicide. He had shot himself. Later, I learned that the bullet had come to rest in the back wall of the skull.

This experience was a genuine synchronistic phenomenon such as is quite often observed in connection with an archetypal situation—in this case, death. By means of a relativization of time and space in the unconscious it could well be that I had perceived something which in reality was taking place elsewhere. The collective unconscious is common to all; it is the foundation of what the ancients called the "sympathy of all things." In this case the unconscious had knowledge of my patient's condition. All that evening, in fact, I had felt curiously restive and nervous, very much in contrast to my usual mood.

I never try to convert a patient to anything, and never exercise any compulsion. What matters most to me is that the patient should reach his own view of things. Under my treatment a pagan becomes a pagan and a Christian a Christian, a Jew a Jew, according to what his destiny prescribes for him.

I well recall the case of a Jewish woman who had lost her faith. It began with a dream of mine in which a young girl, unknown to me, came to me as a patient. She outlined her case to me, and while she was talking, I thought, "I don't understand her at all. I don't understand what it is all about." But suddenly it occurred to me that she must have an unusual father complex. That was the dream.

For the next day I had down in my appointment book a consultation for four o'clock. A young woman appeared. She was Jewish, daughter of a wealthy banker, pretty, chic, and highly intelligent. She had already undergone an analysis, but the doctor acquired a transference to her and finally begged her not to come to him any more, for if she did, it would mean the destruction of his marriage.

The girl had been suffering for years from a severe anxiety neurosis, which this experience naturally worsened. I began with an anamnesis, but could discover nothing special. She was a well-adapted, Westernized Jewess, enlightened down to her bones. At first I could not understand what her trouble was. Suddenly my dream occurred to me, and I thought, "Good Lord, so this is the little girl of my dream." Since, however, I could detect not a trace of a father complex in her, I asked her, as I am in the habit of doing in such cases, about her grandfather. For a brief moment she closed her eyes, and I realized at once that here lay the heart of the problem. I therefore asked her to tell me about this grandfather, and learned that he had been a rabbi and had belonged to a Jewish sect. "Do you mean the Chassidim?" I asked. She said yes. I pursued my questioning. "If he was a rabbi, was he by any chance a zaddik?" "Yes," she replied, "it is said that he was a kind of saint and also possessed second sight. But that is all nonsense. There is no such thing!"

With that I had concluded the anamnesis and understood the history of her neurosis. I explained to her, "Now I am going to tell you something that you may not be able to accept. Your grandfather was a zaddik. Your father became an apostate to the Jewish faith. He betrayed the secret and turned his back on God. And you have your neurosis because the fear of God has got into you." That struck her like a bolt of lightning.

The following night I had another dream. A reception was taking place in my house, and behold, this girl was there too. She came up to me and asked, "Haven't you got an umbrella? It is raining so hard." I actually found an umbrella, fumbled around with it to open it, and was on the point of giving it to her. But what happened instead? I handed it to her on my knees, as if she were a goddess.

I told this dream to her, and in a week the neurosis had vanished.[6] The dream had showed me that she was not just a superficial little girl, but that beneath the surface were the makings of a saint. She had no mythological ideas, and therefore the most essential feature of her nature could find no way to express itself. All her conscious activity was directed toward flirtation, clothes, and sex, because she knew of nothing else. She knew only the intellect and lived a meaningless life. In reality she was a child of God whose destiny was to fulfill His secret will. I had to awaken mythological and religious ideas in her, for she belonged to that class of human beings of whom spiritual ac-

[6] This case is distinguished from most of Jung's cases by the brevity of the treatment.—A. J.

tivity is demanded. Thus her life took on a meaning, and no trace of the neurosis was left.

In this case I had applied no "method," but had sensed the presence of the numen. My explaining this to her had accomplished the cure. Method did not matter here; what mattered was the "fear of God." [7]

I have frequently seen people become neurotic when they content themselves with inadequate or wrong answers to the questions of life. They seek position, marriage, reputation, outward success or money, and remain unhappy and neurotic even when they have attained what they were seeking. Such people are usually confined within too narrow a spiritual horizon. Their life has not sufficient content, sufficient meaning. If they are enabled to develop into more spacious personalities, the neurosis generally disappears. For that reason the idea of development was always of the highest importance to me.

The majority of my patients consisted not of believers but of those who had lost their faith. The ones who came to me were the lost sheep. Even in this day and age the believer has the opportunity, in his church, to live the "symbolic life." We need only think of the experience of the Mass, of baptism, of the *imitatio Christi,* and many other aspects of religion. But to live and experience symbols presupposes a vital participation on the part of the believer, and only too often this is lacking in people today. In the neurotic it is practically always lacking. In such cases we have to observe whether the unconscious will not spontaneously bring up symbols to replace what is lacking. But then the question remains of whether a person who has symbolic dreams or visions will also be able to understand their meaning and take the consequences upon himself.

There is, for example, the case of the theologian which I described in "Archetypes of the Collective Unconscious." [8] He had a certain dream which was frequently repeated. He dreamt that he was standing on a slope from which he had a beautiful

[7] Cf. *The Symbolic Life,* Pastoral Psychology Guild Lecture, No. 80 (London, 1954), p. 18.
[8] *The Archetypes and the Collective Unconscious* (CW 9, i), pp. 17–18.

view of a low valley covered with dense woods. In the dream he knew that in the middle of the woods there was a lake, and he also knew that hitherto something had always prevented him from going there. But this time he wanted to carry out his plan. As he approached the lake, the atmosphere grew uncanny, and suddenly a light gust of wind passed over the surface of the water, which rippled darkly. He awoke with a cry of terror.

At first this dream seems incomprehensible. But as a theologian the dreamer should have remembered the "pool" whose waters were stirred by a sudden wind, and in which the sick were bathed—the pool of Bethesda. An angel descended and touched the water, which thereby acquired curative powers. The light wind is the pneuma which bloweth where it listeth And that terrified the dreamer. An unseen presence is suggested, a numen that lives its own life and in whose presence man shudders. The dreamer was reluctant to accept the association with the pool of Bethesda. He wanted nothing of it, for such things are met with only in the Bible, or at most on Sunday mornings as the subjects of sermons, and have nothing to do with psychology. All very well to speak of the Holy Ghost on occasions—but it is not a phenomenon to be experienced!

I knew that the dreamer should have overcome his fright and, as it were, got over his panic. But I never force the issue if a patient is unwilling to go the way that has been revealed to him and take the consequences. I do not subscribe to the facile assumption that the patient is blocked merely by ordinary resistances. Resistances—especially when they are stubborn—merit attention, for they are often warnings which must not be overlooked. The cure may be a poison that not everyone can take, or an operation which, when it is contraindicated, can prove fatal.

Wherever there is a reaching down into innermost experience, into the nucleus of personality, most people are overcome by fright, and many run away. Such was the case with this theologian. I am of course aware that theologians are in a more difficult situation than others. On the one hand they are closer to religion, but on the other hand they are more bound by church and dogma. The risk of inner experience, the adventure of the spirit, is in any case alien to most human beings. The possibility that such experience might have psychic reality is anathema to them. All very well if it has a supernatural or at least a "historical" foundation. But psychic? Face to face with this question, the patient will often show an unsuspected but profound contempt for the psyche.

In contemporary psychotherapy the demand is often made that the doctor or psychotherapist should "go along" with the patient and his affects. I don't consider that to be always the right course. Sometimes active intervention on the part of the doctor is required.

Once a lady of the aristocracy came to me who was in the habit of slapping her employees—including her doctors. She suffered from a compulsion neurosis and had been under treatment in a sanatorium. Naturally, she had soon dispensed the obligatory slap to the head physician. In her eyes, after all, he was only a superior *valet de chambre*. She was paying the bills, wasn't she? This doctor sent her on to another institution and there the same scene was repeated. Since the lady was not really insane, but evidently had to be handled with kid gloves, the hapless doctor sent her on to me.

She was a very stately and imposing person, six feet tall—and there was power behind her slaps, I can tell you! She came, then, and we had a very good talk. Then came the moment when I had to say something unpleasant to her. Furious, she sprang to her feet and threatened to slap me. I, too, jumped up, and said to her, "Very well, you are the lady. You hit first—ladies first! But then I hit back!" And I meant it. She fell back into her chair and deflated before my eyes. "No one has ever said that to me before!" she protested. From that moment on, the therapy began to succeed.

What this patient needed was a masculine reaction. In this case it would have been entirely wrong to "go along." That would have been worse than useless. She had a compulsion neurosis because she could not impose moral restraint upon herself. Such people must then have some other form of restraint—and along come the compulsive symptoms to serve the purpose.

Years ago I once drew up statistics on the results of my treatments. I no longer recall the figures exactly; but, on a conservative estimate, a third of my cases were really cured, a third considerably improved, and a third not essentially influenced. But it is precisely the unimproved cases which are hardest to judge, because many things are not realized and understood by the patients until years afterward, and only then can they take effect. How often former patients have written to me: "I did not realize what it was really all about until ten years after I had been with you."

I have had a few cases who ran out on me; very rarely indeed have I had to send a patient away. But even among them were some who later sent me positive reports. That is why it is often so difficult to draw conclusions as to the success of a treatment.

It is obvious that in the course of his practice a doctor will come across people who have a great effect on him too. He meets personalities who, for better or worse, never stir the interest of the public and who nevertheless, or for that very reason, possess unusual qualities, or whose destiny it is to pass through unprecedented developments and disasters. Sometimes they are persons of extraordinary talents, who might well inspire another to give his life for them; but these talents may be implanted in so strangely unfavorable a psychic disposition that we cannot tell whether it is a question of genius or of fragmentary development. Frequently, too, in this unlikely soil there flower rare blossoms of the psyche which we would never have thought to find in the flatlands of society. For psychotherapy to be effective a close rapport is needed, so close that the doctor cannot shut his eyes to the heights and depths of human suffering. The rapport consists, after all, in a constant comparison and mutual comprehension, in the dialectical confrontation of two opposing psychic realities. If for some reason these mutual impressions do not impinge on each other, the psychotherapeutic process remains ineffective, and no change is produced. Unless both doctor and patient become a problem to each other, no solution is found.

Among the so-called neurotics of our day there are a good

many who in other ages would not have been neurotic—that is, divided against themselves. If they had lived in a period and in a milieu in which man was still linked by myth with the world of the ancestors, and thus with nature truly experienced and not merely seen from outside, they would have been spared this division with themselves. I am speaking of those who cannot tolerate the loss of myth and who can neither find a way to a merely exterior world, to the world as seen by science, nor rest satisfied with an intellectual juggling with words, which has nothing whatsoever to do with wisdom.

These victims of the psychic dichotomy of our time are merely optional neurotics; their apparent morbidity drops away the moment the gulf between the ego and the unconscious is closed. The doctor who has felt this dichotomy to the depths of his being will also be able to reach a better understanding of the unconscious psychic processes, and will be saved from the danger of inflation to which the psychologist is prone. The doctor who does not know from his own experience the numinosity of the archetypes will scarcely be able to escape their negative effect when he encounters it in his practice. He will tend to over- or underestimate it, since he possesses only an intellectual point of view but no empirical criterion. This is where those perilous aberrations begin, the first of which is the attempt to dominate everything by the intellect. This serves the secret purpose of placing both doctor and patient at a safe distance from the archetypal effect and thus from real experience, and of substituting for psychic reality an apparently secure, artificial, but merely two-dimensional conceptual world in which the reality of life is well covered up by so-called clear concepts. Experience is stripped of its substance, and instead mere names are substituted, which are henceforth put in the place of reality. No one has any obligations to a concept; that is what is so agreeable about conceptuality—it promises protection from experience. The spirit does not dwell in concepts, but in deeds and in facts. Words butter no parsnips; nevertheless, this futile procedure is repeated ad infinitum.

In my experience, therefore, the most difficult as well as the most ungrateful patients, apart from habitual liars, are the so-called intellectuals. With them, one hand never knows what the other hand is doing. They cultivate a "compartment psychology." Anything can be settled by an intellect that is not subject to the control of feeling—and yet the intellectual still suffers from a neurosis if feeling is undeveloped.

From my encounters with patients and with the psychic phenomena which they have paraded before me in an endless stream of images, I have learned an enormous amount—not just knowledge, but above all insight into my own nature. And not the least of what I have learned has come from my errors and defeats. I have had mainly women patients, who often entered into the work with extraordinary conscientiousness, understanding, and intelligence. It was essentially because of them that I was able to strike out on new paths in therapy.

A number of my patients became my disciples in the original sense of the word, and have carried my ideas out into the world. Among them I have made friendships that have endured decade after decade.

My patients brought me so close to the reality of human life that I could not help learning essential things from them. Encounters with people of so many different kinds and on so many different psychological levels have been for me incomparably more important than fragmentary conversations with celebrities. The finest and most significant conversations of my life were anonymous.

· V ·

Sigmund Freud[1]

I EMBARKED on the adventure of my intellectual development by becoming a psychiatrist. In all innocence I began observing mental patients, clinically, from the outside, and thereby came upon psychic processes of a striking nature. I noted and classified these things without the slightest understanding of their contents, which were considered to be adequately evaluated when they were dismissed as "pathological." In the course of time my interest focused more and more upon cases in which I experienced something understandable—that is, cases of paranoia, manic-depressive insanity, and psychogenic disturbances. From the start of my psychiatric career the studies of Breuer and Freud, along with the work of Pierre Janet, provided me with a wealth of suggestions and stimuli. Above all, I found that Freud's technique of dream analysis and dream interpretation cast a valuable light upon schizophrenic forms of expression. As early as 1900 I had read Freud's *The In-*

[1] This chapter should be regarded as a supplement to Jung's numerous writings on Freud. The most important of these are contained in *Freud and Psychoanalysis* (CW 4). Cf. also "Sigmund Freud in His Historical Setting" (1934) and "In Memory of Sigmund Freud" (1939), in *The Spirit in Man, Art, and Literature* (CW 15).

terpretation of Dreams.[2] I had laid the book aside, at the time, because I did not yet grasp it. At the age of twenty-five I lacked the experience to appreciate Freud's theories. Such experience did not come until later. In 1903 I once more took up *The Interpretation of Dreams* and discovered how it all linked up with my own ideas. What chiefly interested me was the application to dreams of the concept of the repression mechanism, which was derived from the psychology of the neuroses. This was important to me because I had frequently encountered repressions in my experiments with word association; in response to certain stimulus words the patient either had no associative answer or was unduly slow in his reaction time. As was later discovered, such a disturbance occurred each time the stimulus word had touched upon a psychic lesion or conflict. In most cases the patient was unconscious of this. When questioned about the cause of the disturbance, he would often answer in a peculiarly artificial manner. My reading of Freud's *The Interpretation of Dreams* showed me that the repression mechanism was at work here, and that the facts I had observed were consonant with his theory. Thus I was able to corroborate Freud's line of argument.

The situation was different when it came to the content of the repression. Here I could not agree with Freud. He considered the cause of the repression to be a sexual trauma. From my practice, however, I was familiar with numerous cases of neurosis in which the question of sexuality played a subordinate part, other factors standing in the foreground—for example, the problem of social adaptation, of oppression by tragic circumstances of life, prestige considerations, and so on. Later I presented such cases to Freud; but he would not grant that factors other than sexuality could be the cause. That was highly unsatisfactory to me.

At the beginning it was not easy for me to assign Freud the proper place in my life, or to take the right attitude toward him. When I became acquainted with his work I was planning an

[2] In his obituary on Freud (1939), Jung calls this work "epoch-making" and "probably the boldest attempt that has ever been made to master the riddles of the unconscious psyche upon the apparently firm ground of empiricism. For us, then young psychiatrists, it was . . . a source of illumination, while for our older colleagues it was an object of mockery."—A. J.

academic career, and was about to complete a paper that was intended to advance me at the university. But Freud was definitely *persona non grata* in the academic world at the time, and any connection with him would have been damaging in scientific circles. "Important people" at most mentioned him surreptitiously, and at congresses he was discussed only in the corridors, never on the floor. Therefore the discovery that my association experiments were in agreement with Freud's theories was far from pleasant to me.

Once, while I was in my laboratory and reflecting again upon these questions, the devil whispered to me that I would be justified in publishing the results of my experiments and my conclusions without mentioning Freud. After all, I had worked out my experiments long before I understood his work. But then I heard the voice of my second personality: "If you do a thing like that, as if you had no knowledge of Freud, it would be a piece of trickery. You cannot build your life upon a lie." With that, the question was settled. From then on I became an open partisan of Freud's and fought for him.

I first took up the cudgels for Freud at a congress in Munich where a lecturer discussed obsessional neuroses but studiously forbore to mention the name of Freud. In 1906, in connection with this incident, I wrote a paper [3] for the *Münchner Medizinische Wochenschrift* on Freud's theory of the neuroses, which had contributed a great deal to the understanding of obsessional neuroses. In response to this article, two German professors wrote to me, warning that if I remained on Freud's side and continued to defend him, I would be endangering my academic career. I replied: "If what Freud says is the truth, I am with him. I don't give a damn for a career if it has to be based on the premise of restricting research and concealing the truth." And I went on defending Freud and his ideas. But on the basis of my own findings I was still unable to feel that all neuroses were caused by sexual repression or sexual traumata. In certain

[3] "Die Hysterielehre Freuds: Eine Erwiderung auf die Aschaffenburgsche Kritik," *Münchener medizinische Wochenschrift*, LIII (November, 1906), 47; English trans.: "Freud's Theory of Hysteria: A Reply to Aschaffenburg," in *Freud and Psychoanalysis* (CW 4).

cases that was so, but not in others. Nevertheless, Freud had opened up a new path of investigation, and the shocked outcries against him at the time seemed to me absurd.[4]

I had not met with much sympathy for the ideas expressed in "The Psychology of Dementia Praecox." In fact, my colleagues laughed at me. But through this book I came to know Freud. He invited me to visit him, and our first meeting took place in Vienna in March 1907. We met at one o'clock in the afternoon and talked virtually without a pause for thirteen hours. Freud was the first man of real importance I had encountered; in my experience up to that time, no one else could compare with him. There was nothing the least trivial in his attitude. I found him extremely intelligent, shrewd, and altogether remarkable. And yet my first impressions of him remained somewhat tangled; I could not make him out.

What he said about his sexual theory impressed me. Nevertheless, his words could not remove my hesitations and doubts. I tried to advance these reservations of mine on several occasions, but each time he would attribute them to my lack of experience. Freud was right; in those days I had not enough experience to support my objections. I could see that his sexual theory was enormously important to him, both personally and philosophically. This impressed me, but I could not decide to what extent this strong emphasis upon sexuality was connected with subjective prejudices of his, and to what extent it rested upon verifiable experiences.

Above all, Freud's attitude toward the spirit seemed to me highly questionable. Wherever, in a person or in a work of art, an expression of spirituality (in the intellectual, not the supernatural sense) came to light, he suspected it, and insinuated that it was repressed sexuality. Anything that could not be directly interpreted as sexuality he referred to as "psychosexual-

[4] In 1906, after Jung sent Freud *Diagnostische Assoziationsstudien* (1906; English trans. of Jung's contributions in *Experimental Researches*, CW 2), the correspondence between the two men began, and went on until 1913. In 1907 Jung sent Freud his book *Über die Psychologie der Dementia Praecox* (English trans.: "The Psychology of Dementia Praecox," in *The Psychogenesis of Mental Disease*, CW 3).—A. J.

ity." I protested that this hypothesis, carried to its logical conclusion, would lead to an annihilating judgment upon culture. Culture would then appear as a mere farce, the morbid consequence of repressed sexuality. "Yes," he assented, "so it is, and that is just a curse of fate against which we are powerless to contend." I was by no means disposed to agree, or to let it go at that, but still I did not feel competent to argue it out with him.

There was something else that seemed to me significant at that first meeting. It had to do with things which I was able to think out and understand only after our friendship was over. There was no mistaking the fact that Freud was emotionally involved in his sexual theory to an extraordinary degree. When he spoke of it, his tone became urgent, almost anxious, and all signs of his normally critical and skeptical manner vanished. A strange, deeply moved expression came over his face, the cause of which I was at a loss to understand. I had a strong intuition that for him sexuality was a sort of *numinosum*. This was confirmed by a conversation which took place some three years later (in 1910), again in Vienna.

I can still recall vividly how Freud said to me, "My dear Jung, promise me never to abandon the sexual theory. That is the most essential thing of all. You see, we must make a dogma of it, an unshakable bulwark." He said that to me with great emotion, in the tone of a father saying, "And promise me this one thing, my dear son: that you will go to church every Sunday." In some astonishment I asked him, "A bulwark—against what?" To which he replied, "Against the black tide of mud"—and here he hesitated for a moment, then added—"of occultism." First of all, it was the words "bulwark" and "dogma" that alarmed me; for a dogma, that is to say, an undisputable confession of faith, is set up only when the aim is to suppress doubts once and for all. But that no longer has anything to do with scientific judgment; only with a personal power drive.

This was the thing that struck at the heart of our friendship. I knew that I would never be able to accept such an attitude. What Freud seemed to mean by "occultism" was virtually everything that philosophy and religion, including the rising contemporary science of parapsychology, had learned about the psyche. To me the sexual theory was just as occult, that is to say, just as unproven an hypothesis, as many other speculative views. As I saw it, a scientific truth was a hypothesis which might be adequate for the moment but was not to be preserved as an article of faith for all time.

Although I did not properly understand it then, I had observed in Freud the eruption of unconscious religious factors. Evidently he wanted my aid in erecting a barrier against these threatening unconscious contents.

The impression this conversation made upon me added to my confusion; until then I had not considered sexuality as a precious and imperiled concept to which one must remain faithful. Sexuality evidently meant more to Freud than to other people. For him it was something to be religiously observed. In the face of such deep convictions one generally becomes shy and reticent. After a few stammering attempts on my part, the conversation soon came to an end.

I was bewildered and embarrassed. I had the feeling that I had caught a glimpse of a new, unknown country from which swarms of new ideas flew to meet me. One thing was clear: Freud, who had always made much of his irreligiosity, had now constructed a dogma; or rather, in the place of a jealous God whom he had lost, he had substituted another compelling image, that of sexuality. It was no less insistent, exacting, domineering, threatening, and morally ambivalent than the original one. Just as the psychically stronger agency is given "divine" or "daemonic" attributes, so the "sexual libido" took over the role of a *deus absconditus*, a hidden or concealed god. The advantage of this transformation for Freud was, apparently, that he was able to regard the new numinous principle as scientifically irreproachable and free from all religious taint. At bottom, however, the numinosity, that is, the psychological qualities of the two rationally incommensurable opposites—Yahweh and sexuality—remained the same. The name alone had changed, and with it, of course, the point of view: the lost god had now to be sought below, not above. But what difference does it make, ultimately, to the stronger agency if it is called now by one name and now by another? If psychology did not exist, but only concrete objects, the one would actually have been destroyed and replaced by the other. But in reality, that is to say, in psychological experience, there is not one whit the less of urgency, anxiety, compulsiveness, etc. The problem still remains: how to overcome or escape our anxiety, bad conscience, guilt, compulsion, unconsciousness, and instinctuality. If we cannot do this from the bright, idealistic side, then perhaps we shall have better luck by approaching the problem from the dark, biological side.

Like flames suddenly flaring up, these thoughts darted through my mind. Much later, when I reflected upon Freud's character, they revealed their significance. There was one characteristic of his that preoccupied me above all: his bitterness. It had struck me at our first encounter, but it remained inexplicable to me until I was able to see it in connection with his attitude toward sexuality. Although, for Freud, sexuality was undoubtedly a *numinosum,* his terminology and theory seemed to define it exclusively as a biological function. It was only the emotionality with which he spoke of it that revealed the deeper elements reverberating within him. Basically, he wanted to teach—or so at least it seemed to me—that, regarded from within, sexuality included spirituality and had an intrinsic meaning. But his concretistic terminology was too narrow to express this idea. He gave me the impression that at bottom he was working against his own goal and against himself; and there is, after all, no harsher bitterness than that of a person who is his own worst enemy. In his own words, he felt himself menaced by a "black tide of mud"—he who more than anyone else had tried to let down his buckets into those black depths.

Freud never asked himself why he was compelled to talk continually of sex, why this idea had taken such possession of him. He remained unaware that his "monotony of interpretation" expressed a flight from himself, or from that other side of him which might perhaps be called mystical. So long as he refused to acknowledge that side, he could never be reconciled with himself. He was blind toward the paradox and ambiguity of the contents of the unconscious, and did not know that everything which arises out of the unconscious has a top and a bottom, an inside and an outside. When we speak of the outside—and that is what Freud did—we are considering only half of the whole, with the result that a countereffect arises out of the unconscious.

There was nothing to be done about this one-sidedness of Freud's. Perhaps some inner experience of his own might have opened his eyes; but then his intellect would have reduced any such experience to "mere sexuality" or "psychosexuality." He remained the victim of the one aspect he could recognize, and for that reason I see him as a tragic figure; for he was a great man, and what is more, a man in the grip of his daimon.

After that second conversation in Vienna I also understood Alfred Adler's power hypothesis, to which I had hitherto paid scant attention. Like many sons, Adler had learned from his "father" not what the father said, but what he did. Instantly, the problem of love (Eros) and power came down upon me like a leaden weight. Freud himself had told me that he had never read Nietzsche; now I saw Freud's psychology as, so to speak, an adroit move on the part of intellectual history, compensating for Nietzsche's deification of the power principle. The problem had obviously to be rephrased not as "Freud versus Adler" but "Freud versus Nietzsche." It was therefore, I thought, more than a domestic quarrel in the domain of psychopathology. The idea dawned on me that Eros and the power drive might be in a sense like the dissident sons of a single father, or the products of a single motivating psychic force which manifested itself empirically in opposing forms, like positive and negative electrical charges, Eros as a *patiens*, the power drive as an *agens*, and vice versa. Eros makes just as great demands upon the power drive as the latter upon the former. Where is the one drive without the other? On the one hand man succumbs to the drive; on the other hand, he tries to master it. Freud shows how the object succumbs to the drive, and Adler how man uses the drive in order to force his will upon the object. Nietzsche, helpless in the hands of his destiny, had to create a "superman" for himself. Freud, I concluded, must himself be so profoundly affected by the power of Eros that he actually wished to elevate it into a dogma—*aere perennius*—like a religious numen. It is no secret that "Zarathustra" is the proclaimer of a gospel, and here was Freud also trying to outdo the church and to canonize a theory. To be sure, he did not do this too loudly; instead, he suspected *me* of wanting to be a prophet. He made his tragic claim and demolished it at the same time. That is how people usually behave with numinosities, and rightly so, for in one respect they are true, in another untrue. Numinous experience elevates and humiliates simultaneously. If Freud had given somewhat more consideration to the psychological truth that sexuality is numinous—both a god and a devil—he would not have remained bound within the confines of a biological concept. And Nietzsche might not have been carried over the brink of the world by his intellectual excesses if he had only held more firmly to the foundations of human existence.

Wherever the psyche is set violently oscillating by a numinous experience, there is a danger that the thread by which one hangs may be torn. Should that happen, one man tumbles into an absolute affirmation, another into an equally absolute negation. *Nirdvandva* (freedom from opposites) is the Orient's remedy for this. I have not forgotten that. The pendulum of the mind oscillates between sense and nonsense, not between right and wrong. The *numinosum* is dangerous because it lures men to extremes, so that a modest truth is regarded as *the* truth and a minor mistake is equated with fatal error. *Tout passe*—yesterday's truth is today's deception, and yesterday's false inference may be tomorrow's revelation. This is particularly so in psychological matters, of which, if truth were told, we still know very little. We are still a long way from understanding what it signifies that nothing has any existence unless some small—and oh, so transitory—consciousness has become aware of it.

My conversation with Freud had shown me that he feared that the numinous light of his sexual insights might be extinguished by a "black tide of mud." Thus a mythological situation had arisen: the struggle between light and darkness. That explains its numinosity, and why Freud immediately fell back on his dogma as a religious means of defense. In my next book, *Wandlungen und Symbole der Libido*,[5] which dealt with the hero's struggle for freedom, Freud's curious reaction prompted me to investigate further this archetypal theme and its mythological background.

What with the sexual interpretation on the one hand and the power drive of dogma on the other I was led, over the years, to a consideration of the problem of typology. It was necessary to study the polarity and dynamics of the psyche. And I also embarked upon an investigation extending over several decades of "the black tide of mud of occultism"—that is to say, I tried to understand the conscious and unconscious historical assumptions underlying our contemporary psychology.

It interested me to hear Freud's views on precognition and on parapsychology in general. When I visited him in Vienna in 1909 I asked him what he thought of these matters. Because of his materialistic prejudice, he rejected this entire complex of questions as nonsensical, and did so in terms of so shallow a positivism that I had difficulty in checking the sharp retort on the tip of my tongue. It was some years before he recognized the seriousness of parapsychology and acknowledged the factuality of "occult" phenomena.

While Freud was going on this way, I had a curious sensation. It was as if my diaphragm were made of iron and were becoming red-hot—a glowing vault. And at that moment there was such a loud report in the bookcase, which stood right next to us, that we both started up in alarm, fearing the thing was going to topple over on us. I said to Freud: "There, that is an example of a so-called catalytic exteriorization phenomenon."

"Oh come," he exclaimed. "That is sheer bosh."

"It is not," I replied. "You are mistaken, Herr Professor. And to prove my point I now predict that in a moment there will be another such loud report!" Sure enough, no sooner had I said the words than the same detonation went off in the bookcase.

[5] Published in 1912; English trans.: *Psychology of the Unconscious* (1917). Rev. edn., *Symbole der Wandlung* (1952); English trans.: *Symbols of Transformation* (CW 5, 1956).

To this day I do not know what gave me this certainty. But I knew beyond all doubt that the report would come again. Freud only stared aghast at me. I do not know what was in his mind, or what his look meant. In any case, this incident aroused his mistrust of me, and I had the feeling that I had done something against him. I never afterward discussed the incident with him.[6]

The year 1909 proved decisive for our relationship. I had been invited to lecture on the association experiment at Clark University in Worcester, Massachusetts.[7] Independently, Freud had also received an invitation, and we decided to travel together. We met in Bremen, where Ferenczi joined us. In Bremen the much-discussed incident of Freud's fainting fit occurred. It was provoked—indirectly—by my interest in the "peat-bog corpses." I knew that in certain districts of Northern Germany these so-called bog corpses were to be found. They are the bodies of prehistoric men who either drowned in the marshes or were buried there. The bog water in which the bodies lie contains humic acid, which consumes the bones and simultaneously tans the skin, so that it and the hair are perfectly preserved. In essence this is a process of natural mummification, in the course of which the bodies are pressed flat by the weight of the peat. Such remains are occasionally turned up by peat diggers in Holstein, Denmark, and Sweden.

Having read about these peat-bog corpses, I recalled them when we were in Bremen, but, being a bit muddled, confused them with the mummies in the lead cellars of the city. This interest of mine got on Freud's nerves. "Why are you so concerned with these corpses?" he asked me several times. He was inordinately vexed by the whole thing and during one such conversation, while we were having dinner together, he suddenly fainted. Afterward he said to me that he was convinced that all this chatter about corpses meant I had death-wishes toward him. I was more than surprised by this interpretation. I was alarmed by the intensity of his fantasies—so strong that, obviously, they could cause him to faint.

In a similar connection Freud once more suffered a fainting

[6] For Freud's reaction to the incident, see Appendix I, pp. 361–63.
[7] See Appendix II, pp. 365–68.

fit in my presence. This was during the Psychoanalytic Congress in Munich in 1912. Someone had turned the conversation to Amenophis IV (Ikhnaton). The point was made that as a result of his negative attitude toward his father he had destroyed his father's cartouches on the steles, and that at the back of his great creation of a monotheistic religion there lurked a father complex. This sort of thing irritated me, and I attempted to argue that Amenophis had been a creative and profoundly religious person whose acts could not be explained by personal resistances toward his father. On the contrary, I said, he had held the memory of his father in honor, and his zeal for destruction had been directed only against the name of the god Amon, which he had everywhere annihilated; it was also chiseled out of the cartouches of his father Amon-hotep. Moreover, other pharaohs had replaced the names of their actual or divine forefathers on monuments and statues by their own, feeling that they had a right to do so since they were incarnations of the same god. Yet they, I pointed out, had inaugurated neither a new style nor a new religion.

At that moment Freud slid off his chair in a faint. Everyone clustered helplessly around him. I picked him up, carried him into the next room, and laid him on a sofa. As I was carrying him, he half came to, and I shall never forget the look he cast at me. In his weakness he looked at me as if I were his father. Whatever other causes may have contributed to this faint—the atmosphere was very tense—the fantasy of father-murder was common to both cases.

At the time Freud frequently made allusions indicating that he regarded me as his successor. These hints were embarrassing to me, for I knew that I would never be able to uphold his views properly, that is to say, as he intended them. On the other hand I had not yet succeeded in working out my criticisms in such a manner that they would carry any weight with him, and my respect for him was too great for me to want to force him to come finally to grips with my own ideas. I was by no means charmed by the thought of being burdened, virtually over my own head, with the leadership of a party. In the first place that sort of thing was not in my nature; in the second place I could not sacrifice my intellectual independence; and in the third place such luster was highly unwelcome to me since it would only deflect me from my real aims. I was concerned with investigating truth, not with questions of personal prestige.

The trip to the United States which began in Bremen in 1909 lasted for seven weeks. We were together every day, and analyzed each other's dreams. At the time I had a number of important ones, but Freud could make nothing of them. I did not regard that as any reflection upon him, for it sometimes happens to the best analyst that he is unable to unlock the riddle of a dream. It was a human failure, and I would never have wanted to discontinue our dream analyses on that account. On the contrary, they meant a great deal to me, and I found our relationship exceedingly valuable. I regarded Freud as an older, more mature and experienced personality, and felt like a son in that respect. But then something happened which proved to be a severe blow to the whole relationship.

Freud had a dream—I would not think it right to air the problem it involved. I interpreted it as best I could, but added that a great deal more could be said about it if he would supply me with some additional details from his private life. Freud's response to these words was a curious look—a look of the utmost suspicion. Then he said, "But I cannot risk my authority!" At that moment he lost it altogether. That sentence burned itself into my memory; and in it the end of our relationship was already foreshadowed. Freud was placing personal authority above truth.

As I have already said, Freud was able to interpret the dreams I was then having only incompletely or not at all. They were dreams with collective contents, containing a great deal of symbolic material. One in particular was important to me, for it led me for the first time to the concept of the "collective unconscious" and thus formed a kind of prelude to my book, *Wandlungen und Symbole der Libido*.[8]

This was the dream. I was in a house I did not know, which had two stories. It was "my house." I found myself in the upper

[8] *Psychology of the Unconscious;* rev. edn.: *Symbols of Transformation* (CW 5).

story, where there was a kind of salon furnished with fine old pieces in rococo style. On the walls hung a number of precious old paintings. I wondered that this should be my house, and thought, "Not bad." But then it occurred to me that I did not know what the lower floor looked like. Descending the stairs, I reached the ground floor. There everything was much older, and I realized that this part of the house must date from about the fifteenth or sixteenth century. The furnishings were medieval; the floors were of red brick. Everywhere it was rather dark. I went from one room to another, thinking, "Now I really must explore the whole house." I came upon a heavy door, and opened it. Beyond it, I discovered a stone stairway that led down into the cellar. Descending again, I found myself in a beautifully vaulted room which looked exceedingly ancient. Examining the walls, I discovered layers of brick among the ordinary stone blocks, and chips of brick in the mortar. As soon as I saw this I knew that the walls dated from Roman times. My interest by now was intense. I looked more closely at the floor. It was of stone slabs, and in one of these I discovered a ring. When I pulled it, the stone slab lifted, and again I saw a stairway of narrow stone steps leading down into the depths. These, too, I descended, and entered a low cave cut into the rock. Thick dust lay on the floor, and in the dust were scattered bones and broken pottery, like remains of a primitive culture. I discovered two human skulls, obviously very old and half disintegrated. Then I awoke.

What chiefly interested Freud in this dream were the two skulls. He returned to them repeatedly, and urged me to find a *wish* in connection with them. What did I think about these skulls? And whose were they? I knew perfectly well, of course, what he was driving at: that secret death-wishes were concealed in the dream. "But what does he really expect of me?" I thought to myself. Toward whom would I have death-wishes? I felt violent resistance to any such interpretation. I also had some intimation of what the dream might really mean. But I did not then trust my own judgment, and wanted to hear Freud's opinion. I wanted to learn from him. Therefore I submitted to his intention and said, "My wife and my sister-in-law"—after all,

I had to name someone whose death was worth the wishing!

I was newly married at the time and knew perfectly well that there was nothing within myself which pointed to such wishes. But I would not have been able to present to Freud my own ideas on an interpretation of the dream without encountering incomprehension and vehement resistance. I did not feel up to quarreling with him, and I also feared that I might lose his friendship if I insisted on my own point of view. On the other hand, I wanted to know what he would make of my answer, and what his reaction would be if I deceived him by saying something that suited his theories. And so I told him a lie.

I was quite aware that my conduct was not above reproach, but *à la guerre, comme à la guerre!* It would have been impossible for me to afford him any insight into my mental world. The gulf between it and his was too great. In fact Freud seemed greatly relieved by my reply. I saw from this that he was completely helpless in dealing with certain kinds of dreams and had to take refuge in his doctrine. I realized that it was up to me to find out the real meaning of the dream.

It was plain to me that the house represented a kind of image of the psyche—that is to say, of my then state of consciousness, with hitherto unconscious additions. Consciousness was represented by the salon. It had an inhabited atmosphere, in spite of its antiquated style.

The ground floor stood for the first level of the unconscious. The deeper I went, the more alien and the darker the scene became. In the cave, I discovered remains of a primitive culture, that is, the world of the primitive man within myself—a world which can scarcely be reached or illuminated by consciousness. The primitive psyche of man borders on the life of the animal soul, just as the caves of prehistoric times were usually inhabited by animals before men laid claim to them.

During this period I became aware of how keenly I felt the difference between Freud's intellectual attitude and mine. I had grown up in the intensely historical atmosphere of Basel at the end of the nineteenth century, and had acquired, thanks to reading the old philosophers, some knowledge of the history of psychology. When I thought about dreams and the contents of the unconscious, I never did so without making historical comparisons; in my student days I always used Krug's old dictionary of philosophy. I was especially familiar with the writers of the eighteenth and early nineteenth century. Theirs was the world which had formed the atmosphere of my first-story salon. By contrast, I had the impression that Freud's intellectual history began with Büchner, Moleschott, Du Bois-Reymond, and Darwin.

The dream pointed out that there were further reaches to the state of consciousness I have just described: the long uninhabited ground floor in medieval style, then the Roman cellar, and finally the prehistoric cave. These signified past times and passed stages of consciousness.

Certain questions had been much on my mind during the days preceding this dream. They were: On what premises is Freudian psychology founded? To what category of human thought does it belong? What is the relationship of its almost exclusive personalism to general historical assumptions? My dream was giving me the answer. It obviously pointed to the foundations of cultural history—a history of successive layers of consciousness. My dream thus constituted a kind of structural diagram of the human psyche; it postulated something of an altogether *impersonal* nature underlying that psyche. It "clicked," as the English have it—and the dream became for me a guiding image which in the days to come was to be corroborated to an extent I could not at first suspect. It was my first inkling of a collective a priori beneath the personal psyche. This I first took to be the traces of earlier modes of functioning. Later, with increasing experience and on the basis of more reliable knowledge, I recognized them as forms of instinct, that is, as archetypes.

I was never able to agree with Freud that the dream is a "façade" behind which its meaning lies hidden—a meaning already known but maliciously, so to speak, withheld from consciousness. To me dreams are a part of nature, which harbors no intention to deceive, but expresses something as best it can, just as a plant grows or an animal seeks its food as best it can. These forms of life, too, have no wish to deceive our eyes, but we may deceive ourselves because our eyes are shortsighted. Or we hear amiss because our ears are rather deaf—but it is not our ears that wish to deceive us. Long before I met Freud I regarded the unconscious, and dreams, which are its direct exponents, as natural processes to which no arbitrariness can be attributed, and above all no legerdemain. I knew no reasons for the assumption that the tricks of consciousness can be extended to the natural processes of the unconscious. On the contrary, daily experience taught me what intense resistance the unconscious opposes to the tendencies of the conscious mind.

The dream of the house had a curious effect upon me: it revived my old interest in archaeology. After I had returned to Zürich I took up a book on Babylonian excavations, and read various works on myths. In the course of this reading I came across Friedrich Creuzer's *Symbolik und Mythologie der alten Völker* [9]—and that fired me! I read like mad, and worked with feverish interest through a mountain of mythological material, then through the Gnostic writers, and ended in total confusion. I found myself in a state of perplexity similar to the one I had experienced at the clinic when I tried to understand the meaning of psychotic states of mind. It was as if I were in an imaginary madhouse and were beginning to treat and analyze all the centaurs, nymphs, gods, and goddesses in Creuzer's book as though they were my patients. While thus occupied I could not help but discover the close relationship between ancient mythology and the psychology of primitives, and this led me to an intensive study of the latter.

In the midst of these studies I came upon the fantasies of a young American altogether unknown to me, Miss Miller. The material had been published by my revered and fatherly friend, Théodore Flournoy, in the *Archives de Psychologie* (Geneva). I was immediately struck by the mythological character of the

[9] *The Symbolism and Mythology of Ancient Peoples* (Leipzig and Darmstadt, 1810–23).

fantasies. They operated like a catalyst upon the stored-up and still disorderly ideas within me. Gradually, there formed out of them, and out of the knowledge of myths I had acquired, my book *Wandlungen und Symbole der Libido*.

While I was working on this book, I had dreams which presaged the forthcoming break with Freud. One of the most significant had its scene in a mountainous region on the Swiss-Austrian border. It was toward evening, and I saw an elderly man in the uniform of an Imperial Austrian customs official. He walked past, somewhat stooped, without paying any attention to me. His expression was peevish, rather melancholic and vexed. There were other persons present, and someone informed me that the old man was not really there, but was the ghost of a customs official who had died years ago. "He is one of those who still couldn't die properly." That was the first part of the dream.

I set about analyzing this dream. In connection with "customs" I at once thought of the word "censorship." In connection with "border" I thought of the border between consciousness and the unconscious on the one hand, and between Freud's views and mine on the other. The extremely rigorous customs examination at the border seemed to me an allusion to analysis. At a border suitcases are opened and examined for contraband. In the course of this examination, unconscious assumptions are discovered. As for the old customs official, his work had obviously brought him so little that was pleasurable and satisfactory that he took a sour view of the world. I could not refuse to see the analogy with Freud.

At that time Freud had lost much of his authority for me. But he still meant to me a superior personality, upon whom I projected the father, and at the time of the dream this projection was still far from eliminated. Where such a projection occurs, we are no longer objective; we persist in a state of divided judgment. On the one hand we are dependent, and on the other we have resistances. When the dream took place I still thought highly of Freud, but at the same time I was critical of him. This divided attitude is a sign that I was still unconscious of the situation and had not come to any resolution of it. This is characteristic of all projections. The dream urged upon me the necessity of clarifying this situation.

Under the impress of Freud's personality I had, as far as possible, cast aside my own judgments and repressed my criticisms. That was the prerequisite for collaborating with him. I had told myself, "Freud is far wiser and more experienced than you. For the present you must simply listen to what he says and learn from him." And then, to my own surprise, I found myself dreaming of him as a peevish official of the Imperial Austrian monarchy, as a defunct and still walking ghost of a customs inspector. Could that be the death-wish which Freud had insinuated I felt toward him? I could find no part of myself that normally might have had such a wish, for I wanted at all costs to be able to work with Freud, and, in a frankly egotistic manner, to partake of his wealth of experience. His friendship meant a great deal to me. I had no reason for wishing him dead. But it was possible that the dream could be regarded as a corrective, as a compensation or antidote for my conscious high opinion and admiration. Therefore the dream recommended a rather more critical attitude toward Freud. I was distinctly shocked by it, although the final sentence of the dream seemed to me an allusion to Freud's potential immortality.

The dream had not reached its end with the episode of the customs official; after a hiatus came a second and far more remarkable part. I was in an Italian city, and it was around noon, between twelve and one o'clock. A fierce sun was beating down upon the narrow streets. The city was built on hills and reminded me of a particular part of Basel, the Kohlenberg. The little streets which lead down into the valley, the Birsigtal, that runs through the city, are partly flights of steps. In the dream, one such stairway descended to Barfüsserplatz. The city was Basel, and yet it was also an Italian city, something like Bergamo. It was summertime; the blazing sun stood at the zenith, and everything was bathed in an intense light. A crowd came streaming toward me, and I knew that the shops were closing and people were on their way home to dinner. In the midst of this stream of people walked a knight in full armor. He mounted the steps toward me. He wore a helmet of the kind that is called a basinet, with eye slits, and chain armor. Over this was a white tunic into which was woven, front and back, a large red cross.

One can easily imagine how I felt: suddenly to see in a modern city, during the noonday rush hour, a crusader coming toward me. What struck me as particularly odd was that none of the many persons walking about seemed to notice him. No one turned his head or gazed after him. It was as though he were completely invisible to everyone but me. I asked myself what this apparition meant, and then it was as if someone answered me—but there was no one there to speak: "Yes, this is a regular apparition. The knight always passes by here between twelve and one o'clock, and has been doing so for a very long time [for centuries, I gathered] and everyone knows about it."

The knight and the customs official were contrasting figures. The customs official was shadowy, someone who "still couldn't die properly"—a fading apparition. The knight, on the other hand, was full of life and completely real. The second part of the dream was numinous in the extreme, whereas the scene on the border had been prosaic and in itself not impressive; I had been struck only by my reflections upon it.

In the period following these dreams I did a great deal of thinking about the mysterious figure of the knight. But it was only much later, after I had been meditating on the dream for a long time, that I was able to get some idea of its meaning. Even in the dream, I knew that the knight belonged to the twelfth century. That was the period when alchemy was beginning and also the quest for the Holy Grail. The stories of the Grail had been of the greatest importance to me ever since I read them, at the age of fifteen, for the first time. I had an inkling that a great secret still lay hidden behind those stories. Therefore it seemed quite natural to me that the dream should conjure up the world of the Knights of the Grail and their quest —for that was, in the deepest sense, my own world, which had scarcely anything to do with Freud's. My whole being was seeking for something still unknown which might confer meaning upon the banality of life.

To me it was a profound disappointment that all the efforts of the probing mind had apparently succeeded in finding nothing more in the depths of the psyche than the all too familiar and "all-too-human" limitations. I had grown up in the country, among peasants, and what I was unable to learn in the stables I found out from the Rabelaisian wit and the untrammeled fantasies of our peasant folklore. Incest and perversions were no remarkable novelties to me, and did not call for any special explanation. Along with criminality, they formed part of the black lees that spoiled the taste of life by showing me only too plainly the ugliness and meaninglessness of human existence. That cabbages thrive in dung was something I had always taken for granted. In all honesty I could discover no helpful insight in such knowledge. "It's just that all of those people are city folks who know nothing about nature and the human stable," I thought, sick and tired of these ugly matters.

People who know nothing about nature are of course neurotic, for they are not adapted to reality. They are too naïve, like children, and it is necessary to tell them the facts of life, so to speak—to make it plain to them that they are human beings like all others. Not that such enlightenment will cure neurotics; they can only regain their health when they climb up out of the mud of the commonplace. But they are only too fond of lingering in what they have earlier repressed. How are they ever to emerge if analysis does not make them aware of something different and better, when even theory holds them fast in it and offers them nothing more than the rational or "reasonable" injunction to abandon such childishness? That is precisely what they cannot do, and how should they be able to if they do not discover something to stand on? One form of life cannot simply be abandoned unless it is exchanged for another. As for a totally rational approach to life, that is, as experience shows, impossible, especially when a person is by nature as unreasonable as a neurotic.

I now realized why Freud's personal psychology was of such burning interest to me. I was eager to know the truth about his "reasonable solution," and I was prepared to sacrifice a good deal in order to obtain the answer. Now I felt that I was on the track of it. Freud himself had a neurosis, no doubt diagnosable and one with highly troublesome symptoms, as I had discovered on our voyage to America. Of course he had taught me that everybody is somewhat neurotic, and that we must practice tolerance. But I was not at all inclined to content myself with that; rather, I wanted to know how one could escape having a neurosis. Apparently neither Freud nor his disciples could understand what it meant for the theory and practice of psychoanalysis if not even the master could deal with his own neurosis. When, then, Freud announced his intention of identifying theory and method and making them into some kind of dogma, I could no longer collaborate with him; there remained no choice for me but to withdraw.

When I was working on my book about the libido and approaching the end of the chapter "The Sacrifice," I knew in advance that its publication would cost me my friendship with Freud. For I planned to set down in it my own conception of incest, the decisive transformation of the concept of libido, and various other ideas in which I differed from Freud. To me incest signified a personal complication only in the rarest cases. Usually incest has a highly religious aspect, for which reason the incest theme plays a decisive part in almost all cosmogonies and in numerous myths. But Freud clung to the literal interpretation of it and could not grasp the spiritual significance of incest as a symbol. I knew that he would never be able to accept any of my ideas on this subject.

I spoke with my wife about this, and told her of my fears. She attempted to reassure me, for she thought that Freud would magnanimously raise no objections, although he might not accept my views. I myself was convinced that he could not do so. For two months I was unable to touch my pen, so tormented was I by the conflict. Should I keep my thoughts to myself, or should I risk the loss of so important a friendship? At last I resolved to go ahead with the writing—and it did indeed cost me Freud's friendship.

After the break with Freud, all my friends and acquaintances dropped away. My book was declared to be rubbish; I was a mystic, and that settled the matter. Riklin and Maeder alone stuck by me. But I had foreseen my isolation and harbored no illusion about the reactions of my so-called friends. That was a point I had thoroughly considered beforehand. I had known that everything was at stake, and that I had to take a stand for my convictions. I realized that the chapter, "The Sacrifice," meant my own sacrifice. Having reached this insight, I was able to write again, even though I knew that my ideas would go uncomprehended.

In retrospect I can say that I alone logically pursued the two problems which most interested Freud: the problem of "archaic vestiges," and that of sexuality. It is a widespread error to imagine that I do not see the value of sexuality. On the contrary, it plays a large part in my psychology as an essential—though not the sole—expression of psychic wholeness. But my main concern has been to investigate, over and above its personal significance and biological function, its spiritual aspect and its numinous meaning, and thus to explain what Freud was so fascinated by but was unable to grasp. My thoughts on this subject are contained in "The Psychology of the Transference" [10] and the *Mysterium Coniunctionis*.[11] Sexuality is of the greatest importance as the expression of the chthonic spirit. That spirit is the "other face of God," the dark side of the God-image. The question of the chthonic spirit has occupied me ever since I began to delve into the world of alchemy. Basically, this interest was awakened by that early conversation with Freud, when, mystified, I felt how deeply stirred he was by the phenomenon of sexuality.

Freud's greatest achievement probably consisted in taking neurotic patients seriously and entering into their peculiar individual psychology. He had the courage to let the case material speak for itself, and in this way was able to penetrate into the real psychology of his patients. He saw with the patient's eyes, so to speak, and so reached a deeper understanding of mental illness than had hitherto been possible. In this respect he was free of bias, courageous, and succeeded in overcoming a host

[10] In *The Practice of Psychotherapy* (CW 16).
[11] CW 14.

of prejudices. Like an Old Testament prophet, he undertook to overthrow false gods, to rip the veils away from a mass of dishonesties and hypocrisies, mercilessly exposing the rottenness of the contemporary psyche. He did not falter in the face of the unpopularity such an enterprise entailed. The impetus which he gave to our civilization sprang from his discovery of an avenue to the unconscious. By evaluating dreams as the most important source of information concerning the unconscious processes, he gave back to mankind a tool that had seemed irretrievably lost. He demonstrated empirically the presence of an unconscious psyche which had hitherto existed only as a philosophical postulate, in particular in the philosophies of C. G. Carus and Eduard von Hartmann.

It may well be said that the contemporary cultural consciousness has not yet absorbed into its general philosophy the idea of the unconscious and all that it means, despite the fact that modern man has been confronted with this idea for more than half a century. The assimilation of the fundamental insight that psychic life has two poles still remains a task for the future.

·VI·

Confrontation
with the Unconscious

A FTER the parting of the ways with Freud, a period of
inner uncertainty began for me. It would be no exaggeration to call it a state of disorientation. I felt totally suspended in mid-air, for I had not yet found my own footing.
Above all, I felt it necessary to develop a new attitude toward
my patients. I resolved for the present not to bring any theoretical premises to bear upon them, but to wait and see what they
would tell of their own accord. My aim became to leave things
to chance. The result was that the patients would spontaneously
report their dreams and fantasies to me, and I would merely ask,
"What occurs to you in connection with that?" or, "How do you
mean that, where does that come from, what do you think about
it?" The interpretations seemed to follow of their own accord
from the patients' replies and associations. I avoided all theoretical points of view and simply helped the patients to understand
the dream-images by themselves, without application of rules
and theories.

Soon I realized that it was right to take the dreams in this way as the basis of interpretation, for that is how dreams are intended. They are the facts from which we must proceed. Naturally, the aspects resulting from this method were so multitudinous that the need for a criterion grew more and more pressing—the need, I might almost put it, for some initial orientation.

About this time I experienced a moment of unusual clarity in which I looked back over the way I had traveled so far. I thought, "Now you possess a key to mythology and are free to unlock all the gates of the unconscious psyche." But then something whispered within me, "Why open all gates?" And promptly the question arose of what, after all, I had accomplished. I had explained the myths of peoples of the past; I had written a book about the hero, the myth in which man has always lived. But in what myth does man live nowadays? In the Christian myth, the answer might be, "Do *you* live in it?" I asked myself. To be honest, the answer was no. For me, it is not what I live by." "Then do we no longer have any myth?" "No, evidently we no longer have any myth." "But then what is your myth—the myth in which you do live?" At this point the dialogue with myself became uncomfortable, and I stopped thinking. I had reached a dead end.

Then, around Christmas of 1912, I had a dream. In the dream I found myself in a magnificent Italian loggia with pillars, a marble floor, and a marble balustrade. I was sitting on a gold Renaissance chair; in front of me was a table of rare beauty. It was made of green stone, like emerald. There I sat, looking out into the distance, for the loggia was set high up on the tower of a castle. My children were sitting at the table too.

Suddenly a white bird descended, a small sea gull or a dove. Gracefully, it came to rest on the table, and I signed to the children to be still so that they would not frighten away the pretty white bird. Immediately, the dove was transformed into a little girl, about eight years of age, with golden blond hair. She ran off with the children and played with them among the colonnades of the castle.

I remained lost in thought, musing about what I had just

experienced. The little girl returned and tenderly placed her arms around my neck. Then she suddenly vanished; the dove was back and spoke slowly in a human voice. "Only in the first hours of the night can I transform myself into a human being, while the male dove is busy with the twelve dead." Then she flew off into the blue air, and I awoke.

I was greatly stirred. What business would a male dove be having with twelve dead people? In connection with the emerald table the story of the Tabula Smaragdina occurred to me, the emerald table in the alchemical legend of Hermes Trismegistos. He was said to have left behind him a table upon which the basic tenets of alchemical wisdom were engraved in Greek.

I also thought of the twelve apostles, the twelve months of the year, the signs of the zodiac, etc. But I could find no solution to the enigma. Finally I had to give it up. All I knew with any certainty was that the dream indicated an unusual activation of the unconscious. But I knew no technique whereby I might get to the bottom of my inner processes, and so there remained nothing for me to do but wait, go on with my life, and pay close attention to my fantasies.

One fantasy kept returning: there was something dead present, but it was also still alive. For example, corpses were placed in crematory ovens, but were then discovered to be still living. These fantasies came to a head and were simultaneously resolved in a dream.

I was in a region like the Alyscamps near Arles. There they have a lane of sarcophagi which go back to Merovingian times. In the dream I was coming from the city, and saw before me a similar lane with a long row of tombs. They were pedestals with stone slabs on which the dead lay. They reminded me of old church burial vaults, where knights in armor lie outstretched. Thus the dead lay in my dream, in their antique clothes, with hands clasped, the difference being that they were not hewn out of stone, but in a curious fashion mummified. I stood still in front of the first grave and looked at the dead man, who was a person of the eighteen-thirties. I looked at his clothes with interest, whereupon he suddenly moved and came to life.

He unclasped his hands; but that was only because I was look-ing at him. I had an extremely unpleasant feeling, but walked on and came to another body. He belonged to the eighteenth century. There exactly the same thing happened: when I looked at him, he came to life and moved his hands. So I went down the whole row, until I came to the twelfth century—that is, to a crusader in chain mail who lay there with clasped hands. His figure seemed carved out of wood. For a long time I looked at him and thought he was really dead. But suddenly I saw that a finger of his left hand was beginning to stir gently.

Of course I had originally held to Freud's view that vestiges of old experiences exist in the unconscious.[1] But dreams like this, and my actual experiences of the unconscious, taught me that such contents are not dead, outmoded forms, but belong to our living being. My work had confirmed this assumption, and in the course of years there developed from it the theory of archetypes.

The dreams, however, could not help me over my feeling of disorientation. On the contrary, I lived as if under constant inner pressure. At times this became so strong that I suspected there was some psychic disturbance in myself. Therefore I twice went over all the details of my entire life, with particular atten-tion to childhood memories; for I thought there might be some-thing in my past which I could not see and which might possibly be the cause of the disturbance. But this retrospection led to nothing but a fresh acknowledgment of my own ignorance. Thereupon I said to myself, "Since I know nothing at all, I shall simply do whatever occurs to me." Thus I consciously submitted myself to the impulses of the unconscious.

The first thing that came to the surface was a childhood mem-ory from perhaps my tenth or eleventh year. At that time I had had a spell of playing passionately with building blocks. I dis-tinctly recalled how I had built little houses and castles, using bottles to form the sides of gates and vaults. Somewhat later I had used ordinary stones, with mud for mortar. These structures had fascinated me for a long time. To my astonishment, this memory was accompanied by a good deal of emotion. "Aha," I

[1] Freud speaks of "archaic vestiges."

said to myself, "there is still life in these things. The small boy is still around, and possesses a creative life which I lack. But how can I make my way to it?" For as a grown man it seemed impossible to me that I should be able to bridge the distance from the present back to my eleventh year. Yet if I wanted to re-establish contact with that period, I had no choice but to return to it and take up once more that child's life with his childish games. This moment was a turning point in my fate, but I gave in only after endless resistances and with a sense of resignation. For it was a painfully humiliating experience to realize that there was nothing to be done except play childish games.

Nevertheless, I began accumulating suitable stones, gathering them partly from the lake shore and partly from the water. And I started building: cottages, a castle, a whole village. The church was still missing, so I made a square building with a hexagonal drum on top of it, and a dome. A church also requires an altar, but I hesitated to build that.

Preoccupied with the question of how I could approach this task, I was walking along the lake as usual one day, picking stones out of the gravel on the shore. Suddenly I caught sight of a red stone, a four-sided pyramid about an inch and a half high. It was a fragment of stone which had been polished into this shape by the action of the water—a pure product of chance. I knew at once: this was the altar! I placed it in the middle under the dome, and as I did so, I recalled the underground phallus of my childhood dream. This connection gave me a feeling of satisfaction.

I went on with my building game after the noon meal every day, whenever the weather permitted. As soon as I was through eating, I began playing, and continued to do so until the patients arrived; and if I was finished with my work early enough in the evening, I went back to building. In the course of this activity my thoughts clarified, and I was able to grasp the fantasies whose presence in myself I dimly felt.

Naturally, I thought about the significance of what I was doing, and asked myself, "Now, really, what are you about? You are building a small town, and doing it as if it were a rite!" I had no answer to my question, only the inner certainty that I was on the way to discovering my own myth. For the building game was only a beginning. It released a stream of fantasies which I later carefully wrote down.

This sort of thing has been consistent with me, and at any time in my later life when I came up against a blank wall, I painted a picture or hewed stone. Each such experience proved to be a *rite d'entrée* for the ideas and works that followed hard upon it. Everything that I have written this year [2] and last year, "The Undiscovered Self," "Flying Saucers: A Modern Myth," "A Psychological View of Conscience," has grown out of the stone sculptures I did after my wife's death.[3] The close of her life, the end, and what it made me realize, wrenched me violently out of myself. It cost me a great deal to regain my footing, and contact with stone helped me.

Toward the autumn of 1913 the pressure which I had felt was in *me* seemed to be moving outward, as though there were something in the air. The atmosphere actually seemed to me darker than it had been. It was as though the sense of oppression no longer sprang exclusively from a psychic situation, but from concrete reality. This feeling grew more and more intense.

In October, while I was alone on a journey, I was suddenly seized by an overpowering vision: I saw a monstrous flood covering all the northern and low-lying lands between the North Sea and the Alps. When it came up to Switzerland I saw that the mountains grew higher and higher to protect our country. I realized that a frightful catastrophe was in progress. I saw the mighty yellow waves, the floating rubble of civilization, and the drowned bodies of uncounted thousands. Then the whole sea turned to blood. This vision lasted about one hour. I was perplexed and nauseated, and ashamed of my weakness.

Two weeks passed; then the vision recurred, under the same conditions, even more vividly than before, and the blood was more emphasized. An inner voice spoke. "Look at it well; it is wholly real and it will be so. You cannot doubt it." That winter someone asked me what I thought were the political prospects

[2] 1957.
[3] November 27, 1955.

of the world in the near future. I replied that I had no thoughts on the matter, but that I saw rivers of blood.

I asked myself whether these visions pointed to a revolution, but could not really imagine anything of the sort. And so I drew the conclusion that they had to do with me myself, and decided that I was menaced by a psychosis. The idea of war did not occur to me at all.

Soon afterward, in the spring and early summer of 1914, I had a thrice-repeated dream that in the middle of summer an Arctic cold wave descended and froze the land to ice. I saw, for example, the whole of Lorraine and its canals frozen and the entire region totally deserted by human beings. All living green things were killed by frost. This dream came in April and May, and for the last time in June, 1914.

In the third dream frightful cold had again descended from out of the cosmos. This dream, however, had an unexpected end. There stood a leaf-bearing tree, but without fruit (my tree of life, I thought), whose leaves had been transformed by the effects of the frost into sweet grapes full of healing juices. I plucked the grapes and gave them to a large, waiting crowd.

At the end of July 1914 I was invited by the British Medical Association to deliver a lecture, "On the Importance of the Unconscious in Psychopathology," at a congress in Aberdeen. I was prepared for something to happen, for such visions and dreams are fateful. In my state of mind just then, with the fears that were pursuing me, it seemed fateful to me that I should have to talk on the importance of the unconscious at such a time!

On August 1 the world war broke out. Now my task was clear: I had to try to understand what had happened and to what extent my own experience coincided with that of mankind in general. Therefore my first obligation was to probe the depths of my own psyche. I made a beginning by writing down the fantasies which had come to me during my building game. This work took precedence over everything else.

An incessant stream of fantasies had been released, and I did my best not to lose my head but to find some way to understand these strange things. I stood helpless before an alien world; everything in it seemed difficult and incomprehensible. I was living in a constant state of tension; often I felt as if gigantic blocks of stone were tumbling down upon me. One thunderstorm followed another. My enduring these storms was a question of brute strength. Others have been shattered by them— Nietzsche, and Hölderlin, and many others. But there was a demonic strength in me, and from the beginning there was no doubt in my mind that I must find the meaning of what I was experiencing in these fantasies. When I endured these assaults of the unconscious I had an unswerving conviction that I was obeying a higher will, and that feeling continued to uphold me until I had mastered the task.

I was frequently so wrought up that I had to do certain yoga exercises in order to hold my emotions in check. But since it was my purpose to know what was going on within myself, I would do these exercises only until I had calmed myself enough to resume my work with the unconscious. As soon as I had the feeling that I was myself again, I abandoned this restraint upon the emotions and allowed the images and inner voices to speak afresh. The Indian, on the other hand, does yoga exercises in order to obliterate completely the multitude of psychic contents and images.

To the extent that I managed to translate the emotions into images—that is to say, to find the images which were concealed in the emotions—I was inwardly calmed and reassured. Had I left those images hidden in the emotions, I might have been torn to pieces by them. There is a chance that I might have succeeded in splitting them off; but in that case I would inexorably have fallen into a neurosis and so been ultimately destroyed by them anyhow. As a result of my experiment I learned how helpful it can be, from the therapeutic point of view, to find the particular images which lie behind emotions.

I wrote down the fantasies as well as I could, and made an earnest effort to analyze the psychic conditions under which they had arisen. But I was able to do this only in clumsy language. First I formulated the things as I had observed them, usually in "high-flown language," for that corresponds to the style of the archetypes. Archetypes speak the language of high rhetoric, even of bombast. It is a style I find embarrassing; it grates on my nerves, as when someone draws his nails down a plaster wall, or scrapes his knife against a plate. But since I did not know what was going on, I had no choice but to write everything down in the style selected by the unconscious itself. Sometimes it was as if I were hearing it with my ears, sometimes feeling it with my mouth, as if my tongue were formulating words; now and then I heard myself whispering aloud. Below the threshold of consciousness everything was seething with life.

From the beginning I had conceived my voluntary confrontation with the unconscious as a scientific experiment which I myself was conducting and in whose outcome I was vitally interested. Today I might equally well say that it was an experiment which was being conducted on *me*. One of the greatest difficulties for me lay in dealing with my negative feelings. I was voluntarily submitting myself to emotions of which I could not really approve, and I was writing down fantasies which often struck me as nonsense, and toward which I had strong resistances. For as long as we do not understand their meaning, such fantasies are a diabolical mixture of the sublime and the ridiculous. It cost me a great deal to undergo them, but I had been challenged by fate. Only by extreme effort was I finally able to escape from the labyrinth.

In order to grasp the fantasies which were stirring in me "underground," I knew that I had to let myself plummet down into them, as it were. I felt not only violent resistance to this, but a distinct fear. For I was afraid of losing command of myself and becoming a prey to the fantasies—and as a psychiatrist I realized only too well what that meant. After prolonged hesitation, however, I saw that there was no other way out. I had to take the chance, had to try to gain power over them; for I realized that if I did not do so, I ran the risk of their gaining power over me. A cogent motive for my making the attempt was the conviction that I could not expect of my patients something I did not dare to do myself. The excuse that a helper stood at their side would not pass muster, for I was well aware that the so-called helper—that is, myself—could not help them unless he knew their fantasy material from his own direct experience, and that at present all he possessed were a few theoretical prejudices of dubious value. This idea—that I was committing myself to a dangerous enterprise not for myself alone, but also for the sake of my patients—helped me over several critical phases.

It was during Advent of the year 1913—December 12, to be exact—that I resolved upon the decisive step. I was sitting at my desk once more, thinking over my fears. Then I let myself drop. Suddenly it was as though the ground literally gave way beneath my feet, and I plunged down into dark depths. I could not fend off a feeling of panic. But then, abruptly, at not too great a depth, I landed on my feet in a soft, sticky mass. I felt great relief, although I was apparently in complete darkness. After a while my eyes grew accustomed to the gloom, which was rather like a deep twilight. Before me was the entrance to a dark cave, in which stood a dwarf with a leathery skin, as if he were mummified. I squeezed past him through the narrow entrance and waded knee deep through icy water to the other end of the cave where, on a projecting rock, I saw a glowing red crystal. I grasped the stone, lifted it, and discovered a hollow underneath. At first I could make out nothing, but then I saw that there was running water. In it a corpse floated by, a youth with blond hair and a wound in the head. He was followed by a gigantic black scarab and then by a red, newborn sun, rising up out of the depths of the water. Dazzled by the light, I wanted to replace the stone upon the opening, but then a fluid welled out. It was blood. A thick jet of it leaped up, and I felt nauseated. It seemed to me that the blood continued to spurt for an unendurably long time. At last it ceased, and the vision came to an end.

I was stunned by this vision. I realized, of course, that it was a hero and solar myth, a drama of death and renewal, the rebirth symbolized by the Egyptian scarab. At the end, the dawn of the new day should have followed, but instead came that intolerable outpouring of blood—an altogether abnormal phenomenon, so it seemed to me. But then I recalled the vision of blood that I had had in the autumn of that same year, and I abandoned all further attempt to understand.

Six days later (December 18, 1913), I had the following

dream. I was with an unknown, brown-skinned man, a savage, in a lonely, rocky mountain landscape. It was before dawn; the eastern sky was already bright, and the stars fading. Then I heard Siegfried's horn sounding over the mountains and I knew that we had to kill him. We were armed with rifles and lay in wait for him on a narrow path over the rocks.

Then Siegfried appeared high up on the crest of the mountain, in the first ray of the rising sun. On a chariot made of the bones of the dead he drove at furious speed down the precipitous slope. When he turned a corner, we shot at him, and he plunged down, struck dead.

Filled with disgust and remorse for having destroyed something so great and beautiful, I turned to flee, impelled by the fear that the murder might be discovered. But a tremendous downfall of rain began, and I knew that it would wipe out all traces of the dead. I had escaped the danger of discovery; life could go on, but an unbearable feeling of guilt remained.

When I awoke from the dream, I turned it over in my mind, but was unable to understand it. I tried therefore to fall asleep again, but a voice within me said, "You *must* understand the dream, and must do so at once!" The inner urgency mounted until the terrible moment came when the voice said, "If you do not understand the dream, you must shoot yourself!" In the drawer of my night table lay a loaded revolver, and I became frightened. Then I began pondering once again, and suddenly the meaning of the dream dawned on me. "Why, that is the problem that is being played out in the world." Siegfried, I thought, represents what the Germans want to achieve, heroically to impose their will, have their own way. "Where there is a will there is a way!" I had wanted to do the same. But now that was no longer possible. The dream showed that the attitude embodied by Siegfried, the hero, no longer suited me. Therefore it had to be killed.

After the deed I felt an overpowering compassion, as though I myself had been shot: a sign of my secret identity with Siegfried, as well as of the grief a man feels when he is forced to sacrifice his ideal and his conscious attitudes. This identity and my heroic idealism had to be abandoned, for there are higher things than the ego's will, and to these one must bow.

These thoughts sufficed for the present, and I fell asleep again.

The small, brown-skinned savage who accompanied me and had actually taken the initiative in the killing was an embodiment of the primitive shadow. The rain showed that the tension between consciousness and the unconscious was being resolved. Although at the time I was not able to understand the meaning of the dream beyond these few hints, new forces were released in me which helped me to carry the experiment with the unconscious to a conclusion.

In order to seize hold of the fantasies, I frequently imagined a steep descent. I even made several attempts to get to the very bottom. The first time I reached, as it were, a depth of about a thousand feet; the next time I found myself at the edge of a cosmic abyss. It was like a voyage to the moon, or a descent into empty space. First came the image of a crater, and I had the feeling that I was in the land of the dead. The atmosphere was that of the other world. Near the steep slope of a rock I caught sight of two figures, an old man with a white beard and a beautiful young girl. I summoned up my courage and approached them as though they were real people, and listened attentively to what they told me. The old man explained that he was Elijah, and that gave me a shock. But the girl staggered me even more, for she called herself Salome! She was blind. What a strange couple: Salome and Elijah. But Elijah assured me that he and Salome had belonged together from all eternity, which completely astounded me. . . . They had a black serpent living with them which displayed an unmistakable fondness for me. I stuck close to Elijah because he seemed to be the most reasonable of the three, and to have a clear intelligence. Of Salome I was distinctly suspicious. Elijah and I had a long conversation which, however, I did not understand.

Naturally I tried to find a plausible explanation for the appearance of Biblical figures in my fantasy by reminding myself that my father had been a clergyman. But that really explained nothing at all. For what did the old man signify? What did Salome signify? Why were they together? Only many years later, when I knew a great deal more than I knew then, did the connection between the old man and the young girl appear perfectly natural to me.

In such dream wanderings one frequently encounters an old man who is accompanied by a young girl, and examples of such couples are to be found in many mythic tales. Thus, according to Gnostic tradition, Simon Magus went about with a young girl whom he had picked up in a brothel. Her name was Helen, and she was regarded as the reincarnation of the Trojan Helen. Klingsor and Kundry, Lao-tzu and the dancing girl, likewise belong to this category.

I have mentioned that there was a third figure in my fantasy besides Elijah and Salome: the large black snake. In myths the snake is a frequent counterpart of the hero. There are numerous accounts of their affinity. For example, the hero has eyes like a snake, or after his death he is changed into a snake and revered as such, or the snake is his mother, etc. In my fantasy, therefore, the presence of the snake was an indication of a hero-myth.

Salome is an anima figure. She is blind because she does not see the meaning of things. Elijah is the figure of the wise old prophet and represents the factor of intelligence and knowledge; Salome, the erotic element. One might say that the two figures are personifications of Logos and Eros. But such a definition would be excessively intellectual. It is more meaningful to let the figures be what they were for me at the time—namely, events and experiences.

Soon after this fantasy another figure rose out of the unconscious. He developed out of the Elijah figure. I called him Philemon. Philemon was a pagan and brought with him an Egypto-Hellenistic atmosphere with a Gnostic coloration. His figure first appeared to me in the following dream.

There was a blue sky, like the sea, covered not by clouds but by flat brown clods of earth. It looked as if the clods were breaking apart and the blue water of the sea were becoming visible between them. But the water was the blue sky. Suddenly there appeared from the right a winged being sailing across the sky.

I saw that it was an old man with the horns of a bull. He held a bunch of four keys, one of which he clutched as if he were about to open a lock. He had the wings of the kingfisher with its characteristic colors.

Since I did not understand this dream-image, I painted it in order to impress it upon my memory. During the days when I was occupied with the painting, I found in my garden, by the lake shore, a dead kingfisher! I was thunderstruck, for kingfishers are quite rare in the vicinity of Zürich and I have never since found a dead one. The body was recently dead—at the most, two or three days—and showed no external injuries.

Philemon and other figures of my fantasies brought home to me the crucial insight that there are things in the psyche which I do not produce, but which produce themselves and have their own life. Philemon represented a force which was not myself. In my fantasies I held conversations with him, and he said things which I had not consciously thought. For I observed clearly that it was he who spoke, not I. He said I treated thoughts as if I generated them myself, but in his view thoughts were like animals in the forest, or people in a room, or birds in the air, and added, "If you should see people in a room, you would not think that you had made those people, or that you were responsible for them." It was he who taught me psychic objectivity, the reality of the psyche. Through him the distinction was clarified between myself and the object of my thought. He confronted me in an objective manner, and I understood that there is something in me which can say things that I do not know and do not intend, things which may even be directed against me.

Psychologically, Philemon represented superior insight. He was a mysterious figure to me. At times he seemed to me quite real, as if he were a living personality. I went walking up and down the garden with him, and to me he was what the Indians call a guru.

Whenever the outlines of a new personification appeared, I felt it almost as a personal defeat. It meant: "Here is something else you didn't know until now!" Fear crept over me that the succession of such figures might be endless, that I might lose

myself in bottomless abysses of ignorance. My ego felt devalued
—although the successes I had been having in worldly affairs
might have reassured me. In my darknesses (*horridas nostrae
mentis purga tenebras*—"cleanse the horrible darknesses of our
mind"—the *Aurora Consurgens* [4] says) I could have wished for
nothing better than a real, live guru, someone possessing superior knowledge and ability, who would have disentangled for
me the involuntary creations of my imagination. This task was
undertaken by the figure of Philemon, whom in this respect I
had willy-nilly to recognize as my psychagogue. And the fact
was that he conveyed to me many an illuminating idea.

More than fifteen years later a highly cultivated elderly Indian visited me, a friend of Gandhi's, and we talked about Indian education—in particular, about the relationship between
guru and chela. I hesitantly asked him whether he could tell me
anything about the person and character of his own guru,
whereupon he replied in a matter-of-fact tone, "Oh yes, he was
Shankaracharya."

"You don't mean the commentator on the Vedas who died
centuries ago?" I asked.

"Yes, I mean him," he said, to my amazement.

"Then you are referring to a spirit?" I asked.

"Of course it was his spirit," he agreed.

At that moment I thought of Philemon.

"There are ghostly gurus too," he added. "Most people have
living gurus. But there are always some who have a spirit for
teacher."

This information was both illuminating and reassuring to me.
Evidently, then, I had not plummeted right out of the human
world, but had only experienced the sort of thing that could
happen to others who made similar efforts.

Later, Philemon became relativized by the emergence of yet
another figure, whom I called Ka. In ancient Egypt the "king's
ka" was his earthly form, the embodied soul. In my fantasy the
ka-soul came from below, out of the earth as if out of a deep
shaft. I did a painting of him, showing him in his earth-bound
form, as a herm with base of stone and upper part of bronze.

[4] An alchemical treatise ascribed to Thomas Aquinas.

High up in the painting appears a kingfisher's wing, and between it and the head of Ka floats a round, glowing nebula of stars. Ka's expression has something demonic about it—one might also say, Mephistophelian. In one hand he holds something like a colored pagoda, or a reliquary, and in the other a stylus with which he is working on the reliquary. He is saying, "I am he who buries the gods in gold and gems."

Philemon had a lame foot, but was a winged spirit, whereas Ka represented a kind of earth demon or metal demon. Philemon was the spiritual aspect, or "meaning." Ka, on the other hand, was a spirit of nature like the Anthroparion of Greek alchemy—with which at the time I was still unfamiliar.[5] Ka was he who made everything real, but who also obscured the halcyon spirit, Meaning, or replaced it by beauty, the "eternal reflection."

In time I was able to integrate both figures through the study of alchemy.

When I was writing down these fantasies, I once asked myself, "What am I really doing? Certainly this has nothing to do with science. But then what is it?" Whereupon a voice within me said, "It is art." I was astonished. It had never entered my head that what I was writing had any connection with art. Then I thought, "Perhaps my unconscious is forming a personality that is not me, but which is insisting on coming through to expression." I knew for a certainty that the voice had come from a woman. I recognized it as the voice of a patient, a talented psychopath who had a strong transference to me. She had become a living figure within my mind.

Obviously what I was doing wasn't science. What then could it be but art? It was as though these were the only alternatives in the world. That is the way a woman's mind works.

I said very emphatically to this voice that my fantasies had

---

[5] The Anthroparion is a tiny man, a kind of homunculus. He is found, for example, in the visions of Zosimos of Panopolis, an important alchemist of the third century. To the group which includes the Anthroparion belong the gnomes, the Dactyls of classical antiquity, and the homunculi of the alchemists. As the spirit of quicksilver, the alchemical Mercurius was also an Anthroparion.—A. J.

nothing to do with art, and I felt a great inner resistance. No voice came through, however, and I kept on writing. Then came the next assault, and again the same assertion: "That is art." This time I caught her and said, "No, it is not art! On the contrary, it is nature," and prepared myself for an argument. When nothing of the sort occurred, I reflected that the "woman within me" did not have the speech centers I had. And so I suggested that she use mine. She did so and came through with a long statement.

I was greatly intrigued by the fact that a woman should interfere with me from within. My conclusion was that she must be the "soul," in the primitive sense, and I began to speculate on the reasons why the name "anima" was given to the soul. Why was it thought of as feminine? Later I came to see that this inner feminine figure plays a typical, or archetypal, role in the unconscious of a man, and I called her the "anima." The corresponding figure in the unconscious of woman I called the "animus."

At first it was the negative aspect of the anima that most impressed me. I felt a little awed by her. It was like the feeling of an invisible presence in the room. Then a new idea came to me: in putting down all this material for analysis I was in effect writing letters to the anima, that is, to a part of myself with a different viewpoint from my conscious one. I got remarks of an unusual and unexpected character. I was like a patient in analysis with a ghost and a woman! Every evening I wrote very conscientiously, for I thought if I did not write, there would be no way for the anima to get at my fantasies. Also, by writing them out I gave her no chance to twist them into intrigues. There is a tremendous difference between intending to tell something and actually telling it. In order to be as honest as possible with myself, I wrote everything down very carefully, following the old Greek maxim: "Give away all that thou hast, then shalt thou receive."

Often, as I was writing, I would have peculiar reactions that threw me off. Slowly I learned to distinguish between myself and the interruption. When something emotionally vulgar or banal came up, I would say to myself, "It is perfectly true that

I have thought and felt this way at some time or other, but I don't have to think and feel that way now. I need not accept this banality of mine in perpetuity; that is an unnecessary humiliation."

The essential thing is to differentiate oneself from these unconscious contents by personifying them, and at the same time to bring them into relationship with consciousness. That is the technique for stripping them of their power. It is not too difficult to personify them, as they always possess a certain degree of autonomy, a separate identity of their own. Their autonomy is a most uncomfortable thing to reconcile oneself to, and yet the very fact that the unconscious presents itself in that way gives us the best means of handling it.

What the anima said seemed to me full of a deep cunning. If I had taken these fantasies of the unconscious as art, they would have carried no more conviction than visual perceptions, as if I were watching a movie. I would have felt no moral obligation toward them. The anima might then have easily seduced me into believing that I was a misunderstood artist, and that my so-called artistic nature gave me the right to neglect reality. If I had followed her voice, she would in all probability have said to me one day, "Do you imagine the nonsense you're engaged in is really art? Not a bit." Thus the insinuations of the anima, the mouthpiece of the unconscious, can utterly destroy a man. In the final analysis the decisive factor is always consciousness, which can understand the manifestations of the unconscious and take up a position toward them.

But the anima has a positive aspect as well. It is she who communicates the images of the unconscious to the conscious mind, and that is what I chiefly valued her for. For decades I always turned to the anima when I felt that my emotional behavior was disturbed, and that something had been constellated in the unconscious. I would then ask the anima: "Now what are you up to? What do you see? I should like to know." After some resistance she regularly produced an image. As soon as the image was there, the unrest or the sense of oppression vanished. The whole energy of these emotions was transformed into interest in and curiosity about the image. I would speak with the anima about the images she communicated to me, for I had to try to understand them as best I could, just like a dream.

Today I no longer need these conversations with the anima, for I no longer have such emotions. But if I did have them, I would deal with them in the same way. Today I am directly conscious of the anima's ideas because I have learned to accept the contents of the unconscious and to understand them. I know how I must behave toward the inner images. I can read their meaning directly from my dreams, and therefore no longer need a mediator to communicate them.

I wrote these fantasies down first in the Black Book; later, I transferred them to the Red Book, which I also embellished with drawings.[6] It contains most of my mandala drawings. In the Red Book I tried an esthetic elaboration of my fantasies, but never finished it. I became aware that I had not yet found the right language, that I still had to translate it into something else. Therefore I gave up this estheticizing tendency in good time, in favor of a rigorous process of *understanding*. I saw that so much fantasy needed firm ground underfoot, and that I must first return wholly to reality. For me, reality meant scientific comprehension. I had to draw concrete conclusions from the insights the unconscious had given me—and that task was to become a life work.

It is of course ironical that I, a psychiatrist, should at almost every step of my experiment have run into the same psychic material which is the stuff of psychosis and is found in the insane. This is the fund of unconscious images which fatally confuse the mental patient. But it is also the matrix of a mythopoeic imagination which has vanished from our rational age. Though such imagination is present everywhere, it is both tabooed and dreaded, so that it even appears to be a risky experiment or a questionable adventure to entrust oneself to the uncertain path that leads into the depths of the unconscious. It is considered the path of error, of equivocation and misunderstanding. I am reminded of Goethe's words: "Now let me dare to open wide the

[6] The Black Book consists of six black-bound, smallish leather notebooks. The Red Book, a folio volume bound in red leather, contains the same fantasies couched in elaborately literary form and language, and set down in calligraphic Gothic script, in the manner of medieval manuscripts.—A. J.

gate/Past which men's steps have ever flinching trod." [7] The second part of *Faust,* too, was more than a literary exercise. It is a link in the *Aurea Catena* [8] which has existed from the beginnings of philosophical alchemy and Gnosticism down to Nietzsche's *Zarathustra.* Unpopular, ambiguous, and dangerous, it is a voyage of discovery to the other pole of the world.

Particularly at this time, when I was working on the fantasies, I needed a point of support in "this world," and I may say that my family and my professional work were that to me. It was most essential for me to have a normal life in the real world as a counterpoise to that strange inner world. My family and my profession remained the base to which I could always return, assuring me that I was an actually existing, ordinary person. The unconscious contents could have driven me out of my wits. But my family, and the knowledge: I have a medical diploma from a Swiss university, I must help my patients, I have a wife and five children, I live at 228 Seestrasse in Küsnacht—these were actualities which made demands upon me and proved to me again and again that I really existed, that I was not a blank page whirling about in the winds of the spirit, like Nietzsche. Nietzsche had lost the ground under his feet because he possessed nothing more than the inner world of his thoughts—which incidentally possessed him more than he it. He was uprooted and hovered above the earth, and therefore he succumbed to exaggeration and irreality. For me, such irreality was the quintessence of horror, for I aimed, after all, at *this* world and *this* life. No matter how deeply absorbed or how blown about I was, I always knew that everything I was experiencing was ultimately directed at this real life of mine. I meant to meet its obligations and fulfill its meanings. My watchword was: *Hic Rhodus, hic salta!*

Thus my family and my profession always remained a joyful reality and a guarantee that I also had a normal existence.

Very gradually the outlines of an inner change began making their appearance within me. In 1916 I felt an urge to give shape

[7] *Faust,* Part One.
[8] The Golden (or Homeric) Chain in alchemy is the series of great wise men, beginning with Hermes Trismegistos, which links earth with heaven.—A. J.

to something. I was compelled from within, as it were, to formulate and express what might have been said by Philemon. This was how the *Septem Sermones ad Mortuos* [9] with its peculiar language came into being.

It began with a restlessness, but I did not know what it meant or what "they" wanted of me. There was an ominous atmosphere all around me. I had the strange feeling that the air was filled with ghostly entities. Then it was as if my house began to be haunted. My eldest daughter saw a white figure passing through the room. My second daughter, independently of her elder sister, related that twice in the night her blanket had been snatched away; and that same night my nine-year-old son had an anxiety dream. In the morning he asked his mother for crayons, and he, who ordinarily never drew, now made a picture of his dream. He called it "The Picture of the Fisherman." Through the middle of the picture ran a river, and a fisherman with a rod was standing on the shore. He had caught a fish. On the fisherman's head was a chimney from which flames were leaping and smoke rising. From the other side of the river the devil came flying through the air. He was cursing because his fish had been stolen. But above the fisherman hovered an angel who said, "You cannot do anything to him; he only catches the bad fish!" My son drew this picture on a Saturday.

Around five o'clock in the afternoon on Sunday the front doorbell began ringing frantically. It was a bright summer day; the two maids were in the kitchen, from which the open square outside the front door could be seen. Everyone immediately looked to see who was there, but there was no one in sight. I was sitting near the doorbell, and not only heard it but saw it moving. We all simply stared at one another. The atmosphere was thick, believe me! Then I knew that something had to happen. The whole house was filled as if there were a crowd present, crammed full of spirits. They were packed deep right up to the door, and the air was so thick it was scarcely possible to breathe. As for myself, I was all a-quiver with the question: "For God's

[9] Privately printed (n.d.) and pseudonymously subtitled "The Seven Sermons to the Dead written by Basilides in Alexandria, the City where the East toucheth the West" (see Appendix V).

sake, what in the world is this?" Then they cried out in chorus, "We have come back from Jerusalem where we found not what we sought." That is the beginning of the *Septem Sermones.*

Then it began to flow out of me, and in the course of three evenings the thing was written. As soon as I took up the pen, the whole ghostly assemblage evaporated. The room quieted and the atmosphere cleared. The haunting was over.

The experience has to be taken for what it was, or as it seems to have been. No doubt it was connected with the state of emotion I was in at the time, and which was favorable to parapsychological phenomena. It was an unconscious constellation whose peculiar atmosphere I recognized as the numen of an archetype. "It walks abroad, it's in the air!" [10] The intellect, of course, would like to arrogate to itself some scientific, physical knowledge of the affair, or, preferably, to write the whole thing off as a violation of the rules. But what a dreary world it would be if the rules were not violated sometimes!

Shortly before this experience I had written down a fantasy of my soul having flown away from me. This was a significant event: the soul, the anima, establishes the relationship to the unconscious. In a certain sense this is also a relationship to the collectivity of the dead; for the unconscious corresponds to the mythic land of the dead, the land of the ancestors. If, therefore, one has a fantasy of the soul vanishing, this means that it has withdrawn into the unconscious or into the land of the dead. There it produces a mysterious animation and gives visible form to the ancestral traces, the collective contents. Like a medium, it gives the dead a chance to manifest themselves. Therefore, soon after the disappearance of my soul the "dead" appeared to me, and the result was the *Septem Sermones.* This is an example of what is called "loss of soul"—a phenomenon encountered quite frequently among primitives.

From that time on, the dead have become ever more distinct for me as the voices of the Unanswered, Unresolved, and Unredeemed; for since the questions and demands which my destiny required me to answer did not come to me from outside,

[10] *Faust*, Part Two.

they must have come from the inner world. These conversations with the dead formed a kind of prelude to what I had to communicate to the world about the unconscious: a kind of pattern of order and interpretation of its general contents.

When I look back upon it all today and consider what happened to me during the period of my work on the fantasies, it seems as though a message had come to me with overwhelming force. There were things in the images which concerned not only myself but many others also. It was then that I ceased to belong to myself alone, ceased to have the right to do so. From then on, my life belonged to the generality. The knowledge I was concerned with, or was seeking, still could not be found in the science of those days. I myself had to undergo the original experience, and, moreover, try to plant the results of my experience in the soil of reality; otherwise they would have remained subjective assumptions without validity. It was then that I dedicated myself to service of the psyche. I loved it and hated it, but it was my greatest wealth. My delivering myself over to it, as it were, was the only way by which I could endure my existence and live it as fully as possible.

Today I can say that I have never lost touch with my initial experiences. All my works, all my creative activity, has come from those initial fantasies and dreams which began in 1912, almost fifty years ago. Everything that I accomplished in later life was already contained in them, although at first only in the form of emotions and images.

My science was the only way I had of extricating myself from that chaos. Otherwise the material would have trapped me in its thicket, strangled me like jungle creepers. I took great care to try to understand every single image, every item of my psychic inventory, and to classify them scientifically—so far as this was possible—and, above all, to realize them in actual life. That is what we usually neglect to do. We allow the images to rise up, and maybe we wonder about them, but that is all. We do not take the trouble to understand them, let alone draw ethical conclusions from them. This stopping-short conjures up the negative effects of the unconscious.

It is equally a grave mistake to think that it is enough to gain some understanding of the images and that knowledge can here make a halt. Insight into them must be converted into an ethical obligation. Not to do so is to fall prey to the power principle, and this produces dangerous effects which are destructive not only to others but even to the knower. The images of the unconscious place a great responsibility upon a man. Failure to understand them, or a shirking of ethical responsibility, deprives him of his wholeness and imposes a painful fragmentariness on his life.

In the midst of this period when I was so preoccupied with the images of the unconscious, I came to the decision to withdraw from the university, where I had lectured for eight years as *Privatdozent* (since 1905). My experience and experiments with the unconscious had brought my intellectual activity to a standstill. After the completion of *The Psychology of the Unconscious* [11] I found myself utterly incapable of reading a scientific book. This went on for three years. I felt I could no longer keep up with the world of the intellect, nor would I have been able to talk about what really preoccupied me. The material brought to light from the unconscious had, almost literally, struck me dumb.[12] I could neither understand it nor give it form. At the university I was in an exposed position, and felt that in order to go on giving courses there I would first have to find an entirely new and different orientation. It would be unfair to continue teaching young students when my own intellectual situation was nothing but a mass of doubts.

I therefore felt that I was confronted with the choice of either continuing my academic career, whose road lay smooth before me, or following the laws of my inner personality, of a higher reason, and forging ahead with this curious task of mine, this experiment in confrontation with the unconscious. But until it was completed I could not appear before the public.

[11] See above, Chap. V, n. 5, p. 155.
[12] During this "fallow period" Jung wrote very little: a handful of papers in English, and the very important first versions of the essays published in English translation as *Two Essays on Analytical Psychology* (CW 7). The period came to an end with the publication of *Psychologische Typen* in 1921 (English trans.: *Psychological Types*, CW 6.)—A.J.

Consciously, deliberately, then, I abandoned my academic career. For I felt that something great was happening to me, and I put my trust in the thing which I felt to be more important *sub specie aeternitatis*. I knew that it would fill my life, and for the sake of that goal I was ready to take any kind of risk.

What, after all, did it matter whether or not I became a professor? Of course it bothered me to have to give this up; in many respects I regretted that I could not confine myself to generally understandable material. I even had moments when I stormed against destiny. But emotions of this kind are transitory, and do not count. The other thing, on the contrary, is important, and if we pay heed to what the inner personality desires and says, the sting vanishes. That is something I have experienced again and again, not only when I gave up my academic career. Indeed, I had my first experiences of this sort as a child. In my youth I was hot-tempered; but whenever the emotion had reached its climax, suddenly it swung around and there followed a cosmic stillness. At such times I was remote from everything, and what had only a moment before excited me seemed to belong to a distant past.

The consequence of my resolve, and my involvement with things which neither I nor anyone else could understand, was an extreme loneliness. I was going about laden with thoughts of which I could speak to no one: they would only have been misunderstood. I felt the gulf between the external world and the interior world of images in its most painful form. I could not yet see that interaction of both worlds which I now understand. I saw only an irreconcilable contradiction between "inner" and "outer."

However, it was clear to me from the start that I could find contact with the outer world and with people only if I succeeded in showing—and this would demand the most intensive effort—that the contents of psychic experience are real, and real not only as my own personal experiences, but as collective experiences which others also have. Later I tried to demonstrate this in my scientific work, and I did all in my power to convey to my intimates a new way of seeing things. I knew that if I did not succeed, I would be condemned to absolute isolation.

It was only toward the end of the First World War that I gradually began to emerge from the darkness. Two events contributed to this. The first was that I broke with the woman who was determined to convince me that my fantasies had artistic value; the second and principal event was that I began to understand mandala drawings. This happened in 1918–19. I had painted the first mandala [13] in 1916 after writing the *Septem Sermones;* naturally I had not, then, understood it.

In 1918–19 I was in Château d'Oex as Commandant de la Région Anglaise des Internés de Guerre. While I was there I sketched every morning in a notebook a small circular drawing, a mandala, which seemed to correspond to my inner situation at the time. With the help of these drawings I could observe my psychic transformations from day to day. One day, for example, I received a letter from that esthetic lady in which she again stubbornly maintained that the fantasies arising from my unconscious had artistic value and should be considered art. The letter got on my nerves. It was far from stupid, and therefore dangerously persuasive. The modern artist, after all, seeks to create art out of the unconscious. The utilitarianism and self-importance concealed behind this thesis touched a doubt in myself, namely, my uncertainty as to whether the fantasies I was producing were really spontaneous and natural, and not ultimately my own arbitrary inventions. I was by no means free from the bigotry and hubris of consciousness which wants to believe that any halfway decent inspiration is due to one's own merit, whereas inferior reactions come merely by chance, or even derive from alien sources. Out of this irritation and disharmony within myself there proceeded, the following day, a changed mandala: part of the periphery had burst open and the symmetry was destroyed.

Only gradually did I discover what the mandala really is:

[13] Reproduced as the frontispiece to *The Archetypes and the Collective Unconscious* (CW 9, i).—A. J.

"Formation, Transformation, Eternal Mind's eternal recreation." [14] And that is the self, the wholeness of the personality, which if all goes well is harmonious, but which cannot tolerate self-deceptions.

My mandalas were cryptograms concerning the state of the self which were presented to me anew each day. In them I saw the self—that is, my whole being—actively at work. To be sure, at first I could only dimly understand them; but they seemed to me highly significant, and I guarded them like precious pearls. I had the distinct feeling that they were something central, and in time I acquired through them a living conception of the self. The self, I thought, was like the monad which I am, and which is my world. The mandala represents this monad, and corresponds to the microcosmic nature of the psyche.

I no longer know how many mandalas I drew at this time. There were a great many. While I was working on them, the question arose repeatedly: What is this process leading to? Where is its goal? From my own experience, I knew by now that I could not presume to choose a goal which would seem trustworthy to me. It had been proved to me that I had to abandon the idea of the superordinate position of the ego. After all, I had been brought up short when I had attempted to maintain it. I had wanted to go on with the scientific analysis of myths which I had begun in *Wandlungen und Symbole*. That was still my goal—but I must not think of that! I was being compelled to go through this process of the unconscious. I had to let myself be carried along by the current, without a notion of where it would lead me. When I began drawing the mandalas, however, I saw that everything, all the paths I had been following, all the steps I had taken, were leading back to a single point—namely, to the mid-point. It became increasingly plain to me that the mandala is the center. It is the exponent of all paths. It is the path to the center, to individuation.

During those years, between 1918 and 1920, I began to understand that the goal of psychic development is the self. There is no linear evolution; there is only a circumambulation of the self.

[14] *Faust*, Part Two, trans. by Philip Wayne (Harmondsworth, England, Penguin Books Ltd., 1959), p. 79.

Uniform development exists, at most, only at the beginning; later, everything points toward the center. This insight gave me stability, and gradually my inner peace returned. I knew that in finding the mandala as an expression of the self I had attained what was for me the ultimate. Perhaps someone else knows more, but not I.

Some years later (in 1927) I obtained confirmation of my ideas about the center and the self by way of a dream. I represented its essence in a mandala which I called "Window on Eternity." The picture is reproduced in *The Secret of the Golden Flower* (Fig. 3).[15] A year later I painted a second picture, likewise a mandala,[16] with a golden castle in the center. When it was finished, I asked myself, "Why is this so Chinese?" I was impressed by the form and choice of colors, which seemed to me Chinese, although there was nothing outwardly Chinese about it. Yet that was how it affected me. It was a strange coincidence that shortly afterward I received a letter from Richard Wilhelm enclosing the manuscript of a Taoist-alchemical treatise entitled *The Secret of the Golden Flower*, with a request that I write a commentary on it. I devoured the manuscript at once, for the text gave me undreamed-of confirmation of my ideas about the mandala and the circumambulation of the center. That was the first event which broke through my isolation. I became aware of an affinity; I could establish ties with something and someone.[17]

In remembrance of this coincidence, this "synchronicity," I wrote underneath the picture which had made so Chinese an impression upon me: "In 1928, when I was painting this picture, showing the golden, well-fortified castle, Richard Wilhelm in Frankfurt sent me the thousand-year-old Chinese text on the yellow castle, the germ of the immortal body."

This is the dream I mentioned earlier: I found myself in a dirty, sooty city. It was night, and winter, and dark, and raining.

[15] Cf. "Concerning Mandala Symbolism," in *The Archetypes and the Collective Unconscious* (CW 9, i,), fig. 6 and pp. 363 ff.
[16] *The Secret of the Golden Flower*, fig. 10. See also "Concerning Mandala Symbolism," fig. 36 and p. 377.
[17] On Richard Wilhelm, see Appendix IV, pp. 373–77.

I was in Liverpool. With a number of Swiss—say, half a dozen—I walked through the dark streets. I had the feeling that there we were coming from the harbor, and that the real city was actually up above, on the cliffs. We climbed up there. It reminded me of Basel, where the market is down below and then you go up through the Totengässchen ("Alley of the Dead"), which leads to a plateau above and so to the Petersplatz and the Peterskirche. When we reached the plateau, we found a broad square dimly illuminated by street lights, into which many streets converged. The various quarters of the city were arranged radially around the square. In the center was a round pool, and in the middle of it a small island. While everything round about was obscured by rain, fog, smoke, and dimly lit darkness, the little island blazed with sunlight. On it stood a single tree, a magnolia, in a shower of reddish blossoms. It was as though the tree stood in the sunlight and were at the same time the source of light. My companions commented on the abominable weather, and obviously did not see the tree. They spoke of another Swiss who was living in Liverpool, and expressed surprise that he should have settled here. I was carried away by the beauty of the flowering tree and the sunlit island, and thought, "I know very well why he has settled here." Then I awoke.

On one detail of the dream I must add a supplementary comment: the individual quarters of the city were themselves arranged radially around a central point. This point formed a small open square illuminated by a larger street lamp, and constituted a small replica of the island. I knew that the "other Swiss" lived in the vicinity of one of these secondary centers.

This dream represented my situation at the time. I can still see the grayish-yellow raincoats, glistening with the wetness of the rain. Everything was extremely unpleasant, black and opaque—just as I felt then. But I had had a vision of unearthly beauty, and that was why I was able to live at all. Liverpool is the "pool of life." The "liver," according to an old view, is the seat of life—that which "makes to live."

This dream brought with it a sense of finality. I saw that here the goal had been revealed. One could not go beyond the center. The center is the goal, and everything is directed toward that center. Through this dream I understood that the self is the principle and archetype of orientation and meaning. Therein lies its healing function. For me, this insight signified an approach to the center and therefore to the goal. Out of it emerged a first inkling of my personal myth.

After this dream I gave up drawing or painting mandalas. The dream depicted the climax of the whole process of development of consciousness. It satisfied me completely, for it gave a total picture of my situation. I had known, to be sure, that I was occupied with something important, but I still lacked understanding, and there had been no one among my associates who could have understood. The clarification brought about by the dream made it possible for me to take an objective view of the things that filled my being.

Without such a vision I might perhaps have lost my orientation and been compelled to abandon my undertaking. But here the meaning had been made clear. When I parted from Freud, I knew that I was plunging into the unknown. Beyond Freud, after all, I knew nothing; but I had taken the step into darkness. When that happens, and then such a dream comes, one feels it as an act of grace.

It has taken me virtually forty-five years to distill within the vessel of my scientific work the things I experienced and wrote down at that time. As a young man my goal had been to accomplish something in my science. But then, I hit upon this stream of lava, and the heat of its fires reshaped my life. That was the primal stuff which compelled me to work upon it, and my works are a more or less successful endeavor to incorporate this incandescent matter into the contemporary picture of the world.

The years when I was pursuing my inner images were the most important in my life—in them everything essential was decided. It all began then; the later details are only supplements and clarifications of the material that burst forth from the unconscious, and at first swamped me. It was the *prima materia* for a lifetime's work.

·VII·

The Work

A<small>S MY LIFE</small> entered its second half, I was already embarked on the confrontation with the contents of the unconscious. My work on this was an extremely long-drawn-out affair, and it was only after some twenty years of it that I reached some degree of understanding of my fantasies.

First I had to find evidence for the historical prefiguration of my inner experiences. That is to say, I had to ask myself, "Where have my particular premises already occurred in history?" If I had not succeeded in finding such evidence, I would never have been able to substantiate my ideas. Therefore, my encounter with alchemy was decisive for me, as it provided me with the historical basis which I had hitherto lacked.

Analytical psychology is fundamentally a natural science, but it is subject far more than any other science to the personal bias of the observer. The psychologist must depend therefore in the highest degree upon historical and literary parallels if he wishes to exclude at least the crudest errors in judgment. Between 1918 and 1926 I had seriously studied the Gnostic writers, for they too had been confronted with the primal world of the unconscious and had dealt with its contents, with images that were obviously

contaminated with the world of instinct. Just how they understood these images remains difficult to say, in view of the paucity
of the accounts—which, moreover, mostly stem from their
opponents, the Church Fathers. It seems to me highly unlikely
that they had a psychological conception of them. But the
Gnostics were too remote for me to establish any link with them
in regard to the questions that were confronting me. As far as I
could see, the tradition that might have connected Gnosis with
the present seemed to have been severed, and for a long time it
proved impossible to find any bridge that led from Gnosticism—
or neo-Platonism—to the contemporary world. But when I began to understand alchemy I realized that it represented the
historical link with Gnosticism, and that a continuity therefore
existed between past and present. Grounded in the natural
philosophy of the Middle Ages, alchemy formed the bridge on
the one hand into the past, to Gnosticism, and on the other into
the future, to the modern psychology of the unconscious.

This had been inaugurated by Freud, who had introduced
along with it the classical Gnostic motifs of sexuality and the
wicked paternal authority. The motif of the Gnostic Yahweh
and Creator-God reappeared in the Freudian myth of the
primal father and the gloomy superego deriving from that father.
In Freud's myth he became a daemon who created a world of
disappointments, illusions, and suffering. But the materialistic
trend which had already come to light in the alchemists' preoccupation with the secrets of matter had the effect of ob-
scuring for Freud that other essential aspect of Gnosticism: the
primordial image of the spirit as another, higher god who gave
to mankind the *krater* (mixing vessel), the vessel of spiritual
transformation.[1] The *krater* is a feminine principle which could
find no place in Freud's patriarchal world. Incidentally, he is
by no means alone in this prejudice. In the realm of Catholic

[1] In the writings of Poimandres, a pagan Gnostic, the *krater* was a vessel filled
with spirit, which the Creator-god sent down to earth so that those who strove
for higher consciousness might be baptized in it. It was a kind of uterus of
spiritual renewal and rebirth, and corresponded to the alchemical *vas* in which
the transformation of substances took place. The parallel to this in Jung's psychology is the inner transformation process known as individuation (see glossary).—A. J.

thought the Mother of God and Bride of Christ has been received into the divine thalamus (bridal chamber) only recently, after centuries of hesitancy, and thus at least been accorded partial recognition.[2] But in the Protestant and Jewish spheres the father continues to dominate as much as ever. In philosophical alchemy, on the other hand, the feminine principle plays a role equal to that of the masculine.

Before I discovered alchemy, I had a series of dreams which repeatedly dealt with the same theme. Beside my house stood another, that is to say, another wing or annex, which was strange to me. Each time I would wonder in my dream why I did not know this house, although it had apparently always been there. Finally came a dream in which I reached the other wing. I discovered there a wonderful library, dating largely from the sixteenth and seventeenth centuries. Large, fat folio volumes, bound in pigskin, stood along the walls. Among them were a number of books embellished with copper engravings of a strange character, and illustrations containing curious symbols such as I had never seen before. At the time I did not know to what they referred; only much later did I recognize them as alchemical symbols. In the dream I was conscious only of the fascination exerted by them and by the entire library. It was a collection of medieval incunabula and sixteenth-century prints.

The unknown wing of the house was a part of my personality, an aspect of myself; it represented something that belonged to me but of which I was not yet conscious. It, and especially the library, referred to alchemy, of which I was ignorant, but which I was soon to study. Some fifteen years later I had assembled a library very like the one in the dream.

The crucial dream anticipating my encounter with alchemy came around 1926: I was in the South Tyrol. It was wartime. I was on the Italian front and driving back from the front line

---

[2] This refers to the Papal Bull of Pius XII, *Munificentissimus Deus* (1950), promulgating the Assumption of the Blessed Virgin Mary. The new dogma affirms that Mary as the Bride is united with the Son in the heavenly bridal chamber, and as Sophia (Wisdom) she is united with the Godhead. Thus the feminine principle is brought into immediate proximity with the masculine Trinity. Cf. Jung, "Answer to Job," in *Psychology and Religion: West and East* (CW 11), pp. 458 ff.—A. J.

with a little man, a peasant, in his horse-drawn wagon. All around us shells were exploding, and I knew that we had to push on as quickly as possible, for it was very dangerous.[3]

We had to cross a bridge and then go through a tunnel whose vaulting had been partially destroyed by the shells. Arriving at the end of the tunnel, we saw before us a sunny landscape, and I recognized it as the region around Verona. Below me lay the city, radiant in full sunlight. I felt relieved, and we drove on out into the green, thriving Lombard plain. The road led through lovely springtime countryside; we saw the rice fields, the olive trees, and the vineyards. Then, diagonally across the road, I caught sight of a large building, a manor house of grand proportions, rather like the palace of a North Italian duke. It was a typical manor house with many annexes and outbuildings. Just as at the Louvre, the road led through a large courtyard and past the palace. The little coachman and myself drove in through a gate, and from here we could see, through a second gate at the far end, the sunlit landscape again. I looked around: to my right was the façade of the manor house, to my left the servants' quarters and the stables, barns, and other outbuildings, which stretched on for a long way.

Just as we reached the middle of the courtyard, in front of the main entrance, something unexpected happened: with a dull clang, both gates flew shut. The peasant leaped down from his seat and exclaimed, "Now we are caught in the seventeenth century." Resignedly I thought, "Well, that's that! But what is there to do about it? Now we shall be caught for years." Then the consoling thought came to me: "Someday, years from now, I shall get out again."

After this dream I plowed through ponderous tomes on the history of the world, of religion, and of philosophy, without finding anything that could help me explain the dream. Not

---

[3] The shells falling from the sky were, interpreted psychologically, missiles coming from the "other side." They were, therefore, effects emanating from the unconscious, from the shadow side of the mind. The happenings in the dream suggested that the war, which in the outer world had taken place some years before, was not yet over, but was continuing to be fought within the psyche. Here, apparently, was to be found the solution of problems which could not be found in the outer world.—C. G. J.

until much later did I realize that it referred to alchemy, for that science reached its height in the seventeenth century. Oddly enough, I had entirely forgotten what Herbert Silberer had written about alchemy.[4] At the time his book was published, I regarded alchemy as something off the beaten track and rather silly, much as I appreciated Silberer's anagogic or constructive point of view. I was in correspondence with him at the time and had let him know how much I valued his work. As his tragic death shows, Silberer's discovery of the problem was not followed by insight into it.[5] He had used in the main late material, which I could make nothing of. The late alchemical texts are fantastic and baroque; only after we have learned how to interpret them can we recognize what treasures they hide.

Light on the nature of alchemy began to come to me only after I had read the text of the *Golden Flower*, that specimen of Chinese alchemy which Richard Wilhelm sent me in 1928. I was stirred by the desire to become more closely acquainted with the alchemical texts. I commissioned a Munich bookseller to notify me of any alchemical books that might fall into his hands. Soon afterward I received the first of them, the *Artis Auriferae Volumina Duo* (1593), a comprehensive collection of Latin treatises among which are a number of the "classics" of alchemy.

I let this book lie almost untouched for nearly two years. Occasionally I would look at the pictures, and each time I would think, "Good Lord, what nonsense! This stuff is impossible to understand." But it persistently intrigued me, and I made up my mind to go into it more thoroughly. The next winter I began, and soon found it provocative and exciting. To be sure, the texts still seemed to me blatant nonsense, but here and there would be passages that seemed significant to me, and occasionally I even found a few sentences which I thought I could understand. Finally I realized that the alchemists were talking in symbols—those old acquaintances of mine. "Why, this is fantastic," I thought. "I simply must learn to decipher all this." By now I was

[4] *Problems of Mysticism and Its Symbolism* (New York, 1917; German edn., Vienna, 1914).
[5] Silberer committed suicide.

completely fascinated, and buried myself in the texts as often
as I had the time. One night, while I was studying them, I
suddenly recalled the dream that I was caught in the seventeenth century. At last I grasped its meaning. "So that's it! Now
I am condemned to study alchemy from the very beginning."

It was a long while before I found my way about in the labyrinth of alchemical thought processes, for no Ariadne had put a
thread into my hand. Reading the sixteenth-century text,
"*Rosarium Philosophorum*," I noticed that certain strange expressions and turns of phrase were frequently repeated. For
example, "*solve et coagula*," "*unum vas*," "*lapis*," "*prima materia*," "*Mercurius*," etc. I saw that these expressions were used
again and again in a particular sense, but I could not make out
what that sense was. I therefore decided to start a lexicon of key
phrases with cross references. In the course of time I assembled
several thousand such key phrases and words, and had volumes
filled with excerpts. I worked along philological lines, as if I
were trying to solve the riddle of an unknown language. In this
way the alchemical mode of expression gradually yielded up its
meaning. It was a task that kept me absorbed for more than a
decade.

I had very soon seen that analytical psychology coincided in a
most curious way with alchemy. The experiences of the alchemists were, in a sense, my experiences, and their world was
my world. This was, of course, a momentous discovery: I had
stumbled upon the historical counterpart of my psychology of
the unconscious. The possibility of a comparison with alchemy,
and the uninterrupted intellectual chain back to Gnosticism,
gave substance to my psychology. When I pored over these old
texts everything fell into place: the fantasy-images, the empirical
material I had gathered in my practice, and the conclusions
I had drawn from it. I now began to understand what these
psychic contents meant when seen in historical perspective.
My understanding of their typical character, which had already
begun with my investigation of myths, was deepened. The
primordial images and the nature of the archetype took a central
place in my researches, and it became clear to me that without
history there can be no psychology, and certainly no psychology

of the unconscious. A psychology of consciousness can, to be sure, content itself with material drawn from personal life, but as soon as we wish to explain a neurosis we require an anamnesis which reaches deeper than the knowledge of consciousness. And when in the course of treatment unusual decisions are called for, dreams occur that need more than personal memories for their interpretation.

I regard my work on alchemy as a sign of my inner relationship to Goethe. Goethe's secret was that he was in the grip of that process of archetypal transformation which has gone on through the centuries. He regarded his *Faust* as an *opus magnum* or *divinum*. He called it his "main business," and his whole life was enacted within the framework of this drama. Thus, what was alive and active within him was a living substance, a suprapersonal process, the great dream of the *mundus archetypus* (archetypal world).

I myself am haunted by the same dream, and from my eleventh year I have been launched upon a single enterprise which is my "main business." My life has been permeated and held together by one idea and one goal: namely, to penetrate into the secret of the personality. Everything can be explained from this central point, and all my works relate to this one theme.

My real scientific work began with the association experiment in 1903. I regard it as my first scientific work in the sense of an undertaking in the field of natural science. *Studies in Word Association* was followed by two psychiatric papers whose origin I have already discussed: "The Psychology of Dementia Praecox" and "The Content of the Psychoses." In 1912 my book *Wandlungen und Symbole der Libido* was published, and my friendship with Freud came to an end. From then on, I had to make my way alone.

I had a starting point in my intense preoccupation with the images of my own unconscious. This period lasted from 1913 to 1917; then the stream of fantasies ebbed away. Not until it had subsided and I was no longer held captive inside the magic mountain was I able to take an objective view of that whole experience and begin to reflect upon it. The first question I asked myself was, "What does one do with the unconscious?" "The Relations between the Ego and the Unconscious" [6] was my answer. In Paris I had delivered a lecture on this subject in 1916; [7] it was, however, not published in German until twelve years later, in greatly expanded form. In it I described some of the typical contents of the unconscious, and showed that it is by no means a matter of indifference what attitude the conscious mind takes toward them.

Simultaneously, I was busy with preparatory work for *Psychological Types*, first published in 1921. This work sprang originally from my need to define the ways in which my outlook differed from Freud's and Adler's. In attempting to answer this question, I came across the problem of types; for it is one's psychological type which from the outset determines and limits a person's judgment. My book, therefore, was an effort to deal with the relationship of the individual to the world, to people and things. It discussed the various aspects of consciousness, the various attitudes the conscious mind might take toward the world, and thus constitutes a psychology of consciousness regarded from what might be called a clinical angle. I worked a great deal of literature into this book. The writings of Spitteler occupied a special place, in particular his *Prometheus and Epimetheus;* [8] but I also discussed Schiller, Nietzsche, and the intellectual history of the classical era and the Middle Ages. I was presumptuous enough to send a copy of my book to Spitteler. He did not answer me, but shortly afterward delivered a lecture in which he declared positively that his *Prometheus and Epimetheus* "meant" nothing, that he might just as well have sung, "Spring is come, tra-la-la-la-la."

The book on types yielded the insight that every judgment made by an individual is conditioned by his personality type and that every point of view is necessarily relative. This raised

---

[6] In *Two Essays on Analytical Psychology* (CW 7).

[7] "La Structure de l'inconscient," *Archives de psychologie,* XVI (Geneva, 1916), 62, 152–79. See CW 7, Appendix 2, "The Structure of the Unconscious."

[8] Carl Spitteler (1845–1924) was a Swiss writer whose best-known works, besides *Prometheus and Epimetheus,* include the epic *Der Olympische Frühling* and the novel *Imago.* In 1919 he was awarded the Nobel Prize for literature.

the question of the unity which must compensate this diversity, and it led me directly to the Chinese concept of Tao. I have already spoken of the interplay between my inner development and Richard Wilhelm's sending me a Taoist text. In 1929 he and I collaborated on *The Secret of the Golden Flower*. It was only after I had reached the central point in my thinking and in my researches, namely, the concept of the *self*, that I once more found my way back to the world. I began delivering lectures and taking a number of journeys. The various essays and lectures formed a kind of counterpoise to the years of interior searching. They also contained answers to the questions that were put to me by my readers and patients.[9]

A subject with which I had been deeply concerned ever since my book *Wandlungen und Symbole* was the theory of the libido. I conceived the libido as a psychic analogue of physical energy, hence as a more or less quantitative concept, which therefore should not be defined in qualitative terms. My idea was to escape from the then prevailing concretism of the libido theory—in other words, I wished no longer to speak of the instincts of hunger, aggression, and sex, but to regard all these phenomena as expressions of psychic energy.

In physics, too, we speak of energy and its various manifestations, such as electricity, light, heat, etc. The situation in psychology is precisely the same. Here, too, we are dealing primarily with energy, that is to say, with measures of intensity, with greater or lesser quantities. It can appear in various guises. If we conceive of libido as energy, we can take a comprehensive and unified view. Qualitative questions as to the nature of the libido—whether it be sexuality, power, hunger, or something else—recede into the background. What I wished to do for psychology was to arrive at some logical and thorough view such as is provided in the physical sciences by the theory of energetics. This is what I was after in my paper "On Psychic Energy" (1928). I see man's drives, for example, as various manifestations of energic processes and thus as forces analogous to heat, light, etc. Just as it would not occur to the modern physicist to derive all forces from, shall we say, heat alone, so the psycholo-

[9] These works are distributed mainly among volumes 4, 8, 10, and 16 of the Collected Works.

gist should beware of lumping all instincts under the concept of
sexuality. This was Freud's initial error which he later corrected
by his assumption of "ego-instincts." Still later he brought in the
superego, and conferred virtual supremacy upon it.

In "The Relations between the Ego and the Unconscious"
I had discussed only my preoccupation with the unconscious,
and something of the nature of that preoccupation, but had not
yet said anything much about the unconscious itself. As I
worked with my fantasies, I became aware that the unconscious
undergoes or produces change. Only after I had familiarized
myself with alchemy did I realize that the unconscious is a
process, and that the psyche is transformed or developed by the
relationship of the ego to the contents of the unconscious. In
individual cases that transformation can be read from dreams
and fantasies. In collective life it has left its deposit principally
in the various religious systems and their changing symbols.
Through the study of these collective transformation processes
and through understanding of alchemical symbolism I arrived
at the central concept of my psychology: *the process of individuation.*

An essential aspect of my work is that it soon began to touch on
the question of one's view of the world, and on the relations
between psychology and religion. I went into these matters in
detail first in "Psychology and Religion" (1938) and then, as a
direct offshoot of this, in *Paracelsica* (1942). The second essay
in this book, "Paracelsus as a Spiritual Phenomenon," is of
particular importance from this point of view. The writings of
Paracelsus contain a wealth of original ideas, including clear
formulations of the questions posed by the alchemists, though
these are set forth in late and baroque dress. Through Paracelsus I was finally led to discuss the nature of alchemy in relation to religion and psychology—or, to put it another way, of
alchemy as a form of religious philosophy. This I did in *Psychology and Alchemy* (1944). Thus I had at last reached the ground
which underlay my own experiences of the years 1913 to 1917;
for the process through which I had passed at that time corresponded to the process of alchemical transformation discussed
in that book.

It is only natural that I should constantly have revolved in my mind the question of the relationship of the symbolism of the unconscious to Christianity as well as to other religions. Not only do I leave the door open for the Christian message, but I consider it of central importance for Western man. It needs, however, to be seen in a new light, in accordance with the changes wrought by the contemporary spirit. Otherwise, it stands apart from the times, and has no effect on man's wholeness. I have endeavored to show this in my writings. I have given a psychological interpretation of the dogma of the Trinity and of the text of the Mass—which, moreover, I compared with the visions described by Zosimos of Panopolis, a third-century alchemist and Gnostic.[10] My attempt to bring analytical psychology into relation with Christianity ultimately led to the question of Christ as a psychological figure. As early as 1944, in *Psychology and Alchemy*, I had been able to demonstrate the parallelism between the Christ figure and the central concept of the alchemists, the *lapis*, or stone.

In 1939 I gave a seminar on the *Spiritual Exercises* of Ignatius Loyola. At the same time I was occupied on the studies for *Psychology and Alchemy*. One night I awoke and saw, bathed in bright light at the foot of my bed, the figure of Christ on the Cross. It was not quite life-size, but extremely distinct; and I saw that his body was made of greenish gold. The vision was marvelously beautiful, and yet I was profoundly shaken by it. A vision as such is nothing unusual for me, for I frequently see extremely vivid hypnagogic images.

I had been thinking a great deal about the *Anima Christi*, one of the meditations from the *Spiritual Exercises*. The vision came to me as if to point out that I had overlooked something in my reflections: the analogy of Christ with the *aurum non vulgi* and the *viriditas* of the alchemists.[11] When I realized that the vision pointed to this central alchemical symbol, and that

[10] Both studies are included in *Psychology and Religion: West and East* (CW 11).
[11] The more serious alchemists realized that the purpose of their work was not the transmutation of base metals into gold, but the production of an *aurum non vulgi* ("not the common gold") or *aurum philosophicum* ("philosophical gold"). In other words, they were concerned with spiritual values and the problem of psychic transformation.—A. J.

I had had an essentially alchemical vision of Christ, I felt comforted.

The green gold is the living quality which the alchemists saw not only in man but also in inorganic nature. It is an expression of the life-spirit, the *anima mundi* or *filius macrocosmi,* the Anthropos who animates the whole cosmos. This spirit has poured himself out into everything, even into inorganic matter; he is present in metal and stone. My vision was thus a union of the Christ-image with his analogue in matter, the *filius macrocosmi.* If I had not been so struck by the greenish-gold, I would have been tempted to assume that something essential was missing from my "Christian" view—in other words, that my traditional Christ-image was somehow inadequate and that I still had to catch up with part of the Christian development. The emphasis on the metal, however, showed me the undisguised alchemical conception of Christ as a union of spiritually alive and physically dead matter.

I took up the problem of Christ again in *Aion.*[12] Here I was concerned not with the various historical parallels but with the relation of the Christ figure to psychology. Nor did I see Christ as a figure stripped of all externalities. Rather, I wished to show the development, extending over the centuries, of the religious content which he represented. It was also important to me to show how Christ could have been astrologically predicted, and how he was understood both in terms of the spirit of his age and in the course of two thousand years of Christian civilization. This was what I wanted to portray, together with all the curious marginal glosses which have accumulated around him in the course of the centuries.

As I delved into all these matters the question of the historical person, of Jesus the man, also came up. It is of importance because the collective mentality of his time—one might also say: the archetype which was already constellated, the primordial image of the Anthropos—was condensed in him, an almost unknown Jewish prophet. The ancient idea of the Anthropos, whose roots lie in Jewish tradition on the one hand

[12] English trans., under same title, in 1959 (CW 9, ii).

and in the Egyptian Horus myth on the other, had taken possession of the people at the beginning of the Christian era, for it was part of the Zeitgeist. It was essentially concerned with the Son of Man, God's own son, who stood opposed to the deified Augustus, the ruler of this world. This idea fastened upon the originally Jewish problem of the Messiah and made it a world problem.

It would be a serious misunderstanding to regard as "mere chance" the fact that Jesus, the carpenter's son, proclaimed the gospel and became the savior of the world. He must have been a person of singular gifts to have been able so completely to express and to represent the general, though unconscious, expectations of his age. No one else could have been the bearer of such a message; it was possible only for this particular man Jesus.

In those times the omnipresent, crushing power of Rome, embodied in the divine Caesar, had created a world where countless individuals, indeed whole peoples, were robbed of their cultural independence and of their spiritual autonomy. Today, individuals and cultures are faced with a similar threat, namely of being swallowed up in the mass. Hence in many places there is a wave of hope in a reappearance of Christ, and a visionary rumor has even arisen which expresses expectations of redemption. The form it has taken, however, is comparable to nothing in the past, but is a typical child of the "age of technology." This is the worldwide distribution of the UFO phenomenon (unidentified flying objects).[13]

Since my aim was to demonstrate the full extent to which my psychology corresponded to alchemy—or vice versa—I wanted to discover, side by side with the religious questions, what special problems of psychotherapy were treated in the work of the alchemists. The main problem of medical psychotherapy is the *transference*. In this matter Freud and I were in complete agreement. I was able to demonstrate that alchemy, too, had something that corresponded to the transference—

[13] Cf. *Flying Saucers: A Modern Myth of Things Seen in the Skies* (New York and London, 1959); also in *Civilization in Transition* (CW 10).

namely, the concept of the *coniunctio*, whose pre-eminent importance had been noted already by Silberer. Evidence for this correspondence is contained in my book, *Psychology and Alchemy*. Two years later, in 1946, I pursued the matter further in "Psychology of the Transference," [14] and finally my researches led to the *Mysterium Coniunctionis*.[15]

As with all problems that concerned me personally or scientifically, that of the *coniunctio* was accompanied or heralded by dreams. In one of these dreams both this and the Christ problem were condensed in a remarkable image.

I dreamed once more that my house had a large wing which I had never visited. I resolved to look at it, and finally entered. I came to a big double door. When I opened it, I found myself in a room set up as a laboratory. In front of the window stood a table covered with many glass vessels and all the paraphernalia of a zoological laboratory. This was my father's workroom. However, he was not there. On shelves along the walls stood hundreds of bottles containing every imaginable sort of fish. I was astonished: so now my father was going in for ichthyology!

As I stood there and looked around I noticed a curtain which bellied out from time to time, as though a strong wind were blowing. Suddenly Hans, a young man from the country, appeared. I told him to look and see whether a window were open in the room behind the curtain. He went, and was gone for some time. When he returned, I saw an expression of terror on his face. He said only, "Yes, there is something. It's haunted in there!"

Then I myself went, and found a door which led to my mother's room. There was no one in it. The atmosphere was uncanny. The room was very large, and suspended from the ceiling were two rows of five chests each, hanging about two feet above the floor. They looked like small garden pavilions, each about six feet in area, and each containing two beds. I knew that this was the room where my mother, who in reality had long been dead, was visited, and that she had set up these

[14] In *The Practice of Psychotherapy* (CW 16).
[15] CW 14.

beds for visiting spirits to sleep. They were spirits who came in
pairs, ghostly married couples, so to speak, who spent the night
or even the day there.

Opposite my mother's room was a door. I opened it and
entered a vast hall; it reminded me of the lobby of a large hotel.
It was fitted out with easy chairs, small tables, pillars, sumptuous
hangings, etc. A brass band was playing loudly; I had heard
music all along in the background, but without knowing where
it came from. There was no one in the hall except the brass band
blaring forth dance tunes and marches.

The brass band in the hotel lobby suggested ostentatious
jollity and worldliness. No one would have guessed that behind
this loud façade was the other world, also located in the same
building. The dream-image of the lobby was, as it were, a
caricature of my bonhomie or worldly joviality. But this was
only the outside aspect; behind it lay something quite different,
which could not be investigated in the blare of the band music:
the fish laboratory and the hanging pavilions for spirits. Both
were awesome places in which a mysterious silence prevailed.
In them I had the feeling: Here is the dwelling of night; whereas
the lobby stood for the daylight world and its superficiality.

The most important images in the dream were the "reception
room for spirits" and the fish laboratory. The former expresses
in somewhat farcial fashion the *coniunctio;* the latter indicates
my preoccupation with Christ, who himself is the fish (*ichthys*).
Both were subjects that were to keep me on the go for more than
a decade.

It is remarkable that the study of fish was attributed to my
father. In the dream he was a caretaker of Christian souls, for,
according to the ancient view, these are fish caught in Peter's
net. It is equally remarkable that in the same dream my mother
was a guardian of departed spirits. Thus both my parents appeared burdened with the problem of the "cure of souls," which
in fact was really my task. Something had remained unfinished
and was still with my parents; that is to say, it was still latent
in the unconscious and hence reserved for the future. I was
being reminded that I had not yet dealt with the major concern
of "philosophical" alchemy, the *coniunctio,* and thus had not

answered the question which the Christian soul put to me. Also the major work on the Grail legend, which my wife had made her life's task, was not completed.[16] I recall how often the quest for the Grail and the fisher king came to my mind while I was working on the *ichthys* symbol in *Aion*. Had it not been for my unwillingness to intrude upon my wife's field, I would unquestionably have had to include the Grail legend in my studies of alchemy.

My memory of my father is of a sufferer stricken with an Amfortas wound, a "fisher king" whose wound would not heal—that Christian suffering for which the alchemists sought the panacea. I as a "dumb" Parsifal was the witness of this sickness during the years of my boyhood, and, like Parsifal, speech failed me. I had only inklings. In actuality my father had never interested himself in theriomorphic Christ-symbolism. On the other hand he had literally lived right up to his death the suffering prefigured and promised by Christ, without ever becoming aware that this was a consequence of the *imitatio Christi*. He regarded his suffering as a personal affliction for which you might ask a doctor's advice; he did not see it as the suffering of the Christian in general. The words of Galatians 2:20: "I live, yet not I, but Christ liveth in me," never penetrated his mind in their full significance, for any thinking about religious matters sent shudders of horror through him. He wanted to rest content with faith, but faith broke faith with him. Such is frequently the reward of the *sacrificium intellectus*. "Not all men can receive this precept, but only those to whom it is given. . . . There are eunuchs who have made themselves eunuchs for the sake of the kingdom of heaven. He who is able to receive this, let him receive it." (Matthew 19:11 f.) Blind acceptance never leads to a solution; at best it leads only to a standstill and is paid for heavily in the next generation.

The theriomorphic attributes of the gods show that the gods extend not only into superhuman regions but also into the sub-

---

[16] After the death of Mrs. Jung in 1955, Dr. Marie-Louise von Franz took up the work on the Grail and brought it to safe harbor in 1958. Cf. Emma Jung and Marie-Louise von Franz: *The Grail Legend*, trans. by Andrea Dykes, New York and London, 1930).—A. J.

human realm. The animals are their shadows, as it were, which nature herself associates with the divine image. The *"pisciculi Christianorum"* show that those who imitate Christ are themselves fish—that is, unconscious souls who require the *cura animarum*. The fish laboratory is a synonym for the ecclesiastical "cure of souls." And just as the wounder wounds himself, so the healer heals himself. Significantly, in the dream the decisive activity is carried out by the dead upon the dead, in the world beyond consciousness, that is, in the unconscious.

At that stage of my life, therefore, I was still not conscious of an essential aspect of my task, nor would I have been able to give a satisfactory interpretation of the dream. I could only sense its meaning. I still had to overcome the greatest inner resistances before I could write *Answer to Job.*

The inner root of this book is to be found in *Aion.* There I had dealt with the psychology of Christianity, and Job is a kind of prefiguration of Christ. The link between them is the idea of suffering. Christ is the suffering servant of God, and so was Job. In the case of Christ the sins of the world are the cause of suffering, and the suffering of the Christian is the general answer. This leads inescapably to the question: Who is responsible for these sins? In the final analysis it is God who created the world and its sins, and who therefore became Christ in order to suffer the fate of humanity.

In *Aion* there are references to the bright and dark side of the divine image. I cited the "wrath of God," the commandment to fear God, and the petition "Lead us not into temptation." The ambivalent God-image plays a crucial part in the Book of Job. Job expects that God will, in a sense, stand by him against God; in this we have a picture of God's tragic contradictoriness. This was the main theme of *Answer to Job.*

There were outside forces, too, which impelled me to write this book. The many questions from the public and from patients had made me feel that I must express myself more clearly about the religious problems of modern man. For years I had hesitated to do so, because I was fully aware of the storm I would be unleashing. But at last I could not help being gripped by the problem, in all its urgency and difficulty, and I found myself compelled to give an answer. I did so in the form in which the problem had presented itself to me, that is, as an experience charged with emotion. I chose this form deliberately, in order to avoid giving the impression that I was bent on proclaiming some eternal truth. My *Answer to Job* was meant to be no more than the utterance of a single individual, who hopes and expects to arouse some thoughtfulness in his public. I was far from wanting to enunciate a metaphysical truth. Yet the theologians tax me with that very thing, because theological thinkers are so used to dealing with eternal truths that they know no other kinds. When the physicist says that the atom is of such and such a composition, and when he sketches a model of it, he too does not intend to express anything like an eternal truth. But theologians do not understand the natural sciences and, particularly, psychological thinking. The material of analytical psychology, its principal facts, consist of *statements* —of statements that occur frequently in consistent form at various places and at various times.

The problem of Job in all its ramifications had likewise been foreshadowed in a dream. It started with my paying a visit to my long-deceased father. He was living in the country—I did not know where. I saw a house in the style of the eighteenth century, very roomy, with several rather large outbuildings. It had originally been, I learned, an inn at a spa, and it seemed that many great personages, famous people and princes, had stopped there. Furthermore, several had died and their sarcophagi were in a crypt belonging to the house. My father guarded these as custodian.

He was, as I soon discovered, not only the custodian but also a distinguished scholar in his own right—which he had never been in his lifetime. I met him in his study, and, oddly enough, Dr. Y.—who was about my age—and his son, both psychiatrists, were also present. I do not know whether I had asked a question or whether my father wanted to explain something of his own accord, but in any case he fetched a big Bible down from a shelf, a heavy folio volume like the Merian Bible in my library. The Bible my father held was bound in shiny fishskin. He opened it at the Old Testament—I guessed that he turned to the Pentateuch—and began interpreting a certain passage. He did this so swiftly and so learnedly that I could not follow him. I noted only that what he said betrayed a vast amount of variegated knowledge, the significance of which I dimly apprehended but could not properly judge or grasp. I saw that Dr. Y. understood nothing at all, and his son began to laugh. They thought that my father was going off the deep end and what he said was simply senile prattle. But it was quite clear to me that it was not due to morbid excitement, and that there was nothing silly about what he was saying. On the contrary, his argument was so intelligent and so learned that we in our stupidity simply could not follow it. It dealt with something extremely important which fascinated him. That was why he was speaking with such intensity; his mind was flooded with profound ideas. I was annoyed and thought it was a pity that he had to talk in the presence of three such idiots as we.

The two psychiatrists represented a limited medical point of view which, of course, also infects me as a physician. They represent my shadow—first and second editions of the shadow, father and son.

Then the scene changed. My father and I were in front of the house, facing a kind of shed where, apparently, wood was stacked. We heard loud thumps, as if large chunks of wood were being thrown down or tossed about. I had the impression that at least two workmen must be busy there, but my father indicated to me that the place was haunted. Some sort of poltergeists were making the racket, evidently.

We then entered the house, and I saw that it had very thick walls. We climbed a narrow staircase to the second floor. There a strange sight presented itself: a large hall which was the exact replica of the *divan-i-kaas* (council hall) of Sultan Akbar at Fatehpur Sikri. It was a high, circular room with a gallery running along the wall, from which four bridges led to a basin-shaped center. The basin rested upon a huge column and formed the sultan's round seat. From this elevated place he spoke to his councilors and philosophers, who sat along the walls in the gallery. The whole was a gigantic mandala. It corresponded precisely to the real *divan-i-kaas*.

In the dream I suddenly saw that from the center a steep flight of stairs ascended to a spot high up on the wall—which no longer corresponded to reality. At the top of the stairs was a small door, and my father said, "Now I will lead you into the highest presence." Then he knelt down and touched his forehead to the floor. I imitated him, likewise kneeling, with great emotion. For some reason I could not bring my forehead quite down to the floor—there was perhaps a millimeter to spare. But at least I had made the gesture with him. Suddenly I knew —perhaps my father had told me—that that upper door led to a solitary chamber where lived Uriah, King David's general, whom David had shamefully betrayed for the sake of his wife Bathsheba, by commanding his soldiers to abandon Uriah in the face of the enemy.

I must make a few explanatory remarks concerning this dream. The initial scene describes how the unconscious task which I had left to my "father," that is, to the unconscious, was working out. He was obviously engrossed in the Bible—Genesis?—and eager to communicate his insights. The fishskin marks the Bible as an unconscious content, for fishes are mute and unconscious. My poor father does not succeed in communicating either, for the audience is in part incapable of understanding, in part maliciously stupid.

After this defeat we cross the street to the "other side," where poltergeists are at work. Poltergeist phenomena usually take place in the vicinity of young people before puberty; that is to say, I am still immature and too unconscious. The Indian ambience illustrates the "other side." When I was in India, the mandala structure of the *divan-i-kaas* had in actual fact powerfully impressed me as the representation of a content related to a center. The center is the seat of Akbar the Great, who rules over a subcontinent, who is a "lord of this world," like David. But even higher than David stands his guiltless victim, his loyal general Uriah, whom he abandoned to the enemy. Uriah is a prefiguration of Christ, the god-man who was abandoned by God. "My God, my God, why hast thou forsaken me?" On top of that, David had "taken unto himself" Uriah's wife. Only later did I understand what this allusion to Uriah signified:

not only was I forced to speak publicly, and very much to my detriment, about the ambivalence of the God-image in the Old Testament; but also, my wife would be taken from me by death.

These were the things that awaited me, hidden in the unconscious. I had to submit to this fate, and ought really to have touched my forehead to the floor, so that my submission would be complete. But something prevented me from doing so entirely, and kept me just a millimeter away. Something in me was saying, "All very well, but not entirely." Something in me was defiant and determined not to be a dumb fish: and if there were not something of the sort in free men, no Book of Job would have been written several hundred years before the birth of Christ. Man always has some mental reservation, even in the face of divine decrees. Otherwise, where would be his freedom? And what would be the use of that freedom if it could not threaten Him who threatens it?

Uriah, then, lives in a higher place than Akbar. He is even, as the dream said, the "highest presence," an expression which properly is used only of God, unless we are dealing in Byzantinisms. I cannot help thinking here of the Buddha and his relationship to the gods. For the devout Asiatic, the Tathagata is the All-Highest, the Absolute. For that reason Hinayana Buddhism has been suspected of atheism—very wrongly so. By virtue of the power of the gods man is enabled to gain an insight into his Creator. He has even been given the power to annihilate Creation in its essential aspect, that is, man's consciousness of the world. Today he can extinguish all higher life on earth by radioactivity. The idea of world annihilation is already suggested by the Buddha: by means of enlightenment the Nidana chain—the chain of causality which leads inevitably to old age, sickness, and death—can be broken, so that the illusion of Being comes to an end. Schopenhauer's negation of the Will points prophetically to a problem of the future that has already come threatingly close. The dream discloses a thought and a premonition that have long been present in humanity: the idea of the creature that surpasses its creator by a small but decisive factor.

After this excursion into the world of dreams, I must once more come back to my writings. In *Aion* I embarked upon a cycle of problems that needed to be dealt with separately. I had attempted to explain how the appearance of Christ coincided with the beginning of a new aeon, the age of the Fishes. A synchronicity exists between the life of Christ and the objective astronomical event, the entrance of the spring equinox into the sign of Pisces. Christ is therefore the "Fish" (just as Hammurabi before him was the "Ram"), and comes forth as the ruler of the new aeon. This led to the problem of synchronicity, which I discussed in my paper "Synchronicity: An Acausal Connecting Principle." [17]

The Christ problem in *Aion* finally led me to the question of how the phenomenon of the Anthropos—in psychological terms, the self—is expressed in the experience of the individual. I attempted to give an answer to this in *Von den Wurzeln des Bewusstseins* (1954).[18] There I was concerned with the interplay between conscious and unconscious, with the development of consciousness from the unconscious, and with the impact of the greater personality, the inner man, upon the life of every individual.

This investigation was rounded out by the *Mysterium Coniunctionis,* in which I once again took up the problem of the transference, but primarily followed my original intention of representing the whole range of alchemy as a kind of psychology of alchemy, or as an alchemical basis for depth psychology. In *Mysterium Coniunctionis* my psychology was at last given its place in reality and established upon its historical foundations. Thus my task was finished, my work done, and now it can stand. The moment I touched bottom, I reached the bounds of scientific understanding, the transcendental, the nature of the archetype per se, concerning which no further scientific statements can be made.

The survey I have given here of my work is, of course, only a brief summary. I really ought to say a great deal more, or a

[17] In C. G. Jung and W. Pauli, *The Interpretation of Nature and the Psyche* (New York and London, 1954); also in *The Structure and Dynamics of the Psyche* (CW 8).
[18] The essays in this book are mostly contained in volumes 8, 9 (i), and 11 of the Collected Works.

great deal less. It is an improvisation, like everything I am relating here. It is born of the moment. Those who know my work may possibly profit by it; others perhaps will be impelled to look into my ideas. My life is what I have done, my scientific work; the one is inseparable from the other. The work is the expression of my inner development; for commitment to the contents of the unconscious forms the man and produces his transformations. My works can be regarded as stations along my life's way.

All my writings may be considered tasks imposed from within; their source was a fateful compulsion. What I wrote were things that assailed me from within myself. I permitted the spirit that moved me to speak out. I have never counted upon any strong response, any powerful resonance, to my writings. They represent a compensation for our times, and I have been impelled to say what no one wants to hear. For that reason, and especially at the beginning, I often felt utterly forlorn. I knew that what I said would be unwelcome, for it is difficult for people of our times to accept the counterweight to the conscious world. Today I can say that it is truly astonishing that I have had as much success as has been accorded me—far more than I ever could have expected. I have the feeling that I have done all that it was possible for me to do. Without a doubt that life work could have been larger, and could have been done better; but more was not within my power.

·VIII·

The Tower

G RADUALLY, through my scientific work, I was able to put my fantasies and the contents of the unconscious on a solid footing. Words and paper, however, did not seem real enough to me; something more was needed. I had to achieve a kind of representation in stone of my innermost thoughts and of the knowledge I had acquired. Or, to put it another way, I had to make a confession of faith in stone. That was the beginning of the "Tower," the house which I built for myself at Bollingen.

It was settled from the start that I would build near the water. I had always been curiously drawn by the scenic charm of the upper lake of Zürich, and so in 1922 I bought some land in Bollingen. It is situated in the area of St. Meinrad and is old church land, having formerly belonged to the monastery of St. Gall.

At first I did not plan a proper house, but merely a kind of primitive one-story dwelling. It was to be a round structure with a hearth in the center and bunks along the walls. I more or less had in mind an African hut where the fire, ringed by a few stones, burns in the middle, and the whole life of the family revolves around this center. Primitive huts concretize an idea of wholeness, a familial wholeness in which all sorts of small domestic animals likewise participate. But I altered the plan even during the first stages of building, for I felt it was too primitive. I realized it would have to be a regular two-story house, not a mere hut crouched on the ground. So in 1923 the first round house was built, and when it was finished I saw that it had become a suitable dwelling tower.

The feeling of repose and renewal that I had in this tower was intense from the start. It represented for me the maternal hearth. But I became increasingly aware that it did not yet express everything that needed saying, that something was still lacking. And so, four years later, in 1927, the central structure was added, with a tower-like annex.

After some time had passed—again the interval was four years—I once more had a feeling of incompleteness. The building still seemed too primitive to me, and so in 1931 the tower-like annex was extended. I wanted a room in this tower where I could exist for myself alone. I had in mind what I had seen in Indian houses, in which there is usually an area—though it may be only a corner of a room separated off by a curtain—to which the inhabitants can withdraw. There they meditate for perhaps a quarter or half an hour, or do Yoga exercises. Such an area of retirement is essential in India, where people live crowded very close together.

In my retiring room I am by myself. I keep the key with me all the time; no one else is allowed in there except with my permission. In the course of the years I have done paintings on the walls, and so have expressed all those things which have carried me out of time into seclusion, out of the present into timelessness. Thus the second tower became for me a place of spiritual concentration.

In 1935, the desire arose in me for a piece of fenced-in land. I needed a larger space that would stand open to the sky and to nature. And so—once again after an interval of four years—I added a courtyard and a loggia by the lake, which formed a fourth element that was separated from the unitary threeness of the house. Thus a quaternity had arisen, four different parts of the building, and, moreover, in the course of twelve years.

After my wife's death in 1955, I felt an inner obligation to become what I myself am. To put it in the language of the Bollingen house, I suddenly realized that the small central section which crouched so low, so hidden, was myself! I could no longer hide myself behind the "maternal" and the "spiritual" towers. So, in that same year, I added an upper story to this section, which represents myself, or my ego-personality. Earlier, I would not have been able to do this; I would have regarded it as presumptuous self-emphasis. Now it signified an extension of consciousness achieved in old age. With that the building was complete. I had started the first tower in 1923, two months after the death of my mother. These two dates are meaningful because the Tower, as we shall see, is connected with the dead.

From the beginning I felt the Tower as in some way a place of maturation—a maternal womb or a maternal figure in which I could become what I was, what I am and will be. It gave me a feeling as if I were being reborn in stone. It is thus a concretization of the individuation process, a memorial *aere perennius*. During the building work, of course, I never considered these matters. I built the house in sections, always following the concrete needs of the moment. It might also be said that I built it in a kind of dream. Only afterward did I see how all the parts fitted together and that a meaningful form had resulted: a symbol of psychic wholeness.

At Bollingen I am in the midst of my true life, I am most deeply myself. Here I am, as it were, the "age-old son of the mother." That is how alchemy puts it, very wisely, for the "old man," the "ancient," whom I had already experienced as a child, is personality No. 2, who has always been and always will be. He exists outside time and is the son of the maternal unconscious. In my fantasies he took the form of Philemon, and he comes to life again at Bollingen.

At times I feel as if I am spread out over the landscape and inside things, and am myself living in every tree, in the plashing of the waves, in the clouds and the animals that come and go, in the procession of the seasons. There is nothing in the Tower that has not grown into its own form over the decades, nothing with which I am not linked. Here everything has its history, and mine; here is space for the spaceless kingdom of the world's and the psyche's hinterland.

I have done without electricity, and tend the fireplace and stove myself. Evenings, I light the old lamps. There is no running water, and I pump the water from the well. I chop the wood and cook the food. These simple acts make man simple; and how difficult it is to be simple!

In Bollingen, silence surrounds me almost audibly, and I live "in modest harmony with nature."[1] Thoughts rise to the surface which reach back into the centuries, and accordingly anticipate a remote future. Here the torment of creation is lessened; creativity and play are close together.

In 1950 I made a kind of monument out of stone to express what the Tower means to me. The story of how this stone came to me is a curious one. I needed stones for building the enclosing wall for the so-called garden, and ordered them from the quarry near Bollingen. I was standing by when the mason gave all the measurements to the owner of the quarry, who wrote them down in his notebook. When the stones arrived by ship and were unloaded, it turned out that the cornerstone had altogether the wrong measurements; instead of a triangular stone, a square block had been sent: a perfect cube of much larger dimensions than had been ordered, about twenty inches thick. The mason was furious and told the barge men to take it right back with them.

But when I saw the stone, I said, "No, that is my stone. I must have it!" For I had seen at once that it suited me perfectly and that I wanted to do something with it. Only I did not yet know what.

The first thing that occurred to me was a Latin verse by the alchemist Arnaldus de Villanova (died 1313). I chiseled this into the stone; in translation it goes:

---

[1] Title of an old Chinese woodcut showing a little old man in a heroic landscape.

> Here stands the mean, uncomely stone,
> 'Tis very cheap in price!
> The more it is despised by fools,
> The more loved by the wise.

This verse refers to the alchemist's stone, the *lapis*, which is despised and rejected.

Soon something else emerged. I began to see on the front face, in the natural structure of the stone, a small circle, a sort of eye, which looked at me. I chiseled it into the stone, and in the center made a tiny homunculus. This corresponds to the "little doll" (*pupilla*)—yourself—which you see in the pupil of another's eye; a kind of Kabir, or the Telesphoros of Asklepios. Ancient statues show him wearing a hooded cloak and carrying a lantern. At the same time he is a pointer of the way. I dedicated a few words to him which came into my mind while I was working. The inscription is in Greek; the translation goes:

Time is a child—playing like a child—playing a board game— the kingdom of the child. This is Telesphoros, who roams through the dark regions of this cosmos and glows like a star out of the depths. He points the way to the gates of the sun and to the land of dreams.[2]

These words came to me—one after the other—while I worked on the stone.

On the third face, the one facing the lake, I let the stone itself speak, as it were, in a Latin inscription. These sayings are more or less quotations from alchemy. This is the translation:

I am an orphan, alone; nevertheless I am found everywhere. I am one, but opposed to myself. I am youth and old man at one and the same time. I have known neither father nor mother, because I have had to be fetched out of the deep like a fish, or fell like a white stone from heaven. In woods and mountains I roam, but I am hidden in the innermost soul of man. I am mortal for everyone, yet I am not touched by the cycle of aeons.

[2] The first sentence is a fragment from Heraclitus; the second sentence alludes to the Mithras liturgy, and the last sentence to Homer (*Odyssey*, Book 24, verse 12).

In conclusion, under the saying of Arnaldus de Villanova, I set down in Latin the words "In remembrance of his seventy-fifth birthday C. G. Jung made and placed this here as a thanks offering, in the year 1950."

When the stone was finished, I looked at it again and again, wondering about it and asking myself what lay behind my impulse to carve it.

The stone stands outside the Tower, and is like an explanation of it. It is a manifestation of the occupant, but one which remains incomprehensible to others. Do you know what I wanted to chisel into the back face of the stone? *"Le cri de Merlin!"* For what the stone expressed reminded me of Merlin's life in the forest, after he had vanished from the world. Men still hear his cries, so the legend runs, but they cannot understand or interpret them.

Merlin represents an attempt by the medieval unconscious to create a parallel figure to Parsifal. Parsifal is a Christian hero, and Merlin, son of the devil and a pure virgin, is his dark brother. In the twelfth century, when the legend arose, there were as yet no premises by which his intrinsic meaning could be understood. Hence he ended in exile, and hence *"le cri de Merlin"* which still sounded from the forest after his death. This cry that no one could understand implies that he lives on in unredeemed form. His story is not yet finished, and he still walks abroad. It might be said that the secret of Merlin was carried on by alchemy, primarily in the figure of Mercurius. Then Merlin was taken up again in my psychology of the unconscious and—remains uncomprehended to this day! That is because most people find it quite beyond them to live on close terms with the unconscious. Again and again I have had to learn how hard this is for people.

I was in Bollingen just as the first tower was being finished. This was the winter of 1923–24. As far as I can recall, there was no snow on the ground; perhaps it was early spring. I had been alone perhaps for a week, perhaps longer. An indescribable stillness prevailed.

One evening—I can still remember it precisely—I was sitting

by the fireplace and had put a big kettle on the fire to make hot water for washing up. The water began to boil and the kettle to sing. It sounded like many voices, or stringed instruments, or even like a whole orchestra. It was just like polyphonic music, which in reality I cannot abide, though in this case it seemed to me peculiarly interesting. It was as though there were one orchestra inside the Tower and another one outside. Now one dominated, now the other, as though they were responding to each other.

I sat and listened, fascinated. For far more than an hour I listened to the concert, to this natural melody. It was soft music, containing, as well, all the discords of nature. And that was right, for nature is not only harmonious; she is also dreadfully contradictory and chaotic. The music was that way too: an outpouring of sounds, having the quality of water and of wind—so strange that it is simply impossible to describe it.

On another such still night when I was alone in Bollingen (it was in the late winter or early spring of 1924) I awoke to the sound of soft footsteps going around the Tower. Distant music sounded, coming closer and closer, and then I heard voices laughing and talking. I thought, "Who can be prowling around? What is this all about? There is only the little footpath along the lake, and scarcely anybody ever walks on it!" While I was thinking these things I became wide awake, and went to the window. I opened the shutters—all was still. There was no one in sight, nothing to be heard—no wind—nothing—nothing at all.

"This is really strange," I thought. I was certain that the footsteps, the laughter and talk, had been real. But apparently I had only been dreaming. I returned to bed and mulled over the way we can deceive ourselves after all, and what might have been the cause of such a strange dream. In the midst of this, I fell asleep again—and at once the same dream began: once more I heard footsteps, talk, laughter, music. At the same time I had a visual image of several hundred dark-clad figures, possibly peasant boys in their Sunday clothes, who had come down from the mountains and were pouring in around the Tower, on both sides, with a great deal of loud trampling, laughing, singing, and playing of accordions. Irritably, I thought, "This is really the limit! I thought it was a dream and now it turns out to be reality!" At this point, I woke up. Once again I jumped up, opened the window and shutters, and found everything just the same as before: a deathly still moonlit night. Then I thought: "Why, this is simply a case of haunting!"

Naturally I asked myself what it meant when a dream was so insistent on its reality and at the same time on my being awake. Usually we experience that only when we see a ghost. Being awake means perceiving reality. The dream therefore represented a situation equivalent to reality, in which it created a kind of wakened state. In this sort of dream, as opposed to ordinary dreams, the unconscious seems bent on conveying a powerful impression of reality to the dreamer, an impression which is emphasized by repetition. The sources of such realities are known to be physical sensations on the one hand, and archetypal figures on the other.

That night everything was so completely real, or at least seemed to be so, that I could scarcely sort out the two realities. Nor could I make anything of the dream itself. What was the meaning of these music-making peasant boys passing by in a long procession? It seemed to me they had come out of curiosity, in order to look at the Tower.

Never again did I experience or dream anything similar, and I cannot recall ever having heard of a parallel to it. It was only much later that I found an explanation. This was when I came across the seventeenth-century Lucerne chronicle by Rennward Cysat. He tells the following story: On a high pasture of Mount Pilatus, which is particularly notorious for spooks—it is said that Wotan to this day practices his magic arts there—Cysat, while climbing the mountain, was disturbed one night by a procession of men who poured past his hut on both sides, playing music and singing—precisely what I had experienced at the Tower.

The next morning Cysat asked the herdsman with whom he had spent that night what could have been the meaning of it. The man had a ready explanation: those must be the departed folk—*sälig Lüt*, in Swiss dialect; the phrase also means blessed folk—namely, Wotan's army of departed souls. These, he said, were in the habit of walking abroad and showing themselves.

It may be suggested that this is a phenomenon of solitude, the outward emptiness and silence being compensated by the image of a crowd of people. This would put it in the same class with the hallucinations of hermits, which are likewise compensatory. But do we know what realities such stories may be founded on? It is also possible that I had been so sensitized by the solitude that I was able to perceive the procession of "departed folk" who passed by.

The explanation of this experience as a psychic compensation never entirely satisfied me, and to say that it was a hallucination seemed to me to beg the question. I felt obliged to consider the possibility of its reality, especially in view of the seventeenth-century account which had come my way.

It would seem most likely to have been a synchronistic phenomenon. Such phenomena demonstrate that premonitions or visions very often have some correspondence in external reality. There actually existed, as I discovered, a real parallel to my experience. In the Middle Ages just such gatherings of young men took place. These were the *Reisläufer* (mercenaries) who usually assembled in spring, marched from Central Switzerland to Locarno, met at the Casa di Ferro in Minusio and then marched on together to Milan. In Italy they served as soldiers, fighting for foreign princes. My vision, therefore, might have been one of these gatherings which took place regularly each spring when the young men, with singing and jollity, bade farewell to their native land.

When we began to build at Bollingen in 1923, my eldest daughter came to see the spot, and exclaimed, "What, you're building here? There are corpses about!" Naturally I thought, "Ridiculous! Nothing of the sort!" But when we were constructing the annex four years later, we did come upon a skeleton. It lay at a depth of seven feet in the ground. An old rifle bullet was imbedded in the elbow. From various indications it seemed evident that the body had been thrown into the grave in an advanced state of decay. It belonged to one of the many dozens of French soldiers who were drowned in the Linth in 1799 and were later washed up on the shores of the Upper Lake. These men were drowned when the Austrians blew up the bridge of Grynau which the French were storming. A photograph of the open grave with the skeleton and the date of its discovery—August 22, 1927—is preserved at the Tower.

I arranged a regular burial on my property, and fired a gun three times over the soldier's grave. Then I set up a gravestone with an inscription for him. My daughter had sensed the presence of the dead body. Her power to sense such things is something she inherits from my grandmother on my mother's side.

In the winter of 1955–56 I chiseled the names of my paternal ancestors on three stone tablets and placed them in the courtyard of the Tower. I painted the ceiling with motifs from my own and my wife's arms, and from those of my sons-in-law. The Jung family originally had a phoenix for its arms, the bird obviously being connected with "young," "youth," "rejuvenation." My grandfather changed the elements of the arms, probably out of a spirit of resistance toward his father. He was an ardent Freemason and Grand Master of the Swiss lodge. This had a good deal to do with the changes he made in the armorial bearings. I mention this point, in itself of no consequence, because it belongs in the historical nexus of my thinking and my life.

In keeping with this revision of my grandfather's, my coat of arms no longer contains the original phoenix. Instead there is a cross azure in chief dexter and in base sinister a blue bunch of grapes in a field d'or; separating these is an estoile d'or in a fess azure.[3] The symbolism of these arms is Masonic, or Rosicrucian. Just as cross and rose represent the Rosicrucian problem of opposites (*"per crucem ad rosam"*), that is, the Christian and Dionysian elements, so cross and grapes are symbols of the heavenly and the chthonic spirit. The uniting symbol is the gold star, the *aurum philosophorum.*

The Rosicrucians derived from Hermetic or alchemical philosophy. One of their founders was Michael Maier (1568–1622), a well-known alchemist and younger contemporary of the rela-

[3] Translated from the language of heraldry: a blue cross in the upper right and blue grapes in the lower left in a field of gold; a blue bar with a gold star.

tively unknown but more important Gerardus Dorneus (end of the sixteenth century), whose treatises fill the first volume of the *Theatrum Chemicum* of 1602. The two men lived in Frankfurt, which seems to have been a center of alchemical philosophy at the time. In any case, as Count Palatine and court physician to Rudolph II, Michael Maier was something of a local celebrity. In neighboring Mainz at that time lived Dr. med. et. jur. Carl Jung (died 1654), of whom nothing else is known, since the family tree breaks off with my great-great-grandfather who lived at the beginning of the eighteenth century. This was Sigmund Jung, a *civis Moguntinus,* citizen of Mainz. The hiatus is due to the fact that the municipal archives of Mainz were burned in the course of a siege during the War of the Spanish Succession. It is a safe surmise that this evidently learned Dr. Carl Jung was familiar with the writings of the two alchemists, for the pharmacology of the day was still very much under the influence of Paracelsus. Dorneus was an outspoken Paracelsist and even composed a voluminous commentary on the Paracelsan treatise, *De Vita Longa.* He also, more than all the other alchemists, dealt with the process of individuation. In view of the fact that a large part of my life work has revolved around the study of the problem of opposites, and especially their alchemical symbolism, all this is not without a certain interest.

When I was working on the stone tablets, I became aware of the fateful links between me and my ancestors. I feel very strongly that I am under the influence of things or questions which were left incomplete and unanswered by my parents and grandparents and more distant ancestors. It often seems as if there were an impersonal karma within a family, which is passed on from parents to children. It has always seemed to me that I had to answer questions which fate had posed to my forefathers, and which had not yet been answered, or as if I had to complete, or perhaps continue, things which previous ages had left unfinished. It is difficult to determine whether these questions are more of a personal or more of a general (collective) nature. It seems to me that the latter is the case. A collective problem, if not recognized as such, always appears as a personal problem, and in individual cases may give the impression that something is out of order in the realm of the personal psyche. The personal sphere is indeed disturbed, but such disturbances need not be primary; they may well be secondary, the consequence of an insupportable change in the social atmosphere. The cause of disturbance is, therefore, not to be sought in the personal surroundings, but rather in the collective situation. Psychotherapy has hitherto taken this matter far too little into account.

Like anyone who is capable of some introspection, I had early taken it for granted that the split in my personality was my own purely personal affair and responsibility. Faust, to be sure, had made the problem somewhat easier for me by confessing, "Two souls, alas, are housed within my breast"; but he had thrown no light on the cause of this dichotomy. His insight seemed, in a sense, directed straight at me. In the days when I first read *Faust* I could not remotely guess the extent to which Goethe's strange heroic myth was a collective experience and that it prophetically anticipated the fate of the Germans. Therefore I felt personally implicated, and when Faust, in his hubris and self-inflation, caused the murder of Philemon and Baucis, I felt guilty, quite as if I myself in the past had helped commit the murder of the two old people. This strange idea alarmed me, and I regarded it as my responsibility to atone for this crime, or to prevent its repetition.

My false conclusion was further supported by a bit of odd information that I picked up during those early years. I heard that it had been bruited about that my grandfather Jung had been an illegitimate son of Goethe's.[4] This annoying story made an impression upon me insofar as it at once corroborated and seemed to explain my curious reactions to *Faust*. It is true that I did not believe in reincarnation, but I was instinctively familiar with that concept which the Indians call karma. Since in those days I had no idea of the existence of the unconscious, I could not have had any psychological understanding of my reactions. I also did not know—no more than, even today, it is generally known—that the future is unconsciously prepared long in ad-

[4] See above, Chap. II, n. 1, pp. 35–36.

vance and therefore can be guessed by clairvoyants. Thus, when the news arrived of the crowning of Kaiser Wilhelm I at Versailles, Jakob Burckhardt exclaimed, "That is the doom of Germany." The archetypes of Wagner were already knocking at the gates, and along with them came the Dionysian experience of Nietzsche—which might better be ascribed to the god of ecstasy, Wotan. The hubris of the Wilhelmine era alienated Europe and paved the way for the disaster of 1914.

In my youth (around 1890) I was unconsciously caught up by this spirit of the age, and had no methods at hand for extricating myself from it. *Faust* struck a chord in me and pierced me through in a way that I could not but regard as personal. Most of all, it awakened in me the problem of opposites, of good and evil, of mind and matter, of light and darkness. Faust, the inept, purblind philosopher, encounters the dark side of his being, his sinister shadow, Mephistopheles, who in spite of his negating disposition represents the true spirit of life as against the arid scholar who hovers on the brink of suicide. My own inner contradictions appeared here in dramatized form; Goethe had written virtually a basic outline and pattern of my own conflicts and solutions. The dichotomy of Faust-Mephistopheles came together within myself into a single person, and I was that person. In other words, I was directly struck, and recognized that this was my fate. Hence, all the crises of the drama affected me personally; at one point I had passionately to agree, at another to oppose. No solution could be a matter of indifference to me. Later I consciously linked my work to what Faust had passed over: respect for the eternal rights of man, recognition of "the ancient," and the continuity of culture and intellectual history.[5]

Our souls as well as our bodies are composed of individual elements which were all already present in the ranks of our ancestors. The "newness" in the individual psyche is an endlessly varied recombination of age-old components. Body and soul therefore have an intensely historical character and find no

---

[5] Jung's attitude is shown in the inscription he placed over the gate of the Tower: *Philemonis Sacrum—Fausti Poenitentia* (Shrine of Philemon—Repentance of Faust). When the gate was walled up, he put the same words above the entrance to the second tower.—A. J.

proper place in what is new, in things that have just come into being. That is to say, our ancestral components are only partly at home in such things. We are very far from having finished completely with the Middle Ages, classical antiquity, and primitivity, as our modern psyches pretend. Nevertheless, we have plunged down a cataract of progress which sweeps us on into the future with ever wilder violence the farther it takes us from our roots. Once the past has been breached, it is usually annihilated, and there is no stopping the forward motion. But it is precisely the loss of connection with the past, our uprootedness, which has given rise to the "discontents" of civilization and to such a flurry and haste that we live more in the future and its chimerical promises of a golden age than in the present, with which our whole evolutionary background has not yet caught up. We rush impetuously into novelty, driven by a mounting sense of insufficiency, dissatisfaction, and restlessness. We no longer live on what we have, but on promises, no longer in the light of the present day, but in the darkness of the future, which, we expect, will at last bring the proper sunrise. We refuse to recognize that everything better is purchased at the price of something worse; that, for example, the hope of greater freedom is canceled out by increased enslavement to the state, not to speak of the terrible perils to which the most brilliant discoveries of science expose us. The less we understand of what our fathers and forefathers sought, the less we understand ourselves, and thus we help with all our might to rob the individual of his roots and his guiding instincts, so that he becomes a particle in the mass, ruled only by what Nietzsche called the spirit of gravity.

Reforms by advances, that is, by new methods or gadgets, are of course impressive at first, but in the long run they are dubious and in any case dearly paid for. They by no means increase the contentment or happiness of people on the whole. Mostly, they are deceptive sweetenings of existence, like speedier communications which unpleasantly accelerate the tempo of life and leave us with less time than ever before. *Omnis festinatio ex parte diaboli est*—all haste is of the devil, as the old masters used to say.

Reforms by retrogressions, on the other hand, are as a rule less expensive and in addition more lasting, for they return to the simpler, tried and tested ways of the past and make the sparsest use of newspapers, radio, television, and all supposedly timesaving innovations.

In this book I have devoted considerable space to my subjective view of the world, which, however, is not a product of rational thinking. It is rather a vision such as will come to one who undertakes, deliberately, with half-closed eyes and somewhat closed ears, to see and hear the form and voice of being. If our impressions are too distinct, we are held to the hour and minute of the present and have no way of knowing how our ancestral psyches listen to and understand the present—in other words, how our unconscious is responding to it. Thus we remain ignorant of whether our ancestral components find an elementary gratification in our lives, or whether they are repelled. Inner peace and contentment depend in large measure upon whether or not the historical family which is inherent in the individual can be harmonized with the ephemeral conditions of the present.

In the Tower at Bollingen it is as if one lived in many centuries simultaneously. The place will outlive me, and in its location and style it points backward to things of long ago. There is very little about it to suggest the present. If a man of the sixteenth century were to move into the house, only the kerosene lamp and the matches would be new to him; otherwise, he would know his way about without difficulty. There is nothing to disturb the dead, neither electric light nor telephone. Moreover, my ancestors' souls are sustained by the atmosphere of the house, since I answer for them the questions that their lives once left behind. I carve out rough answers as best I can. I have even drawn them on the walls. It is as if a silent, greater family, stretching down the centuries, were peopling the house. There I live in my second personality and see life in the round, as something forever coming into being and passing on.

· IX ·

Travels

A T THE BEGINNING of 1920 a friend told me that he had a business trip to make to Tunis, and would I like to accompany him? I said yes immediately. We set out in March, going first to Algiers. Following the coast, we reached Tunis and from there Sousse, where I left my friend to his business affairs.

At last I was where I had longed to be: in a non-European country where no European language was spoken and no Christian conceptions prevailed, where a different race lived and a different historical tradition and philosophy had set its stamp upon the face of the crowd. I had often wished to be able for once to see the European from outside, his image reflected back at him by an altogether foreign milieu. To be sure, there was my ignorance of the Arabic language, which I deeply regretted; but to make up for this I was all the more attentive in observing the people and their behavior. Frequently I sat for hours in an Arab coffee house, listening to conversations of which I understood not a word. But I studied the people's gestures, and especially their expression of emotions; I observed the subtle change

238

in their gestures when they spoke with a European, and thus learned to see to some extent with different eyes and to know the white man outside his own environment.

What the Europeans regard as Oriental calm and apathy seemed to me a mask; behind it I sensed a restlessness, a degree of agitation, which I could not explain. Strangely, in setting foot upon Moorish soil, I found myself haunted by an impression which I myself could not understand: I kept thinking that the land smelled queer. It was the smell of blood, as though the soil were soaked with blood. This strip of land, it occurred to me, had already borne the brunt of three civilizations: Carthaginian, Roman, and Christian. What the technological age will do with Islam remains to be seen.

When I left Sousse, I traveled south to Sfax, and thence into the Sahara, to the oasis city of Tozeur. The city lies on a slight elevation, on the margin of a plateau, at whose foot lukewarm, slightly saline springs well up profusely and irrigate the oasis through a thousand little canals. Towering date palms formed a green, shady roof overhead, under which peach, apricot, and fig trees flourished, and beneath these alfalfa of an unbelievable green. Several kingfishers, shining like jewels, flitted through the foliage. In the comparative coolness of this green shade strolled figures clad in white, among them a great number of affectionate couples holding one another in close embrace— obviously homosexual friendships. I felt suddenly transported to the times of classical Greece, where this inclination formed the cement of a society of men and of the *polis* based on that society. It was clear that men spoke to men and women to women here. Only a few of the latter were to be seen, nunlike, heavily veiled figures. I saw a few without veils. These, my dragoman explained, were prostitutes. On the main streets the scene was dominated by men and children.

My dragoman confirmed my impression of the prevalence of homosexuality, and of its being taken for granted, and promptly made me offers. The good fellow could have no notion of the thoughts which had struck me like a flash of lightning, suddenly illuminating my point of observation. I felt cast back many centuries to an infinitely more naïve world of adolescents who were preparing, with the aid of a slender knowledge of the Koran, to emerge from their original state of twilight consciousness, in which they had existed from time immemorial, and to become aware of their own existence, in self-defense against the forces threatening them from the North.

While I was still caught up in this dream of a static, age-old existence, I suddenly thought of my pocket watch, the symbol of the European's accelerated tempo. This, no doubt, was the dark cloud that hung threateningly over the heads of these unsuspecting souls. They suddenly seemed to me like game who do not see the hunter but, vaguely uneasy, scent him—"him" being the god of time who will inevitably chop into the bits and pieces of days, hours, minutes, and seconds that duration which is still the closest thing to eternity.

From Tozeur I went on to the oasis of Nefta. I rode off with my dragoman early in the morning, shortly after sunrise. Our mounts were large, swift-footed mules, on which we made rapid progress. As we approached the oasis, a single rider, wholly swathed in white, came toward us. With proud bearing he rode by without offering us any greeting, mounted on a black mule whose harness was banded and studded with silver. He made an impressive, elegant figure. Here was a man who certainly possessed no pocket watch, let alone a wrist watch; for he was obviously and unself-consciously the person he had always been. He lacked that faint note of foolishness which clings to the European. The European is, to be sure, convinced that he is no longer what he was ages ago; but he does not know what he has since become. His watch tells him that since the "Middle Ages" time and its synonym, progress, have crept up on him and irrevocably taken something from him. With lightened baggage he continues his journey, with steadily increasing velocity, toward nebulous goals. He compensates for the loss of gravity and the corresponding *sentiment d'incomplétitude* by the illusion of his triumphs, such as steamships, railroads, airplanes, and rockets, that rob him of his duration and transport him into another reality of speeds and explosive accelerations.

The deeper we penetrated into the Sahara, the more time slowed down for me; it even threatened to move backward. The shimmering heat waves rising up contributed a good deal to my dreamy state, and when we reached the first palms and dwellings of the oasis, it seemed to me that everything here was exactly the way it should be and the way it had always been.

Early the next morning I was awakened by the various unfamiliar noises outside my inn. There was a large open square which had been empty the night before, but which was now crowded with people, camels, mules, and donkeys. The camels groaned and announced in manifold variations of tone their chronic discontent, and the donkeys competed with cacophonous screams. The people ran around in a great state of excitement, shouting and gesticulating. They looked savage and rather alarming. My dragoman explained that a great festival was being celebrated that day. Several desert tribes had come in during the night to do two days of field work for the marabout. The marabout was the administrator of poor relief and owned many fields in the oasis. The people were to lay out a new field and irrigation canals to match.

At the farther end of the square there suddenly rose a cloud of dust; a green flag unfolded, and drums rolled. At the head of a long procession of hundreds of wild-looking men carrying baskets and short, wide hoes appeared a white-bearded, venerable old man. He radiated inimitable natural dignity, as though he were a hundred years old. This was the marabout, astride a white mule. The men danced around him, beating small drums. The scene was one of wild excitement, hoarse shouting, dust, and heat. With fanatic purposefulness the procession swarmed by, out into the oasis, as if going to battle.

I followed this horde at a cautious distance, and my dragoman made no attempt to encourage me to approach closer until we reached the spot where the "work" was going on. Here, if possible, even greater excitement prevailed; people were beating drums and shouting wildly; the site of the work resembled a disturbed anthill; everything was being done with the utmost haste. Carrying their baskets filled with heavy loads of earth, men danced along to the rhythm of the drums; others hacked into the ground at a furious rate, digging ditches and erecting dams. Through this wild tumult the marabout rode along on his white mule, evidently issuing instructions with the dignified, mild, and weary gestures of advanced age. Wherever he came, the haste, shouting, and rhythm intensified, forming the background against which the calm figure of the holy man stood out with extraordinary effectiveness. Toward evening the crowd was visibly overcome by exhaustion; the men soon dropped down beside their camels into deep sleep. During the night, after the usual stupendous concert of the dogs, utter stillness prevailed, until at the first rays of the rising sun the invocation of the muezzin—which always deeply stirred me—summoned the people to their morning prayer.

This scene taught me something: these people live from their affects, are moved and have their being in emotions. Their consciousness takes care of their orientation in space and transmits impressions from outside, and it is also stirred by inner impulses and affects. But it is not given to reflection; the ego has almost no autonomy. The situation is not so different with the European; but we are, after all, somewhat more complicated. At any rate the European possesses a certain measure of will and directed intention. What we lack is intensity of life.

Without wishing to fall under the spell of the primitive, I nevertheless had been psychically infected. This manifested itself outwardly in an infectious enteritis which cleared up after a few days, thanks to the local treatment of rice water and calomel.

Overcharged with ideas, I finally went back to Tunis. The night before we embarked from Marseilles I had a dream which, I sensed, summed up the whole experience. This was just as it should be, for I had accustomed myself to living always on two planes simultaneously, one conscious, which attempted to understand and could not, and one unconscious, which wanted to express something and could not formulate it any better than by a dream.

I dreamt that I was in an Arab city, and as in most such cities there was a citadel, a casbah. The city was situated in a broad plain, and had a wall all around it. The shape of the wall was square, and there were four gates.

The casbah in the interior of the city was surrounded by a

wide moat (which is not the way it really is in Arab countries).
I stood before a wooden bridge leading over the water to a dark,
horseshoe-shaped portal, which was open. Eager to see the
citadel from the inside also, I stepped out on the bridge. When I
was about halfway across it, a handsome, dark Arab of aristocratic, almost royal bearing came toward me from the gate. I
knew that this youth in the white burnoose was the resident
prince of the citadel. When he came up to me, he attacked me
and tried to knock me down. We wrestled. In the struggle we
crashed against the railing; it gave way and both of us fell into
the moat, where he tried to push my head under water to drown
me. No, I thought, this is going too far. And in my turn I pushed
his head under water. I did so although I felt great admiration
for him; but I did not want to let myself be killed. I had no intention of killing him; I wanted only to make him unconscious
and incapable of fighting.

Then the scene of the dream changed, and he was with me in
a large vaulted octagonal room in the center of the citadel. The
room was all white, very plain and beautiful. Along the light-
colored marble walls stood low divans, and before me on the
floor lay an open book with black letters written in magnificent
calligraphy on milky-white parchment. It was not Arabic script;
rather, it looked to me like the Uigurian script of West Turke-
stan, which was familiar to me from the Manichaean fragments
from Turfan. I did not know the contents, but nevertheless I had
the feeling that this was *"my* book," that I had written it. The
young prince with whom I had just been wrestling sat to the
right of me on the floor. I explained to him that now that I had
overcome him he must read the book. But he resisted. I placed
my arm around his shoulders and forced him, with a sort of
paternal kindness and patience, to read the book. I knew that
this was absolutely essential, and at last he yielded.

In this dream, the Arab youth was the double of the proud
Arab who had ridden past us without a greeting. As an inhabitant of the casbah he was a figuration of the self, or rather,
a messenger or emissary of the self. For the casbah from which
he came was a perfect mandala: a citadel surrounded by a
square wall with four gates. His attempt to kill me was an echo

of the motif of Jacob's struggle with the angel; he was—to use
the language of the Bible—like an angel of the Lord, a messenger of God who wished to kill men because he did not know
them.

Actually, the angel ought to have had his dwelling in me. But
he knew only angelic truth and understood nothing about man.
Therefore he first came forward as my enemy; however, I held
my own against him. In the second part of the dream I was the
master of the citadel; he sat at my feet and had to learn to
understand my thoughts, or rather, learn to know man.

Obviously, my encounter with Arab culture had struck me
with overwhelming force. The emotional nature of these unreflective people who are so much closer to life than we are exerts
a strong suggestive influence upon those historical layers in ourselves which we have just overcome and left behind, or which
we think we have overcome. It is like the paradise of childhood
from which we imagine we have emerged, but which at the
slightest provocation imposes fresh defeats upon us. Indeed, our
cult of progress is in danger of imposing on us even more childish dreams of the future, the harder it presses us to escape from
the past.

On the other hand, a characteristic of childhood is that,
thanks to its naïveté and unconsciousness, it sketches a more
complete picture of the self, of the whole man in his pure individuality, than adulthood. Consequently, the sight of a child
or a primitive will arouse certain longings in adult, civilized
persons—longings which relate to the unfulfilled desires and
needs of those parts of the personality which have been blotted
out of the total picture in favor of the adapted persona.

In traveling to Africa to find a psychic observation post outside the sphere of the European, I unconsciously wanted to find
that part of my personality which had become invisible under
the influence and the pressure of being European. This part
stands in unconscious opposition to myself, and indeed I attempt to suppress it. In keeping with its nature, it wishes to make
me unconscious (force me under water) so as to kill me; but my
aim is, through insight, to make it more conscious, so that we
can find a common modus vivendi. The Arab's dusky complexion

marks him as a "shadow," but not the personal shadow, rather an ethnic one associated not with my persona but with the totality of my personality, that is, with the self. As master of the casbah, he must be regarded as a kind of shadow of the self. The predominantly rationalistic European finds much that is human alien to him, and he prides himself on this without realizing that his rationality is won at the expense of his vitality, and that the primitive part of his personality is consequently condemned to a more or less underground existence.

The dream reveals how my encounter with North Africa affected me. First of all there was the danger that my European consciousness would be overwhelmed by an unexpectedly violent assault of the unconscious psyche. Consciously, I was not a bit aware of any such situation; on the contrary, I could not help feeling superior because I was reminded at every step of my Europeanism. That was unavoidable; my being European gave me a certain perspective on these people who were so differently constituted from myself, and utterly marked me off from them. But I was not prepared for the existence of unconscious forces within myself which would take the part of these strangers with such intensity, so that a violent conflict ensued. The dream expressed this conflict in the symbol of an attempted murder.

I was not to recognize the real nature of this disturbance until some years later, when I stayed in tropical Africa. It had been, in fact, the first hint of "going black under the skin," a spiritual peril which threatens the uprooted European in Africa to an extent not fully appreciated. "Where danger is, there is salvation also"—these words of Hölderlin often came to my mind in such situations. The salvation lies in our ability to bring the unconscious urges to consciousness with the aid of warning dreams. These dreams show that there is something in us which does not merely submit passively to the influence of the unconscious, but on the contrary rushes eagerly to meet it, identifying itself with the shadow. Just as a childhood memory can suddenly take possession of consciousness with so lively an emotion that we feel wholly transported back to the original situation, so these seemingly alien and wholly different Arab surroundings awaken an archetypal memory of an only too well known prehistoric past which apparently we have entirely forgotten. We are remembering a potentiality of life which has been overgrown by civilization, but which in certain places is still existent. If we were to relive it naïvely, it would constitute a relapse into barbarism. Therefore we prefer to forget it. But should it appear to us again in the form of a conflict, then we should keep it in our consciousness and test the two possibilities against each other—the life we live and the one we have forgotten. For what has apparently been lost does not come to the fore again without sufficient reason. In the living psychic structure, nothing takes place in a merely mechanical fashion; everything fits into the economy of the whole, relates to the whole. That is to say, it is all purposeful and has meaning. But because consciousness never has a view of the whole, it usually cannot understand this meaning. We must therefore content ourselves for the time being with noting the phenomenon and hoping that the future, or further investigation, will reveal the significance of this clash with the shadow of the self. In any case, I did not at the time have any glimmering of the nature of this archetypal experience, and knew still less about the historical parallels. Yet though I did not then grasp the full meaning of the dream, it lingered in my memory, along with the liveliest wish to go to Africa again at the next opportunity. That wish was not to be fulfilled for another five years.

ii. AMERICA: THE PUEBLO INDIANS
(*Extract from an unpublished MS.*)

We always require an outside point to stand on, in order to apply the lever of criticism. This is especially so in psychology, where by the nature of the material we are much more subjectively involved than in any other science. How, for example, can we become conscious of national peculiarities if we have never had the opportunity to regard our own nation from outside? Regarding it from outside means regarding it from the standpoint of another nation. To do so, we must acquire sufficient knowledge of the foreign collective psyche, and in the course of this process of assimilation we encounter all those incompatibilities which constitute the national bias and the national peculiarity. Everything that irritates us about others can lead us to an understanding of ourselves. I understand England only when I see where I, as a Swiss, do not fit in. I understand Europe, our greatest problem, only when I see where I as a European do not fit into the world. Through my acquaintance with many Americans, and my trips to and in America, I have obtained an enormous amount of insight into the European character; it has always seemed to me that there can be nothing more useful for a European than some time or another to look out at Europe from the top of a skyscraper. When I contemplated for the first time the European spectacle from the Sahara, surrounded by a civilization which has more or less the same relationship to ours as Roman antiquity has to modern times, I became aware of how completely, even in America, I was still caught up and imprisoned in the cultural consciousness of the white man. The desire then grew in me to carry the historical comparisons still farther by descending to a still lower cultural level.

On my next trip to the United States I went with a group of American friends to visit the Indians of New Mexico, the city-building Pueblos. "City," however, is too strong a word. What they build are in reality only villages; but their crowded houses piled one atop the other suggest the word "city," as do their language and their whole manner. There for the first time I had the good fortune to talk with a non-European, that is, to a non-white. He was a chief of the Taos pueblos, an intelligent man between the ages of forty and fifty. His name was Ochwiay Biano (Mountain Lake). I was able to talk with him as I have rarely been able to talk with a European. To be sure, he was caught up in his world just as much as a European is in his, but what a world it was! In talk with a European, one is constantly running up on the sand bars of things long known but never understood; with this Indian, the vessel floated freely on deep, alien seas. At the same time, one never knows which is more enjoyable: catching sight of new shores, or discovering new approaches to age-old knowledge that has been almost forgotten.

"See," Ochwiay Biano said, "how cruel the whites look. Their lips are thin, their noses sharp, their faces furrowed and distorted by folds. Their eyes have a staring expression; they are always seeking something. What are they seeking? The whites always want something; they are always uneasy and restless. We do not know what they want. We do not understand them. We think that they are mad."

I asked him why he thought the whites were all mad.

"They say that they think with their heads," he replied.

"Why of course. What do you think with?" I asked him in surprise.

"We think here," he said, indicating his heart.

I fell into a long meditation. For the first time in my life, so it seemed to me, someone had drawn for me a picture of the real white man. It was as though until now I had seen nothing but sentimental, prettified color prints. This Indian had struck our vulnerable spot, unveiled a truth to which we are blind. I felt rising within me like a shapeless mist something unknown and yet deeply familiar. And out of this mist, image upon image detached itself: first Roman legions smashing into the cities of Gaul, and the keenly incised features of Julius Caesar, Scipio Africanus, and Pompey. I saw the Roman eagle on the North Sea and on the banks of the White Nile. Then I saw St. Augustine transmitting the Christian creed to the Britons on the tips of Roman lances, and Charlemagne's most glorious forced conversions of the heathen; then the pillaging and murdering bands of the Crusading armies. With a secret stab I realized the hollowness of that old romanticism about the Crusades. Then followed Columbus, Cortes, and the other conquistadors who with fire, sword, torture, and Christianity came down upon even these remote pueblos dreaming peacefully in the Sun, their Father. I saw, too, the peoples of the Pacific islands decimated by firewater, syphilis, and scarlet fever carried in the clothes the missionaries forced on them.

It was enough. What we from our point of view call colonization, missions to the heathen, spread of civilization, etc., has another face—the face of a bird of prey seeking with cruel intentness for distant quarry—a face worthy of a race of pirates and highwaymen. All the eagles and other predatory creatures that adorn our coats of arms seem to me apt psychological representatives of our true nature.

Something else that Ochwiay Biano said to me stuck in my mind. It seems to me so intimately connected with the peculiar atmosphere of our interview that my account would be incomplete if I failed to mention it. Our conversation took place on the roof of the fifth story of the main building. At frequent intervals figures of other Indians could be seen on the roofs, wrapped in their woolen blankets, sunk in contemplation of the wandering sun that daily rose into a clear sky. Around us were grouped the low-built square buildings of air-dried brick (adobe), with the characteristic ladders that reach from the ground to the roof, or from roof to roof of the higher stories. (In earlier, dangerous times the entrance used to be through the roof.) Before us the rolling plateau of Taos (about seven thousand feet above sea level) stretched to the horizon, where several conical peaks (ancient volcanoes) rose to over twelve thousand feet. Behind us a clear stream purled past the houses, and on its opposite bank stood a second pueblo of reddish adobe houses, built one atop the other toward the center of the settlement, thus strangely anticipating the perspective of an American metropolis with its skyscrapers in the center. Perhaps half an hour's journey upriver rose a mighty isolated mountain, *the* mountain, which has no name. The story goes that on days when the mountain is wrapped in clouds the men vanish in that direction to perform mysterious rites.

The Pueblo Indians are unusually closemouthed, and in matters of their religion absolutely inaccessible. They make it a policy to keep their religious practices a secret, and this secret is so strictly guarded that I abandoned as hopeless any attempt at direct questioning. Never before had I run into such an atmosphere of secrecy; the religions of civilized nations today are all accessible; their sacraments have long ago ceased to be mysteries. Here, however, the air was filled with a secret known to all the communicants, but to which whites could gain no access. This strange situation gave me an inkling of Eleusis, whose secret was known to one nation and yet never betrayed. I understood what Pausanias or Herodotus felt when he wrote:

"I am not permitted to name the name of that god." This was not, I felt, mystification, but a vital mystery whose betrayal might bring about the downfall of the community as well as of the individual. Preservation of the secret gives the Pueblo Indian pride and the power to resist the dominant whites. It gives him cohesion and unity; and I feel sure that the Pueblos as an individual community will continue to exist as long as their mysteries are not desecrated.

It was astonishing to me to see how the Indian's emotions change when he speaks of his religious ideas. In ordinary life he shows a degree of self-control and dignity that borders on fatalistic equanimity. But when he speaks of things that pertain to his mysteries, he is in the grip of a surprising emotion which he cannot conceal—a fact which greatly helped to satisfy my curiosity. As I have said, direct questioning led to nothing. When, therefore, I wanted to know about essential matters, I made tentative remarks and observed my interlocutor's expression for those affective movements which are so very familiar to me. If I had hit on something essential, he remained silent or gave an evasive reply, but with all the signs of profound emotion; frequently tears would fill his eyes. Their religious conceptions are not theories to them (which, indeed, would have to be very curious theories to evoke tears from a man), but facts, as important and moving as the corresponding external realities.

As I sat with Ochwiay Biano on the roof, the blazing sun rising higher and higher, he said, pointing to the sun, "Is not he who moves there our father? How can anyone say differently? How can there be another god? Nothing can be without the sun." His excitement, which was already perceptible, mounted still higher; he struggled for words, and exclaimed at last, "What would a man do alone in the mountains? He cannot even build his fire without him."

I asked him whether he did not think the sun might be a fiery ball shaped by an invisible god. My question did not even arouse astonishment, let alone anger. Obviously it touched nothing within him; he did not even think my question stupid. It merely left him cold. I had the feeling that I had come upon an insurmountable wall. His only reply was, "The sun is God. Everyone can see that."

Although no one can help feeling the tremendous impress of the sun, it was a novel and deeply affecting experience for me to see these mature, dignified men in the grip of an overmastering emotion when they spoke of it.

Another time I stood by the river and looked up at the mountains, which rise almost another six thousand feet above the plateau. I was just thinking that this was the roof of the American continent, and that people lived here in the face of the sun like the Indians who stood wrapped in blankets on the highest roofs of the pueblo, mute and absorbed in the sight of the sun. Suddenly a deep voice, vibrant with suppressed emotion, spoke from behind me into my left ear: "Do you not think that all life comes from the mountain?" An elderly Indian had come up to me, inaudible in his moccasins, and had asked me this heaven knows how far-reaching question. A glance at the river pouring down from the mountain showed me the outward image that had engendered this conclusion. Obviously all life came from the mountain, for where there is water, there is life. Nothing could be more obvious. In his question I felt a swelling emotion connected with the word "mountain," and thought of the tale of secret rites celebrated on the mountain. I replied, "Everyone can see that you speak the truth."

Unfortunately, the conversation was soon interrupted, and so I did not succeed in attaining any deeper insight into the symbolism of water and mountain.

I observed that the Pueblo Indians, reluctant as they were to speak about anything concerning their religion, talked with great readiness and intensity about their relations with the Americans. "Why," Mountain Lake said, "do the Americans not let us alone? Why do they want to forbid our dances? Why do they make difficulties when we want to take our young people from school in order to lead them to the *kiva* (site of the rituals), and instruct them in our religion? We do nothing to harm the Americans!" After a prolonged silence he continued, "The Americans want to stamp out our religion. Why can they not let us alone? What we do, we do not only for ourselves but for the Americans also. Yes, we do it for the whole world. Everyone benefits by it."

I could observe from his excitement that he was alluding to some extremely important element of his religion. I therefore asked him: "You think, then, that what you do in your religion benefits the whole world?" He replied with great animation, "Of course. If we did not do it, what would become of the world?" And with a significant gesture he pointed to the sun.

I felt that we were approaching extremely delicate ground here, verging on the mysteries of the tribe. "After all," he said, "we are a people who live on the roof of the world; we are the sons of Father Sun, and with our religion we daily help our father to go across the sky. We do this not only for ourselves, but for the whole world. If we were to cease practicing our religion, in ten years the sun would no longer rise. Then it would be night forever."

I then realized on what the "dignity," the tranquil composure of the individual Indian, was founded. It springs from his being a son of the sun; his life is cosmologically meaningful, for he helps the father and preserver of all life in his daily rise and descent. If we set against this our own self-justifications, the meaning of our own lives as it is formulated by our reason, we cannot help but see our poverty. Out of sheer envy we are obliged to smile at the Indians' naïveté and to plume ourselves on our cleverness; for otherwise we would discover how impoverished and down at the heels we are. Knowledge does not enrich us; it removes us more and more from the mythic world in which we were once at home by right of birth.

If for a moment we put away all European rationalism and transport ourselves into the clear mountain air of that solitary plateau, which drops off on one side into the broad continental prairies and on the other into the Pacific Ocean; if we also set aside our intimate knowledge of the world and exchange it for a horizon that seems immeasurable, and an ignorance of what lies beyond it, we will begin to achieve an inner comprehension of the Pueblo Indian's point of view. "All life comes from the mountain" is immediately convincing to him, and he is equally certain that he lives upon the roof of an immeasurable world, closest to God. He above all others has the Divinity's ear, and his ritual act will reach the distant sun soonest of all. The holiness of mountains, the revelation of Yahweh upon Sinai, the inspiration that Nietzsche was vouchsafed in the Engadine—all speak the same language. The idea, absurd to us, that a ritual act can magically affect the sun is, upon closer examination, no less irrational but far more familiar to us than might at first be assumed. Our Christian religion—like every other, incidentally —is permeated by the idea that special acts or a special kind of action can influence God—for example, through certain rites or by prayer, or by a morality pleasing to the Divinity.

The ritual acts of man are an answer and reaction to the action of God upon man; and perhaps they are not only that, but are also intended to be "activating," a form of magic coercion. That man feels capable of formulating valid replies to the overpowering influence of God, and that he can render back something which is essential even to God, induces pride, for it raises the human individual to the dignity of a metaphysical factor. "God and us"—even if it is only an unconscious *sous-entendu*— this equation no doubt underlies that enviable serenity of the Pueblo Indian. Such a man is in the fullest sense of the word in his proper place.

iii. KENYA AND UGANDA

Tout est bien sortant des mains de l'Auteur des choses—Rousseau.

When I visited the Wembley Exhibition in London (1925), I was deeply impressed by the excellent survey of the tribes under British rule, and resolved to take a trip to tropical Africa in the near future.

In the autumn of that year I set out with two friends, an Englishman and an American, for Mombassa. We traveled on a Woerman steamer, together with many young Englishmen going out to posts in various African colonies. It was evident from the atmosphere aboard ship that these passengers were not traveling for pleasure, but were entering upon their destiny.

To be sure, there was a good deal of gay exuberance, but the serious undertone was also evident. As a matter of fact, I heard of the fate of several of my fellow voyagers even before my own return trip. Several met death in the tropics in the course of the next two months. They died of tropical malaria, amoebic dysentery, and pneumonia. Among those who died was the young man who sat opposite me at table. Another was Dr. Akley, who had made a name for himself as the founder of the Gorilla Reservation in Central Africa and whom I had met in New York shortly before this voyage.

Mombassa remains in my memory as a humidly hot, European, Indian, and Negro settlement hidden in a forest of palms and mango trees. It has an extremely picturesque setting, on a natural harbor, with an old Portuguese fort towering over it. We stayed there two days, and left toward evening on a narrow-gauge railroad for Nairobi in the interior, plunging almost immediately into the tropical night.

Along the coastal strip we passed by numerous Negro villages where the people sat talking around tiny fires. Soon the train began to climb. The settlements ceased, and the night became inky black. Gradually it turned cooler, and I fell asleep. When the first ray of sunlight announced the onset of day, I awoke. The train, swathed in a red cloud of dust, was just making a turn around a steep red cliff. On a jagged rock above us a slim, brownish-black figure stood motionless, leaning on a long spear, looking down at the train. Beside him towered a gigantic candelabrum cactus.

I was enchanted by this sight—it was a picture of something utterly alien and outside my experience, but on the other hand a most intense *sentiment du déjà vu*. I had the feeling that I had already experienced this moment and had always known this world which was separated from me only by distance in time. It was as if I were this moment returning to the land of my youth, and as if I knew that dark-skinned man who had been waiting for me for five thousand years.

The feeling-tone of this curious experience accompanied me throughout my whole journey through savage Africa. I can recall only one other such recognition of the immemorially known.

That was when I first observed a parapsychological phenomenon, together with my former chief, Professor Eugen Bleuler. Beforehand I had imagined that I would be dumfounded if I were to see so fantastic a thing. But when it happened, I was not surprised at all; I felt it was perfectly natural, something I could take for granted because I had long since been acquainted with it.

I could not guess what string within myself was plucked at the sight of that solitary dark hunter. I knew only that his world had been mine for countless millennia.

Somewhat bemused, I arrived around noon in Nairobi, situated at an altitude of six thousand feet. There was a dazzling plethora of light that reminded me of the glare of sunlight in the Engadine as one comes up out of the winter fogs of the lowlands. To my astonishment the swarm of "boys" assembled at the railroad station wore the old-fashioned gray and white woolen ski caps which I had seen worn or worn myself in the Engadine. They are highly esteemed because the upturned rim can be let down like a visor—in the Alps, good protection against the icy wind; here, against the blazing heat.

From Nairobi we used a small Ford to visit the Athi Plains, a great game preserve. From a low hill in this broad savanna a magnificent prospect opened out to us. To the very brink of the horizon we saw gigantic herds of animals: gazelle, antelope, gnu, zebra, warthog, and so on. Grazing, heads nodding, the herds moved forward like slow rivers. There was scarcely any sound save the melancholy cry of a bird of prey. This was the stillness of the eternal beginning, the world as it had always been, in the state of non-being; for until then no one had been present to know that it was this world. I walked away from my companions until I had put them out of sight, and savored the feeling of being entirely alone. There I was now, the first human being to recognize that this was the world, but who did not know that in this moment he had first really created it.

There the cosmic meaning of consciousness became overwhelmingly clear to me. "What nature leaves imperfect, the art perfects," say the alchemists. Man, I, in an invisible act of creation put the stamp of perfection on the world by giving it objective existence. This act we usually ascribe to the Creator alone, without considering that in so doing we view life as a machine calculated down to the last detail, which, along with the human psyche, runs on senselessly, obeying foreknown and predetermined rules. In such a cheerless clockwork fantasy there is no drama of man, world, and God; there is no "new day" leading to "new shores," but only the dreariness of calculated processes. My old Pueblo friend came to my mind. He thought that the *raison d'être* of his pueblo had been to help their father, the sun, to cross the sky each day. I had envied him for the fullness of meaning in that belief, and had been looking about without hope for a myth of our own. Now I knew what it was, and knew even more: that man is indispensable for the completion of creation; that, in fact, he himself is the second creator of the world, who alone has given to the world its objective existence—without which, unheard, unseen, silently eating, giving birth, dying, heads nodding through hundreds of millions of years, it would have gone on in the profoundest night of non-being down to its unknown end. Human consciousness created objective existence and meaning, and man found his indispensable place in the great process of being.

By the Uganda railroad, which was then being built, we traveled to its provisional terminus, Station Sigistifour (sixty-four). The boys unloaded our quantities of equipment. I sat down on a chop box, a crate containing provisions, each one a man's head-load, and lit a pipe, meditating on the fact that here we had, as it were, reached the edge of the *oikumene*, the inhabited earth, from which trails stretched endlessly over the continent. After a while an elderly Englishman, obviously a squatter, joined me, sat down, and likewise took out a pipe. He asked where we were going. When I outlined our various destinations, he asked, "Is this the first time you have been in Africa? I have been here for forty years."

"Yes," I told him. "At least in this part of Africa."

"Then may I give you a piece of advice? You know, mister, this here country is not man's country, it's God's country. So if anything should happen, just sit down and don't worry." Whereupon he rose and without another word was lost in the horde of Negroes swarming around us.

His words struck me as somehow significant, and I tried to visualize the psychological state from which they had sprung. Evidently they represented the quintessence of his experience; not man but God was in command here—in other words, not will and intention, but inscrutable design.

I had not come to the end of my meditation when our two automobiles were ready to set off. Our party piled in with the baggage, eight men strong, and we held on as best we could. The shaking I received for the next several hours left no room for reflection. It was much farther than I had thought to the next settlement; Kakamegas, seat of a D.C. (District Commissioner), headquarters of a small garrison of the African Rifles, and site of a hospital and—fantastically enough—a small insane asylum. Evening approached, and suddenly night had fallen. All at once, a tropical storm came up, with almost incessant flashes of lightning, thunder, and a cloudburst which instantly soaked us from head to foot and made every brook a raging torrent.

It was half an hour after midnight, with the sky beginning to clear, when we reached Kakamegas. We were exhausted, and the D.C. helpfully received us with whisky in his drawing room. A jolly and oh-so-welcome fire was burning in the fireplace. In the center of the handsome room stood a large table with a display of English journals. The place might easily have been a country house in Sussex. In my tiredness I no longer knew whether I had been transported from reality into a dream, or from a dream to reality. Then we had still to pitch our tents—for the first time. Luckily, nothing was missing.

Next morning I awoke with a touch of feverish laryngitis, and had to stay in bed for a day. To this circumstance I owe my memorable acquaintanceship with the "brain-fever bird," a creature remarkable for being able to sing a correct scale, but leaving out the last note and starting again from the beginning. To listen to this when one is down with a fever is to have one's nerves strained to the breaking point.

Another feathered inhabitant of the banana plantations has a cry which consists of two of the sweetest and most melodious flute tones with a third, frightful sour note for an ending. "What nature leaves imperfect . . ." The song of the "bell bird," however, was one of unalloyed beauty. When it sang, it was as though a bell were drifting along the horizon.

Next day, with the aid of the D.C., we rounded up our column of bearers, which was supplemented by a military escort of three Askaris. And now began the trek to Mt. Elgon, whose fourteen-thousand-foot crater wall we soon saw on the horizon. The track led through relatively dry savanna covered with umbrella acacias. The whole district was densely covered with small, round tumuli between six and ten feet high—old termite colonies.

For travelers there were resthouses along the track—round, grass-roofed, rammed-earth huts, open and empty. At night a burning lantern was placed in the entrance as protection against intruders. Our cook had no lantern; but as a compensation he had a miniature hut all to himself, with which he was highly pleased. But it nearly proved fatal to him. The previous day he had slaughtered in front of his hut a sheep that we had bought for five Uganda shillings, and had prepared excellent mutton chops for our evening meal. After dinner, while we were sitting around the fire, smoking, we heard strange noises in the distance. The sounds came closer. They sounded now like the growling of bears, now like the barking and yapping of dogs; then again the sounds became shrill, like shrieks and hysterical laughter. My first impression was: This is like a comic turn at Barnum and Bailey's. Before long, however, the scene became more menacing: we were surrounded on all sides by a huge pack of hungry hyenas who had obviously smelled the sheep's blood. They performed an infernal concert, and in the glow of the fire their eyes could be seen glittering from the tall elephant grass.

In spite of our lofty knowledge of the nature of hyenas, which are alleged not to attack man, we did not feel altogether sure of ourselves—and suddenly a frightful human scream came from behind the resthouse. We snatched up our arms (a nine-mm. Mannlicher rifle and a shotgun) and fired several rounds in the direction of those glittering lights. As we did so, our cook came rushing panic-stricken into our midst and babbled that a *fizi* had come into his hut and almost killed him. The whole camp was in an uproar. The excitement, it seemed, so frightened the pack of hyenas that they quit the scene, protesting noisily. The bearers went on laughing for a long time, after-which the rest of the night passed quietly, without further disturbance. Early next morning the local chief appeared with a gift of two chickens and a basketful of eggs. He implored us to stay another day to shoot the hyenas. The day before, he said, they had dragged out an old man asleep in his hut and eaten him. *De Africa nihil certum!*

At daybreak roars of laughter began again in the boys' quarters. It appeared that they were re-enacting the events of the night. One of them played the sleeping cook, and one of the soldiers played the creeping hyena, approaching the sleeper with murderous intent. This playlet was repeated I don't know how many times, to the utter delight of the audience.

From then on the cook bore the nickname "Fizi." We three whites already had our "trade-marks." My friend, the Englishman, was called "Red Neck"—to the native mind, all Englishmen had red necks. The American, who sported an impressive wardrobe, was known as *"bwana maredadi* (the dapper gentleman). Because I already had gray hair at the time (I was then fifty), I was the *"mzee,"* the old man, and was regarded as a hundred years old. Advanced age was rare in those parts; I saw very few white-haired men. Mzee is also a title of honor and was accorded to me in my capacity as head of the "Bugishu Psychological Expedition"—an appellation imposed by the Foreign Office in London as a *lucus a non lucendo*. We did visit the Bugishus, but spent a much longer time with the Elgonyis.

All in all, Negroes proved to be excellent judges of character. One of their avenues to insight lay in their talent for mimicry. They could imitate with astounding accuracy the manner of expression, the gestures, the gaits of people, thus, to all intents and purposes, slipping into their skins. I found their understanding of the emotional nature of others altogether surprising. I would always take the time to engage in the long palavers for which they had a pronounced fondness. In this way I learned a great deal.

Our traveling semi-officially proved advantageous, since in this way we found it easier to recruit bearers, and we were also given a military escort. The latter was by no means superfluous, since we were going to travel in territories that were not under white control. A corporal and two privates accompanied our safari to Mt. Elgon.

We could not help the chief by hunting the hyenas, and continued on our way after the adventure. The terrain sloped gently upward. Signs of Tertiary lava beds increased. We passed through glorious stretches of jungle with huge Nandi flame trees flaunting their red blossoms. Enormous beetles and even larger brilliantly colored butterflies enlivened the clearings and the edges of the jungle. Branches were shaken by inquisitive monkeys as we advanced further into the bush. It was a paradisal world. Most of the way we still traversed flat savanna with deep red soil. We tramped mostly along the native trails which meandered in strikingly sharp turns. Our route led us into the Nandi region, and through the Nandi Forest, a sizable area of jungle. Without incident we reached a resthouse at the foot of Mt. Elgon, which had been towering higher and higher above our heads for days. Here the climb began, along a narrow path. We were greeted by the local chief, who was the son of the *laibon,* the medicine man. He rode a pony—the only horse we had so far seen. From him we learned that his tribe belonged to the Masai, but lived in isolation here on the slopes of Mt. Elgon.

There a letter awaited us from the governor of Uganda, requesting us to take under our protection an English lady who was on her way back to Egypt via the Sudan. The governor was aware that we were following the same itinerary, and since we had already met the lady in Nairobi we knew that she would be a congenial companion. Moreover, we were under considerable obligation to the governor for his having helped us in all sorts of ways.

I mention this episode to suggest the subtle modes by which

an archetype influences our actions. We were three men; that was a matter of pure chance. I had asked another friend of mine to join us, which would have made a fourth. But circumstances had prevented him from accepting. That sufficed to produce an unconscious or fated constellation: the archetype of the triad, which calls for the fourth to complete it, as we have seen again and again in the history of this archetype.

Since I am inclined to accept chance when it comes my way, I welcomed the lady to our group of three men. Hardy and intrepid, she proved a useful counterpoise to our one-sided masculinity. When one of our party came down with a bad case of tropical malaria, we were grateful for the experience she had acquired as a nurse during the First World War.

After a few hours of climbing we reached a lovely large clearing, bisected by a clear, cool brook with a waterfall about ten feet in height. The pool at the bottom of the waterfall became our bath. Our campsite was situated about three hundred yards away, on a gentle, dry slope, shadowed by umbrella acacias. Nearby—that is, about fifteen minutes' walk away—was a native kraal which consisted of a few huts and a *boma*—a yard surrounded by a hedge of wait-a-bit thorn. This kraal provided us with our water bearers, a woman and her two half-grown daughters, who were naked except for a belt of cowries. They were chocolate-brown and strikingly pretty, with fine slim figures and an aristocratic leisureliness about their movements. It was a pleasure for me each morning to hear the soft *cling-clang* of their iron ankle rings as they came up from the brook, and soon afterward to see their swaying gait as they emerged from the tall yellow elephant grass, balancing the amphorae of water on their heads. They were adorned with ankle rings, brass bracelets and necklaces, earrings of copper or wood in the shape of small spools. Their lower lips were pierced with either a bone or iron nail. They had very good manners, and always greeted us with shy, charming smiles.

With a single exception, which I shall mention shortly, I never spoke to a native woman, this being what was expected of me. As in Southern Europe, men speak to men, women to women. Anything else signifies love-making. The white who goes in for this not only forfeits his authority, but runs the serious risk of "going black." I observed several highly instructive examples of this. Quite often I heard the natives pass judgment upon a certain white: "He is a bad man." When I asked why, the reply was invariably, "He sleeps with our women."

Among my Elgonyis, the men busied themselves with the cattle and with hunting; the women were identified with the *shamba*, a field of bananas, sweet potatoes, kaffir (grain sorghum), and maize. They kept children, goats, and chickens in the same round hut in which the family lived. Their dignity and naturalness flow from their function in the economy; they are intensely active business partners. The concept of equal rights for women is the product of an age in which such partnership has lost its meaning. Primitive society is regulated by an unconscious egoism and altruism; both attitudes are wisely given their due. This unconscious order breaks up at once if any disturbance ensues which has to be remedied by a conscious act.

It gives me pleasure to recall one of my important informants on family relations among the Elgonyi. He was a strikingly handsome youth by the name of Gibroat—the son of a chief, charming and distinguished in manners, whose confidence I had evidently won. To be sure, he gladly accepted my cigarettes, but he was not greedy for them, as the others were for all sorts of gifts. From time to time he would pay me a gentlemanly visit and tell me all sorts of interesting things. I felt that he had something in mind, some request that he somehow could not voice. Not until we had known each other for some time did he astonish me by asking me to meet his family. I knew that he himself was still unmarried, and that his parents were dead. The family in question was that of an elder sister; she was married as a second wife, and had four children. Gibroat very much wanted me to pay her a visit, so that she would have the opportunity to meet me. Evidently she filled the place of a mother in his life. I agreed, because I hoped in this social way to obtain some insight into native family life.

"Madame était chez elle"—she came out of the hut when we arrived, and greeted me with utter naturalness. She was a good-looking woman, middle-aged—that is, about thirty. Aside from

the obligatory cowrie belt, she wore arm and ankle rings, some copper ornaments hanging from the greatly extended ear lobe, and the skin of some small game animal over her breast. She had locked her four little *"mtotos"* in the hut; they peered out through cracks in the door, giggling excitedly. At my request she let them out; but it took some time before they dared to emerge. She had the same excellent manners as her brother, who was beaming joyfully at the success of his coup.

We did not sit down, since there was nowhere to sit except on the dusty ground, which was covered with chicken droppings and goat pellets. The conversation moved in the conventional framework of semi-familial drawing-room talk, revolving around family, children, house, and garden. Her elder co-wife, whose property bordered on hers, had six children. The *boma* of this "sister" was some eighty yards away. Approximately halfway between the two women's huts, at the apex of a triangle, stood the husband's hut, and behind that, about fifty yards away, a small hut occupied by the first wife's already grown son. Each of the two women had her own *shamba*. My hostess was obviously proud of hers.

I had the feeling that the confidence and self-assurance of her manner were founded to a great extent upon her identity with her own wholeness, her private world made up of children, house, small livestock, *shamba* and—last but not least—her not-unattractive physique. The husband was referred to only in an allusive way. It seemed that he was sometimes here, sometimes not here. At the moment he was staying at some unknown place. My hostess was plainly and unproblematically the embodiment of stability, a veritable *pied-à-terre* for the husband. The question did not seem to be whether or not *he* was there, but rather whether *she* was present in her wholeness, providing a geomagnetic center for the husband who wandered over the land with his herds. What goes on in the interior of these "simple" souls is not conscious, is therefore unknown, and we can only deduce it from comparative evidence of "advanced" European differentiation.

I asked myself whether the growing masculinization of the white woman is not connected with the loss of her natural wholeness (*shamba*, children, livestock, house of her own, hearth fire); whether it is not a compensation for her impoverishment; and whether the feminizing of the white man is not a further consequence. The more rational the polity, the more blurred is the difference between the sexes. The role homosexuality plays in modern society is enormous. It is partly the consequence of the mother-complex, partly a purposive phenomenon (prevention of reproduction).

My companions and I had the good fortune to taste the world of Africa, with its incredible beauty and its equally incredible suffering, before the end came. Our camp life proved to be one of the loveliest interludes in my life. I enjoyed the "divine peace" of a still primeval country. Never had I seen so clearly "man and the other animals" (Herodotus). Thousands of miles lay between me and Europe, mother of all demons. The demons could not reach me here—there were no telegrams, no telephone calls, no letters, no visitors. My liberated psychic forces poured blissfully back to the primeval expanses.

It was easy for us to arrange a palaver each morning with the natives who squatted all day long around our camp and watched our doings with never-fading interest. My headman, Ibrahim, had initiated me into the etiquette of the palaver. All the men (the women never came near) had to sit on the ground. Ibrahim had obtained for me a small four-legged chief's stool of mahogany on which I had to sit. Then I began with an address and set forth the *shauri*, that is, the agenda of the palaver. Most of the natives spoke a tolerable pidgin Swahili; and I for my part would manage to speak to them by making ample use of a small dictionary. This little book was the object of unwearying admiration. My limited vocabulary imposed upon me a needful simplicity. Often the conversation resembled an amusing game of guessing riddles, for which reason the palavers enjoyed great popularity. The sessions seldom lasted longer than an hour or an hour and a half, because the men grew visibly tired, and would complain, with dramatic gestures, "Alas, we are so tired."

I was naturally much interested in the natives' dreams, but at first could not get them to tell me any. I offered small rewards, cigarettes, matches, safety pins, and such things, which they were eager to have. But nothing helped. I could never completely explain their shyness about telling dreams. I suspect the reason was fear and distrust. It is well known that Negroes are afraid of being photographed; they fear that anyone who takes a picture of them is robbing them of their soul, and perhaps they likewise fear that harm may come to them from anyone who has knowledge of their dreams. This, incidentally, did not apply to our boys, who were coastal Somalis and Swahilis. They had an Arab dream book which they daily consulted during the trek. If they were in doubt about an interpretation, they would actually come to me for advice. They termed me a "man of the Book" because of my knowledge of the Koran. To their minds, I was a disguised Mohammedan.

One time we had a palaver with the *laibon,* the old medicine man. He appeared in a splendid cloak made of the skins of blue monkeys—a valuable article of display. When I asked him about his dreams, he answered with tears in his eyes, "In old days the *laibons* had dreams, and knew whether there is war or sickness or whether rain comes and where the herds should be driven." His grandfather, too, had still dreamed. But since the whites were in Africa, he said, no one had dreams any more. Dreams were no longer needed because now the English knew everything!

His reply showed me that the medicine man had lost his *raison d'être*. The divine voice which counseled the tribe was no longer needed because "the English know better." Formerly the medicine man had negotiated with the gods or the power of destiny, and had advised his people. He exerted great influence, just as in ancient Greece the word of the Pythia possessed the highest authority. Now the medicine man's authority was replaced by that of the D.C. The value of life now lay wholly in this world, and it seemed to me only a question of time and of the vitality of the black race before the Negroes would become conscious of the importance of physical power.

Far from being an imposing personality, our *laibon* was only a somewhat tearful old gentleman. He was the living embodiment of the spreading disintegration of an undermined, outmoded, unrestorable world.

On numerous occasions I brought the conversation around to the numina, especially to rites and ceremonies. Concerning these, I had only a single piece of evidence. In front of an empty hut, in the middle of a busy village street, I had seen a carefully swept spot several yards in diameter. In the center lay a cowrie belt, arm and ankle rings, earrings, the shards of all sorts of pots, and a digging stick. All that we were able to learn about this was the fact that a woman had died in this hut. Nothing whatsoever was said about a funeral.

In the palaver the people assured me with considerable emphasis that their neighbors to the west were "bad" people. If someone died there, the next village was informed, and in the evening the body was brought to the midpoint between the two villages. From the other side, presents of various sorts were brought to the same spot, and in the morning the corpse was no longer there. It was plainly insinuated that the other village devoured the dead. Such things never happened among the Elgonyi, they said. To be sure, their dead were laid out in the bush, where the hyenas took care of them in the course of the night. In point of fact we never found any signs of burial of the dead.

I was informed, however, that when a man dies, his body is placed on the floor in the middle of the hut. The *laibon* walks around the body, sprinkling milk from a bowl on to the floor, murmuring, *"Ayík adhísta, adhísta ayík!"*

I knew the meaning of these words from a memorable palaver that had taken place earlier. At the end of that palaver an old man had suddenly exclaimed, "In the morning, when the sun comes, we go out of the huts, spit into our hands, and hold them up to the sun." I had him show me the ceremony and describe it exactly. They held their hands in front of their mouths, spat or blew vigorously, then turned the palms upward toward the sun. I asked what this meant, why they blew or spat into their hands. My questioning was in vain. "We've always done it," they said. It was impossible to obtain any explanation, and I realized that they actually knew only that they did it, not what they were doing. They themselves saw no meaning in this action. But we, too, perform ceremonies without realizing what we are doing—such as lighting Christmas tree candles, hiding Easter eggs, etc.

The old man said that this was the true religion of all peoples, that all Kevirondos, all Buganda, all tribes for as far as the eye could see from the mountain and endlessly farther, worshiped *adhísta*—that is, the sun at the moment of rising. Only then was the sun *mungu,* God. The first delicate golden crescent of the new moon in the purple of the western sky was also God. But only at that time; otherwise not.

Evidently, the meaning of the Elgonyi ceremony was that an offering was being made to the sun divinity at the moment of its rising. If the gift was spittle, it was the substance which in the view of primitives contains the personal mana, the power of healing, magic, and life. If it was breath, then it was *roho*—Arabic, *ruch,* Hebrew, *ruach,* Greek, *pneuma*—wind and spirit. The act was therefore saying: I offer to God my living soul. It was a wordless, acted-out prayer which might equally well be rendered: "Lord, into thy hands I commend my spirit."

Besides *adhísta* the Elgonyi—we were further informed—also venerate *ayík,* the spirit who dwells in the earth and is a *sheitan* (devil). He is the creator of fear, a cold wind who lies in wait for the nocturnal traveler. The old man whistled a kind of Loki motif to convey vividly how the *ayík* creeps through the tall, mysterious grass of the bush.

In general the people asseverated that the Creator had made everything good and beautiful. He was beyond good and evil. He was *m'zuri,* that is, beautiful, and everything he did was *m'zuri.*

When I asked: "But what about the wicked animals who kill your cattle?" they said, "The lion is good and beautiful." "And your horrible diseases?" They said, "You lie in the sun and it is good."

I was impressed by this optimism. But at six o'clock in the evening this optimism was suddenly over, as I soon discovered. From sunset on, it was a different world—the dark world of *ayík,* of evil, danger, fear. The optimistic philosophy gave way to fear of ghosts and magical practices intended to secure pro-

tection from evil. Without any inner contradiction the optimism
returned at dawn.

It was a profoundly stirring experience for me to find, at the
sources of the Nile, this reminder of the ancient Egyptian conception of the two acolytes of Osiris, Horus and Set. Here, evidently, was a primordial African experience that had flowed
down to the coasts of the Mediterranean along with the sacred
waters of the Nile: *adhísta*, the rising sun, the principle of light
like Horus; *ayík*, the principle of darkness, the breeder of fear.
In the simple rites performed for the dead, the *laibon*'s words
and his sprinkling of milk unite the opposites; he simultaneously
sacrifices to these two principles, which are of equal power and
significance since the time of their dominance, the rule of day
and of night, each visibly lasts for twelve hours. The important
thing, however, is the moment when, with the typical suddenness of the tropics, the first ray of light shoots forth like an
arrow and night passes into life-filled light.

The sunrise in these latitudes was a phenomenon that overwhelmed me anew every day. The drama of it lay less in the
splendor of the sun's shooting up over the horizon than in what
happened afterward. I formed the habit of taking my camp
stool and sitting under an umbrella acacia just before dawn. Before me, at the bottom of the little valley, lay a dark, almost
black-green strip of jungle, with the rim of the plateau on the
opposite side of the valley towering above it. At first, the contrasts between light and darkness would be extremely sharp.
Then objects would assume contour and emerge into the light
which seemed to fill the valley with a compact brightness. The
horizon above became radiantly white. Gradually the swelling
light seemed to penetrate into the very structure of objects,
which became illuminated from within until at last they shone
translucently, like bits of colored glass. Everything turned to
flaming crystal. The cry of the bell bird rang around the horizon. At such moments I felt as if I were inside a temple. It was
the most sacred hour of the day. I drank in this glory with
insatiable delight, or rather, in a timeless ecstasy.

Near my observation point was a high cliff inhabited by big
baboons. Every morning they sat quietly, almost motionless, on

the ridge of the cliff facing the sun, whereas throughout the rest of the day they ranged noisily through the forest, screeching and chattering. Like me, they seemed to be waiting for the sunrise. They reminded me of the great baboons of the temple of Abu Simbel in Egypt, which perform the gesture of adoration. They tell the same story: for untold ages men have worshiped the great god who redeems the world by rising out of the darkness as a radiant light in the heavens.

At that time I understood that within the soul from its primordial beginnings there has been a desire for light and an irrepressible urge to rise out of the primal darkness. When the great night comes, everything takes on a note of deep dejection, and every soul is seized by an inexpressible longing for light. That is the pent-up feeling that can be detected in the eyes of primitives, and also in the eyes of animals. There is a sadness in animals' eyes, and we never know whether that sadness is bound up with the soul of the animal or is a poignant message which speaks to us out of that still unconscious existence. That sadness also reflects the mood of Africa, the experience of its solitudes. It is a maternal mystery, this primordial darkness. That is why the sun's birth in the morning strikes the natives as so overwhelmingly meaningful. The *moment* in which light comes *is* God. That moment brings redemption, release. To say that the *sun* is God is to blur and forget the archetypal experience of that moment. "We are glad that the night when the spirits are abroad is over now," the natives will say—but that is already a rationalization. In reality a darkness altogether different from natural night broods over the land. It is the psychic primal night which is the same today as it has been for countless millions of years. The longing for light is the longing for consciousness.

Our blissful stay on Mt. Elgon neared its end. With heavy hearts we struck our tents, promising ourselves that we would return. I could not have brought myself to think that this would be the first and the last time I would experience this unlooked-for glory. Since then, gold has been discovered near Kakamegas, mining has begun, the Mau-Mau movement has arisen among those innocent and friendly natives, and we too have known a rude awakening from the dream of civilization.

We trekked along the southern slope of Mt. Elgon. Gradually the character of the landscape changed. Higher mountains, covered with dense jungle, verged on the plain. The color of the inhabitants grew blacker; their bodies became clumsier and more massive, lacking the grace of the Masai. We were entering the territory of the Bugishu, where we stayed some time in the resthouse of Bunambale. It is situated at a high altitude, and we had a splendid view of the broad Nile valley. From there we went on to Mbala, where we were met by two Ford trucks that took us to Jinja, on Lake Victoria. We loaded our baggage onto a train of the narrow-gauge railroad; once every two weeks it went to Lake Kioga. A paddle-wheel steamer whose boiler was fired by wood picked us up and after a number of incidents brought us to Masindi Port. There we transferred to a truck and so reached Masindi Town, which is situated on the plateau that separates Lake Kioga from Albert Nyanza.

In a village on the way from Lake Albert to Rejâf in the Sudan we had a very exciting experience. The local chief, a tall, still quite young man, appeared with his retinue. These were the blackest Negroes I had ever seen. There was something about the group which was not exactly reassuring. The *mamur*[1] of Nimule had given us three askaris as an escort, but I saw that they as well as our own boys did not feel at all easy. After all, they had only three cartridges each for their rifles. Their presence, consequently, was a merely symbolic gesture on the part of the government.

When the chief proposed that he give a *n'goma* (dance) in the evening, I assented gladly. I hoped that the frolic would bring their better nature to the fore. Night had fallen and we were all longing for sleep when we heard drums and horn blasts. Soon some sixty men appeared, martially equipped with flashing lances, clubs, and swords. They were followed at some distance by the women and children; even the infants were present, carried on their mothers' backs. This was obviously to be a

---

[1] *El mamur,* literally, prefect or governor.

grand social occasion. In spite of the heat, which still hovered around ninety-three degrees, a big fire was kindled, and women and children formed a circle around it. The men formed an outer ring around them, as I had once observed a nervous herd of elephants do. I did not know whether I ought to feel pleased or anxious about this mass display. I looked around for our boys and the government soldiers—they had vanished completely from the camp! As a gesture of good will, I distributed cigarettes, matches, and safety pins. The men's chorus began to sing, vigorous, bellicose melodies, not unharmonious, and at the same time began to swing their legs. The women and children tripped around the fire; the men danced toward it, waving their weapons, then drew back again, and then advanced anew, amid savage singing, drumming, and trumpeting.

It was a wild and stirring scene, bathed in the glow of the fire and magical moonlight. My English friend and I sprang to our feet and mingled with the dancers. I swung my rhinoceros whip, the only weapon I had, and danced with them. By their beaming faces I could see that they approved of our taking part. Their zeal redoubled; the whole company stamped, sang, shouted, sweating profusely. Gradually the rhythm of the dance and the drumming accelerated.

In dances such as these, accompanied by such music, the natives easily fall into a virtual state of possession. That was the case now. As eleven o'clock approached, their excitement began to get out of bounds, and suddenly the whole affair took on a highly curious aspect. The dancers were being transformed into a wild horde, and I became worried about how it would end. I signed to the chief that it was time to stop, and that he and his people ought to go to sleep. But he kept wanting "just another one."

I remembered that a countryman of mine, one of the Sarasin cousins, on an exploratory expedition in Celebes had been struck by a stray spear in the course of such a *n'goma*. And so, disregarding the chief's pleas, I called the people together, distributed cigarettes, and then made the gesture of sleeping. Then I swung my rhinoceros whip threateningly, but at the same time laughing, and for lack of any better language I swore at them loudly in Swiss German that this was enough and they must go home to bed and sleep now. It was apparent to the people that I was to some extent pretending my anger, but that seems to have struck just the right note. General laughter arose; capering, they scattered in all directions and vanished into the night. For a long time we heard their jovial howls and drumming in the distance. At last silence fell, and we dropped into the sleep of exhaustion.

Our trek came to an end in Rejâf on the Nile. There we stowed our gear onto a paddle-wheel steamer which just succeeded in docking at Rejâf; the water level was almost too low for it. By this time I was feeling burdened by all that I had experienced. A thousand thoughts were whirling around me, and it became painfully clear to me that my capacity to digest new impressions was quickly approaching its limits. The thing to do was to go over all my observations and experiences and discover their inner connections. I had written down everything worth noting.

During the entire trip my dreams stubbornly followed the tactic of ignoring Africa. They drew exclusively upon scenes from home, and thus seemed to say that they considered—if it is permissible to personify the unconscious processes to this extent—the African journey not as something real, but rather as a symptomatic or symbolic act. Even the most impressive events of the trip were rigorously excluded from my dreams. Only once during the entire expedition did I dream of a Negro. His face appeared curiously familiar to me, but I had to reflect a long time before I could determine where I had met him before. Finally it came to me: he had been my barber in Chattanooga, Tennessee! An American Negro. In the dream he was holding a tremendous, red-hot curling iron to my head, intending to make my hair kinky—that is, to give me Negro hair. I could already feel the painful heat, and awoke with a sense of terror.

I took this dream as a warning from the unconscious; it was saying that the primitive was a danger to me. At that time I was obviously all too close to "going black." I was suffering an attack of sandfly fever which probably reduced my psychic resistance. In order to represent a Negro threatening me, my unconscious had invoked a twelve-year-old memory of my Negro barber in America, just in order to avoid any reminder of the present.

This curious behavior of my dreams corresponds, incidentally, to a phenomenon which was noted during the First World War. Soldiers in the field dreamt far less of the war than of their homes. Military psychiatrists considered it a basic principle that a man should be pulled out of the front lines when he started dreaming too much of war scenes, for that meant he no longer possessed any psychic defenses against the impressions from outside.

Parallel to my involvement with this demanding African environment, an interior line was being successfully secured within my dreams. The dreams dealt with my personal problems. The only thing I could conclude from this was that my European personality must under all circumstances be preserved intact.

To my astonishment, the suspicion dawned on me that I had undertaken my African adventure with the secret purpose of escaping from Europe and its complex of problems, even at the risk of remaining in Africa, as so many before me had done, and as so many were doing at this very time. The trip revealed itself as less an investigation of primitive psychology ("Bugishu Psychological Expedition," B.P.E., black letters on the chop boxes!) than a probing into the rather embarrassing question: What is going to happen to Jung the psychologist in the wilds of Africa? This was a question I had constantly sought to evade, in spite of my intellectual intention to study the European's reaction to primitive conditions. It became clear to me that this study had been not so much an objective scientific project as an intensely personal one, and that any attempt to go deeper into it touched every possible sore spot in my own psychology. I had to admit to myself that it was scarcely the Wembley Exhibition which had begotten my decision to travel, but rather the fact that the atmosphere had become too highly charged for me in Europe.

Amid such thoughts I glided on the peaceful waters of the Nile toward the north—toward Europe, toward the future. The voyage ended at Khartoum. There Egypt began. And thus I fulfilled my desire and my plan to approach this cultural realm not from the west, from the direction of Europe and Greece, but from the south, from the sources of the Nile. I was less interested in the complex Asiatic elements in Egyptian culture than in the Hamitic contribution. By following the geographical course of the Nile, and hence the stream of time, I could find out something about that for myself. My greatest illumination in this respect had been my discovery of the Horus principle among the Elgonyi. That whole episode, and all that it meant, was dramatically called to mind again when I saw the sculptured cynocephali (dog-faced baboons) of Abu Simbel, the southern gate of Egypt.

The myth of Horus is the age-old story of the newly risen divine light. It is a myth which must have been told after human culture—that is, consciousness—had for the first time released men from the darkness of prehistoric times. Thus the journey from the heart of Africa to Egypt became, for me, a kind of drama of the birth of light. That drama was intimately connected with me, with my psychology. I realized this, but felt incapable of formulating it in words. I had not known in advance what Africa would give me; but here lay the satisfying answer, the fulfilling experience. It was worth more to me than any ethnological yield would have been, any collection of weapons, ornaments, pottery, or hunting trophies. I had wanted to know how Africa would affect me, and I had found out.

iv. INDIA [2]

My journey to India, in 1938, was not taken on my own initiative. It arose out of an invitation from the British Government of India to take part in the celebrations connected with the twenty-fifth anniversary of the University of Calcutta.

By that time I had read a great deal about Indian philosophy and religious history, and was deeply convinced of the value of

[2] On his return from India, Jung contributed two articles to the magazine *Asia* (New York, January and February issues, 1939): "The Dreamlike World of India," and "What India Can Teach Us." They are included in *Civilization in Transition* (CW 10).—A. J.

Oriental wisdom. But I had to travel in order to form my own conclusions, and remained within myself like a homunculus in the retort. India affected me like a dream, for I was and remained in search of myself, of the truth peculiar to myself.

The journey formed an intermezzo in the intensive study of alchemical philosophy on which I was engaged at the time. This had so strong a grip upon me that I took along the first volume of the *Theatrum Chemicum* of 1602, which contains the principal writings of Gerardus Dorneus. In the course of the voyage I studied the book from beginning to end. Thus it was that this material belonging to the fundamental strata of European thought was constantly counterpointed by my impressions of a foreign mentality and culture. Both had emerged from original psychic experiences of the unconscious, and therefore had produced the same, similar, or at least comparable insights.

India gave me my first direct experience of an alien, highly differentiated culture. Altogether different elements had ruled my Central African journey; culture had not predominated. As for North Africa, I had never had the opportunity there to talk with a person capable of putting his culture into words. In India, however, I had the chance to speak with representatives of the Indian mentality, and to compare it with the European. I had searching talks with S. Subramanya Iyer, the guru of the Maharajah of Mysore, whose guest I was for some time; also with many others, whose names unfortunately have escaped me. On the other hand, I studiously avoided all so-called "holy men." I did so because I had to make do with my own truth, not accept from others what I could not attain on my own. I would have felt it as a theft had I attempted to learn from the holy men and to accept their truth for myself. Neither in Europe can I make any borrowings from the East, but must shape my life out of myself—out of what my inner being tells me, or what nature brings to me.

In India I was principally concerned with the question of the psychological nature of evil. I had been very much impressed by the way this problem is integrated in Indian spiritual life, and I saw it in a new light. In a conversation with a cultivated Chinese I was also impressed, again and again, by the fact that these people are able to integrate so-called "evil" without "losing face." In the West we cannot do this. For the Oriental the problem of morality does not appear to take first place, as it does for us. To the Oriental, good and evil are meaningfully contained in nature, and are merely varying degrees of the same thing.

I saw that Indian spirituality contains as much of evil as of good. The Christian strives for good and succumbs to evil; the Indian feels himself to be outside good and evil, and seeks to realize this state by meditation or yoga. My objection is that, given such an attitude, neither good nor evil takes on any real outline, and this produces a certain stasis. One does not really believe in evil, and one does not really believe in good. Good or evil are then regarded at most as *my* good or *my* evil, as whatever seems to me good or evil—which leaves us with the paradoxical statement that Indian spirituality lacks both evil and good, or is so burdened by contradictions that it needs *nirdvandva*, the liberation from opposites and from the ten thousand things.

The Indian's goal is not moral perfection, but the condition of *nirdvandva*. He wishes to free himself from nature; in keeping with this aim, he seeks in meditation the condition of imagelessness and emptiness. I, on the other hand, wish to persist in the state of lively contemplation of nature and of the psychic images. I want to be freed neither from human beings, nor from myself, nor from nature; for all these appear to me the greatest of miracles. Nature, the psyche, and life appear to me like divinity unfolded—and what more could I wish for? To me the supreme meaning of Being can consist only in the fact that it *is*, not that it is not or is no longer.

To me there is no liberation *à tout prix*. I cannot be liberated from anything that I do not possess, have not done or experienced. Real liberation becomes possible for me only when I have done all that I was able to do, when I have completely devoted myself to a thing and participated in it to the utmost. If I withdraw from participation, I am virtually amputating the corresponding part of my psyche. Naturally, there may be good reasons for my not immersing myself in a given experience. But then I am forced to confess my inability, and must know that I may have neglected to do something of vital importance. In this way I make amends for the lack of a positive act by the clear knowledge of my incompetence.

A man who has not passed through the inferno of his passions has never overcome them. They then dwell in the house next door, and at any moment a flame may dart out and set fire to his own house. Whenever we give up, leave behind, and forget too much, there is always the danger that the things we have neglected will return with added force.

In Konarak (Orissa) I met a pandit who obligingly offered to come with me on my visit to the temple and the great temple car. The pagoda is covered from base to pinnacle with exquisitely obscene sculptures. We talked for a long time about this extraordinary fact, which he explained to me as a means to achieve spiritualization. I objected—pointing to a group of young peasants who were standing open-mouthed before the monument, admiring these splendors—that such young men were scarcely undergoing spiritualization at the moment, but were much more likely having their heads filled with sexual fantasies. Whereupon he replied, "But that is just the point. How can they ever become spiritualized if they do not first fulfill their karma? These admittedly obscene images are here for the very purpose of recalling to the people their dharma [law]; otherwise these unconscious fellows might forget it."

I thought it an odd notion that young men might forget their sexuality, like animals out of rutting time. My sage, however, resolutely maintained that they were as unconscious as animals and actually in need of urgent admonishments. To this end, he said, before they set foot inside the temple they were reminded of their dharma by the exterior decorations; for unless they were made conscious of their dharma and fulfilled it, they could not partake of spiritualization.

As we entered through the gate of the temple, my companion pointed to the two "temptresses," statues of two dancing girls with seductively curved hips who smilingly greeted all who entered. "Do you see these two dancing girls?" he said. "Their meaning is the same. Naturally, this does not apply to people like you and me, for we have attained to a level of consciousness which is above this sort of thing. But for these peasant boys it is an indispensable instruction and admonishment."

When we left the temple and were walking down a lingam lane, he suddenly said, "Do you see these stones? Do you know what they mean? I will tell you a great secret." I was astonished, for I thought that the phallic nature of these monuments was known to every child. But he whispered into my ear with the greatest seriousness, "These stones are man's private parts." I had expected him to tell me that they signified the great god Shiva. I looked at him dumfounded, but he only nodded self-importantly, as if to say, "Yes, that is how it is. No doubt you in your European ignorance would never have thought so!" When I told this story to Heinrich Zimmer, he exclaimed in delight, "At last I have heard something real about India for a change!"

When I visited the stupas of Sanchi, where Buddha delivered his fire sermon, I was overcome by a strong emotion of the kind that frequently develops in me when I encounter a thing, person, or idea of whose significance I am still unconscious. The stupas are situated on a rocky hill whose peak can be reached by a pleasant path of great stone slabs laid down through a green meadow. The stupas are tombs or containers of relics, hemispherical in shape, like two gigantic rice bowls placed one on top of the other (concavity upon concavity), according to the prescripts of the Buddha himself in the *Mahâ-Parinibbâna-Sutta*. The British have done their restoration work in a most respectful spirit. The largest of these buildings is surrounded by a wall which has four elaborate gates. You come in by one of these and the path turns to the left, then leads into a clockwise circumambulation around the stupa. At the four cardinal points stand statues of the Buddha. When you have completed one circumambulation, you enter a second, higher circuit which runs in the same direction. The distant prospect over the plain, the stupas themselves, the temple ruins, and the solitary stillness of this holy site held me in a spell. I took leave of my companion and submerged myself in the overpowering mood of the place.

After a while I heard rhythmic gong tones approaching from the distance. A group of Japanese pilgrims came marching up one behind the other, each striking a small gong. They were beating out the rhythm of the age-old prayer *Om mani padme hum,* the stroke of the gong falling upon the *hum.* Outside the stupas they bowed low, then passed through the gate. There they bowed again before the statue of the Buddha, intoning a chorale-like song. They completed the double circumambulation, singing a hymn before each statue of the Buddha. As I watched them, my mind and spirit were with them, and something within me silently thanked them for having so wonderfully come to the aid of my inarticulate feelings.

The intensity of my emotion showed that the hill of Sanchi meant something central to me. A new side of Buddhism was revealed to me there. I grasped the life of the Buddha as the reality of the self which had broken through and laid claim to a personal life. For Buddha, the self stands above all gods, a *unus mundus* which represents the essence of human existence and of the world as a whole. The self embodies both the aspect of intrinsic being and the aspect of its being known, without which no world exists. Buddha saw and grasped the cosmogonic dignity of human consciousness; for that reason he saw clearly that if a man succeeded in extinguishing this light, the world would sink into nothingness. Schopenhauer's great achievement lay in his also recognizing this, or rediscovering it independently.

Christ—like Buddha—is an embodiment of the self, but in an altogether different sense. Both stood for an overcoming of the world: Buddha out of rational insight; Christ as a foredoomed sacrifice. In Christianity more is suffered, in Buddhism more is seen and done. Both paths are right, but in the Indian sense Buddha is the more complete human being. He is a historical personality, and therefore easier for men to understand. Christ is at once a historical man and God, and therefore much more difficult to comprehend. At bottom he was not comprehensible even to himself; he knew only that he had to sacrifice himself, that this course was imposed upon him from within. His sacrifice happened to him like an act of destiny. Buddha lived out his life and died at an advanced age, whereas Christ's activity as Christ probably lasted no more than a year.

Later, Buddhism underwent the same transformation as Christianity: Buddha became, as it were, the image of the development of the self; he became a model for men to imitate, whereas actually he had preached that by overcoming the Nidana-chain every human being could become an illuminate, a buddha. Similarly, in Christianity, Christ is an exemplar who dwells in every Christian as his integral personality. But historical trends led to the *imitatio Christi,* whereby the individual does not pursue his own destined road to wholeness, but attempts to imitate the way taken by Christ. Similarly in the East, historical trends led to a devout imitation of the Buddha. That Buddha should have become a model to be imitated was in itself a weakening of his idea, just as the *imitatio Christi* was a forerunner of the fateful stasis in the evolution of the Christian idea. As Buddha, by virtue of his insight, was far in advance of the Brahma gods, so Christ cried out to the Jews, "You are gods" (John 10:34); but men were incapable of understanding what he meant. Instead we find that the so-called Christian West, far from creating a new world, is moving with giant strides toward the possibility of destroying the world we have.[3]

India honored me with three doctorates, from Allahabad, Benares, and Calcutta—representatives of Islam, of Hinduism, and of British-Indian medicine and science. It was a little too much of a good thing, and I needed a retreat. A ten-day spell in the hospital offered it to me, for in Calcutta I finally came down with dysentery. This was a blessed island in the wild sea of new impressions, and I found a place to stand on from which I could contemplate the ten thousand things and their bewildering turmoil.

When I returned to the hotel, in tolerably good health, I had a dream so characteristic that I wish to set it down here. I found myself, with a large number of my Zürich friends and acquaintances, on an unknown island, presumably situated not far off the coast of southern England. It was small and almost uninhabited. The island was narrow, a strip of land about twenty miles long, running in a north-south direction. On the rocky coast at the southern end of the island was a medieval castle.

[3] On the problem of the *imitatio,* cf. *Psychology and Alchemy,* Part I (CW 12).

We stood in its courtyard, a group of sightseeing tourists. Before us rose an imposing *belfroi*, through whose gate a wide stone staircase was visible. We could just manage to see that it terminated above in a columned hall. This hall was dimly illuminated by candlelight. I understood that this was the castle of the Grail, and that this evening there would be a "celebration of the Grail" here. This information seemed to be of a secret character, for a German professor among us, who strikingly resembled old Mommsen, knew nothing about it. I talked most animatedly with him, and was impressed by his learning and sparkling intelligence. Only one thing disturbed me: he spoke constantly about a dead past and lectured very learnedly on the relationship of the British to the French sources of the Grail story. Apparently he was not conscious of the meaning of the legend, nor of its living presentness, whereas I was intensely aware of both. Also, he did not seem to perceive our immediate, actual surroundings, for he behaved as though he were in a classroom, lecturing to his students. In vain I tried to call his attention to the peculiarity of the situation. He did not see the stairs or the festive glow in the hall.

I looked around somewhat helplessly, and discovered that I was standing by the wall of a tall castle; the lower portion of the wall was covered by a kind of trellis, not made of the usual wood, but of black iron artfully formed into a grapevine complete with leaves, twining tendrils, and grapes. At intervals of six feet on the horizontal branches were tiny houses, likewise of iron, like birdhouses. Suddenly I saw a movement in the foliage; at first it seemed to be that of a mouse, but then I saw distinctly a tiny, iron, hooded gnome, a *cucullatus*, scurrying from one little house to the next. "Well," I exclaimed in astonishment to the professor, "now look at that, will you . . ."

At that moment a hiatus occurred, and the dream changed. We—the same company as before, but without the professor—were outside the castle, in a treeless, rocky landscape. I knew that something had to happen, for the Grail was not yet in the castle and still had to be celebrated that same evening. It was said to be in the northern part of the island, hidden in a small, uninhabited house, the only house there. I knew that it was our task to bring the Grail to the castle. There were about six of us who set out and tramped northward.

After several hours of strenuous hiking, we reached the narrowest part of the island, and I discovered that the island was actually divided into two halves by an arm of the sea. At the smallest part of this strait the width of the water was about a hundred yards. The sun had set, and night descended. Wearily, we camped on the ground. The region was unpopulated and desolate; far and wide there was not a tree or shrub, nothing but grass and rocks. There was no bridge, no boat. It was very cold; my companions fell asleep, one after the other. I considered what could be done, and came to the conclusion that I alone must swim across the channel and fetch the Grail. I took off my clothes. At that point I awoke.

Here was this essentially European dream emerging when I had barely worked my way out of the overwhelming mass of Indian impressions. Some ten years before, I had discovered that in many places in England the myth of the Grail was still a living thing, in spite of all the scholarship that has accumulated around this tradition. This fact had impressed me all the more when I realized the concordance between this poetic myth and what alchemy had to say about the *unum vas,* the *una medicina,* and the *unus lapis.* Myths which day has forgotten continue to be told by night, and powerful figures which consciousness has reduced to banality and ridiculous triviality are recognized again by poets and prophetically revived; therefore they can also be recognized "in changed form" by the thoughtful person. The great ones of the past have not died, as we think; they have merely changed their names. "Small and slight, but great in might," the veiled Kabir enters a new house.

Imperiously, the dream wiped away all the intense impressions of India and swept me back to the too-long-neglected concerns of the Occident, which had formerly been expressed in the quest for the Holy Grail as well as in the search for the philosophers' stone. I was taken out of the world of India, and reminded that India was not my task, but only a part of the way —admittedly a significant one—which should carry me closer to my goal. It was as though the dream were asking me, "What are you doing in India? Rather seek for yourself and your fellows the healing vessel, the *servator mundi,* which you urgently need. For your state is perilous; you are all in imminent danger of destroying all that centuries have built up."

Ceylon, the last stage of my journey, struck me as no longer India; there is already something of the South Seas about it, and a touch of paradise, in which one cannot linger too long. Colombo is a busy international port where every day between five and six o'clock a massive downpour descends from a clear sky. We soon left it behind and headed for the hilly country of the interior. There Kandy, the old royal city, is swathed in a fine mist whose tepid humidity sustains a luxuriant vegetation. The Dalada-Maligawa Temple, which contains the relic of the Holy Tooth (of Buddha), is small, but radiates a special charm. I spent a considerable time in its library, talking with the monks, and looking at the texts of the Buddhist canon engraved on silver leaves.

There I witnessed a memorable evening ceremony. Young men and girls poured out enormous mounds of jasmine flowers in front of the altars, at the same time singing a prayer under their breath: *a mantram.* I thought they were praying to Buddha, but the monk who was guiding me explained, "No, Buddha is no more; He is in nirvana; we cannot pray to him. They are singing: 'This life is transitory as the beauty of these flowers. May my God⁴ share with me the merit of this offering.'"

As a prelude to the ceremony a one-hour drum concert was performed in the *mandapam,* or what in Indian temples is called the hall of waiting. There were five drummers; one stood in each corner of the square hall, and the fifth, a young man, stood in the middle. He was the soloist, and a very fine drummer. Naked to the waist, his dark-brown trunk glistening, with a red girdle, white *shoka* (a long skirt reaching to the feet), and white turban, arms covered with shining bracelets, he stepped up to the golden Buddha, bearing a double drum, "to sacrifice the music." There, with beautiful movements of body and arms, he drummed alone a strange melody, artistically perfect. I watched

⁴ God = *deva* = guardian angel.

him from behind; he stood in front of the entrance to the *mandapam*, which was covered with little oil lamps. The drum speaks the ancient language of the belly and solar plexus; the belly does not "pray" but engenders the "meritorious" *mantram* or meditative utterance. It is therefore not adoration of a non-existent Buddha, but one of the many acts of self-redemption performed by the awakened human being.

Toward the beginning of spring I set out on my homeward voyage, with such a plethora of impressions that I did not have any desire to leave the ship to see Bombay. Instead, I buried myself in my Latin alchemical texts. But India did not pass me by without a trace; it left tracks which lead from one infinity into another infinity.

v. RAVENNA AND ROME

Even on the occasion of my first visit to Ravenna in 1913, the tomb of Galla Placidia seemed to me significant and unusually fascinating. The second time, twenty years later, I had the same feeling. Once more I fell into a strange mood in the tomb of Galla Placidia; once more I was deeply stirred. I was there with an acquaintance, and we went directly from the tomb into the Baptistery of the Orthodox.

Here, what struck me first was the mild blue light that filled the room; yet I did not wonder about this at all. I did not try to account for its source, and so the wonder of this light without any visible source did not trouble me. I was somewhat amazed because, in place of the windows I remembered having seen on my first visit, there were now four great mosaic frescoes of incredible beauty which, it seemed, I had entirely forgotten. I was vexed to find my memory so unreliable. The mosaic on the south side represented the baptism in the Jordan; the second picture, on the north, was of the passage of the Children of Israel through the Red Sea; the third, on the east, soon faded from my memory. It might have shown Naaman being cleansed of leprosy in the Jordan; there was a picture on this theme in the old Merian Bible in my library, which was much like the mosaic.

The fourth mosaic, on the west side of the baptistery, was the most impressive of all. We looked at this one last. It represented Christ holding out his hand to Peter, who was sinking beneath the waves. We stopped in front of this mosaic for at least twenty minutes and discussed the original ritual of baptism, especially the curious archaic conception of it as an initiation connected with real peril of death. Such initiations were often connected with the peril of death and so served to express the archetypal idea of death and rebirth. Baptism had originally been a real submersion which at least suggested the danger of drowning.

I retained the most distinct memory of the mosaic of Peter sinking, and to this day can see every detail before my eyes: the blue of the sea, individual chips of the mosaic, the inscribed scrolls proceeding from the mouths of Peter and Christ, which I attempted to decipher. After we left the baptistery, I went promptly to Alinari to buy photographs of the mosaics, but could not find any. Time was pressing—this was only a short visit—and so I postponed the purchase until later. I thought I might order the pictures from Zürich.

When I was back home, I asked an acquaintance who was going to Ravenna to obtain the pictures for me. He could not locate them, for he discovered that the mosaics I had described did not exist.

Meanwhile, I had already spoken at a seminar about the original conception of baptism, and on this occasion had also mentioned the mosaics that I had seen in the Baptistery of the Orthodox.[5] The memory of those pictures is still vivid to me. The lady who had been there with me long refused to believe that what she had "seen with her own eyes" had not existed.

As we know, it is very difficult to determine whether, and to what extent, two persons simultaneously see the same thing. In this case, however, I was able to ascertain that at least the main features of what we both saw had been the same.

This experience in Ravenna is among the most curious events in my life. It can scarcely be explained. A certain light may possibly be cast on it by an incident in the story of Empress

[5] Tantra Yoga Seminar, 1932.

Galla Placidia (d. 450). During a stormy crossing from Byzantium to Ravenna in the worst of winter, she made a vow that if she came through safely, she would build a church and have the perils of the sea represented in it. She kept this vow by building the basilica of San Giovanni in Ravenna and having it adorned with mosaics. In the early Middle Ages, San Giovanni, together with its mosaics, was destroyed by fire; but in the Ambrosiana in Milan is still to be found a sketch representing Galla Placidia in a boat.

I had, from the first visit, been personally affected by the figure of Galla Placidia, and had often wondered how it must have been for this highly cultivated, fastidious woman to live at the side of a barbarian prince. Her tomb seemed to me a final legacy through which I might reach her personality. Her fate and her whole being were vivid presences to me; with her intense nature, she was a suitable embodiment for my anima.[6]

The anima of a man has a strongly historical character. As a personification of the unconscious she goes back into prehistory, and embodies the contents of the past. She provides the individual with those elements that he ought to know about his prehistory. To the individual, the anima is all life that has been in the past and is still alive in him. In comparison to her I have always felt myself to be a barbarian who really has no history—like a creature just sprung out of nothingness, with neither a past nor a future.

In the course of my confrontation with the anima I had actually had a brush with those perils which I saw represented in the mosaics. I had come close to drowning. The same thing happened to me as to Peter, who cried for help and was rescued by Jesus. What had been the fate of Pharaoh's army could have been mine. Like Peter and like Naaman, I came away unscathed, and the integration of the unconscious contents made an essential contribution to the completion of my personality.

[6] Jung himself explained the vision as a momentary new creation by the unconscious, arising out of his thoughts about archetypal initiation. The immediate cause of the concretization lay, in his opinion, in a projection of his anima upon Galla Placidia.—A. J.

What happens within oneself when one integrates previously unconscious contents with the consciousness is something which can scarcely be described in words. It can only be experienced. It is a subjective affair quite beyond discussion; we have a particular feeling about ourselves, about the way we are, and that is a fact which it is neither possible nor meaningful to doubt. Similarly, we convey a particular feeling to others, and that too is a fact that cannot be doubted. So far as we know, there is no higher authority which could eliminate the probable discrepancies between all these impressions and opinions. Whether a change has taken place as the result of integration, and what the nature of that change is, remains a matter of subjective conviction. To be sure, it is not a fact which can be scientifically verified and therefore finds no place in an official view of the world. Yet it nevertheless remains a fact which is in practice uncommonly important and fraught with consequences. Realistic psychotherapists, at any rate, and psychologists interested in therapy, can scarcely afford to overlook facts of this sort.

Since my experience in the baptistery in Ravenna, I know with certainty that something interior can seem to be exterior, and that something exterior can appear to be interior. The actual walls of the baptistery, though they must have been seen by my physical eyes, were covered over by a vision of some altogether different sight which was as completely real as the unchanged baptismal font. Which was real at that moment?

My case is by no means the only one of its kind. But when that sort of thing happens to oneself, one cannot help taking it more seriously than something heard or read about. In general, with anecdotes of that kind, one is quick to think of all sorts of explanations which dispose of the mystery. I have come to the conclusion that before we settle upon any theories in regard to the unconscious, we require many, many more experiences of it.

I have traveled a great deal in my life, and I should very much have liked to go to Rome, but I felt that I was not really up to the impression the city would have made upon me. Pompeii alone was more than enough; the impressions very nearly exceeded my powers of receptivity. I was able to visit Pompeii only after I had acquired, through my studies of 1910 to 1912, some insight into the psychology of classical antiquity. In 1912 I was on a ship sailing from Genoa to Naples. As the vessel neared the latitude of Rome, I stood at the railing. Out there lay Rome, the still smoking and fiery hearth from which ancient cultures had spread, enclosed in the tangled rootwork of the Christian and Occidental Middle Ages. There classical antiquity still lived in all its splendor and ruthlessness.

I always wonder about people who go to Rome as they might go, for example, to Paris or to London. Certainly Rome as well as these other cities can be enjoyed esthetically; but if you are affected to the depths of your being at every step by the spirit that broods there, if a remnant of a wall here and a column there gaze upon you with a face instantly recognized, then it becomes another matter entirely. Even in Pompeii unforeseen vistas opened, unexpected things became conscious, and questions were posed which were beyond my powers to handle.

In my old age—in 1949—I wished to repair this omission, but was stricken with a faint while I was buying tickets. After that, the plans for a trip to Rome were once and for all laid aside.

· X ·

Visions

A T T H E B E G I N N I N G of 1944 I broke my foot, and this misadventure was followed by a heart attack. In a state of unconsciousness I experienced deliriums and visions which must have begun when I hung on the edge of death and was being given oxygen and camphor injections. The images were so tremendous that I myself concluded that I was close to death. My nurse afterward told me, "It was as if you were surrounded by a bright glow." That was a phenomenon she had sometimes observed in the dying, she added. I had reached the outermost limit, and do not know whether I was in a dream or an ecstasy. At any rate, extremely strange things began to happen to me.

It seemed to me that I was high up in space. Far below I saw the globe of the earth, bathed in a gloriously blue light. I saw the deep blue sea and the continents. Far below my feet lay Ceylon, and in the distance ahead of me the subcontinent of India. My field of vision did not include the whole earth, but its global shape was plainly distinguishable and its outlines shone with a silvery gleam through that wonderful blue light. In many places the globe seemed colored, or spotted dark green like oxydized silver. Far away to the left lay a broad expanse—the reddish-yellow desert of Arabia; it was as though the silver of the earth had there assumed a reddish-gold hue. Then came the Red Sea, and far, far back—as if in the upper left of a map—I could just make out a bit of the Mediterranean. My gaze was directed chiefly toward that. Everything else appeared indistinct. I could also see the snow-covered Himalayas, but in that direction it was foggy or cloudy. I did not look to the right at all. I knew that I was on the point of departing from the earth.

Later I discovered how high in space one would have to be to have so extensive a view—approximately a thousand miles! The sight of the earth from this height was the most glorious thing I had ever seen.

After contemplating it for a while, I turned around. I had been standing with my back to the Indian Ocean, as it were, and my face to the north. Then it seemed to me that I made a turn to the south. Something new entered my field of vision. A short distance away I saw in space a tremendous dark block of stone, like a meteorite. It was about the size of my house, or even bigger. It was floating in space, and I myself was floating in space.

I had seen similar stones on the coast of the Gulf of Bengal. They were blocks of tawny granite, and some of them had been hollowed out into temples. My stone was one such gigantic dark block. An entrance led into a small antechamber. To the right of the entrance, a black Hindu sat silently in lotus posture upon a stone bench. He wore a white gown, and I knew that he expected me. Two steps led up to this antechamber, and inside, on the left, was the gate to the temple. Innumerable tiny niches, each with a saucer-like concavity filled with coconut oil and small burning wicks, surrounded the door with a wreath of bright flames. I had once actually seen this when I visited the Temple of the Holy Tooth at Kandy in Ceylon; the gate had been framed by several rows of burning oil lamps of this sort.

As I approached the steps leading up to the entrance into the rock, a strange thing happened: I had the feeling that everything was being sloughed away; everything I aimed at or wished for or thought, the whole phantasmagoria of earthly existence, fell away or was stripped from me—an extremely painful process. Nevertheless something remained; it was as if I now carried along with me everything I had ever experienced or done, everything that had happened around me. I might also say: it was with me, and I was it. I consisted of all that, so to speak. I consisted of my own history, and I felt with great certainty: this is what I am. "I am this bundle of what has been, and what has been accomplished."

This experience gave me a feeling of extreme poverty, but at the same time of great fullness. There was no longer anything I wanted or desired. I existed in an objective form; I was what I had been and lived. At first the sense of annihilation predominated, of having been stripped or pillaged; but suddenly that became of no consequence. Everything seemed to be past; what remained was a *fait accompli*, without any reference back to what had been. There was no longer any regret that something had dropped away or been taken away. On the contrary: I had everything that I was, and that was everything.

Something else engaged my attention: as I approached the temple I had the certainty that I was about to enter an illuminated room and would meet there all those people to whom I belong in reality. There I would at last understand—this too was a certainty—what historical nexus I or my life fitted into. I would know what had been before me, why I had come into being, and where my life was flowing. My life as I lived it had often seemed to me like a story that has no beginning and no end. I had the feeling that I was a historical fragment, an excerpt for which the preceding and succeeding text was missing. My life seemed to have been snipped out of a long chain of events, and many questions had remained unanswered. Why had it taken this course? Why had I brought these particular assumptions with me? What had I made of them? What will follow? I felt sure that I would receive an answer to all these questions as soon as I entered the rock temple. There I would learn why everything had been thus and not otherwise. There I would meet the people who knew the answer to my question about what had been before and what would come after.

While I was thinking over these matters, something happened

that caught my attention. From below, from the direction of Europe, an image floated up. It was my doctor, Dr. H.—or, rather, his likeness—framed by a golden chain or a golden laurel wreath. I knew at once: "Aha, this is my doctor, of course, the one who has been treating me. But now he is coming in his primal form, as a *basileus* of Kos.[1] In life he was an avatar of this *basileus*, the temporal embodiment of the primal form, which has existed from the beginning. Now he is appearing in that primal form."

Presumably I too was in my primal form, though this was something I did not observe but simply took for granted. As he stood before me, a mute exchange of thought took place between us. Dr. H. had been delegated by the earth to deliver a message to me, to tell me that there was a protest against my going away. I had no right to leave the earth and must return. The moment I heard that, the vision ceased.

I was profoundly disappointed, for now it all seemed to have been for nothing. The painful process of defoliation had been in vain, and I was not to be allowed to enter the temple, to join the people in whose company I belonged.

In reality, a good three weeks were still to pass before I could truly make up my mind to live again. I could not eat because all food repelled me. The view of city and mountains from my sickbed seemed to me like a painted curtain with black holes in it, or a tattered sheet of newspaper full of photographs that meant nothing. Disappointed, I thought, "Now I must return to the 'box system' again." For it seemed to me as if behind the horizon of the cosmos a three-dimensional world had been artificially built up, in which each person sat by himself in a little box. And now I should have to convince myself all over again that this was important! Life and the whole world struck me as a prison, and it bothered me beyond measure that I should again be finding all that quite in order. I had been so glad to shed it all, and now it had come about that I—along with everyone else—would again be hung up in a box by a thread. While I floated in space, I had been weightless, and there had been

[1] *Basileus* = king. Kos was famous in antiquity as the site of the temple of Asklepios, and was the birthplace of Hippocrates.—A. J.

nothing tugging at me. And now all that was to be a thing of the past!

I felt violent resistance to my doctor because he had brought me back to life. At the same time, I was worried about him. "His life is in danger, for heaven's sake! He has appeared to me in his primal form! When anybody attains this form it means he is going to die, for already he belongs to the 'greater company'!" Suddenly the terrifying thought came to me that Dr. H. would have to die in my stead. I tried my best to talk to him about it, but he did not understand me. Then I became angry with him. "Why does he always pretend he doesn't know he is a *basileus* of Kos? And that he has already assumed his primal form? He wants to make me believe that he doesn't know!" That irritated me. My wife reproved me for being so unfriendly to him. She was right; but at the time I was angry with him for stubbornly refusing to speak of all that had passed between us in my vision. "Damn it all, he ought to watch his step. He has no right to be so reckless! I want to tell him to take care of himself." I was firmly convinced that his life was in jeopardy.

In actual fact I was his last patient. On April 4, 1944—I still remember the exact date—I was allowed to sit up on the edge of my bed for the first time since the beginning of my illness, and on this same day Dr. H. took to his bed and did not leave it again. I heard that he was having intermittent attacks of fever. Soon afterward he died of septicemia. He was a good doctor; there was something of the genius about him. Otherwise he would not have appeared to me as a prince of Kos.

During those weeks I lived in a strange rhythm. By day I was usually depressed. I felt weak and wretched, and scarcely dared to stir. Gloomily, I thought, "Now I must go back to this drab world." Toward evening I would fall asleep, and my sleep would last until about midnight. Then I would come to myself and lie awake for about an hour, but in an utterly transformed state. It was as if I were in an ecstasy. I felt as though I were floating in space, as though I were safe in the womb of the universe—in a tremendous void, but filled with the highest possible feeling of happiness. "This is eternal bliss," I thought. "This cannot be described; it is far too wonderful!"

Everything around me seemed enchanted. At this hour of the night the nurse brought me some food she had warmed—for only then was I able to take any, and I ate with appetite. For a time it seemed to me that she was an old Jewish woman, much older than she actually was, and that she was preparing ritual kosher dishes for me. When I looked at her, she seemed to have a blue halo around her head. I myself was, so it seemed, in the Pardes Rimmonim, the garden of pomegranates,[2] and the wedding of Tifereth with Malchuth was taking place. Or else I was Rabbi Simon ben Jochai, whose wedding in the afterlife was being celebrated. It was the mystic marriage as it appears in the Cabbalistic tradition. I cannot tell you how wonderful it was. I could only think continually, "Now this is the garden of pomegranates! Now this is the marriage of Malchuth with Tifereth!" I do not know exactly what part I played in it. At bottom it was I myself: I was the marriage. And my beatitude was that of a blissful wedding.

Gradually the garden of pomegranates faded away and changed. There followed the Marriage of the Lamb, in a Jerusalem festively bedecked. I cannot describe what it was like in detail. These were ineffable states of joy. Angels were present, and light. I myself was the "Marriage of the Lamb."

That, too, vanished, and there came a new image, the last vision. I walked up a wide valley to the end, where a gentle chain of hills began. The valley ended in a classical amphitheater. It was magnificently situated in the green landscape. And there, in this theater, the *hierosgamos* was being celebrated. Men and women dancers came onstage, and upon a flower-decked couch All-father Zeus and Hera consummated the mystic marriage, as it is described in the *Iliad*.

All these experiences were glorious. Night after night I floated in a state of purest bliss, "thronged round with images of all creation."[3] Gradually, the motifs mingled and paled. Usu-

<hr>

[2] *Pardes Rimmonim* is the title of an old Cabbalistic tract by Moses Cordovero (sixteenth century). In Cabbalistic doctrine Malchuth and Tifereth are two of the ten spheres of divine manifestation in which God emerges from his hidden state. They represent the female and male principles within the Godhead.

[3] *Faust*, Part Two.

ally the visions lasted for about an hour; then I would fall asleep again. By the time morning drew near, I would feel: Now gray morning is coming again; now comes the gray world with its boxes! What idiocy, what hideous nonsense! Those inner states were so fantastically beautiful that by comparison this world appeared downright ridiculous. As I approached closer to life again, they grew fainter, and scarcely three weeks after the first vision they ceased altogether.

It is impossible to convey the beauty and intensity of emotion during those visions. They were the most tremendous things I have ever experienced. And what a contrast the day was: I was tormented and on edge; everything irritated me; everything was too material, too crude and clumsy, terribly limited both spatially and spiritually. It was all an imprisonment, for reasons impossible to divine, and yet it had a kind of hypnotic power, a cogency, as if it were reality itself, for all that I had clearly perceived its emptiness. Although my belief in the world returned to me, I have never since entirely freed myself of the impression that this life is a segment of existence which is enacted in a three-dimensional boxlike universe especially set up for it.

There is something else I quite distinctly remember. At the beginning, when I was having the vision of the garden of pomegranates, I asked the nurse to forgive me if she were harmed. There was such sanctity in the room, I said, that it might be harmful to her. Of course she did not understand me. For me the presence of sanctity had a magical atmosphere; I feared it might be unendurable to others. I understood then why one speaks of the odor of sanctity, of the "sweet smell" of the Holy Ghost. This was it. There was a *pneuma* of inexpressible sanctity in the room, whose manifestation was the *mysterium coniunctionis*.

I would never have imagined that any such experience was possible. It was not a product of imagination. The visions and experiences were utterly real; there was nothing subjective about them; they all had a quality of absolute objectivity.

We shy away from the word "eternal," but I can describe the experience only as the ecstasy of a non-temporal state in which present, past, and future are one. Everything that happens in time had been brought together into a concrete whole. Nothing was distributed over time, nothing could be measured by temporal concepts. The experience might best be defined as a state of feeling, but one which cannot be produced by imagination. How can I imagine that I exist simultaneously the day before yesterday, today, and the day after tomorrow? There would be things which would not yet have begun, other things which would be indubitably present, and others again which would already be finished—and yet all this would be one. The only thing that feeling could grasp would be a sum, an iridescent whole, containing all at once expectation of a beginning, surprise at what is now happening, and satisfaction or disappointment with the result of what has happened. One is interwoven into an indescribable whole and yet observes it with complete objectivity.

I experienced this objectivity once again later on. That was after the death of my wife. I saw her in a dream which was like a vision. She stood at some distance from me, looking at me squarely. She was in her prime, perhaps about thirty, and wearing the dress which had been made for her many years before by my cousin the medium. It was perhaps the most beautiful thing she had ever worn. Her expression was neither joyful nor sad, but, rather, objectively wise and understanding, without the slightest emotional reaction, as though she were beyond the mist of affects. I knew that it was not she, but a portrait she had made or commissioned for me. It contained the beginning of our relationship, the events of fifty-three years of marriage, and the end of her life also. Face to face with such wholeness one remains speechless, for it can scarcely be comprehended.

The objectivity which I experienced in this dream and in the visions is part of a completed individuation. It signifies detachment from valuations and from what we call emotional ties. In general, emotional ties are very important to human beings. But they still contain projections, and it is essential to withdraw these projections in order to attain to oneself and to objectivity. Emotional relationships are relationships of desire, tainted by coercion and constraint; something is expected from the other person, and that makes him and ourselves unfree. Objective cognition lies hidden behind the attraction of the emotional relationship; it seems to be the central secret. Only through objective cognition is the real *coniunctio* possible.

After the illness a fruitful period of work began for me. A good many of my principal works were written only then. The insight I had had, or the vision of the end of all things, gave me the courage to undertake new formulations. I no longer attempted to put across my own opinion, but surrendered myself to the current of my thoughts. Thus one problem after the other revealed itself to me and took shape.

Something else, too, came to me from my illness. I might formulate it as an affirmation of things as they are: an unconditional "yes" to that which is, without subjective protests—acceptance of the conditions of existence as I see them and understand them, acceptance of my own nature, as I happen to be. At the beginning of the illness I had the feeling that there was something wrong with my attitude, and that I was to some extent responsible for the mishap. But when one follows the path of individuation, when one lives one's own life, one must take mistakes into the bargain; life would not be complete without them. There is no guarantee—not for a single moment —that we will not fall into error or stumble into deadly peril. We may think there is a sure road. But that would be the road of death. Then nothing happens any longer—at any rate, not the right things. Anyone who takes the sure road is as good as dead.

It was only after the illness that I understood how important it is to affirm one's own destiny. In this way we forge an ego that does not break down when incomprehensible things happen; an ego that endures, that endures the truth, and that is capable of coping with the world and with fate. Then, to experience defeat is also to experience victory. Nothing is disturbed— neither inwardly nor outwardly, for one's own continuity has withstood the current of life and of time. But that can come to pass only when one does not meddle inquisitively with the workings of fate.

I have also realized that one must accept the thoughts that go on within oneself of their own accord as part of one's reality. The categories of true and false are, of course, always present; but because they are not binding they take second place. The presence of thoughts is more important than our subjective judgment of them. But neither must these judgments be suppressed, for they also are existent thoughts which are part of our wholeness.

·XI·

On Life after Death

WHAT I HAVE to tell about the hereafter, and about life after death, consists entirely of memories, of images in which I have lived and of thoughts which have buffeted me. These memories in a way also underlie my works; for the latter are fundamentally nothing but attempts, ever renewed, to give an answer to the question of the interplay between the "here" and the "hereafter." Yet I have never written expressly about a life after death; for then I would have had to document my ideas, and I have no way of doing that. Be that as it may, I would like to state my ideas now.

Even now I can do no more than tell stories—"mythologize." Perhaps one has to be close to death to acquire the necessary freedom to talk about it. It is not that I wish we had a life after death. In fact, I would prefer not to foster such ideas. Still, I must state, to give reality its due, that, without my wishing and without my doing anything about it, thoughts of this nature move about within me. I can't say whether these thoughts are true or false, but I do know they are there, and can be given utterance, if I do not repress them out of some prejudice. Prejudice cripples and injures the full phenomenon of psychic life.

And I know too little about psychic life to feel that I can set it right out of superior knowledge. Critical rationalism has apparently eliminated, along with so many other mythic conceptions, the idea of life after death. This could only have happened because nowadays most people identify themselves almost exclusively with their consciousness, and imagine that they are only what they know about themselves. Yet anyone with even a smattering of psychology can see how limited this knowledge is. Rationalism and doctrinairism are the disease of our time; they pretend to have all the answers. But a great deal will yet be discovered which our present limited view would have ruled out as impossible. Our concepts of space and time have only approximate validity, and there is therefore a wide field for minor and major deviations. In view of all this, I lend an attentive ear to the strange myths of the psyche, and take a careful look at the varied events that come my way, regardless of whether or not they fit in with my theoretical postulates.

Unfortunately, the mythic side of man is given short shrift nowadays. He can no longer create fables. As a result, a great deal escapes him; for it is important and salutary to speak also of incomprehensible things. Such talk is like the telling of a good ghost story, as we sit by the fireside and smoke a pipe.

What the myths or stories about a life after death really mean, or what kind of reality lies behind them, we certainly do not know. We cannot tell whether they possess any validity beyond their indubitable value as anthropomorphic projections. Rather, we must hold clearly in mind that there is no possible way for us to attain certainty concerning things which pass our understanding.

We cannot visualize another world ruled by quite other laws, the reason being that we live in a specific world which has helped to shape our minds and establish our basic psychic conditions. We are strictly limited by our innate structure and therefore bound by our whole being and thinking to this world of ours. Mythic man, to be sure, demands a "going beyond all that," but scientific man cannot permit this. To the intellect, all my mythologizing is futile speculation. To the emotions, however, it is a healing and valid activity; it gives existence a glamour which we would not like to do without. Nor is there any good reason why we should.

Parapsychology holds it to be a scientifically valid proof of an afterlife that the dead manifest themselves—either as ghosts, or through a medium—and communicate things which they alone could possibly know. But even though there do exist such well-documented cases, the question remains whether the ghost or the voice is identical with the dead person or is a psychic projection, and whether the things said really derive from the deceased or from knowledge which may be present in the unconscious.[1]

Leaving aside the rational arguments against any certainty in these matters, we must not forget that for most people it means a great deal to assume that their lives will have an indefinite continuity beyond their present existence. They live more sensibly, feel better, and are more at peace. One has centuries, one has an inconceivable period of time at one's disposal. What then is the point of this senseless mad rush?

Naturally, such reasoning does not apply to everyone. There are people who feel no craving for immortality, and who shudder at the thought of sitting on a cloud and playing the harp for ten thousand years! There are also quite a few who have been so buffeted by life, or who feel such disgust for their own existence, that they far prefer absolute cessation to continuance. But in the majority of cases the question of immortality is so urgent, so immediate, and also so ineradicable that we must make an effort to form some sort of view about it. But how?

My hypothesis is that we can do so with the aid of hints sent to us from the unconscious—in dreams, for example. Usually we dismiss these hints because we are convinced that the question is not susceptible to answer. In response to this understandable skepticism, I suggest the following considerations. If there is something we cannot know, we must necessarily abandon it as an intellectual problem. For example, I do not know for what reason the universe has come into being, and shall never know.

---

[1] Concerning "absolute knowledge" in the unconscious, cf. "Synchronicity: An Acausal Connecting Principle," in *The Structure and Dynamics of the Psyche* (CW 8), pp. 481 ff.

Therefore I must drop this question as a scientific or intellectual problem. But if an idea about it is offered to me—in dreams or in mythic traditions—I ought to take note of it. I even ought to build up a conception on the basis of such hints, even though it will forever remain a hypothesis which I know cannot be proved.

A man should be able to say he has done his best to form a conception of life after death, or to create some image of it—even if he must confess his failure. Not to have done so is a vital loss. For the question that is posed to him is the age-old heritage of humanity: an archetype, rich in secret life, which seeks to add itself to our own individual life in order to make it whole. Reason sets the boundaries far too narrowly for us, and would have us accept only the known—and that too with limitations —and live in a known framework, just as if we were sure how far life actually extends. As a matter of fact, day after day we live far beyond the bounds of our consciousness; without our knowledge, the life of the unconscious is also going on within us. The more the critical reason dominates, the more impoverished life becomes; but the more of the unconscious, and the more of myth we are capable of making conscious, the more of life we integrate. Overvalued reason has this in common with political absolutism: under its dominion the individual is pauperized.

The unconscious helps by communicating things to us, or making figurative allusions. It has other ways, too, of informing us of things which by all logic we could not possibly know. Consider synchronistic phenomena, premonitions, and dreams that come true. I recall one time during the Second World War when I was returning home from Bollingen. I had a book with me, but could not read, for the moment the train started to move I was overpowered by the image of someone drowning. This was a memory of an accident that had happened while I was on military service. During the entire journey I could not rid myself of it. It struck me as uncanny, and I thought, "What has happened? Can there have been an accident?"

I got out at Erlenbach and walked home, still troubled by this memory. My second daughter's children were in the garden.

The family was living with us, having returned to Switzerland from Paris because of the war. The children stood looking rather upset, and when I asked, "Why, what is the matter?" they told me that Adrian, then the youngest of the boys, had fallen into the water in the boathouse. It is quite deep there, and since he could not really swim he had almost drowned. His older brother had fished him out. This had taken place at exactly the time I had been assailed by that memory in the train. The unconscious had given me a hint. Why should it not be able to inform me of other things also?

I had a somewhat similar experience before a death in my wife's family. I dreamed that my wife's bed was a deep pit with stone walls. It was a grave, and somehow had a suggestion of classical antiquity about it. Then I heard a deep sigh, as if someone were giving up the ghost. A figure that resembled my wife sat up in the pit and floated upward. It wore a white gown into which curious black symbols were woven. I awoke, roused my wife, and checked the time. It was three o'clock in the morning. The dream was so curious that I thought at once that it might signify a death. At seven o'clock came the news that a cousin of my wife had died at three o'clock in the morning.

Frequently foreknowledge is there, but not recognition. Thus I once had a dream in which I was attending a garden party. I saw my sister there, and that greatly surprised me, for she had died some years before. A deceased friend of mine was also present. The rest were people who were still alive. Presently I saw that my sister was accompanied by a lady I knew well. Even in the dream I had drawn the conclusion that the lady was going to die. "She is already marked," I thought. In the dream I knew exactly who she was. I knew also that she lived in Basel. But as soon as I woke up I could no longer, with the best will in the world, recall who she was, although the whole dream was still vivid in my mind. I pictured all my acquaintances in Basel to see whether the memory images would ring a bell. Nothing!

A few weeks later I received news that a friend of mine had had a fatal accident. I knew at once that she was the person I had seen in the dream but had been unable to identify. My recollection of her was perfectly clear and richly detailed, since she had been my patient for a considerable time up to a year before her death. In my attempt to recall the person in my dream, however, hers was the one picture which did not appear in my portrait gallery of Basel acquaintances, although by rights it should have been one of the first.

When one has such experiences—and I will tell of others like them—one acquires a certain respect for the potentialities and arts of the unconscious. Only, one must remain critical and be aware that such communications may have a subjective meaning as well. They may be in accord with reality, and then again they may not. I have, however, learned that the views I have been able to form on the basis of such hints from the unconscious have been most rewarding. Naturally, I am not going to write a book of revelations about them, but I will acknowledge that I have a "myth" which encourages me to look deeper into this whole realm. Myths are the earliest form of science. When I speak of things after death, I am speaking out of inner prompting, and can go no farther than to tell you dreams and myths that relate to this subject.

Naturally, one can contend from the start that myths and dreams concerning continuity of life after death are merely compensating fantasies which are inherent in our natures—all life desires eternity. The only argument I can adduce in answer to this is the myth itself.

However, there are indications that at least a part of the psyche is not subject to the laws of space and time. Scientific proof of that has been provided by the well-known J. B. Rhine experiments.[2] Along with numerous cases of spontaneous foreknowledge, non-spatial perceptions, and so on—of which I have given a number of examples from my own life—these experiments prove that the psyche at times functions outside of the spatio-temporal law of causality. This indicates that our conceptions of space and time, and therefore of causality also, are incomplete. A complete picture of the world would require the addition of still another dimension; only then could the totality of phenomena be given a unified explanation. Hence it is that

[2] *Extra-sensory Perception* (Boston, 1934); *The Reach of the Mind* (New York, 1947).

the rationalists insist to this day that parapsychological experiences do not really exist; for their world-view stands or falls by this question. If such phenomena occur at all, the rationalistic picture of the universe is invalid, because incomplete. Then the possibility of an other-valued reality behind the phenomenal world becomes an inescapable problem, and we must face the fact that our world, with its time, space, and causality, relates to another order of things lying behind or beneath it, in which neither "here and there" nor "earlier and later" are of importance. I have been convinced that at least a part of our psychic existence is characterized by a relativity of space and time. This relativity seems to increase, in proportion to the distance from consciousness, to an absolute condition of timelessness and spacelessness.

Not only my own dreams, but also occasionally the dreams of others, helped to shape, revise, or confirm my views on a life after death. I attach particular importance to a dream which a pupil of mine, a woman of sixty, dreamed about two months before her death. She had entered the hereafter. There was a class going on, and various deceased women friends of hers sat on the front bench. An atmosphere of general expectation prevailed. She looked around for a teacher or lecturer, but could find none. Then it became plain that she herself was the lecturer, for immediately after death people had to give accounts of the total experience of their lives. The dead were extremely interested in the life experiences that the newly deceased brought with them, just as if the acts and experiences taking place in earthly life, in space and time, were the decisive ones.

In any case, the dream describes a most unusual audience whose like could scarcely be found on earth: people burningly interested in the final psychological results of a human life that was in no way remarkable, any more than were the conclusions that could be drawn from it—to our way of thinking. If, however, the "audience" existed in a state of relative non-time, where "termination," "event," and "development" had become questionable concepts, they might very well be most interested precisely in what was lacking in their own condition.

At the time of this dream the lady was afraid of death and

did her best to fend off any thoughts about it. Yet death is an important interest, especially to an aging person. A categorical question is being put to him, and he is under an obligation to answer it. To this end he ought to have a myth about death, for reason shows him nothing but the dark pit into which he is descending. Myth, however, can conjure up other images for him, helpful and enriching pictures of life in the land of the dead. If he believes in them, or greets them with some measure of credence, he is being just as right or just as wrong as someone who does not believe in them. But while the man who despairs marches toward nothingness, the one who has placed his faith in the archetype follows the tracks of life and lives right into his death. Both, to be sure, remain in uncertainty, but the one lives against his instincts, the other with them.

The figures from the unconscious are uninformed too, and need man, or contact with consciousness, in order to attain to knowledge. When I began working with the unconscious, I found myself much involved with the figures of Salome and Elijah. Then they receded, but after about two years they reappeared. To my enormous astonishment, they were completely unchanged; they spoke and acted as if nothing had happened in the meanwhile. In actuality the most incredible things had taken place in my life. I had, as it were, to begin from the beginning again, to tell them all about what had been going on, and explain things to them. At the time I had been greatly surprised by this situation. Only later did I understand what had happened: in the interval the two had sunk back into the unconscious and into themselves—I might equally well put it, into timelessness. They remained out of contact with the ego and the ego's changing circumstances, and therefore were ignorant of what had happened in the world of consciousness.

Quite early I had learned that it was necessary for me to instruct the figures of the unconscious, or that other group which is often indistinguishable from them, the "spirits of the departed." The first time I experienced this was on a bicycle trip through upper Italy which I took with a friend in 1911. On the way home we cycled from Pavia to Arona, on the lower part of Lake Maggiore, and spent the night there. We had intended to pedal on along the lake and then through the Tessin as far as Faido, where we were going to take the train to Zürich. But in Arona I had a dream which upset our plans.

In the dream I was in an assemblage of distinguished spirits of earlier centuries; the feeling was similar to the one I had later toward the "illustrious ancestors" in the black rock temple of my 1944 vision. The conversation was conducted in Latin. A gentleman with a long, curly wig addressed me and asked a difficult question, the gist of which I could no longer recall after I woke up. I understood him, but did not have a sufficient command of the language to answer him in Latin. I felt so profoundly humiliated by this that the emotion awakened me.

At the very moment of awakening I thought of the book I was then working on, *Wandlungen und Symbole der Libido,* and had such intense inferiority feelings about the unanswered question that I immediately took the train home in order to get back to work. It would have been impossible for me to continue the bicycle trip and lose another three days. I had to work, to find the answer.

Not until years later did I understand the dream and my reaction. The bewigged gentleman was a kind of ancestral spirit, or spirit of the dead, who had addressed questions to me —in vain! It was still too soon, I had not yet come so far, but I had an obscure feeling that by working on my book I would be answering the question that had been asked. It had been asked by, as it were, my spiritual forefathers, in the hope and expectation that they would learn what they had not been able to find out during their time on earth, since the answer had first to be created in the centuries that followed. If question and answer had already been in existence in eternity, had always been there, no effort on my part would have been necessary, and it could all have been discovered in any other century. There does seem to be unlimited knowledge present in nature, it is true, but it can be comprehended by consciousness only when the time is ripe for it. The process, presumably, is like what happens in the individual psyche: a man may go about for many years with an inkling of something, but grasps it clearly only at a particular moment.

Later, when I wrote the *Septem Sermones ad Mortuos,* once again it was the dead who addressed crucial questions to me. They came—so they said—"back from Jerusalem, where they found not what they sought." This had surprised me greatly at the time, for according to the traditional views the dead are the possessors of great knowledge. People have the idea that the dead know far more than we, for Christian doctrine teaches that in the hereafter we shall "see face to face." Apparently, however, the souls of the dead "know" only what they knew at the moment of death, and nothing beyond that. Hence their endeavor to penetrate into life in order to share in the knowledge of men. I frequently have a feeling that they are standing directly behind us, waiting to hear what answer we will give to them, and what answer to destiny. It seems to me as if they were dependent on the living for receiving answers to their questions, that is, on those who have survived them and exist in a world of change: as if omniscience or, as I might put it, omni-consciousness, were not at their disposal, but could flow only into the psyche of the living, into a soul bound to a body. The mind of the living appears, therefore, to hold an advantage over that of the dead in at least one point: in the capacity for attaining clear and decisive cognitions. As I see it, the three-dimensional world in time and space is like a system of co-ordinates; what is here separated into ordinates and abscissae may appear "there," in space-timelessness, as a primordial image with many aspects, perhaps as a diffuse cloud of cognition surrounding an archetype. Yet a system of co-ordinates is necessary if any distinction of discrete contents is to be possible. Any such operation seems to us unthinkable in a state of diffuse omniscience, or, as the case may be, of subjectless consciousness, with no spatio-temporal demarcations. Cognition, like generation, presupposes an opposition, a here and there, an above and below, a before and after.

If there were to be a conscious existence after death, it would, so it seems to me, have to continue on the level of consciousness attained by humanity, which in any age has an upper though variable limit. There are many human beings who throughout their lives and at the moment of death lag behind their own potentialities and—even more important—behind the knowledge which has been brought to consciousness by other human beings during their own lifetimes. Hence their demand to attain in death that share of awareness which they failed to win in life.

I have come to this conclusion through observation of dreams about the dead. I dreamed once that I was paying a visit to a friend who had died about two weeks before. In life, this friend had never espoused anything but a conventional view of the world, and had remained stuck in this unreflecting attitude. In the dream his home was on a hill similar to the Tüllinger hill near Basel. The walls of an old castle surrounded a square consisting of a small church and a few smaller buildings. It reminded me of the square in front of the castle of Rapperswil. It was autumn. The leaves of the ancient trees had turned gold, and the whole scene was transfigured by gentle sunlight. My friend sat at a table with his daughter, who had studied psychology in Zürich. I knew that she was telling him about psychology. He was so fascinated by what she was saying that he greeted me only with a casual wave of the hand, as though to intimate: "Don't disturb me." The greeting was at the same time a dismissal. The dream told me that now, in a manner which of course remains incomprehensible to me, he was required to grasp the reality of his psychic existence, which he had never been capable of doing during his life.

I had another experience of the evolution of the soul after death when—about a year after my wife's death—I suddenly awoke one night and knew that I had been with her in the south of France, in Provence, and had spent an entire day with her. She was engaged on studies of the Grail there. That seemed significant to me, for she had died before completing her work on this subject. Interpretation on the subjective level—that my anima had not yet finished with the work she had to do—yielded nothing of interest; I know quite well that I am not yet finished with that. But the thought that my wife was continuing after death to work on her further spiritual development—however that may be conceived—struck me as meaningful and held a measure of reassurance for me.

Ideas of this sort are, of course, inaccurate, and give a wrong picture, like a body projected on a plane or, conversely, like the construction of a four-dimensional model out of a three-dimensional body. They use the terms of a three-dimensional world in order to represent themselves to us. Mathematics goes to great pains to create expressions for relationships which pass empirical comprehension. In much the same way, it is all-important for a disciplined imagination to build up images of intangibles by logical principles and on the basis of empirical data, that is, on the evidence of dreams. The method employed is what I have called "the method of the necessary statement." It represents the principle of *amplification* in the interpretation of dreams, but can most easily be demonstrated by the statements implicit in simple whole numbers.

One, as the first numeral, is unity. But it is also *"the* unity," the One, All-Oneness, individuality and non-duality—not a numeral but a philosophical concept, an archetype and attribute of God, the monad. It is quite proper that the human intellect should make these statements; but at the same time the intellect is determined and limited by its conception of oneness and its implications. In other words, these statements are not arbitrary. They are governed by the nature of oneness and therefore are necessary statements. Theoretically, the same logical operation could be performed for each of the following conceptions of number, but in practice the process soon comes to an end because of the rapid increase in complications, which become too numerous to handle.

Every further unit introduces new properties and new modifications. Thus, it is a property of the number four that equations of the fourth degree can be solved, whereas equations of the fifth degree cannot. The necessary statement of the number four, therefore, is that, among other things, it is an apex and simultaneously the end of a preceding ascent. Since with each additional unit one or more new mathematical properties appear, the statements attain such a complexity that they can no longer be formulated.

The infinite series of natural numbers corresponds to the infinite number of individual creatures. That series likewise consists of individuals, and the properties even of its first ten members represent—if they represent anything at all—an abstract cosmogony derived from the monad. The properties of numbers are, however, simultaneously properties of matter, for which reason certain equations can anticipate its behavior.

Therefore I submit that other than mathematical statements (i.e., statements implicit in nature) are likewise capable of pointing to irrepresentable realities beyond themselves—such, for example, as those products of the imagination which enjoy universal acceptance or are distinguished by the frequency of their occurrence, like the whole class of archetypal motifs. Just as in the case of some factors in mathematical equations we cannot say to what physical realities they correspond, so in the case of some mythological products we do not know at first to what psychic realities they refer. Equations governing the turbulence of heated gases existed long before the problems of such gases had been precisely investigated. Similarly, we have long been in possession of mythologems which express the dynamics of certain subliminal processes, though these processes were only given names in very recent times.

The maximum awareness which has been attained anywhere forms, so it seems to me, the upper limit of knowledge to which the dead can attain. That is probably why earthly life is of such great significance, and why it is that what a human being "brings over" at the time of his death is so important. Only here, in life on earth, where the opposites clash together, can the general level of consciousness be raised. That seems to be man's metaphysical task—which he cannot accomplish without "mythologizing." Myth is the natural and indispensable intermediate stage between unconscious and conscious cognition. True, the unconscious knows more than consciousness does; but it is knowledge of a special sort, knowledge in eternity, usually without reference to the here and now, not couched in language of the intellect. Only when we let its statements amplify themselves, as has been shown above by the example of numerals, does it come within the range of our understanding; only then does a new aspect become perceptible to us. This process is convincingly repeated in every successful dream analysis. That

is why it is so important not to have any preconceived, doctrinaire opinions about the statements made by dreams. As soon
as a certain "monotony of interpretation" strikes us, we know
that our approach has become doctrinaire and hence sterile.

Although there is no way to marshal valid proof of continuance of the soul after death, there are nevertheless experiences
which make us thoughtful. I take them as hints, and do not
presume to ascribe to them the significance of insights.

One night I lay awake thinking of the sudden death of a
friend whose funeral had taken place the day before. I was
deeply concerned. Suddenly I felt that he was in the room. It
seemed to me that he stood at the foot of my bed and was asking
me to go with him. I did not have the feeling of an apparition;
rather, it was an inner visual image of him, which I explained to
myself as a fantasy. But in all honesty I had to ask myself, "Do I
have any proof that this is a fantasy? Suppose it is not a fantasy,
suppose my friend is really here and I decided he was only a
fantasy—would that not be abominable of me?" Yet I had
equally little proof that he stood before me as an apparition.
Then I said to myself, "Proof is neither here nor there! Instead
of explaining him away as a fantasy, I might just as well give him
the benefit of the doubt and for experiment's sake credit him
with reality." The moment I had that thought, he went to the
door and beckoned me to follow him. So I was going to have to
play along with him! That was something I hadn't bargained
for. I had to repeat my argument to myself once more. Only then
did I follow him in my imagination.

He led me out of the house, into the garden, out to the road,
and finally to his house. (In reality it was several hundred yards
away from mine.) I went in, and he conducted me into his
study. He climbed on a stool and showed me the second of five
books with red bindings which stood on the second shelf from
the top. Then the vision broke off. I was not acquainted with his
library and did not know what books he owned. Certainly I
could never have made out from below the titles of the books he
had pointed out to me on the second shelf from the top.

This experience seemed to me so curious that next morning I

went to his widow and asked whether I could look up something in my friend's library. Sure enough, there was a stool standing under the bookcase I had seen in my vision, and even before I came closer I could see the five books with red bindings. I stepped up on the stool so as to be able to read the titles. They were translations of the novels of Emile Zola. The title of the second volume read: "The Legacy of the Dead." The contents seemed to me of no interest. Only the title was extremely significant in connection with this experience.

Equally important to me were the dream-experiences I had before my mother's death. News of her death came to me while I was staying in the Tessin. I was deeply shaken, for it had come with unexpected suddenness. The night before her death I had a frightening dream. I was in a dense, gloomy forest; fantastic, gigantic boulders lay about among huge jungle-like trees. It was a heroic, primeval landscape. Suddenly I heard a piercing whistle that seemed to resound through the whole universe. My knees shook. Then there were crashings in the underbrush, and a gigantic wolfhound with a fearful, gaping maw burst forth. At the sight of it, the blood froze in my veins. It tore past me, and I suddenly knew: the Wild Huntsman had commanded it to carry away a human soul. I awoke in deadly terror, and the next morning I received the news of my mother's passing.

Seldom has a dream so shaken me, for upon superficial consideration it seemed to say that the devil had fetched her. But to be accurate the dream said that it was the Wild Huntsman, the *"Grünhütl,"* or Wearer of the Green Hat, who hunted with his wolves that night—it was the season of Föhn storms in January. It was Wotan, the god of my Alemannic forefathers, who had gathered my mother to her ancestors—negatively to the "wild horde," but positively to the *"sälig lüt,"* the blessed folk. It was the Christian missionaries who made Wotan into a devil. In himself he is an important god—a Mercury or Hermes, as the Romans correctly realized, a nature spirit who returned to life again in the Merlin of the Grail legend and became, as the *spiritus Mercurialis,* the sought-after arcanum of the alchemists. Thus the dream says that the soul of my mother was taken into that greater territory of the self which lies beyond the segment of Christian morality, taken into that wholeness of nature and spirit in which conflicts and contradictions are resolved.

I went home immediately, and while I rode in the night train I had a feeling of great grief, but in my heart of hearts I could not be mournful, and this for a strange reason: during the entire journey I continually heard dance music, laughter, and jollity, as though a wedding were being celebrated. This contrasted violently with the devastating impression the dream had made on me. Here was gay dance music, cheerful laughter, and it was impossible to yield entirely to my sorrow. Again and again it was on the point of overwhelming me, but the next moment I would find myself once more engulfed by the merry melodies. One side of me had a feeling of warmth and joy, and the other of terror and grief; I was thrown back and forth between these contrasting emotions.

This paradox can be explained if we suppose that at one moment death was being represented from the point of view of the ego, and at the next from that of the psyche. In the first case it appeared as a catastrophe; that is how it so often strikes us, as if wicked and pitiless powers had put an end to a human life.

And so it is—death is indeed a fearful piece of brutality; there is no sense pretending otherwise. It is brutal not only as a physical event, but far more so psychically: a human being is torn away from us, and what remains is the icy stillness of death. There no longer exists any hope of a relationship, for all the bridges have been smashed at one blow. Those who deserve a long life are cut off in the prime of their years, and good-for-nothings live to a ripe old age. This is a cruel reality which we have no right to sidestep. The actual experience of the cruelty and wantonness of death can so embitter us that we conclude there is no merciful God, no justice, and no kindness.

From another point of view, however, death appears as a joyful event. In the light of eternity, it is a wedding, a *mysterium coniunctionis*. The soul attains, as it were, its missing half, it achieves wholeness. On Greek sarcophagi the joyous element was represented by dancing girls, on Etruscan tombs by banquets. When the pious Cabbalist Rabbi Simon ben Jochai came to die, his friends said that he was celebrating his wedding. To this day it is the custom in many regions to hold a picnic on the graves on All Souls' Day. Such customs express the feeling that death is really a festive occasion.

Several months before my mother's death, in September 1922, I had a dream which presaged it. It concerned my father, and made a deep impression upon me. I had not dreamed of my father since his death in 1896. Now he once more appeared in a dream, as if he had returned from a distant journey. He looked rejuvenated, and had shed his appearance of paternal authoritarianism. I went into my library with him, and was greatly pleased at the prospect of finding out what he had been up to. I was also looking forward with particular joy to introducing my wife and children to him, to showing him my house, and to telling him all that had happened to me and what I had become in the meanwhile. I wanted also to tell him about my book on psychological types, which had recently been published. But I quickly saw that all this would be inopportune, for my father looked preoccupied. Apparently he wanted something from me. I felt that plainly, and so I refrained from talking about my own concerns.

He then said to me that since I was after all a psychologist, he would like to consult me about marital psychology. I made ready to give him a lengthy lecture on the complexities of marriage, but at this point I awoke. I could not properly understand the dream, for it never occurred to me that it might refer to my mother's death. I realized that only when she died suddenly in January 1923.

My parents' marriage was not a happy one, but full of trials and difficulties and tests of patience. Both made the mistakes typical of many couples. My dream was a forecast of my mother's death, for here was my father who, after an absence of twenty-six years, wished to ask a psychologist about the newest insights and information on marital problems, since he would soon have to resume this relationship again. Evidently he had acquired no better understanding in his timeless state and therefore had to appeal to someone among the living who, enjoying the benefits of changed times, might have a fresh approach to the whole thing.

Such was the dream's message. Undoubtedly, I could have found out a good deal more by looking into its subjective meaning—but why did I dream it just before the death of my mother, which I did not foresee? It plainly referred to my father, with whom I felt a sympathy that deepened as I grew older.

Since the unconscious, as the result of its spatio-temporal relativity, possesses better sources of information than the conscious mind—which has only sense perceptions available to it—we are dependent for our myth of life after death upon the meager hints of dreams and similar spontaneous revelations from the unconscious. As I have already said, we cannot attribute to these allusions the value of knowledge, let alone proof. They can, however, serve as suitable bases for mythic amplifications; they give the probing intellect the raw material which is indispensable for its vitality. Cut off the intermediary world of mythic imagination, and the mind falls prey to doctrinaire rigidities. On the other hand, too much traffic with these germs of myth is dangerous for weak and suggestible minds, for they are led to mistake vague intimations for substantial knowledge, and to hypostatize mere phantasms.

One widespread myth of the hereafter is formed by the ideas and images centering on reincarnation. In one country whose intellectual culture is highly complex and much older than ours —I am, of course, referring to India—the idea of reincarnation is as much taken for granted as, among us, the idea that God created the world, or that there is a *spiritus rector*. Cultivated Hindus know that we do not share their ideas about this, but that does not trouble them. In keeping with the spirit of the East, the succession of birth and death is viewed as an endless continuity, as an eternal wheel rolling on forever without a goal. Man lives and attains knowledge and dies and begins again from the beginning. Only with the Buddha does the idea of a goal emerge, namely, the overcoming of earthly existence.

The mythic needs of the Occidental call for an evolutionary cosmogony with a *beginning* and a *goal*. The Occidental rebels against a cosmogony with a beginning and mere *end,* just as he cannot accept the idea of a static, self-contained, eternal cycle of events. The Oriental, on the other hand, seems able to come to terms with this idea. Apparently there is no unanimous feeling about the nature of the world, any more than there is general agreement among contemporary astronomers on this question. To Western man, the meaninglessness of a merely static universe is unbearable. He must assume that it has meaning. The Oriental does not need to make this assumption; rather, he himself embodies it. Whereas the Occidental feels the need to complete the meaning of the world, the Oriental strives for the fulfillment of meaning in man, stripping the world and existence from himself (Buddha).

I would say that both are right. Western man seems predominantly extraverted, Eastern man predominantly introverted. The former projects the meaning and considers that it exists in objects; the latter feels the meaning in himself. But the meaning is both without and within.

The idea of rebirth is inseparable from that of karma. The crucial question is whether a man's karma is personal or not. If it is, then the preordained destiny with which a man enters life represents an achievement of previous lives, and a personal continuity therefore exists. If, however, this is not so, and an impersonal karma is seized upon in the act of birth, then that karma is incarnated again without there being any personal continuity.

Buddha was twice asked by his disciples whether man's karma is personal or not. Each time he fended off the question, and did not go into the matter; to know this, he said, would not contribute to liberating oneself from the illusion of existence. Buddha considered it far more useful for his disciples to meditate upon the Nidana chain, that is, upon birth, life, old age, and death, and upon the cause and effect of suffering.

I know no answer to the question of whether the karma which I live is the outcome of my past lives, or whether it is not rather the achievement of my ancestors, whose heritage comes together in me. Am I a combination of the lives of these ancestors and do I embody these lives again? Have I lived before in the past as a specific personality, and did I progress so far in that life that I am now able to seek a solution? I do not know. Buddha left the question open, and I like to assume that he himself did not know with certainty.

I could well imagine that I might have lived in former centuries and there encountered questions I was not yet able to answer; that I had to be born again because I had not fulfilled the task that was given to me. When I die, my deeds will follow along with me—that is how I imagine it. I will bring with me what I have done. In the meantime it is important to insure that I do not stand at the end with empty hands. Buddha, too, seems to have had this thought when he tried to keep his disciples from wasting time on useless speculation.

The meaning of my existence is that life has addressed a question to me. Or, conversely, I myself am a question which is addressed to the world, and I must communicate my answer, for otherwise I am dependent upon the world's answer. That is a suprapersonal life task, which I accomplish only by effort and with difficulty. Perhaps it is a question which preoccupied my ancestors, and which they could not answer. Could that be why I am so impressed by the fact that the conclusion of *Faust* contains no solution? Or by the problem on which Nietzsche foundered: the Dionysian side of life, to which the Christian seems to have lost the way? Or is it the restless Wotan-Hermes of my Alemannic and Frankish ancestors who poses challenging riddles?

What I feel to be the resultant of my ancestors' lives, or a karma acquired in a previous personal life, might perhaps equally well be an impersonal archetype which today presses hard on everyone and has taken a particular hold upon me—an archetype such as, for example, the development over the centuries of the divine triad and its confrontation with the feminine principle; or the still pending answer to the Gnostic question as to the origin of evil, or, to put it another way, the incompleteness of the Christian God-image.

I also think of the possibility that through the achievement of an individual a question enters the world, to which he must provide some kind of answer. For example, my way of posing the question as well as my answer may be unsatisfactory. That being so, someone who has my karma—or I myself—would have to be reborn in order to give a more complete answer. It might happen that I would not be reborn again so long as the world needed no such answer, and that I would be entitled to several hundred years of peace until someone was once more needed who took an interest in these matters and could profitably tackle the task anew. I imagine that for a while a period of rest could ensue, until the stint I had done in my lifetime needed to be taken up again.

The question of karma is obscure to me, as is also the problem of personal rebirth or of the transmigration of souls. "With a free and open mind" I listen attentively to the Indian doctrine of rebirth, and look around in the world of my own experience to see whether somewhere and somehow there is some authentic sign pointing toward reincarnation. Naturally, I do not count the relatively numerous testimonies, here in the West, to the belief in reincarnation. A belief proves to me only the phenomenon of belief, not the content of the belief. This I must see revealed empirically in order to accept it. Until a few years ago I could not discover anything convincing in this respect, although I kept a sharp lookout for any such signs. Recently, however, I observed in myself a series of dreams which would seem to describe the process of reincarnation in a deceased person of my acquaintance. But I have never come across any such dreams in other persons, and therefore have no basis for comparison. Since this observation is subjective and unique, I prefer only to mention its existence and not to go into it any further. I must confess, however, that after this experience I view the problem of reincarnation with somewhat different eyes, though without being in a position to assert a definite opinion.

If we assume that life continues "there," we cannot conceive of any other form of existence except a psychic one; for the life of the psyche requires no space and no time. Psychic existence, and above all the inner images with which we are here concerned, supply the material for all mythic speculations about a life in the hereafter, and I imagine that life as a continuance in the world of images. Thus the psyche might be that existence in which the hereafter or the land of the dead is located.

From the psychological point of view, life in the hereafter would seem to be a logical continuation of the psychic life of old age. With increasing age, contemplation, and reflection, the inner images naturally play an ever greater part in man's life. "Your old men shall dream dreams." [3] That, to be sure, presupposes that the psyches of the old men have not become wooden, or entirely petrified—*sero medicina paratur cum mala per longas convaluere moras.*[4] In old age one begins to let memories unroll before the mind's eye and, musing, to recognize oneself in the inner and outer images of the past. This is like a preparation for an existence in the hereafter, just as, in Plato's view, philosophy is a preparation for death.

The inner images keep me from getting lost in personal retrospection. Many old people become too involved in their reconstruction of past events. They remain imprisoned in these memories. But if it is reflective and is translated into images, retrospection can be a *reculer pour mieux sauter*. I try to see the line which leads through my life into the world, and out of the world again.

In general, the conception people form of the hereafter is largely made up of wishful thinking and prejudices. Thus in most conceptions the hereafter is pictured as a pleasant place. That does not seem so obvious to me. I hardly think that after death we shall be spirited to some lovely flowering meadow. If everything were pleasant and good in the hereafter, surely there would be some friendly communication between us and the blessed spirits, and an outpouring upon us of goodness and beauty from the prenatal state. But there is nothing of the sort. Why is there this insurmountable barrier between the departed and the living? At least half the reports of encounters with the dead tell of terrifying experiences with dark spirits; and it is the

[3] Acts 2:17; Joel 2:28.
[4] The medicine is prepared too late, when the illness has grown strong by long delay.

rule that the land of the dead observes icy silence, unperturbed by the grief of the bereaved.

To follow out the thought that involuntarily comes to me: the world, I feel, is far too unitary for there to be a hereafter in which the rule of opposites is completely absent. There, too, is nature, which after its fashion is also God's. The world into which we enter after death will be grand and terrible, like God and like all of nature that we know. Nor can I conceive that suffering should entirely cease. Granted that what I experienced in my 1944 visions—liberation from the burden of the body, and perception of meaning—gave me the deepest bliss. Nevertheless, there was darkness too, and a strange cessation of human warmth. Remember the black rock to which I came! It was dark and of the hardest granite. What does that mean? If there were no imperfections, no primordial defect in the ground of creation, why should there be any urge to create, any longing for what must yet be fulfilled? Why should the gods be the least bit concerned about man and creation? About the continuation of the Nidâna chain to infinity? After all, the Buddha opposes to the painful illusion of existence his *quod non,* and the Christian hopes for the swift coming of this world's end.

It seems probable to me that in the hereafter, too, there exist certain limitations, but that the souls of the dead only gradually find out where the limits of the liberated state lie. Somewhere "out there" there must be a determinant, a necessity conditioning the world, which seeks to put an end to the after-death state. This creative determinant—so I imagine it—must decide what souls will plunge again into birth. Certain souls, I imagine, feel the state of three-dimensional existence to be more blissful than that of Eternity. But perhaps that depends upon how much of completeness or incompleteness they have taken across with them from their human existence.

It is possible that any further spell of three-dimensional life would have no more meaning once the soul had reached a certain stage of understanding; it would then no longer have to return, fuller understanding having put to rout the desire for re-embodiment. Then the soul would vanish from the three-dimensional world and attain what the Buddhists call nirvana. But if a karma still remains to be disposed of, then the soul relapses again into desires and returns to life once more, perhaps even doing so out of the realization that something remains to be completed.

In my case it must have been primarily a passionate urge toward understanding which brought about my birth. For that is the strongest element in my nature. This insatiable drive toward understanding has, as it were, created a consciousness in order to know what is and what happens, and in order to piece together mythic conceptions from the slender hints of the unknowable.

We lack concrete proof that anything of us is preserved for eternity. At most we can say that there is some probability that something of our psyche continues beyond physical death. Whether what continues to exist is conscious of itself, we do not know either. If we feel the need to form some opinion on this question, we might possibly consider what has been learned from the phenomena of psychic dissociation. In most cases where a split-off complex manifests itself it does so in the form of a personality, as if the complex had a consciousness of itself. Thus the voices heard by the insane are personified. I dealt long ago with this phenomenon of personified complexes in my doctoral dissertation. We might, if we wish, adduce these complexes as evidence for a continuity of consciousness. Likewise in favor of such an assumption are certain astonishing observations in cases of profound syncope after acute injuries to the brain and in severe states of collapse. In both situations, total loss of consciousness can be accompanied by perceptions of the outside world and vivid dream experiences. Since the cerebral cortex, the seat of consciousness, is not functioning at these times, there is as yet no explanation for such phenomena. They may be evidence for at least a subjective persistence of the capacity for consciousness—even in a state of apparent unconsciousness.[5]

The thorny problem of the relationship between eternal man,

[5] Cf. "Synchronicity: An Acausal Connecting Principle," in *The Structure and Dynamics of the Psyche* (CW 8), pp. 506 ff.

the self and earthly man in time and space was illuminated by two dreams of mine.

In one dream, which I had in October 1958, I caught sight from my house of two lens-shaped metallically gleaming disks, which hurtled in a narrow arc over the house and down to the lake. They were two UFOs (Unidentified Flying Objects). Then another body came flying directly toward me. It was a perfectly circular lens, like the objective of a telescope. At a distance of four or five hundred yards it stood still for a moment, and then flew off. Immediately afterward, another came speeding through the air: a lens with a metallic extension which led to a box—a magic lantern. At a distance of sixty or seventy yards it stood still in the air, pointing straight at me. I awoke with a feeling of astonishment. Still half in the dream, the thought passed through my head: "We always think that the UFOs are projections of ours. Now it turns out that we are their projections. I am projected by the magic lantern as C. G. Jung. But who manipulates the apparatus?"

I had dreamed once before of the problem of the self and the ego. In that earlier dream I was on a hiking trip. I was walking along a little road through a hilly landscape; the sun was shining and I had a wide view in all directions. Then I came to a small wayside chapel. The door was ajar, and I went in. To my surprise there was no image of the Virgin on the altar, and no crucifix either, but only a wonderful flower arrangement. But then I saw that on the floor in front of the altar, facing me, sat a yogi—in lotus posture, in deep meditation. When I looked at him more closely, I realized that he had my face. I started in profound fright, and awoke with the thought: "Aha, so he is the one who is meditating me. He has a dream, and I am it." I knew that when he awakened, I would no longer be.

I had this dream after my illness in 1944. It is a parable: My self retires into meditation and meditates my earthly form. To put it another way: it assumes human shape in order to enter three-dimensional existence, as if someone were putting on a diver's suit in order to dive into the sea. When it renounces existence in the hereafter, the self assumes a religious posture, as the chapel in the dream shows. In earthly form it can pass through the experiences of the three-dimensional world, and by greater awareness take a further step toward realization.

The figure of the yogi, then, would more or less represent my unconscious prenatal wholeness, and the Far East, as is often the case in dreams, a psychic state alien and opposed to our own. Like the magic lantern, the yogi's meditation "projects" my empirical reality. As a rule, we see this causal relationship in reverse: in the products of the unconscious we discover mandala symbols, that is, circular and quaternary figures which express wholeness, and whenever we wish to express wholeness, we employ just such figures. Our basis is ego-consciousness, our world the field of light centered upon the focal point of the ego. From that point we look out upon an enigmatic world of obscurity, never knowing to what extent the shadowy forms we see are caused by our consciousness, or possess a reality of their own. The superficial observer is content with the first assumption. But closer study shows that as a rule the images of the unconscious are not produced by consciousness, but have a reality and spontaneity of their own. Nevertheless, we regard them as mere marginal phenomena.

The aim of both these dreams is to effect a reversal of the relationship between ego-consciousness and the unconscious, and to represent the unconscious as the generator of the empirical personality. This reversal suggests that in the opinion of the "other side," our unconscious existence is the real one and our conscious world a kind of illusion, an apparent reality constructed for a specific purpose, like a dream which seems a reality as long as we are in it. It is clear that this state of affairs resembles very closely the Oriental conception of Maya.[6]

Unconscious wholeness therefore seems to me the true *spiritus rector* of all biological and psychic events. Here is a principle which strives for total realization—which in man's case signifies the attainment of total consciousness. Attainment of conscious-

---

[6] A tendency to question the locus of reality manifested itself early in Jung's life, when as a child he sat upon the stone and toyed with the idea that the stone was saying, or *was*, "I." Cf. the well-known butterfly dream in Chuangtzu. —A. J.

ness is culture in the broadest sense, and self-knowledge is therefore the heart and essence of this process. The Oriental attributes unquestionably divine significance to the self, and according to the ancient Christian view self-knowledge is the road to knowledge of God.

The decisive question for man is: Is he related to something infinite or not? That is the telling question of his life. Only if we know that the thing which truly matters is the infinite can we avoid fixing our interest upon futilities, and upon all kinds of goals which are not of real importance. Thus we demand that the world grant us recognition for qualities which we regard as personal possessions: our talent or our beauty. The more a man lays stress on false possessions, and the less sensitivity he has for what is essential, the less satisfying is his life. He feels limited because he has limited aims, and the result is envy and jealousy. If we understand and feel that here in this life we already have a link with the infinite, desires and attitudes change. In the final analysis, we count for something only because of the essential we embody, and if we do not embody that, life is wasted. In our relationships to other men, too, the crucial question is whether an element of boundlessness is expressed in the relationship.

The feeling for the infinite, however, can be attained only if we are bounded to the utmost. The greatest limitation for man is the "self"; it is manifested in the experience: "I am *only* that!" Only consciousness of our narrow confinement in the self forms the link to the limitlessness of the unconscious. In such awareness we experience ourselves concurrently as limited and eternal, as both the one and the other. In knowing ourselves to be unique in our personal combination—that is, ultimately limited —we possess also the capacity for becoming conscious of the infinite. But only then!

In an era which has concentrated exclusively upon extension of living space and increase of rational knowledge at all costs, it is a supreme challenge to ask man to become conscious of his uniqueness and his limitation. Uniqueness and limitation are synonymous. Without them, no perception of the unlimited is possible—and, consequently, no coming to consciousness either —merely a delusory identity with it which takes the form of intoxication with large numbers and an avidity for political power.

Our age has shifted all emphasis to the here and now, and thus brought about a daemonization of man and his world. The phenomenon of dictators and all the misery they have wrought springs from the fact that man has been robbed of transcendence by the shortsightedness of the super-intellectuals. Like them, he has fallen a victim to unconsciousness. But man's task is the exact opposite: to become conscious of the contents that press upward from the unconscious. Neither should he persist in his unconsciousness, nor remain identical with the unconscious elements of his being, thus evading his destiny, which is to create more and more consciousness. As far as we can discern, the sole purpose of human existence is to kindle a light in the darkness of mere being. It may even be assumed that just as the unconscious affects us, so the increase in our consciousness affects the unconscious.

·XII·

Late Thoughts

ANY BIOGRAPHY of myself, must, I think, take account of the following reflections. It is true that they may well strike others as highly theoretical, but making "theory"[1] of this sort is as much a part of me, as vital a function of mine, as eating and drinking.

I

What is remarkable about Christianity is that in its system of dogma it anticipates a metamorphosis in the divinity, a process of historic change on the "other side." It does this in the form of the new myth of dissension in heaven, first alluded to in the creation myth in which a serpent-like antagonist of the Creator appears, and lures man to disobedience by the promise of increased conscious knowledge (*scientes bonum et malum*). The second allusion is to the fall of the angels, a premature invasion of the human world by unconscious contents. The angels are a strange genus: they are precisely what they are and cannot be anything else. They are in themselves soulless beings who

[1] In the original sense of the Greek *theorein*, "looking about the world," or the German *Weltanschauung.*—A. J.

represent nothing but the thoughts and intuitions of their Lord. Angels who fall, then, are exclusively "bad" angels. These release the well-known effect of "inflation," which we can also observe nowadays in the megalomania of dictators: the angels beget with men a *race of giants* which ends by threatening to devour mankind, as is told in the book of Enoch.

The third and decisive stage of the myth, however, is the self-realization of God in human form, in fulfillment of the Old Testament idea of the divine marriage and its consequences. As early as the period of primitive Christianity, the idea of the incarnation had been refined to include the intuition of "Christ within us." Thus the unconscious wholeness penetrated into the psychic realm of inner experience, and man was made aware of all that entered into his true configuration. This was a decisive step, not only for man, but also for the Creator—Who, in the eyes of those who had been delivered from darkness, cast off His dark qualities and became the *summum bonum*.

This myth remained unassailably vital for a millennium—until the first signs of a further transformation of consciousness began appearing in the eleventh century.[2] From then on, the symptoms of unrest and doubt increased, until at the end of the second millennium the outlines of a universal catastrophe became apparent, at first in the form of a threat to consciousness. This threat consists in giantism—in other words, a hubris of consciousness—in the assertion: "Nothing is greater than man and his deeds." The otherworldliness, the transcendence of the Christian myth was lost, and with it the view that wholeness is achieved in the other world.

Light is followed by shadow, the other side of the Creator. This development reached its peak in the twentieth century. The Christian world is now truly confronted by the principle of evil, by naked injustice, tyranny, lies, slavery, and coercion of conscience. This manifestation of naked evil has assumed apparently permanent form in the Russian nation; but its first violent eruption came in Germany. That outpouring of evil revealed to what extent Christianity has been undermined in

[2] See *Aion* (CW 9, ii), pp. 82 ff.

the twentieth century. In the face of that, evil can no longer be minimized by the euphemism of the *privatio boni*. Evil has become a determinant reality. It can no longer be dismissed from the world by a circumlocution. We must learn how to handle it, since it is here to stay. How we can live with it without terrible consequences cannot for the present be conceived.

In any case, we stand in need of a reorientation, a *metanoia*. Touching evil brings with it the grave peril of succumbing to it. We must, therefore, no longer succumb to anything at all, not even to good. A so-called good to which we succumb loses its ethical character. Not that there is anything bad in it on that score, but to have succumbed to it may breed trouble. Every form of addiction is bad, no matter whether the narcotic be alcohol or morphine or idealism. We must beware of thinking of good and evil as absolute opposites. The criterion of ethical action can no longer consist in the simple view that good has the force of a categorical imperative, while so-called evil can resolutely be shunned. Recognition of the reality of evil necessarily relativizes the good, and the evil likewise, converting both into halves of a paradoxical whole.

In practical terms, this means that good and evil are no longer so self-evident. We have to realize that each represents a *judgment*. In view of the fallibility of all human judgment, we cannot believe that we will always judge rightly. We might so easily be the victims of misjudgment. The ethical problem is affected by this principle only to the extent that we become somewhat uncertain about moral evaluations. Nevertheless we have to make ethical decisions. The relativity of "good" and "evil" by no means signifies that these categories are invalid, or do not exist. Moral judgment is always present and carries with it characteristic psychological consequences. I have pointed out many times that as in the past, so in the future the wrong we have done, thought, or intended will wreak its vengeance on our souls. Only the contents of judgment are subject to the differing conditions of time and place and, therefore, take correspondingly different forms. For moral evaluation is always founded upon the apparent certitudes of a moral code which pretends to know precisely what is good and what evil. But once we know how uncertain the foundation is, ethical decision becomes a subjective, creative act. We can convince ourselves of its validity only *Deo concedente*—that is, there must be a spontaneous and decisive impulse on the part of the unconscious. Ethics itself, the decision between good and evil, is not affected by this impulse, only made more difficult for us. Nothing can spare us the torment of ethical decision. Nevertheless, harsh as it may sound, we must have the freedom in some circumstances to avoid the known moral good and do what is considered to be evil, if our ethical decision so requires. In other words, again: we must not succumb to either of the opposites. A useful pattern is provided by the *neti-neti* of Indian philosophy. In given cases, the moral code is undeniably abrogated and ethical choice is left to the individual. In itself there is nothing new about this idea; in pre-psychology days such difficult choices were also known and came under the heading of "conflict of duties."

As a rule, however, the individual is so unconscious that he altogether fails to see his own potentialities for decision. Instead he is constantly and anxiously looking around for external rules and regulations which can guide him in his perplexity. Aside from general human inadequacy, a good deal of the blame for this rests with education, which promulgates the old generalizations and says nothing about the secrets of private experience. Thus, every effort is made to teach idealistic beliefs or conduct which people know in their hearts they can never live up to, and such ideals are preached by officials who know that they themselves have never lived up to these high standards and never will. What is more, nobody ever questions the value of this kind of teaching.

Therefore the individual who wishes to have an answer to the problem of evil, as it is posed today, has need, first and foremost, of *self-knowledge*, that is, the utmost possible knowledge of his own wholeness. He must know relentlessly how much good he can do, and what crimes he is capable of, and must beware of regarding the one as real and the other as illusion. Both are elements within his nature, and both are bound to come to light in him, should he wish—as he ought—to live without self-deception or self-delusion.

In general, however, most people are hopelessly ill equipped for living on this level, although there are also many persons today who have the capacity for profounder insight into themselves. Such self-knowledge is of prime importance, because through it we approach that fundamental stratum or core of human nature where the instincts dwell. Here are those preexistent dynamic factors which ultimately govern the ethical decisions of our consciousness. This core is the unconscious and its contents, concerning which we cannot pass any final judgment. Our ideas about it are bound to be inadequate, for we are unable to comprehend its essence cognitively and set rational limits to it. We achieve knowledge of nature only through science, which enlarges consciousness; hence deepened self-knowledge also requires science, that is, psychology. No one builds a telescope or microscope with one turn of the wrist, out of good will alone, without a knowledge of optics.

Today we need psychology for reasons that involve our very existence. We stand perplexed and stupefied before the phenomenon of Nazism and Bolshevism because we know nothing about man, or at any rate have only a lopsided and distorted picture of him. If we had self-knowledge, that would not be the case. We stand face to face with the terrible question of evil and do not even know what is before us, let alone what to pit against it. And even if we did know, we still could not understand "how it could happen here." With glorious naïveté a statesman comes out with the proud declaration that he has no "imagination for evil." Quite right: *we* have no imagination for evil, but evil *has us in its grip.* Some do not want to know this, and others are identified with evil. That is the psychological situation in the world today: some call themselves Christian and imagine that they can trample so-called evil underfoot by merely willing to; others have succumbed to it and no longer see the good. Evil today has become a visible Great Power. One half of humanity battens and grows strong on a doctrine fabricated by human ratiocination; the other half sickens from the lack of a myth commensurate with the situation. The Christian nations have come to a sorry pass; their Christianity slumbers and has neglected to develop its myth further in the course of the centuries.

Those who gave expression to the dark stirrings of growth in mythic ideas were refused a hearing; Gioacchino da Fiore, Meister Eckhart, Jacob Boehme, and many others have remained obscurantists for the majority. The only ray of light is Pius XII and his dogma.[3] But people do not even know what I am referring to when I say this. They do not realize that a myth is dead if it no longer lives and grows.

Our myth has become mute, and gives no answers. The fault lies not in it as it is set down in the Scriptures, but solely in us, who have not developed it further, who, rather, have suppressed any such attempts. The original version of the myth offers ample points of departure and possibilities of development. For example, the words are put into Christ's mouth: "Be ye therefore wise as serpents, and harmless as doves." For what purpose do men need the cunning of serpents? And what is the link between this cunning and the innocence of the dove? "Except ye become as little children . . ." Who gives thought to what children are like in reality? By what morality did the Lord justify the taking of the ass which he needed in order to ride in triumph into Jerusalem? How was it that, shortly afterward, he put on a display of childish bad temper and cursed the fig tree? What kind of morality emerges from the parable of the unjust steward, and what profound insight, of such far-reaching significance for our own predicament, from the apocryphal logion: "Man, if thou knowest what thou dost, thou art blessed; but if thou knowest not, thou art accursed and a transgressor of the law"?[4] What, finally, does it mean when St. Paul confesses: "The evil which I would not, that I do"? I will not discuss the transparent prophecies of the Book of Revelation, because no one believes in them and the whole subject is felt to be an embarrassing one.

The old question posed by the Gnostics, "Whence comes evil?" has been given no answer by the Christian world, and Origen's cautious suggestion of a possible redemption of the devil was termed a heresy. Today we are compelled to meet that question; but we stand empty-handed, bewildered, and perplexed, and cannot even get it into our heads that no myth will come to our

[3] See above, Chap. VII, n. 2, p. 202.
[4] *Codex Bezae ad Lucam* 6, 4.

aid although we have such urgent need of one. As the result of the political situation and the frightful, not to say diabolic, triumphs of science, we are shaken by secret shudders and dark forebodings; but we know no way out, and very few persons indeed draw the conclusion that this time the issue is the long-since-forgotten *soul of man.*

A further development of myth might well begin with the outpouring of the Holy Spirit upon the apostles, by which they were made into sons of God, and not only they, but all others who through them and after them received the *filiatio*—sonship of God—and thus partook of the certainty that they were more than autochthonous *animalia* sprung from the earth, that as the twice-born they had their roots in the divinity itself. Their visible, physical life was on this earth; but the invisible inner man had come from and would return to the primordial image of wholeness, to the eternal Father, as the Christian myth of salvation puts it.

Just as the Creator is whole, so His creature, His son, ought to be whole. Nothing can take away from the concept of divine wholeness. But unbeknownst to all, a splitting of that wholeness ensued; there emerged a realm of light and a realm of darkness. This outcome, even before Christ appeared, was clearly prefigured, as we may observe *inter alia* in the experience of Job, or in the widely disseminated Book of Enoch, which belongs to immediate pre-Christian times. In Christianity, too, this metaphysical split was plainly perpetuated: Satan, who in the Old Testament still belonged to the intimate entourage of Yahweh, now formed the diametrical and eternal opposite of the divine world. He could not be uprooted. It is therefore not surprising that as early as the beginning of the eleventh century the belief arose that the devil, not God, had created the world. Thus the keynote was struck for the second half of the Christian aeon, after the myth of the fall of the angels had already explained that these fallen angels had taught men a dangerous knowledge of science and the arts. What would these old storytellers have to say about Hiroshima?

The visionary genius of Jacob Boehme recognized the paradoxical nature of the God-image and thus contributed to the further development of the myth. The mandala symbol sketched by Boehme [5] is a representation of the split God, for the inner circle is divided into two semicircles standing back to back.

Since dogma holds that God is wholly present in each of the three Persons, He is also wholly present in each part of the out-poured Holy Spirit; thus every man can partake of the whole of God and hence of the filiation. The *complexio oppositorum* of the God-image thus enters into man, and not as unity, but as conflict, the dark half of the image coming into opposition with the accepted view that God is "Light." This very process is tak-ing place in our own times, albeit scarcely recognized by the official teachers of humanity whose task, supposedly, is to un-derstand such matters. There is the general feeling, to be sure, that we have reached a significant turning point in the ages, but people imagine that the great change has to do with nuclear fission and fusion, or with space rockets. What is concurrently taking place in the human psyche is usually overlooked.

Insofar as the God-image is, from the psychological point of view, a manifestation of the ground of the psyche, and insofar as the cleavage in that image is becoming clear to mankind as a profound dichotomy which penetrates even into world politics, a compensation has arisen. This takes the form of circular symbols of unity which represent a synthesis of the opposites within the psyche. I refer to the worldwide rumors of Unidentified Flying Objects, of which we began to hear as early as 1945. These ru-mors are founded either upon visions or upon actual phenomena. The usual story about the UFOs is that they are some kind of spacecraft coming from other planets or even from the fourth dimension.

More than twenty years earlier (in 1918), in the course of my investigations of the collective unconscious, I discovered the presence of an apparently universal symbol of a similar type—the mandala symbol. To make sure of my case, I spent more than a decade amassing additional data, before announcing my dis-covery for the first time. [6] The mandala is an archetypal image

[5] Reproduced in *The Archetypes and the Collective Unconscious* (CW 9, i), p. 297.
[6] In the commentary to *The Secret of the Golden Flower* (1931) (CW 13).

whose occurrence is attested throughout the ages. It signifies the *wholeness of the self*. This circular image represents the wholeness of the psychic ground or, to put it in mythic terms, the divinity incarnate in man. In contrast to Boehme's mandala, the modern ones strive for unity; they represent a compensation of the psychic cleavage, or an anticipation that the cleavage will be surmounted. Since this process takes place in the collective unconscious, it manifests itself everywhere. The worldwide stories of the UFOs are evidence of that; they are the symptom of a universally present psychic disposition.

Insofar as analytical treatment makes the "shadow" conscious, it causes a cleavage and a tension of opposites which in their turn seek compensation in unity. The adjustment is achieved through symbols. The conflict between the opposites can strain our psyche to the breaking point, if we take them seriously, or if they take us seriously. The *tertium non datur* of logic proves its worth: no solution can be seen. If all goes well, the solution, seemingly of its own accord, appears out of nature. Then and then only is it convincing. It is felt as "grace." Since the solution proceeds out of the confrontation and clash of opposites, it is usually an unfathomable mixture of conscious and unconscious factors, and therefore a symbol, a coin split into two halves which fit together precisely.[7] It represents the result of the joint labors of consciousness and the unconscious, and attains the likeness of the God-image in the form of the mandala, which is probably the simplest model of a concept of wholeness, and one which spontaneously arises in the mind as a representation of the struggle and reconciliation of opposites. The clash, which is at first of a purely personal nature, is soon followed by the insight that the subjective conflict is only a single instance of the universal conflict of opposites. Our psyche is set up in accord with the structure of the universe, and what happens in the macrocosm likewise happens in the infinitesimal and most subjective reaches of the psyche. For that reason the God-image is always a projection of the inner experience of a powerful *vis-à-vis*. This is symbolized by objects from which

[7] One of the meanings of *symbolon* is the *tessera hospitalitatis* between host and guest, the broken coin which is shared between two parting friends.—A. J.

the inner experience has taken its initial impulse, and which from then on preserve numinous significance, or else it is characterized by its numinosity and the overwhelming force of that numinosity. In this way the imagination liberates itself from the concretism of the object and attempts to sketch the image of the invisible as something which stands behind the phenomenon. I am thinking here of the simplest basic form of the mandala, the circle, and the simplest (mental) division of the circle, the quadrant or, as the case may be, the cross.

Such experiences have a helpful or, it may be, annihilating effect upon man. He cannot grasp, comprehend, dominate them; nor can he free himself or escape from them, and therefore feels them as overpowering. Recognizing that they do not spring from his conscious personality, he calls them mana, daimon, or God. Science employs the term "the unconscious," thus admitting that it knows nothing about it, for it can know nothing about the substance of the psyche when the sole means of knowing anything is the psyche. Therefore the validity of such terms as mana, daimon, or God can be neither disproved nor affirmed. We can, however, establish that the sense of strangeness connected with the experience of something objective, apparently outside the psyche, is indeed authentic.

We know that something unknown, alien, does come our way, just as we know that we do not ourselves *make* a dream or an inspiration, but that it somehow arises of its own accord. What does happen to us in this manner can be said to emanate from mana, from a daimon, a god, or the unconscious. The first three terms have the great merit of including and evoking the emotional quality of numinosity, whereas the latter—the unconscious—is banal and therefore closer to reality. This latter concept includes the empirical realm—that is, the commonplace reality we know so well. The unconscious is too neutral and rational a term to give much impetus to the imagination. The term, after all, was coined for scientific purposes, and is far better suited to dispassionate observation which makes no metaphysical claims than are the transcendental concepts, which are controversial and therefore tend to breed fanaticism.

Hence I prefer the term "the unconscious," knowing that I

might equally well speak of "God" or "daimon" if I wished to express myself in mythic language. When I do use such mythic language, I am aware that "mana," "daimon," and "God" are synonyms for the unconscious—that is to say, we know just as much or just as little about them as about the latter. People only *believe* they know much more about them—and for certain purposes that belief is far more useful and effective than a scientific concept. The great advantage of the concepts "daimon" and "God" lies in making possible a much better objectification of the *vis-à-vis*, namely, a *personification* of it. Their emotional quality confers life and effectuality upon them. Hate and love, fear and reverence, enter the scene of the confrontation and raise it to a drama. What has merely been "displayed" becomes "acted." [8] The whole man is challenged and enters the fray with his total reality. Only then can he become whole and only then can "God be born," that is, enter into human reality and associate with man in the form of "man." By this act of incarnation man—that is, his ego—is inwardly replaced by "God," and God becomes outwardly man, in keeping with the saying of Jesus: "Who sees me, sees the Father."

It is at this point that the shortcomings of mythic terminology become apparent. The Christian's ordinary conception of God is of an omnipotent, omniscient, and all-merciful Father and Creator of the world. If this God wishes to become man, an incredible *kenosis* (emptying) [9] is required of Him, in order to reduce His totality to the infinitesimal human scale. Even then it is hard to see why the human frame is not shattered by the incarnation. Theological thinkers have therefore felt it necessary to equip Jesus with qualities which raise him above ordinary human existence. Above all he lacks the *macula peccati* (stain of original sin). For that reason, if for no other, he is at least a god-man or a demigod. The Christian God-image cannot become incarnate in empirical man without contradictions—quite apart from the fact that man with all his external characteristics seems little suited to representing a god.

[8] Cf. "Transformation Symbolism in the Mass," in *Psychology and Religion: West and East* (CW 11), pp. 249–50.
[9] Philippians 2:6.

The myth must ultimately take monotheism seriously and put aside its dualism, which, however much repudiated officially, has persisted until now and enthroned an eternal dark antagonist alongside the omnipotent Good. Room must be made within the system for the philosophical *complexio oppositorum* of Nicholas of Cusa and the moral ambivalence of Jacob Boehme; only thus can the One God be granted the wholeness and the synthesis of opposites which should be His. It is a fact that symbols, by their very nature, can so unite the opposites that these no longer diverge or clash, but mutually supplement one another and give meaningful shape to life. Once that has been experienced, the ambivalence in the image of a nature-god or Creator-god ceases to present difficulties. On the contrary, the myth of the necessary incarnation of God—the essence of the Christian message—can then be understood as man's creative confrontation with the opposites and their synthesis in the self, the wholeness of his personality. The unavoidable internal contradictions in the image of a Creator-god can be reconciled in the unity and wholeness of the self as the *coniunctio oppositorum* of the alchemists or as a *unio mystica*. In the experience of the self it is no longer the opposites "God" and "man" that are reconciled, as it was before, but rather the opposites within the God-image itself. That is the meaning of divine service, of the service which man can render to God, that light may emerge from the darkness, that the Creator may become conscious of His creation, and man conscious of himself.

That is the goal, or one goal, which fits man meaningfully into the scheme of creation, and at the same time confers meaning upon it. It is an explanatory myth which has slowly taken shape within me in the course of the decades. It is a goal I can acknowledge and esteem, and which therefore satisfies me.

By virtue of his reflective faculties, man is raised out of the animal world, and by his mind he demonstrates that nature has put a high premium precisely upon the development of consciousness. Through consciousness he takes possession of nature by recognizing the existence of the world and thus, as it were, confirming the Creator. The world becomes the phenomenal world, for without conscious reflection it would not be. If the Creator were conscious of Himself, He would not need conscious creatures; nor is it probable that the extremely indirect methods of creation, which squander millions of years upon the development of countless species and creatures, are the outcome of purposeful intention. Natural history tells us of a haphazard and casual transformation of species over hundreds of millions of years of devouring and being devoured. The biological and political history of man is an elaborate repetition of the same thing. But the history of the mind offers a different picture. Here the miracle of reflecting consciousness intervenes—the second cosmogony. The importance of consciousness is so great that one cannot help suspecting the element of *meaning* to be concealed somewhere within all the monstrous, apparently senseless biological turmoil, and that the road to its manifestation was ultimately found on the level of warm-blooded vertebrates possessed of a differentiated brain—found as if by chance, unintended and unforeseen, and yet somehow sensed, felt and groped for out of some dark urge.

I do not imagine that in my reflections on the meaning of man and his myth I have uttered a final truth, but I think that this is what can be said at the end of our aeon of the Fishes, and perhaps must be said in view of the coming aeon of Aquarius (the Water Bearer), who has a human figure and is next to the sign of the Fishes. This is a *coniunctio oppositorum* composed of two fishes in reverse. The Water Bearer seems to represent the self. With a sovereign gesture he pours the contents of his jug into the mouth of *Piscis austrinus*,[10] which symbolizes a son, a still unconscious content. Out of this unconscious content will emerge, after the passage of another aeon of more than two thousand years, a future whose features are indicated by the symbol of Capricorn: an *aigokeros*, the monstrosity of the Goat-Fish,[11] symbolizing the mountains and the depths of the sea, a polarity

[10] Constellation of the "Southern Fish." Its mouth is formed by Fomalhaut (Arabic for "mouth of the fish") below the constellation of the Water Bearer.
[11] The constellation of Capricorn was originally called the "Goat-Fish."

339

made up of two undifferentiated animal elements which have grown together. This strange being could easily be the primordial image of a Creator-god confronting "man," the Anthropos. On this question there is a silence within me, as there is in the empirical data at my disposal—the products of the unconscious of other people with which I am acquainted, or historical documents. If insight does not come by itself, speculation is pointless. It makes sense only when we have objective data comparable to our material on the aeon of Aquarius.

We do not know how far the process of coming to consciousness can extend, or where it will lead. It is a new element in the story of creation, and there are no parallels we can look to. We therefore cannot know what potentialities are inherent in it. Neither can we know the prospects for the species Homo sapiens. Will it imitate the fate of other species, which once flourished on the earth and now are extinct? Biology can advance no reasons why this should not be so.

The need for mythic statements is satisfied when we frame a view of the world which adequately explains the meaning of human existence in the cosmos, a view which springs from our psychic wholeness, from the co-operation between conscious and unconscious. Meaninglessness inhibits fullness of life and is therefore equivalent to illness. Meaning makes a great many things endurable—perhaps everything. No science will ever replace myth, and a myth cannot be made out of any science. For it is not that "God" is a myth, but that myth is the revelation of a divine life in man. It is not we who invent myth, rather it speaks to us as a Word of God. The Word of God comes to us, and we have no way of distinguishing whether and to what extent it is different from God. There is nothing about this Word that could not be considered known and human, except for the manner in which it confronts us spontaneously and places obligations upon us. It is not affected by the arbitrary operation of our will. We cannot explain an inspiration. Our chief feeling about it is that it is not the result of our own ratiocinations, but that it came to us from elsewhere. And if we happen to have a precognitive dream, how can we possibly ascribe it to our own powers? After all, often we do not even know, until some time afterward, that the dream represented foreknowledge, or knowledge of something that happened at a distance.

The Word happens to us; we suffer it, for we are victims of a profound uncertainty: with God as a *complexio oppositorum*, all things are possible, in the fullest meaning of the phrase. Truth and delusion, good and evil, are equally possible. Myth is or can be equivocal, like the oracle of Delphi or like a dream. We cannot and ought not to repudiate reason; but equally we must cling to the hope that instinct will hasten to our aid—in which case God is supporting us against God, as Job long ago understood. Everything through which the "other will" is expressed proceeds from man—his thinking, his words, his images, and even his limitations. Consequently he has the tendency to refer everything to himself, when he begins to think in clumsy psychological terms, and decides that everything proceeds out of his intentions and out of himself. With childlike naïveté he assumes that he knows all his own reaches and knows what he is "in himself." Yet all the while he is fatally handicapped by the weakness of his consciousness and the corresponding fear of the unconscious. Therefore he is utterly unable to separate what he has carefully reasoned out from what has spontaneously flowed to him from another source. He has no objectivity toward himself and cannot yet regard himself as a phenomenon which he finds in existence and with which, for better or worse, he is identical. At first everything is thrust upon him, everything happens to him, and it is only by great effort that he finally succeeds in conquering and holding for himself an area of relative freedom.

Only when he has won his way to this achievement, and then only, is he in a position to recognize that he is confronting his instinctive foundations, given him from the beginning, which he cannot make disappear, however much he would like to. His beginnings are not by any means mere pasts; they live with him as the constant substratum of his existence, and his consciousness is as much molded by them as by the physical world around him.

These facts assail man from without and from within with overwhelming force. He has summed them up under the idea of divinity, has described their effects with the aid of myth, and has interpreted this myth as the "Word of God," that is, as the inspiration and revelation of the numen from the "other side."

II

There is no better means of intensifying the treasured feeling of individuality than the possession of a secret which the individual is pledged to guard. The very beginnings of societal structures reveal the craving for secret organizations. When no valid secrets really exist, mysteries are invented or contrived to which privileged initiates are admitted. Such was the case with the Rosicrucians and many other societies. Among these pseudo-secrets there are—ironically—real secrets of which the initiates are entirely unaware—as, for example, in those societies which borrowed their "secret" primarily from the alchemical tradition.

The need for ostentatious secrecy is of vital importance on the primitive level, for the shared secret serves as a cement binding the tribe together. Secrets on the tribal level constitute a helpful compensation for lack of cohesion in the individual personality, which is constantly relapsing into the original unconscious identity with other members of the group. Attainment of the human goal—an individual who is conscious of his own peculiar nature—thus becomes a long, almost hopeless process of education. For even the individuals whose initiation into certain secrets has marked them out in some way are fundamentally obeying the laws of group identity, though in their case the group is a socially differentiated one.

The secret society is an intermediary stage on the way to individuation. The individual is still relying on a collective organization to effect his differentiation for him; that is, he has not yet recognized that it is really the individual's task to differentiate himself from all the others and stand on his own feet. All collective identities, such as membership in organizations, support of "isms," and so on, interfere with the fulfillment of this task. Such collective identities are crutches for the lame, shields for the timid, beds for the lazy, nurseries for the irresponsible; but they are equally shelters for the poor and weak, a home port for the shipwrecked, the bosom of a family for orphans, a land of promise for disillusioned vagrants and weary pilgrims, a herd and a safe fold for lost sheep, and a mother providing nourishment and growth. It would therefore be wrong to regard this intermediary stage as a trap; on the contrary, for a long time to come it will represent the only possible form of existence for the individual, who nowadays seems more than ever threatened by anonymity. Collective organization is still so essential today that many consider it, with some justification, to be the final goal; whereas to call for further steps along the road to autonomy appears like arrogance or hubris, fantasticality, or simply folly.

Nevertheless it may be that for sufficient reasons a man feels he must set out on his own feet along the road to wider realms. It may be that in all the garbs, shapes, forms, modes, and manners of life offered to him he does not find what is peculiarly necessary for him. He will go alone and be his own company. He will serve as his own group, consisting of a variety of opinions and tendencies—which need not necessarily be marching in the same direction. In fact, he will be at odds with himself, and will find great difficulty in uniting his own multiplicity for purposes of common action. Even if he is outwardly protected by the social forms of the intermediary stage, he will have no defense against his inner multiplicity. The disunion within himself may cause him to give up, to lapse into identity with his surroundings.

Like the initiate of a secret society who has broken free from the undifferentiated collectivity, the individual on his lonely path needs a secret which for various reasons he may not or cannot reveal. Such a secret reinforces him in the isolation of his individual aims. A great many individuals cannot bear this isolation. They are the neurotics, who necessarily play hide-and-seek with others as well as with themselves, without being able to take the game really seriously. As a rule they end by surrendering their individual goal to their craving for collective conformity—a procedure which all the opinions, beliefs, and ideals of their environment encourage. Moreover, no rational arguments prevail against the environment. Only a secret which the individual cannot betray—one which he fears to give away, or which he cannot formulate in words, and which therefore seems to belong to the category of crazy ideas—can prevent the otherwise inevitable retrogression.

The need for such a secret is in many cases so compelling that the individual finds himself involved in ideas and actions for which he is no longer responsible. He is being motivated neither by caprice nor arrogance, but by a *dira necessitas* which he himself cannot comprehend. This necessity comes down upon him with savage fatefulness, and perhaps for the first time in his life demonstrates to him *ad oculos* the presence of something alien and more powerful than himself in his own most personal domain, where he thought himself the master. A vivid example is the story of Jacob, who wrestled with the angel and came away with a dislocated hip, but by his struggle prevented a murder. In those fortunate days, Jacob's story was believed without question. A contemporary Jacob, telling such a tale, would be treated to meaningful smiles. He would prefer not to speak of such matters, especially if he were inclined to have his private views about the nature of Yahweh's messenger. Thus he would find himself willy-nilly in possession of a secret that could not be discussed, and would become a deviant from the collectivity. Naturally, his mental reservation would ultimately come to light, unless he succeeded in playing the hypocrite all his life. But anyone who attempts to do both, to adjust to his group and at the same time pursue his individual goal, becomes neurotic. Our modern Jacob would be concealing from himself the fact that the angel was after all the stronger of the two—as he certainly was, for no claims were ever made that the angel, too, came away with a limp.

The man, therefore, who, driven by his daimon, steps beyond the limits of the intermediary stage, truly enters the "untrodden, untreadable regions," [12] where there are no charted ways and no shelter spreads a protecting roof over his head. There are no precepts to guide him when he encounters an unforeseen situation—for example, a conflict of duties. For the most part, these

[12] *Faust*, Part Two.

sallies into no man's land last only as long as no such conflicts occur, and come swiftly to an end as soon as conflict is sniffed from afar. I cannot blame the person who takes to his heels at once. But neither can I approve his finding merit in his weakness and cowardice. Since my contempt can do him no further harm, I may as well say that I find nothing praiseworthy about such capitulations.

But if a man faced with a conflict of duties undertakes to deal with them absolutely on his own responsibility, and before a judge who sits in judgment on him day and night, he may well find himself in an isolated position. There is now an authentic secret in his life which cannot be discussed—if only because he is involved in an endless inner trial in which he is his own counsel and ruthless examiner, and no secular or spiritual judge can restore his easy sleep. If he were not already sick to death of the decisions of such judges, he would never have found himself in a conflict. For such a conflict always presupposes a higher sense of responsibility. It is this very quality which keeps its possessor from accepting the decision of a collectivity. In his case the court is transposed to the inner world where the verdict is pronounced behind closed doors.

Once this happens, the psyche of the individual acquires heightened importance. It is not only the seat of his well-known and socially defined ego; it is also the instrument for measuring what it is worth in and for itself. Nothing so promotes the growth of consciousness as this inner confrontation of opposites. Quite unsuspected facts turn up in the indictment, and the defense is obliged to discover arguments hitherto unknown. In the course of this, a considerable portion of the outer world reaches the inner, and by that very fact the outer world is impoverished or relieved. On the other hand, the inner world has gained that much weight by being raised to the rank of a tribunal for ethical decisions. However, the once unequivocal ego loses the prerogative of being merely the prosecutor; it must also learn the role of defendant. The ego becomes ambivalent and ambiguous, and is caught between hammer and anvil. *It becomes aware of a polarity superordinate to itself.*

By no means every conflict of duties, and perhaps not even a single one, is ever really "solved," though it may be argued over, weighed, and counterweighed till doomsday. Sooner or later the decision is simply there, the product, it would seem, of some kind of short-circuit. Practical life cannot be suspended in an everlasting contradiction. The opposites and the contradictions between them do not vanish, however, even when for a moment they yield before the impulse to action. They constantly threaten the unity of the personality, and entangle life again and again in their dichotomies.

Insight into the dangers and the painfulness of such a state might well decide one to stay at home, that is, never to leave the safe fold and the warm cocoon, since these alone promise protection from inner stress. Those who do not *have* to leave father and mother are certainly safest with them. A good many persons, however, find themselves thrust out upon the road to individuation. In no time at all they will become acquainted with the positive and negative aspects of human nature.

Just as all energy proceeds from opposition, so the psyche too possesses its inner polarity, this being the indispensable prerequisite for its aliveness, as Heraclitus realized long ago. Both theoretically and practically, polarity is inherent in all living things. Set against this overpowering force is the fragile unity of the ego, which has come into being in the course of millennia only with the aid of countless protective measures. That an ego was possible at all appears to spring from the fact that all opposites seek to achieve a state of balance. This happens in the exchange of energy which results from the collision of hot and cold, high and low, and so on. The energy underlying conscious psychic life is pre-existent to it and therefore at first unconscious. As it approaches consciousness it first appears projected in figures like mana, gods, daimons, etc., whose numen seems to be the vital source of energy, and in point of fact is so as long as these supernatural figures are accepted. But as these fade and lose their force, the ego—that is, the empirical man—seems to come into possession of this source of energy, and does so in the fullest meaning of this ambiguous statement: on the one hand he seeks to seize this energy, to possess it, and even imagines that he does possess it; and on the other hand he is possessed by it.

This grotesque situation can, to be sure, occur only when the contents of consciousness are regarded as the sole form of psychic existence. Where this is the case, there is no preventing inflation by projections coming home to roost. But where the existence of an unconscious psyche is admitted, the contents of projection can be received into the inborn instinctive forms which predate consciousness. Their objectivity and autonomy are thereby preserved, and inflation is avoided. The archetypes, which are pre-existent to consciousness and condition it, appear in the part they actually play in reality: as a priori structural forms of the stuff of consciousness. They do not in any sense represent things as they are in themselves, but rather the forms in which things can be perceived and conceived. Naturally, it is not merely the archetypes that govern the particular nature of perceptions. They account only for the collective component of a perception. As an attribute of instinct they partake of its dynamic nature, and consequently possess a specific energy which causes or compels definite modes of behavior or impulses; that is, they may under certain circumstances have a possessive or obsessive force (numinosity!). The conception of them as *daimonia* is therefore quite in accord with their nature.

If anyone is inclined to believe that any aspect of the *nature* of things is changed by such formulations, he is being extremely credulous about words. The real facts do not change, whatever names we give them. Only we ourselves are affected. If one were to conceive of "God" as "pure Nothingness," that has nothing whatsoever to do with the fact of a superordinate principle. We are just as much possessed as before; the change of name has removed nothing at all from reality. At most we have taken a false attitude toward reality if the new name implies a denial. On the other hand, a positive name for the unknowable has the merit of putting us into a correspondingly positive attitude. If, therefore, we speak of "God" as an "archetype," we are saying nothing about His real nature but are letting it be known that "God" already has a place in that part of our psyche which is pre-existent to consciousness and that He therefore cannot be considered an invention of consciousness. We neither make Him more remote nor eliminate Him, but bring Him closer to the possibility of being experienced. This latter circumstance is by no means unimportant, for a thing which cannot be experienced may easily be suspected of non-existence. This suspicion is so inviting that so-called believers in God see nothing but atheism in my attempt to reconstruct the primitive unconscious psyche. Or if not atheism, then Gnosticism—anything, heaven forbid, but a psychic reality like the unconscious. If the unconscious is anything at all, it must consist of earlier evolutionary stages of our conscious psyche. The assumption that man in his whole glory was created on the sixth day of Creation, without any preliminary stages, is after all somewhat too simple and archaic to satisfy us nowadays. There is pretty general agreement on that score. In regard to the psyche, however, the archaic conception holds on tenaciously: the psyche has no antecedents, is a *tabula rasa*, arises anew at birth, and is only what it imagines itself to be.

Consciousness is phylogenetically and ontogenetically a secondary phenomenon. It is time this obvious fact were grasped at last. Just as the body has an anatomical prehistory of millions of years, so also does the psychic system. And just as the human body today represents in each of its parts the result of this evolution, and everywhere still shows traces of its earlier stages—so the same may be said of the psyche. Consciousness began its evolution from an animal-like state which seems to us unconscious, and the same process of differentiation is repeated in every child. The psyche of the child in its preconscious state is anything but a *tabula rasa;* it is already preformed in a recognizably individual way, and is moreover equipped with all specifically human instincts, as well as with the a priori foundations of the higher functions.

On this complicated base, the ego arises. Throughout life the ego is sustained by this base. When the base does not function, stasis ensues and then death. Its life and its reality are of vital importance. Compared to it, even the external world is secondary, for what does the world matter if the endogenous impulse to grasp it and manipulate it is lacking? In the long run no conscious will can ever replace the life instinct. This instinct comes to us from within, as a compulsion or will or command, and if—as has more or less been done from time immemorial—we give it the name of a personal daimon we are at least aptly expressing the psychological situation. And if, by employing the concept of the archetype, we attempt to define a little more closely the point at which the daimon grips us, we have not abolished anything, only approached closer to the source of life.

It is only natural that I as a psychiatrist (doctor of the soul) should espouse such a view, for I am primarily interested in how I can help my patients find their healthy base again. To do that, a great variety of knowledge is needed, as I have learned. Medicine in general has, after all, proceeded in like manner. It has not made its advances through the discovery of some single trick of healing, thus phenomenally simplifying its methods. On the contrary, it has evolved into a science of enormous complexity—not the least of the reasons being that it has made borrowings from all possible fields. Hence I am not concerned with proving anything to other disciplines; I am merely attempting to put their knowledge to good use in my own field. Naturally, it is incumbent upon me to report on such applications and their consequences. For certain new things come to light when one transfers the knowledge of one field to another and applies it in practice. Had X-rays remained the exclusive property of the physicist and not been applied in medicine, we would know far less. Then again, if radiation therapy has in some circumstances dangerous consequences, that is interesting to the physician; but it is not necessarily of interest to the physicist, who uses radiation in an altogether different manner and for other purposes. Nor will he think that the physician has poached upon his territory when the latter points out certain harmful or salutary properties of the invisible rays.

If I, for example, apply historical or theological insights in psychotherapy, they naturally appear in a different light and lead to conclusions other than those to which they lead when restricted to their proper fields, where they serve other purposes.

The fact, therefore, that a polarity underlies the dynamics of the psyche means that the whole problem of opposites in its broadest sense, with all its concomitant religious and philosophical aspects, is drawn into the psychological discussion. These aspects lose the autonomous character they have in their own field—inevitably so, since they are approached in terms of psychological questions; that is, they are no longer viewed from the angle of religious or philosophical truth, but are examined for their psychological validity and significance. Leaving aside their claim to be independent truths, the fact remains that regarded empirically—which is to say, scientifically—they are primarily *psychic phenomena*. This fact seems to me incontestable. That they claim a justification for themselves is in keeping with the psychological approach, which does not brand such a claim unjustified, but on the contrary treats it with special consideration. Psychology has no room for judgments like "only religious" or "only philosophical," despite the fact that we too often hear the charge of something's being "only psychological"—especially from theologians.

All conceivable statements are made by the psyche. Among other things, the psyche appears as a dynamic process which rests on a foundation of antithesis, on a flow of energy between two poles. It is a general rule of logic that "principles are not to be multiplied beyond the necessary." Therefore, since interpretation in terms of energy has proved a generally valid principle of explanation in the natural sciences, we must limit ourselves to it in psychology also. No firm facts are available which would recommend some other view; moreover, the antithetical or polaristic nature of the psyche and its contents is verified by psychological experience.[13]

Now if the dynamic conception of the psyche is correct, all statements which seek to overstep the limits of the psyche's polarity—statements about a metaphysical reality, for example—must be paradoxical if they are to lay claim to any sort of validity.

The psyche cannot leap beyond itself. It cannot set up any absolute truths, for its own polarity determines the relativity of its

[13] Cf. "On Psychic Energy," in *The Structure and Dynamics of the Psyche* (CW 8).

statements. Wherever the psyche does announce absolute truths—such as, for example, "God is motion," or "God is One" —it necessarily falls into one or the other of its own antitheses. For the two statements might equally well be: "God is rest," or "God is All." Through one-sidedness the psyche disintegrates and loses its capacity for cognition. It becomes an unreflective (because unreflectable) succession of psychic states, each of which fancies itself its own justification because it does not, or does not yet, see any other state.

In saying this we are not expressing a value judgment, but only pointing out that the limit is very frequently overstepped. Indeed, this is inevitable, for, as Heraclitus says, "Everything is flux." Thesis is followed by antithesis, and between the two is generated a third factor, a lysis which was not perceptible before. In this the psyche once again merely demonstrates its antithetical nature and at no point has really got outside itself.

In my effort to depict the limitations of the psyche I do not mean to imply that *only* the psyche exists. It is merely that, so far as perception and cognition are concerned, we cannot see beyond the psyche. Science is tacitly convinced that a non-psychic, transcendental object exists. But science also knows how difficult it is to grasp the real nature of the object, especially when the organ of perception fails or is lacking, and when the appropriate modes of thought do not exist or have still to be created. In cases where neither our sense organs nor their artificial aids can attest the presence of a real object, the difficulties mount enormously, so that one feels tempted to assert that there is simply no real object present. I have never drawn this overhasty conclusion, for I have never been inclined to think that our senses were capable of perceiving all forms of being. I have, therefore, even hazarded the postulate that the phenomenon of archetypal configurations—which are psychic events *par excellence*—may be founded upon a *psychoid* base, that is, upon an only partially psychic and possibly altogether different form of being. For lack of empirical data I have neither knowledge nor understanding of such forms of being, which are commonly called spiritual. From the point of view of science, it is immaterial what I may *believe* on that score, and I must accept my ignorance. But insofar as the archetypes act upon me, they are real and actual to me, even though I do not know what their real nature is. This applies, of course, not only to the archetypes but to the nature of the psyche in general. Whatever it may state about itself, it will never get beyond itself. All comprehension and all that is comprehended is in itself psychic, and to that extent we are hopelessly cooped up in an exclusively psychic world. Nevertheless, we have good reason to suppose that behind this veil there exists the uncomprehended absolute object which affects and influences us—and to suppose it even, or particularly, in the case of psychic phenomena about which no verifiable statements can be made. Statements concerning possibility or impossibility are valid only in specialized fields; outside those fields they are merely arrogant presumptions.

Prohibited though it may be from an objective point of view to make statements out of the blue—that is, without sufficient reason—there are nevertheless some statements which apparently have to be made without objective reasons. The justification here is a psychodynamic one, of the sort usually termed subjective and regarded as a purely personal matter. But that is to commit the mistake of failing to distinguish whether the statement really proceeds only from an isolated subject, and is prompted by exclusively personal motives, or whether it occurs generally and springs from a collectively present dynamic pattern. In that case it should not be classed as subjective, but as psychologically objective, since an indefinite number of individuals find themselves prompted by an inner impulse to make an identical statement, or feel a certain view to be a vital necessity. Since the archetype is not just an inactive form, but a real force charged with a specific energy, it may very well be regarded as the *causa efficiens* of such statements, and be understood as the subject of them. In other words, it is not the personal human being who is making the statement, but the archetype speaking through him. If these statements are stifled or disregarded, both medical experience and common knowledge demonstrate that psychic troubles are in store. These will appear either as neurotic symptoms or, in the case of persons who are incapable of neurosis, as collective delusions.

Archetypal statements are based upon instinctive precondi-
tions and have nothing to do with reason; they are neither rationally grounded nor can they be banished by rational arguments. They have always been part of the world scene—*repré-
sentations collectives,* as Lévy-Bruhl rightly called them.
Certainly the ego and its will have a great part to play in life;
but what the ego wills is subject in the highest degree to the interference, in ways of which the ego is usually unaware, of the
autonomy and numinosity of archetypal processes. Practical
consideration of these processes is the essence of religion, insofar
as religion can be approached from a psychological point of
view.

III

At this point the fact forces itself on my attention that beside
the field of reflection there is another equally broad if not
broader area in which rational understanding and rational
modes of representation find scarcely anything they are able to
grasp. This is the realm of Eros. In classical times, when such
things were properly understood, Eros was considered a god
whose divinity transcended our human limits, and who therefore could neither be comprehended nor represented in any
way. I might, as many before me have attempted to do, venture
an approach to this daimon, whose range of activity extends
from the endless spaces of the heavens to the dark abysses of
hell; but I falter before the task of finding the language which
might adequately express the incalculable paradoxes of love.
Eros is a *kosmogonos,* a creator and father-mother of all higher
consciousness. I sometimes feel that Paul's words—"Though I
speak with the tongues of men and of angels, and have not love"
—might well be the first condition of all cognition and the
quintessence of divinity itself. Whatever the learned interpretation may be of the sentence "God is love," the words affirm
the *complexio oppositorum* of the Godhead. In my medical experience as well as in my own life I have again and again been
faced with the mystery of love, and have never been able to
explain what it is. Like Job, I had to "lay my hand on my
mouth. I have spoken once, and I will not answer." (Job 40:4 f.)

Here is the greatest and smallest, the remotest and nearest, the highest and lowest, and we cannot discuss one side of it without also discussing the other. No language is adequate to this paradox. Whatever one can say, no words express the whole. To speak of partial aspects is always too much or too little, for only the whole is meaningful. Love "bears all things" and "endures all things" (1 Cor. 13:7). These words say all there is to be said; nothing can be added to them. For we are in the deepest sense the victims and the instruments of cosmogonic "love." I put the word in quotation marks to indicate that I do not use it in its connotations of desiring, preferring, favoring, wishing, and similar feelings, but as something superior to the individual, a unified and undivided whole. Being a part, man cannot grasp the whole. He is at its mercy. He may assent to it, or rebel against it; but he is always caught up by it and enclosed within it. He is dependent upon it and is sustained by it. Love is his light and his darkness, whose end he cannot see. "Love ceases not"—whether he speaks with the "tongues of angels," or with scientific exactitude traces the life of the cell down to its uttermost source. Man can try to name love, showering upon it all the names at his command, and still he will involve himself in endless self-deceptions. If he possesses a grain of wisdom, he will lay down his arms and name the unknown by the more unknown, *ignotum per ignotius*—that is, by the name of God. That is a confession of his subjection, his imperfection, and his dependence; but at the same time a testimony to his freedom to choose between truth and error.

Retrospect

WHEN PEOPLE SAY I am wise, or a sage, I cannot accept it. A man once dipped a hatful of water from a stream. What did that amount to? I am not that stream. I am at the stream, but I do nothing. Other people are at the same stream, but most of them find they have to do something with it. I do nothing. I never think that I am the one who must see to it that cherries grow on stalks. I stand and behold, admiring what nature can do.

There is a fine old story about a student who came to a rabbi and said, "In the olden days there were men who saw the face of God. Why don't they any more?" The rabbi replied, "Because nowadays no one can stoop so low."

One must stoop a little in order to fetch water from the stream.

The difference between most people and myself is that for me the "dividing walls" are transparent. That is my peculiarity. Others find these walls so opaque that they see nothing behind them and therefore think nothing is there. To some extent I perceive the processes going on in the background, and that gives me an inner certainty. People who see nothing have no cer-

355

tainties and can draw no conclusions—or do not trust them even if they do. I do not know what started me off perceiving the stream of life. Probably the unconscious itself. Or perhaps my early dreams. They determined my course from the beginning.

Knowledge of processes in the background early shaped my relationship to the world. Basically, that relationship was the same in my childhood as it is to this day. As a child I felt myself to be alone, and I am still, because I know things and must hint at things which others apparently know nothing of, and for the most part do not want to know. Loneliness does not come from having no people about one, but from being unable to communicate the things that seem important to oneself, or from holding certain views which others find inadmissible. The loneliness began with the experiences of my early dreams, and reached its climax at the time I was working on the unconscious. If a man knows more than others, he becomes lonely. But loneliness is not necessarily inimical to companionship, for no one is more sensitive to companionship than the lonely man, and companionship thrives only when each individual remembers his individuality and does not identify himself with others.

It is important to have a secret, a premonition of things unknown. It fills life with something impersonal, a *numinosum*. A man who has never experienced that has missed something important. He must sense that he lives in a world which in some respects is mysterious; that things happen and can be experienced which remain inexplicable; that not everything which happens can be anticipated. The unexpected and the incredible belong in this world. Only then is life whole. For me the world has from the beginning been infinite and ungraspable.

I have had much trouble getting along with my ideas. There was a daimon in me, and in the end its presence proved decisive. It overpowered me, and if I was at times ruthless it was because I was in the grip of the daimon. I could never stop at anything once attained. I had to hasten on, to catch up with my vision. Since my contemporaries, understandably, could not perceive my vision, they saw only a fool rushing ahead.

I have offended many people, for as soon as I saw that they did not understand me, that was the end of the matter so far as

I was concerned. I had to move on. I had no patience with people—aside from my patients. I had to obey an inner law which was imposed on me and left me no freedom of choice. Of course I did not always obey it. How can anyone live without inconsistency?

For some people I was continually present and close to them so long as they were related to my inner world; but then it might happen that I was no longer with them, because there was nothing left which would link me to them. I had to learn painfully that people continued to exist even when they had nothing more to say to me. Many excited in me a feeling of living humanity, but only when they appeared within the magic circle of psychology; next moment, when the spotlight cast its beam elsewhere, there was nothing to be seen. I was able to become intensely interested in many people; but as soon as I had seen through them, the magic was gone. In this way I made many enemies. A creative person has little power over his own life. He is not free. He is captive and driven by his daimon.

> *"Shamefully*
> *A power wrests away the heart from us,*
> *For the Heavenly Ones each demand sacrifice;*
> *But if it should be withheld*
> *Never has that led to good,"*

says Hölderlin.

This lack of freedom has been a great sorrow to me. Often I felt as if I were on a battlefield, saying, "Now you have fallen, my good comrade, but I must go on." For "shamefully a power wrests away the heart from us." I am fond of you, indeed I love you, but I cannot stay. There is something heart-rending about that. And I myself am the victim; I *cannot* stay. But the daimon manages things so that one comes through, and blessed inconsistency sees to it that in flagrant contrast to my "disloyalty" I can keep faith in unsuspected measure.

Perhaps I might say: I need people to a higher degree than others, and at the same time much less. When the daimon is at work, one is always too close and too far. Only when it is silent can one achieve moderation.

The daimon of creativity has ruthlessly had its way with me. The ordinary undertakings I planned usually had the worst of it—though not always and not everywhere. By way of compensation, I think, I am conservative to the bone. I fill my pipe from my grandfather's tobacco jar and still keep his alpenstock, topped with a chamois horn, which he brought back from Pontresina after having been one of the first guests at that newly opened *Kurort*.

I am satisfied with the course my life has taken. It has been bountiful, and has given me a great deal. How could I ever have expected so much? Nothing but unexpected things kept happening to me. Much might have been different if I myself had been different. But it was as it had to be; for all came about because I am as I am. Many things worked out as I planned them to, but that did not always prove of benefit to me. But almost everything developed naturally and by destiny. I regret many follies which sprang from my obstinacy; but without that trait I would not have reached my goal. And so I am disappointed and not disappointed. I am disappointed with people and disappointed with myself. I have learned amazing things from people, and have accomplished more than I expected of myself. I cannot form any final judgment because the phenomenon of life and the phenomenon of man are too vast. The older I have become, the less I have understood or had insight into or known about myself.

I am astonished, disappointed, pleased with myself. I am distressed, depressed, rapturous. I am all these things at once, and cannot add up the sum. I am incapable of determining ultimate worth or worthlessness; I have no judgment about myself and my life. There is nothing I am quite sure about. I have no definite convictions—not about anything, really. I know only that I was born and exist, and it seems to me that I have been carried along. I exist on the foundation of something I do not know. In spite of all uncertainties, I feel a solidity underlying all existence and a continuity in my mode of being.

The world into which we are born is brutal and cruel, and at the same time of divine beauty. Which element we think outweighs the other, whether meaninglessness or meaning, is a matter of temperament. If meaninglessness were absolutely preponderant, the meaningfulness of life would vanish to an increasing degree with each step in our development. But that is —or seems to me—not the case. Probably, as in all metaphysical questions, both are true: Life is—or has—meaning and meaninglessness. I cherish the anxious hope that meaning will preponderate and win the battle.

When Lao-tzu says: "All are clear, I alone am clouded," he is expressing what I now feel in advanced old age. Lao-tzu is the example of a man with superior insight who has seen and experienced worth and worthlessness, and who at the end of his life desires to return into his own being, into the eternal unknowable meaning. The archetype of the old man who has seen enough is eternally true. At every level of intelligence this type appears, and its lineaments are always the same, whether it be an old peasant or a great philosopher like Lao-tzu. This is old age, and a limitation. Yet there is so much that fills me: plants, animals, clouds, day and night, and the eternal in man. The more uncertain I have felt about myself, the more there has grown up in me a feeling of kinship with all things. In fact it seems to me as if that alienation which so long separated me from the world has become transferred into my own inner world, and has revealed to me an unexpected unfamiliarity with myself.

Appendix I

Vienna IX, Berggasse 19
April 16, 1909

DEAR FRIEND,

. . . It is remarkable that on the same evening that I formally adopted you as an eldest son, anointing you as my successor and crown prince—*in partibus infidelium*—that then and there you should have divested me of my paternal dignity, and that the divesting seems to have given you as much pleasure as investing your person gave me. Now I am afraid that I must fall back again into the role of father toward you in giving you my views on poltergeist phenomena. I must do this because these things are different from what you would like to think.

I do not deny that your comments and your experiment made a powerful impression upon me. After your departure I determined to make some observations, and here are the results. In my front room there are continual creaking noises, from where the two heavy Egyptian steles rest on the oak boards of the bookcase, so that's obvious. In the second room, where we heard the crash, such noises are very rare. At first I was inclined to ascribe some meaning to it if the noise we heard so frequently when you were here were never heard again after your departure. But since then it has happened over and over again, yet never in connection with my thoughts and never when I was considering you or your special problem. (Not now, either, I add by way of challenge.) The phenomenon was soon deprived of all significance for me by something else. My credulity, or at least my readiness to believe, vanished along with the spell of your personal presence; once again, for various inner reasons, it seems to me wholly

[1] Reproduced with the kind permission of Ernst Freud, London.

implausible that anything of the sort should occur. The furniture stands before me spiritless and dead, like nature silent and godless before the poet after the passing of the gods of Greece.

I therefore don once more my horn-rimmed paternal spectacles and warn my dear son to keep a cool head and rather not understand something than make such great sacrifices for the sake of understanding. I also shake my wise gray locks over the question of psychosynthesis and think: Well, that is how the young folks are; they really enjoy things only when they need not drag us along with them, where with our short breath and weary legs we cannot follow.

Now I shall exercise the privilege of my years to turn loquacious and tell you about one more matter between heaven and earth which cannot be understood. A few years ago I took it into my head that I would die between the ages of 61 and 62, which at that time seemed to leave me a decent period of grace. (Today that leaves me only eight years still to go.) Shortly afterward I made a trip to Greece with my brother, and it was absolutely uncanny to see how the number 61, or 60 in conjunction with 1 and 2, kept cropping up on anything that had a number, especially on vehicles. I conscientiously noted down these occasions. By the time we came to Athens, I was feeling depressed. At our hotel we were assigned rooms on the second floor, and I hoped I could breathe again—at least there could be no chance of No. 61. However, it turned out that my room was No. 31 (which, with fatalistic license, I regarded as after all half of 61–62). This wilier and nimbler figure proved to be even better at dogging me than the first.

From that day until very recently the number 31 remained faithful to me, with a 2 all too readily associated with it. But since I also have in my psychic system regions in which I am merely avid for knowledge and not at all superstitious, I have attempted to analyze this conviction. Here it is. My conviction began in 1899. Two events coincided at that time. The first was my writing *The Interpretation of Dreams* (which, you know, is dated ahead to 1900); the second, my being assigned a new telephone number, which I have to this day: 14362. It is easy to establish the link between these two facts: in the year 1899, when I wrote *The Interpretation of Dreams*, I was 43 years old. What should be more obvious than that the other figures in my telephone number were intended to signify the end of my life, hence, 61 or 62? Suddenly there appears a method in this madness. The superstition that I would die between 61 and 62 turns out to be equivalent to the conviction that with the book on dreams I had completed my life work, needed to say no more, and could die in peace. You will grant that after this analysis it no longer sounds so non-sensical. Incidentally, the influence of Wilhelm Fliess plays a part in this; the superstitition dates from the year of his attack on me.

Here is another instance where you will find confirmation of the specifically Jewish character of my mysticism. Apart from this, I only want to say that adventures such as mine with the number 62 can be explained by two things. The first is an enormously intensified alertness on the part of the unconscious, so that one is led like Faust to see a Helen in every woman. The second is the undeniable "co-operation of chance," which plays the same role in the formation of delusions as somatic co-operation in hysterical symptoms or linguistic co-operation in puns.

I therefore look forward to hearing more about your investigations of the spook-complex, my interest being the interest one has in a lovely delusion which one does not share oneself.

With cordial regards to yourself,
your wife and children,
Yours,
Freud.

Vienna IX, Berggasse 19
May 12, 1911

DEAR FRIEND,

. . . I know that your deepest inclinations are impelling you toward a study of the occult, and do not doubt that you will return home with a rich cargo. There is no stopping that, and it is always right for a person to follow the biddings of his own impulses. The reputation you have won with your *Dementia* [2] will stand against the charge of "mystic" for quite a while. Only don't stay too long away from us in those lush tropical colonies; it is necessary to govern at home. . . .

With cordial greetings and the hope that you will write me again after a shorter interval this time.

Your faithful
Freud.

[2] See above, Chap. V, n. 4, p. 149.

Vienna IX, Berggasse 19
June 15, 1911

DEAR FRIEND,

. . . In matters of occultism I have become humble ever since the great lesson I received from Ferenczi's experiences.[8] I promise to believe everything that can be made to seem the least bit reasonable. As you know, I do not do so gladly. But my hubris has been shattered. I should like to have you and F. acting in consonance when one of you is ready to take the perilous step of publication, and I imagine that this would be quite compatible with complete independence during the progress of the work. . . .

Cordial regards to you and the beautiful house
from Your faithful
Freud

[8] Cf. Ernest Jones, *Life and Work of Sigmund Freud* (New York, 1953–57), III, pp. 387 f.

Appendix II

September 6, 1909, Monday
At Prof. Stanley Hall's
Clark University, Worcester

. . . . So now we are safely arrived in Worcester! I have to tell you
about the trip. Last Saturday there was dreary weather in New York.
All three of us were afflicted with diarrhea and had pretty bad
stomach aches. . . . In spite of feeling physically miserable and in
spite of not eating anything, I went to the paleontological collection,
where all the old monsters, the Lord God's anxiety dreams of Creation, are to be seen. The collection is absolutely unique for the
phylogenesis of Tertiary mammals. I cannot possibly tell you all I saw
there. Then I met Jones, who had just arrived from Europe. Around
half-past three we took the elevated and rode from 42nd Street to the
piers. There we boarded a fantastically huge structure of a steamer
that had some five white decks. We took cabins, and our vessel set
sail from the West River around the point of Manhattan with all its
tremendous skyscrapers, then up the East River under the Brooklyn
and Manhattan Bridges, right through the endless tangle of tugs,
ferryboats, etc., and through the Sound behind Long Island. It was
damp and chilly, we had belly aches and diarrhea and were suffering
from hunger besides, so we crawled into bed. Early on Sunday
morning we were already on land in Fall River City, where in the rain
we took the train to Boston and immediately went on to Worcester.
While we were en route, the weather cleared. The countryside was
utterly charming, low hills, a great deal of forest, swamp, small lakes,
innumerable huge erratic rocks, tiny villages with wooden houses,
painted red, green, or gray, with windows framed in white (Hol-

land!), tucked away under large, beautiful trees. By 11:30 we were in Worcester. We found the Standish Hotel a very pleasant place to stay, and cheap also, "on the American plan," as they say here—that is, with board. At six in the evening, after a well-deserved rest, we called on Stanley Hall. He is a refined, distinguished old gentleman close on seventy who received us with the kindest hospitality. He has a plump, jolly, good-natured, and extremely ugly wife who, however, serves wonderful food. She promptly took over Freud and me as her "boys" and plied us with delicious nourishment and noble wine, so that we began visibly to recover. We slept very well that night in the hotel, and this morning we have moved over to the Halls'. The house is furnished in an incredibly amusing fashion, everything roomy and comfortable. There is a splendid studio filled with thousands of books, and boxes of cigars everywhere. Two pitch-black Negroes in dinner jackets, the extreme of grotesque solemnity, perform as servants. Carpets everywhere, all the doors open, even the bathroom door and the front door; people going in and out all over the place; all the windows extend down to the floor. The house is surrounded by an English lawn, no garden fence. Half the city (about a hundred and eighty thousand inhabitants) stands in a regular forest of old trees which shade all the streets. Most of the houses are smaller than ours, charmingly surrounded by flowers and flowering shrubs, overgrown with virginia creeper and wisteria; everything well tended, clean, cultivated, and exceedingly peaceful and congenial. A wholly different America! This is what they call New England. The city was founded as long ago as 1690, so it is very old. Much prosperity. The university, richly endowed, is small but distinguished, and has a real, though plain, elegance. This morning was the opening session. Prof. X had first turn, with boring stuff. We soon decamped and took a delightful walk through the outskirts of the town, which is surrounded on all sides by small and minute lakes and cool woods. We were ecstatic over the peaceful beauty of the surroundings. It is refreshing and reviving after the life in New York. . . .

Clark University
Worcester, Massachusetts
Wednesday, September 8, 1909

. . . The people here are all exceedingly amiable and on a decent cultural level. We are beautifully taken care of at the Halls' and daily recovering from the exertions of New York. My stomach is almost back to normal now; from time to time there is a little twitch, but aside from that, my general health is excellent. Yesterday Freud began the lectures and received great applause. We are gaining ground here, and our following is growing slowly but surely. Today I had a talk about psychoanalysis with two highly cultivated elderly ladies who proved to be very well informed and free-thinking. I was greatly surprised, since I had prepared myself for opposition. Recently we had a large garden party with fifty people present, in the course of which I surrounded myself with five ladies. I was even able to make jokes in English—though what English! Tomorrow comes my first lecture; all my dread of it has vanished, since the audience is harmless and merely eager to hear new things, which is certainly what we can supply them with. It is said that we shall be awarded honorary doctorates by the university next Saturday, with a great deal of pomp and circumstance. In the evening there will be a "formal reception." Today's letter has to be short, since the Halls have invited some people for five o'clock to meet us. We have also been interviewed by the *Boston Evening Transcript*. In fact we are the men of the hour here. It is very good to be able to spread oneself in this way once in a while. I can feel that my libido is gulping it in with vast enjoyment . . .

Clark University
Worcester, Mass.
September 14, 1909

. . . Last night there was a tremendous amount of ceremony and fancy dress, with all sorts of red and black gowns and gold-tasseled square caps. In a grand and festive assemblage I was appointed Doctor of Laws *honoris causa* and Freud likewise. Now I may place an L.L.D. after my name. Impressive, what? . . . Today Prof. M. drove us by automobile out to lunch at a beautiful lake. The landscape was utterly lovely. This evening there is one more "private conference" in Hall's house on the "psychology of sex." Our time is dreadfully crammed. The Americans are really masters at that; they hardly leave one time to catch one's breath. Right now I am rather worn out from all the fabulous things we have been through, and am longing for the quiet of the mountains. My head is spinning. Last night at the awarding of the doctorate I had to deliver an impromptu talk before some three hundred persons. . . . Freud is in seventh heaven, and I am glad with all my heart to see him so. . . .

I am looking forward enormously to getting back to the sea again, where the overstimulated psyche can recover in the presence of that infinite peace and spaciousness. Here one is in an almost constant whirlwind. But I have, thank God, completely regained my capacity for enjoyment, so that I can look forward to everything with zest. Now I am going to take everything that comes along by storm, and then I shall settle down again, satiated . . .

Albany, N. Y.
September 18, 1909

. . . Two more days before departure! Everything is taking place in a whirl. Yesterday I stood upon a bare rocky peak nearly 5600 feet high, in the midst of tremendous virgin forests, looking far out into the blue infinities of America and shivering to the bone in the icy wind, and today I am in the midst of the metropolitan bustle of Albany, the capital of the State of New York! The hundred thousand enormously deep impressions I am taking back with me from this wonderland cannot be described with the pen. Everything is too big, too immeasurable. Something that has gradually been dawning upon me in the past few days is the recognition that here an ideal potentiality of life has become reality. Men are as well off here as the culture permits; women badly off. We have seen things here that inspire enthusiastic admiration, and things that make one ponder social evolution deeply. As far as technological culture is concerned, we lag miles behind America. But all that is frightfully costly and already carries the germ of the end in itself. I must tell you a great, great deal. I shall never forget the experiences of this journey. Now we are tired of America. Tomorrow morning we are off to New York, and on September 21 we sail! . . .

Steamer Kaiser Wilhelm der Grosse

North German Lloyd
BREMEN

September 22, 1909

. . . Yesterday morning I shook the dust of America from my feet, with a light heart and an aching head, for the Y.'s plied us with wonderful champagne. . . . As far as abstinence goes, I've arrived on very shaky ground indeed, in point of principle, so that I am honorably withdrawing from my various teetotal societies. I confess myself an honest sinner and only hope that I can endure the sight of a glass of wine without emotion—an undrunk glass, of course. That is always so; only the forbidden attracts. I think I must not forbid myself too much. . . .

Well, then, at ten o'clock yesterday morning we sailed, to our left the towering whitish and reddish heaven-storming towers of New York City, to our right the smoking chimneys, docks, etc., of Hoboken. The morning was misty; New York soon disappeared, and before long the big swells of the ocean began. At the fireship we dropped the American pilot and then sailed on out "into the mournful wasteland of the sea." It is, as always, of cosmic grandeur and simplicity, compelling silence; for what has man to say here, especially at night when the ocean is alone with the starry sky? One looks out silently, surrendering all self-importance, and many old sayings and images scurry through the mind; a low voice says something about the age-oldness and infinitude of the "far-swelling, murmurous sea," of "the waves of the sea and of love," of Leukothea, the lovely goddess who appears in the foam of the seething waves to travel-weary Odysseus and gives him the pearly veil which saves him from Poseidon's storm. The sea is like music; it has all the dreams of the soul within itself and sounds them over. The beauty and grandeur of the sea consists in our being forced down into the fruitful bottomlands of our own psyches, where we confront and re-create ourselves in the animation of the "mournful wasteland of the sea." Now we are still worn out from the "torment of these last days." We brood over the past few months, and the unconscious has a lot of work to do, putting in order all the things America has churned up within us. . . .

Steamer Kaiser Wilhelm der Grosse

North German Lloyd
BREMEN

September 25, 1909

. . . . Yesterday there was a storm that lasted all day until nearly
midnight. Most of the day I stood up front, under the bridge, on a
protected and elevated spot, and admired the magnificent spectacle
as the mountainous waves rolled up and poured a whirling cloud of
foam over the ship. The ship began to roll fearfully, and several times
we were soaked by a salty shower. It turned cold, and we went in for
a cup of tea. Inside, however, the brain flowed down the spinal
canal and tried to come out again from under the stomach. Consequently I retired to my bed, where I soon felt fine again and later
was able to consume a pleasant supper. Outside from time to time a
wave thundered against the ship. The objects in my cabin had all
come to life: the sofa cushion crawled about on the floor in the semi-
darkness; a recumbent shoe sat up, looked around in astonishment,
and then shuffled quietly off under the sofa; a standing shoe turned
wearily on its side and followed its mate. Now the scene changed. I
realized that the shoes had gone under the sofa to fetch my bag and
brief case. The whole company paraded over to join the big trunk
under the bed. One sleeve of my shirt on the sofa waved longingly
after them, and from inside the chests and drawers came rumbles
and rattles. Suddenly there was a terrible crash under my floor, a
rattling, clattering, and tinkling. One of the kitchens is underneath
me. There, at one blow, five hundred plates had been awakened
from their deathlike torpor and with a single bold leap had put a
sudden end to their dreary existence as slaves. In all the cabins round
about, unspeakable groans betrayed the secrets of the menu. I
slept like a top, and this morning the wind is beginning to blow
from another side. . . .

Appendix III

LETTER TO EMMA JUNG
FROM NORTH AFRICA
(1920)

Grand Hotel   *Sousse*
Sousse   *Monday, March 15, 1920*

This Africa is incredible

. . . Unfortunately I cannot write coherently to you, for it is all too much. Only sidelights. After cold, heavy weather at sea, a sparkling morning in Algiers. Bright houses and streets, dark green clumps of trees, tall palms' crowns rising among them. White burnooses, red fezzes, and among these the yellow uniforms of the Tirailleurs d'Afrique, the red of the Spahis, then the Botanical Gardens, an enchanted tropical forest, an Indian vision, holy *acvatta* trees with gigantic aerial roots like monsters, fantastic dwellings of the gods, enormous in extent, heavy, dark green foliage rustling in the sea wind.

Then thirty hours by rail to Tunis. The Arab city is classical antiquity and Moorish middle ages, Granada and the fairy tale of Baghdad. You no longer think of yourself; you are dissolved in this potpourri which cannot be evaluated, still less described: a Roman column stands here as part of a wall; an old Jewess of unspeakable ugliness goes by in white baggy breeches; a crier with a load of burnooses pushes through the crowd, shouting in gutturals that might have come straight from the canton of Zürich; a patch of deep blue sky, a snow-white mosque dome; a shoemaker busily stitching away at shoes in a small vaulted niche, with a hot, dazzling patch of sunlight on the mat before him; blind musicians with a drum and tiny three-stringed lute; a beggar who consists of nothing but rags; smoke from oil cakes, and swarms of flies; up above, on a white

minaret in the blissful ether, a muezzin sings the midday chant; below, a cool, shady, colonnaded yard with horseshoe portal framed in
glazed tiles; on the wall a mangy cat lies in the sun; a coming and
going of red, white, yellow, blue, brown mantles, white turbans, red
fezzes, uniforms, faces ranging from white and light yellow to deep
black; a shuffling of yellow and red slippers, a noiseless scurrying of
naked black feet, and so on and so on.

In the morning the great god rises and fills both horizons with his
joy and power, and all living things obey him. At night the moon is so
silvery and glows with such divine clarity that no one can doubt the
existence of Astarte.

Between Algiers and Tunis lie 550 miles of African soil, towering
up to the noble and spreading shapes of the great Atlas range, wide
valleys and plateaus bursting with grapes and grain, dark green
forests of cork oak. Today Horus rose out of distant, pale mountains
over an unending green and brown plain, and from the desert there
sprang up a mighty wind which blew out to the dark blue sea. On
rolling, gray-green hills yellow-brown remains of whole Roman cities,
small flocks of black goats grazing around them, nearby a Bedouin
camp with black tents, camels, and donkeys. The train runs into a
camel which cannot make up its mind to get off the tracks; the beast
is killed; there is a great running up, shrieking, and gesticulating of
white-clad figures; and always the sea, now deep blue, now hurting
the eyes with its glitter in the sunlight. Out of olive groves and palms
and hedges of giant cactus floating in the flickering, sun-shot air rises
a snow-white city with divinely white domes and towers, gloriously
spread out over a hill. Then comes Sousse, with white walls and
towers, the harbor below; beyond the harbor wall the deep blue sea,
and in the port lies the sailing ship with two lateen sails which I
once painted!!!!

You stumble over Roman remains; with my cane I dug a piece of
Roman pottery out of the ground.

This is all nothing but miserable stammering; I do not know what
Africa is really saying to me, but it speaks. Imagine a tremendous sun,
air clear as in the highest mountains, a sea bluer than any you have
ever seen, all colors of incredible power. In the markets you can
still buy the amphorae of antiquity—things like that—and the
moon!!!! . . .

Appendix IV

RICHARD WILHELM

I first met Richard Wilhelm at Count Keyserling's during a meeting of the "School of Wisdom" in Darmstadt. That was in the early twenties. In 1923 we invited him to Zürich and he spoke on the *I Ching*[1] at the Psychology Club.

Even before meeting him I had been interested in Oriental philosophy, and around 1920 had begun experimenting with the *I Ching*. One summer in Bollingen I resolved to make an all-out attack on the riddle of this book. Instead of traditional stalks of yarrow required by the classical method, I cut myself a bunch of reeds. I would sit for hours on the ground beneath the hundred-year-old pear tree, the *I Ching* beside me, practicing the technique by referring the resultant oracles to one another in an interplay of questions and answers. All sorts of undeniably remarkable results emerged—meaningful connections with my own thought processes which I could not explain to myself.

The only subjective intervention in this experiment consists in the experimenter's arbitrarily—that is, without counting—dividing up the bundle of forty-nine stalks at a single swoop. He does not know how many stalks are contained in each bundle, and yet the result depends upon their numerical relationship. All other manipulations proceed mechanically and leave no room for interference by the will. If a psychic causal connection is present at all, it can only consist in the chance division of the bundle (or, in the other method, the chance fall of the coins).

During the whole of those summer holidays I was preoccupied with the question: Are the *I Ching*'s answers meaningful or not? If

[1] *The I Ching, or Book of Changes:* English trans. by Cary F. Baynes, from the German version of R. Wilhelm (New York and London, 1950). The origins of this ancient Chinese book of wisdom and oracles go back to the fourth millennium B.C.

they are, how does the connection between the psychic and the physical sequence of events come about? Time and again I encountered amazing coincidences which seemed to suggest the idea of an acausal parallelism (a synchronicity, as I later called it). So fascinated was I by these experiments that I altogether forgot to take notes, which I afterward greatly regretted. Later, however, when I often used to carry out the experiment with my patients, it became quite clear that a significant number of answers did indeed hit the mark. I remember, for example, the case of a young man with a strong mother complex. He wanted to marry, and had made the acquaintance of a seemingly suitable girl. However, he felt uncertain, fearing that under the influence of his complex he might once more find himself in the power of an overwhelming mother. I conducted the experiment with him. The text of his hexagram read: "The maiden is powerful. One should not marry such a maiden."

In the mid-thirties I met the Chinese philosopher Hu Shih. I asked him his opinion of the *I Ching*, and received the reply: "Oh, that's nothing but an old collection of magic spells, without significance." He had had no experience with it—or so he said. Only once, he remembered, had he come across it in practice. One day on a walk with a friend, the friend had told him about his unhappy love affair. They were just passing by a Taoist temple. As a joke, he had said to his friend: "Here you can consult the oracle!" No sooner said than done. They went into the temple together and asked the priest for an *I Ching* oracle. But he had not the slightest faith in this nonsense.

I asked him whether the oracle had been correct. Whereupon he replied reluctantly, "Oh yes, it was, of course . . ." Remembering the well-known story of the "good friend" who does everything one does not wish to do oneself, I cautiously asked him whether he had not profited by this opportunity. "Yes," he replied, "as a joke I asked a question too."

"And did the oracle give you a sensible answer?" I asked.

He hesitated. "Oh well, yes, if you wish to put it that way." The subject obviously made him uncomfortable.

A few years after my first experiments with the reeds, the *I Ching* was published with Wilhelm's commentary. I instantly obtained the book, and found to my gratification that Wilhelm took much the same view of the meaningful connections as I had. But he knew the entire literature and could therefore fill in the gaps which had been outside my competence. When Wilhelm came to Zürich, I had the opportunity to discuss the matter with him at length, and we talked a great deal about Chinese philosophy and religion. What he told me, out of his wealth of knowledge of the Chinese mentality, clarified some of the most difficult problems that the European unconscious had posed for me. On the other hand, what I had to tell him about the results of my investigations of the unconscious caused him no little surprise; for he recognized in them things he had considered to be the exclusive possession of the Chinese philosophical tradition.

As a young man Wilhelm had gone to China in the service of a Christian mission, and there the mental world of the Orient had opened its doors wide to him. Wilhelm was a truly religious spirit, with an unclouded and farsighted view of things. He had the gift of being able to listen without bias to the revelations of a foreign mentality, and to accomplish that miracle of empathy which enabled him to make the intellectual treasures of China accessible to Europe. He was deeply influenced by Chinese culture, and once said to me, "It is a great satisfaction to me that I never baptized a single Chinese!" In spite of his Christian background, he could not help recognizing the logic and clarity of Chinese thought. "Influenced" is not quite the word to describe its effect upon him; it had overwhelmed and assimilated him. His Christian views receded into the background, but did not vanish entirely; they formed a kind of mental reservation, a moral proviso that was later to have fateful consequences.

In China he had the good fortune to meet a sage of the old school whom the revolution had driven out of the interior. This sage, Lau Nai Süan, introduced him to Chinese yoga philosophy and the psychology of the *I Ching*. To the collaboration of these two men we owe the edition of the *I Ching* with its excellent commentary. For the first time this profoundest work of the Orient was introduced to the West in a living and comprehensible fashion. I consider this publication Wilhelm's most important work. Clear and unmistakably Western as his mentality was, in his *I Ching* commentary he manifested a degree of adaptation to Chinese psychology which is altogether unmatched.

When the last page of the translation was finished and the first printer's proofs were coming in, the old master Lau Nai Süan died. It was as if his work were completed and he had delivered the last message of the old, dying China to Europe. And Wilhelm had been the perfect disciple, a fulfillment of the wish-dream of the sage.

Wilhelm, when I met him, seemed completely Chinese, in outward manner as much as in his way of writing and speaking. The Oriental point of view and ancient Chinese culture had penetrated him through and through. Upon his arrival in Europe, he entered the faculty of the China Institute in Frankfurt am Main. Both in his teaching work and in his lectures to laymen, however, he seemed to feel the pressure of the European spirit. Christian views and forms of thought moved steadily into the foreground. I went to hear some lectures of his and they turned out to be scarcely any different from conventional sermons.

This reversion to the past seemed to me somewhat unreflective and therefore dangerous. I saw it as a reassimilation to the West, and felt that as a result of it Wilhelm must come into conflict with himself. Since it was, so I thought, a passive assimilation, that is to say, a succumbing to the influence of the environment, there was the danger of a relatively unconscious conflict, a clash between his Western and Eastern psyche. If, as I assumed, the Christian attitude had originally given way to the influence of China, the reverse might well be taking place now: the European element might be gaining the upper hand over the Orient once again. If such a process takes place without a strong, conscious attempt to come to terms with it, the unconscious conflict can seriously affect the physical state of health.

After attending the lectures, I attempted to call his attention to the danger threatening him. My words to him were: "My dear Wilhelm, please do not take this amiss, but I have the feeling that the West is taking possession of you again, and that you are becoming unfaithful to your mission of transmitting the East to the West."

He replied, "I think you are right—something here is overpowering me. But what can be done?"

A few years later Wilhelm was staying as a guest in my house, and came down with an attack of amoebic dysentery. It was a disease he had had twenty years before. His condition grew worse during the following months, and then I heard that Wilhelm was in the hospital. I went to Frankfurt to visit him, and found a very sick man. The doctors had not yet given up hope, and Wilhelm, too, spoke of plans he wished to carry out when he got well. I shared his hopes, but had my forebodings. What he confided to me at the time confirmed my conjectures. In his dreams, he revisited the endless stretches of desolate Asiatic steppes—the China he had left behind. He was groping his way back to the problem which China had set before him, the answer to which had been blocked for him by the West. By now he was conscious of this question, but had been unable to find a solution. His illness dragged on for months.

A few weeks before his death, when I had had no news from him for a considerable time, I was awakened, just as I was on the point of falling asleep, by a vision. At my bed stood a Chinese in a dark blue gown, hands crossed in the sleeves. He bowed low before me, as if he wished to give me a message. I knew what it signified. The vision was extraordinarily vivid. Not only did I see every wrinkle in the man's face, but every thread in the fabric of his gown.

Wilhelm's problem might also be regarded as a conflict between consciousness and the unconscious, which in his case took the form of a clash between West and East. I believed I understood his situation, since I myself had the same problem as he and knew what it meant to be involved in this conflict. It is true that even at our last meeting Wilhelm did not speak plainly. Though he was intensely interested when I introduced the psychological point of view, his interest lasted only so long as my remarks concerned objective matters such as meditation or questions posed by the psychology of religion. So far, so good. But whenever I attempted to touch the actual problem of his inner conflict, I immediately sensed a drawing back, an inward shutting himself off—because such matters went straight to the bone. This is a phenomenon I have observed in many men of importance. There is, as Goethe puts it in *Faust,* an "untrodden, untreadable" region whose precincts cannot and should not be entered by force; a destiny which will brook no human intervention.

Appendix V

Septem Sermones ad Mortuos
(1916)

Jung allowed *Septem Sermones ad Mortuos* (Seven Sermons to the Dead) to be published privately as a booklet. He occasionally gave copies to friends; it was never obtainable at bookstores. Later he described it as a sin of his youth and regretted it.

The language is more or less in the style of the Red Book. But compared with the endless conversations with inner figures in the Red Book, the Seven Sermons form a self-contained whole. They convey an impression, if only a fragmentary one, of what Jung went through in the years 1913–1917, and of what he was bringing to birth.

The Sermons contain hints or anticipations of ideas that were to figure later in his scientific writings, more particularly concerning the polaristic nature of the psyche, of life in general, and of all psychological statements. It was their thinking in paradoxes that drew Jung to the Gnostics. That is why he identifies himself here with the Gnostic writer Basilides (early second century A.D.) and even takes over some of his terminology—for example, God as Abraxas. It was a deliberate game of mystification.

Jung consented to the publication of Seven Sermons in his Memoirs only hesitantly and only "for the sake of honesty." He never disclosed the key to the anagram at the end of the book.

The Seven Sermons to the Dead written by Basilides in Alexandria, the City where the East toucheth the West

Sermo I

The dead came back from Jerusalem, where they found not what they sought. They prayed me let them in and besought my word, and thus I began my teaching.

Harken: I begin with nothingness. Nothingness is the same as fullness. In infinity full is no better than empty. Nothingness is both empty and full. As well might ye say anything else of nothingness, as for instance, white is it, or black, or again, it is not, or it is. A thing that is infinite and eternal hath no qualities, since it hath all qualities.

This nothingness or fullness we name the PLEROMA. Therein both thinking and being cease, since the eternal and infinite possess no qualities. In it no being is, for he then would be distinct from the pleroma, and would possess qualities which would distinguish him as something distinct from the pleroma.

In the pleroma there is nothing and everything. It is quite fruitless to think about the pleroma, for this would mean self-dissolution.

CREATURA is not in the pleroma, but in itself. The pleroma is both beginning and end of created beings. It pervadeth them, as the light of the sun everywhere pervadeth the air. Although the pleroma pervadeth altogether, yet hath created being no share thereof, just as a wholly transparent body becometh neither light nor dark through the light which pervadeth it. We are, however, the pleroma itself, for we are a part of the eternal and infinite. But we have no share thereof, as we are from the pleroma infinitely removed; not spiritually or temporally, but essentially, since we are distinguished from the pleroma in our essence as creatura, which is confined within time and space.

Yet because we are parts of the pleroma, the pleroma is also in us. Even in the smallest point is the pleroma endless, eternal, and entire, since small and great are qualities which are contained in it. It is that nothingness which is everywhere whole and continuous. Only figuratively, therefore, do I speak of created being as a part of the pleroma. Because, actually, the pleroma is nowhere divided, since it is nothingness. We are also the whole pleroma, because, figuratively, the pleroma is the smallest point (assumed only, not existing) in us and the boundless firmament about us. But wherefore, then, do we speak of the pleroma at all, since it is thus everything and nothing?

I speak of it to make a beginning somewhere, and also to free you from the delusion that somewhere, either without or within, there standeth something fixed, or in some way established, from the beginning. Every so-called fixed and certain thing is only relative. That alone is fixed and certain which is subject to change.

What is changeable, however, is creatura. Therefore is it the one thing which is fixed and certain; because it hath qualities: it is even quality itself.

The question ariseth: How did creatura originate? Created beings came to pass, not creatura; since created being is the very quality of the pleroma, as much as non-creation which is the eternal death. In all times and places is creation, in all times and places is death. The pleroma hath all, distinctiveness and non-distinctiveness.

Distinctiveness is creatura. It is distinct. Distinctiveness is its essence, and therefore it distinguisheth. Therefore man discriminateth because his nature is distinctiveness. Wherefore also he distinguisheth qualities of the pleroma which are not. He distinguisheth them out of his own nature. Therefore must he speak of qualities of the pleroma which are not.

What use, say ye, to speak of it? Saidst thou not thyself, there is no profit in thinking upon the pleroma?

That said I unto you, to free you from the delusion that we are able to think about the pleroma. When we distinguish qualities of the pleroma, we are speaking from the ground of our own distinctiveness and concerning our own distinctiveness. But we have said nothing concerning the pleroma. Concerning our own distinctiveness, however, it is needful to speak, whereby we may distinguish ourselves enough. Our very nature is distinctiveness. If we are not true to this nature we do not distinguish ourselves enough. Therefore must we make distinctions of qualities.

What is the harm, ye ask, in not distinguishing oneself? If we do not distinguish, we get beyond our own nature, away from creatura. We fall into indistinctiveness, which is the other quality of the pleroma. We fall into the pleroma itself and cease to be creatures. We are given over to dissolution in the nothingness. This is the death of the creature. Therefore we die in such measure as we do not distinguish. Hence the natural striving of the creature goeth towards distinctiveness, fighteth against primeval, perilous sameness. This is called the PRINCIPIUM INDIVIDUATIONIS. This principle is the essence of the creature. From this you can see why indistinctiveness and non-distinction are a great danger for the creature.

We must, therefore, distinguish the qualities of the pleroma. The qualities are PAIRS OF OPPOSITES, such as—

> The Effective and the Ineffective.
> Fullness and Emptiness.
> Living and Dead.
> Difference and Sameness.
> Light and Darkness.
> The Hot and the Cold.

Force and Matter.
Time and Space.
Good and Evil.
Beauty and Ugliness.
The One and the Many.   etc.

The pairs of opposites are qualities of the pleroma which are not, because each balanceth each. As we are the pleroma itself, we also have all these qualities in us. Because the very ground of our nature is distinctiveness, therefore we have these qualities in the name and sign of distinctiveness, which meaneth—

1. These qualities are distinct and separate in us one from the other; therefore they are not balanced and void, but are effective. Thus are we the victims of the pairs of opposites. The pleroma is rent in us.

2. The qualities belong to the pleroma, and only in the name and sign of distinctiveness can and must we possess or live them. We must distinguish ourselves from qualities. In the pleroma they are balanced and void; in us not. Being distinguished from them delivereth us.

When we strive after the good or the beautiful, we thereby forget our own nature, which is distinctiveness, and we are delivered over to the qualities of the pleroma, which are pairs of opposites. We labor to attain to the good and the beautiful, yet at the same time we also lay hold of the evil and the ugly, since in the pleroma these are one with the good and the beautiful. When, however, we remain true to our own nature, which is distinctiveness, we distinguish ourselves from the good and the beautiful, and, therefore, at the same time, from the evil and the ugly. And thus we fall not into the pleroma, namely, into nothingness and dissolution.

Thou sayest, ye object, that difference and sameness are also qualities of the pleroma. How would it be, then, if we strive after difference? Are we, in so doing, not true to our own nature? And must we none the less be given over to sameness when we strive after difference?

Ye must not forget that the pleroma hath no qualities. We create them through thinking. If, therefore, ye strive after difference or sameness, or any qualities whatsoever, ye pursue thoughts which flow to you out of the pleroma; thoughts, namely, concerning non-existing qualities of the pleroma. Inasmuch as ye run after these thoughts, ye fall again into the pleroma, and reach difference and sameness at the same time. Not your thinking, but your being, is distinctiveness. Therefore not after difference, as ye think it, must ye strive; but after YOUR OWN BEING. At bottom, therefore, there is only one striving, namely, the striving after your own being. If ye had this striving ye would not need to know anything about the pleroma and its qualities, and yet would ye come to your right goal by virtue of your own being. Since, however, thought estrangeth from being, that knowledge must I teach you wherewith ye may be able to hold your thought in leash.

Sermo II

In the night the dead stood along the wall and cried:

We would have knowledge of god. Where is god? Is god dead?

God is not dead. Now, as ever, he liveth. God is creatura, for he is something definite, and therefore distinct from the pleroma. God is quality of the pleroma, and everything which I said of creatura also is true concerning him.

He is distinguished, however, from created beings through this, that he is more indefinite and indeterminable than they. He is less distinct than created beings, since the ground of his being is effective fullness. Only in so far as he is definite and distinct is he creatura, and in like measure is he the manifestation of the effective fullness of the pleroma.

Everything which we do not distinguish falleth into the pleroma and is made void by its opposite. If, therefore, we do not distinguish god, effective fullness is for us extinguished.

Moreover god is the pleroma itself, as likewise each smallest point in the created and uncreated is the pleroma itself.

Effective void is the nature of the devil. God and devil are the first manifestations of nothingness, which we call the pleroma. It is indifferent whether the pleroma is or is not, since in everything it is balanced and void. Not so creatura. In so far as god and devil are creatura they do not extinguish each other, but stand one against the other as effective opposites. We need no proof of their existence. It is enough that we must always be speaking of them. Even if both were not, creatura, of its own essential distinctiveness, would forever distinguish them anew out of the pleroma.

Everything that discrimination taketh out of the pleroma is a pair of opposites. To god, therefore, always belongeth the devil.

This inseparability is as close and, as your own life hath made you see, as indissoluble as the pleroma itself. Thus it is that both stand very close to the pleroma, in which all opposites are extinguished and joined.

God and devil are distinguished by the qualities fullness and emptiness, generation and destruction. EFFECTIVENESS is common to both. Effectiveness joineth them. Effectiveness, therefore, standeth above both; is a god above god, since in its effect it uniteth fullness and emptiness.

This is a god whom ye knew not, for mankind forgot it. We name it by its name ABRAXAS. It is more indefinite still than god and devil.

That god may be distinguished from it, we name god HELIOS or Sun. Abraxas is effect. Nothing standeth opposed to it but the ineffective; hence its effective nature freely unfoldeth itself. The ineffective is not, therefore resisteth not. Abraxas standeth above the sun and above the devil. It is improbable probability, unreal reality. Had the pleroma a being, Abraxas would be its manifestation. It is the effective itself, not any particular effect, but effect in general.

It is unreal reality, because it hath no definite effect.

It is also creatura, because it is distinct from the pleroma.

The sun hath a definite effect, and so hath the devil. Wherefore do they appear to us more effective than indefinite Abraxas.

It is force, duration, change.

The dead now raised a great tumult, for they were Christians.

Sermo III

Like mists arising from a marsh, the dead came near and cried: Speak further unto us concerning the supreme god.

Hard to know is the deity of Abraxas. Its power is the greatest, because man perceiveth it not. From the sun he draweth the *summum bonum;* from the devil the *infimum malum;* but from Abraxas LIFE, altogether indefinite, the mother of good and evil.

Smaller and weaker life seemeth to be than the *summum bonum;* wherefore is it also hard to conceive that Abraxas transcendeth even the sun in power, who is himself the radiant source of all the force of life.

Abraxas is the sun, and at the same time the eternally sucking gorge of the void, the belittling and dismembering devil.

The power of Abraxas is twofold; but ye see it not, because for your eyes the warring opposites of this power are extinguished.

What the god-sun speaketh is life.

What the devil speaketh is death.

But Abraxas speaketh that hallowed and accursed word which is life and death at the same time.

Abraxas begetteth truth and lying, good and evil, light and darkness, in the same word and in the same act. Wherefore is Abraxas terrible.

It is splendid as the lion in the instant he striketh down his victim. It is beautiful as a day of spring. It is the great Pan himself and also the small one. It is Priapos.

It is the monster of the under-world, a thousand-armed polyp, coiled knot of winged serpents, frenzy.

It is the hermaphrodite of the earliest beginning.

It is the lord of the toads and frogs, which live in the water and go up on the land, whose chorus ascendeth at noon and at midnight.

It is abundance that seeketh union with emptiness.

It is holy begetting.

It is love and love's murder.

It is the saint and his betrayer.

It is the brightest light of day and the darkest night of madness.

To look upon it, is blindness.

To know it, is sickness.

To worship it, is death.

To fear it, is wisdom.

To resist it not, is redemption.

God dwelleth behind the sun, the devil behind the night. What god bringeth forth out of the light the devil sucketh into the night. But Abraxas is the world, its becoming and its passing. Upon every gift that cometh from the god-sun the devil layeth his curse.

Everything that ye entreat from the god-sun begetteth a deed of the devil.

Everything that ye create with the god-sun giveth effective power to the devil.

That is terrible Abraxas.

It is the mightiest creature, and in it the creature is afraid of itself.

It is the manifest opposition of creatura to the pleroma and its nothingness.

It is the son's horror of the mother.

It is the mother's love for the son.

It is the delight of the earth and the cruelty of the heavens.

Before its countenance man becometh like stone.

Before it there is no question and no reply.

It is the life of creatura.

It is the operation of distinctiveness.

It is the love of man.

It is the speech of man.

It is the appearance and the shadow of man.
It is illusory reality.

Now the dead howled and raged, for they were unperfected.

Sermo IV

The dead filled the place murmuring and said:
Tell us of gods and devils, accursed one!

The god-sun is the highest good; the devil is the opposite. Thus have ye two gods. But there are many high and good things and many great evils. Among these are two god-devils; the one is the BURNING ONE, the other the GROWING ONE.

The burning one is EROS, who hath the form of flame. Flame giveth light because it consumeth.

The growing one is the TREE OF LIFE. It buddeth, as in growing it heapeth up living stuff.

Eros flameth up and dieth. But the tree of life groweth with slow and constant increase through unmeasured time.

Good and evil are united in the flame.

Good and evil are united in the increase of the tree. In their divinity stand life and love opposed.

Innumerable as the host of the stars is the number of gods and devils.

Each star is a god, and each space that a star filleth is a devil. But the empty-fullness of the whole is the pleroma.

The operation of the whole is Abraxas, to whom only the ineffective standeth opposed.

Four is the number of the principal gods, as four is the number of the world's measurements.

One is the beginning, the god-sun.

Two is Eros; for he bindeth twain together and outspreadeth himself in brightness.

Three is the Tree of Life, for it filleth space with bodily forms.

Four is the devil, for he openeth all that is closed. All that is formed of bodily nature doth he dissolve; he is the destroyer in whom everything is brought to nothing.

For me, to whom knowledge hath been given of the multiplicity and diversity of the gods, it is well. But woe unto you, who replace these incompatible many by a single god. For in so doing ye beget the torment which is bred from not understanding, and ye mutilate the creature whose nature and aim is distinctiveness. How can ye be true to your own nature when ye try to change the many into one? What ye do unto the gods is done likewise unto you. Ye all become equal and thus is your nature maimed.

Equality shall prevail not for god, but only for the sake of man. For the gods are many, whilst men are few. The gods are mighty and can endure their manifoldness. For like the stars they abide in solitude, parted one from the other by immense distances. But men are weak and cannot endure their manifold nature. Therefore they dwell together and need communion, that they may bear their separateness. For redemption's sake I teach you the rejected truth, for the sake of which I was rejected.

The multiplicity of the gods correspondeth to the multiplicity of man.

Numberless gods await the human state. Numberless gods have been men. Man shareth in the nature of the gods. He cometh from the gods and goeth unto god.

Thus, just as it serveth not to reflect upon the pleroma, it availeth not to worship the multiplicity of the gods. Least of all availeth it to worship the first god, the effective abundance and the *summum bonum*. By our prayer we can add to it nothing, and from it nothing take; because the effective void swalloweth all.

The bright gods form the celestial world. It is manifold and infinitely spreading and increasing. The god-sun is the supreme lord of that world.

The dark gods form the earth-world. They are simple and infinitely diminishing and declining. The devil is the earth-world's lowest lord, the moon-spirit, satellite of the earth, smaller, colder, and more dead than the earth.

There is no difference between the might of the celestial gods and those of the earth. The celestial gods magnify, the earth-gods diminish. Measureless is the movement of both.

Sermo V

The dead mocked and cried: Teach us, fool, of the church and holy communion.

The world of the gods is made manifest in spirituality and in sexuality. The celestial ones appear in spirituality, the earthly in sexuality.

Spirituality conceiveth and embraceth. It is womanlike and therefore we call it MATER COELESTIS, the celestial mother. Sexuality engendereth and createth. It is manlike, and therefore we call it PHALLOS, the earthly father.

The sexuality of man is more of the earth, the sexuality of woman is more of the spirit.

The spirituality of man is more of heaven, it goeth to the greater.

The spirituality of woman is more of the earth, it goeth to the smaller.

Lying and devilish is the spirituality of the man which goeth to the smaller.

Lying and devilish is the spirituality of the woman which goeth to the greater.

Each must go to its own place.

Man and woman become devils one to the other when they divide not their spiritual ways, for the nature of creatura is distinctiveness.

The sexuality of man hath an earthward course, the sexuality of woman a spiritual. Man and woman become devils one to the other if they distinguish not their sexuality.

Man shall know of the smaller, woman the greater.

Man shall distinguish himself both from spirituality and from sexuality. He shall call spirituality Mother, and set her between heaven and earth. He shall call sexuality Phallos, and set him between himself and earth. For the Mother and the Phallos are superhuman daemons which reveal the world of the gods. They are for us more effective than the gods, because they are closely akin to our own nature. Should ye not distinguish yourselves from sexuality and from spirituality, and not regard them as of a nature both above you and beyond, then are ye delivered over to them as qualities of the pleroma. Spirituality and sexuality are not your qualities, not things which ye possess and contain. But they possess and contain you; for they are powerful daemons, manifestations of the gods, and are, therefore, things which reach beyond you, existing in themselves. No man hath a spirituality unto himself, or a sexuality unto himself. But he standeth under the law of spirituality and of sexuality.

No man, therefore, escapeth these daemons. Ye shall look upon them as daemons, and as a common task and danger, a common burden which life hath laid upon you. Thus is life for you also a common task and danger, as are the gods, and first of all terrible Abraxas.

Man is weak, therefore is communion indispensable. If your communion be not under the sign of the Mother, then is it under the sign of the Phallos. No communion is suffering and sickness. Communion in everything is dismemberment and dissolution.

Distinctiveness leadeth to singleness. Singleness is opposed to communion. But because of man's weakness over against the gods and daemons and their invincible law is communion needful. Therefore shall there be as much communion as is needful, not for man's sake, but because of the gods. The gods force you to communion. As much as they force you, so much is communion needed, more is evil.

In communion let every man submit to others, that communion be maintained; for ye need it.

In singleness the one man shall be superior to the others, that every man may come to himself and avoid slavery.

In communion there shall be continence.

In singleness there shall be prodigality.

Communion is depth.

Singleness is height.

Right measure in communion purifieth and preserveth.

Right measure in singleness purifieth and increaseth.

Communion giveth us warmth, singleness giveth us light.

Sermo VI

The daemon of sexuality approacheth our soul as a serpent. It is half human and appeareth as thought-desire.

The daemon of spirituality descendeth into our soul as the white bird. It is half human and appeareth as desire-thought.

The serpent is an earthy soul, half daemonic, a spirit, and akin to the spirits of the dead. Thus too, like these, she swarmeth around in the things of earth, making us either to fear them or pricking us with intemperate desires. The serpent hath a nature like unto woman. She seeketh ever the company of the dead who are held by the spell of the earth, they who found not the way beyond that leadeth to singleness. The serpent is a whore. She wantoneth with the devil and with evil spirits; a mischievous tyrant and tormentor, ever seducing to evilest company. The white bird is a half-celestial soul of man. He bideth with the Mother, from time to time descending. The bird hath a nature like unto man, and is effective thought. He is chaste and solitary, a messenger of the Mother. He flieth high above earth. He commandeth singleness. He bringeth knowledge from the distant ones who went before and are perfected. He beareth our word above to the Mother. She intercedeth, she warneth, but against the gods she hath no power. She is a vessel of the sun. The serpent goeth below and with her cunning she lameth the phallic daemon, or else goadeth him on. She yieldeth up the too crafty thoughts of the earthy one, those thoughts which creep through every hole and cleave to all things with desirousness. The serpent, doubtless, willeth it not, yet she must be of use to us. She fleeth our grasp, thus showing us the way, which with our human wits we could not find.

With disdainful glance the dead spake: Cease this talk of gods and daemons and souls. At bottom this hath long been known to us.

Sermo VII

Yet when night was come the dead again approached with lamentable mien and said: There is yet one matter we forgot to mention. Teach us about man.

Man is a gateway, through which from the outer world of gods, daemons, and souls ye pass into the inner world; out of the greater into the smaller world. Small and transitory is man. Already is he behind you, and once again ye find yourselves in endless space, in the smaller or innermost infinity. At immeasurable distance standeth one single Star in the zenith.

This is the one god of this one man. This is his world, his pleroma, his divinity.

In this world is man Abraxas, the creator and the destroyer of his own world.

This Star is the god and the goal of man.

This is his one guiding god. In him goeth man to his rest. Toward him goeth the long journey of the soul after death. In him shineth forth as light all that man bringeth back from the greater world. To this one god man shall pray.

Prayer increaseth the light of the Star. It casteth a bridge over death. It prepareth life for the smaller world and assuageth the hopeless desires of the greater.

When the greater world waxeth cold, burneth the Star.

Between man and his one god there standeth nothing, so long as man can turn away his eyes from the flaming spectacle of Abraxas.

Man here, god there.

Weakness and nothingness here, there eternally creative power.

Here nothing but darkness and chilling moisture.

There wholly sun.

Whereupon the dead were silent and ascended like the smoke above the herdsman's fire, who through the night kept watch over his flock.

ANAGRAMMA:

> NAHTRIHECCUNDE
> GAHINNEVERAHTUNIN
> ZEHGESSURKLACH
> ZUNNUS.

(Translated by H. G. Baynes)

Glossary

Amplification. Elaboration and clarification of a dream-image by means of directed association (*q.v.*) and of parallels from the human sciences (symbology, mythology, mysticism, folklore, history of religion, ethnology, etc.).

Anima and Animus. Personification of the feminine nature of a man's unconscious and the masculine nature of a woman's. This psychological bisexuality is a reflection of the biological fact that it is the larger number of male (or female) genes which is the decisive factor in the determination of sex. The smaller number of contrasexual genes seems to produce a corresponding contrasexual character, which usually remains unconscious. Anima and animus manifest themselves most typically in personified form as figures in dreams and fantasies ("dream girl," "dream lover"), or in the irrationalities of a man's *feeling* and a woman's *thinking*. As regulators of behavior they are two of the most influential archetypes (*q.v.*).

C. G. JUNG: "Every man carries within him the eternal image of woman, not the image of this or that particular woman, but a definitive feminine image. This image is fundamentally unconscious, an hereditary factor of primordial origin engraved in the living organic system of the man, an imprint or 'archetype' [*q.v.*] of all the ancestral experiences of the female, a deposit, as it were, of all the impressions ever made by woman . . . Since this image is unconscious, it is always unconsciously projected upon the person of the beloved, and is one of the chief reasons for passionate attraction or aversion."

(*The Development of Personality*, CW 17, p. 198)

"In its primary 'unconscious' form the animus is a compound of spontaneous, unpremeditated opinions which exercise a powerful influence on the woman's emotional life, while the anima is similarly compounded of feelings which thereafter influence or distort the man's understanding ('she has turned his head'). Consequently the animus likes to project itself upon 'intellectuals' and all kinds of 'heroes,' including tenors, artists, sporting celebrities, etc. The anima has a predilection for everything that is unconscious, dark, equivocal, and unrelated in woman, and also for her vanity, frigidity, helplessness, and so forth."

(*The Practice of Psychotherapy*, CW 16, par. 521)

". . . no man can converse with an animus for five minutes without becoming the victim of his own anima. Anyone who still had enough sense of humour to listen objectively to the ensuing dialogue would be staggered by the vast number of commonplaces, misapplied truisms, clichés from newspapers and novels, shop-soiled platitudes of every description interspersed with vulgar abuse and brain-splitting lack of logic. It is a dialogue which, irrespective of its participants, is repeated millions and millions of times in all languages of the world and always remains essentially the same."   (*Aion*, CW 9, ii, p. 15)

"The natural function of the animus (as well as of the anima) is to remain in [their] place between individual consciousness and the collective unconscious [*q.v.*]; exactly as the persona [*q.v.*] is a sort of stratum between the ego-consciousness and the objects of the external world. The animus and the anima should function as a bridge, or a door, leading to the images of the collective unconscious, as the persona should be a sort of bridge into the world."

(Unpublished Seminar Notes. "Visions" I, p. 116)

Archetype. C. G. JUNG: "The concept of the archetype . . . is derived from the repeated observation that, for instance, the myths and fairytales of world literature contain definite motifs which crop up everywhere. We meet these same motifs in the fantasies, dreams, deliria, and delusions of individuals living today. These typical images and associations are what I call archetypal ideas. The more vivid they are, the more they will be coloured by particularly strong feeling-tones . . . They impress, influence, and fascinate us. They have their origin in the archetype, which in itself is an irrepresentable, unconscious, pre-existent form that seems to be part of the inherited structure of the psyche and can therefore manifest itself spontaneously anywhere, at any time. Because of its instinctual nature, the archetype underlies the feeling-toned complexes [*q.v.*] and shares their autonomy."   (*Civilization in Transition*, CW 10, par. 847)

"Again and again I encounter the mistaken notion that an archetype is determined in regard to its content, in other words that it is a kind of unconscious idea (if such an expression be admissible). It is necessary to point out once more that archetypes are not determined as regards their content, but only as regards their form and then only to a very limited degree. A primordial image [*q.v.*] is determined as to its content only when it has become conscious and is therefore filled out with the material of conscious experience. Its form, however, . . . might perhaps be compared to the axial system of a crystal, which, as it were, preforms the crystalline structure in the mother liquid, although it has no material existence of its own. This first appears according to the specific way in which the ions and molecules aggregate. The archetype in itself is empty and purely formal, nothing but a *facultas praeformandi*, a possibility of representation which is given *a priori*. The representations themselves are not inherited, only the forms, and in that respect they correspond in every way to the instincts, which are also determined in form only. The existence of the instincts can no more be proved than the existence of the archetypes, so long as they do not manifest themselves concretely."

(*The Archetypes and the Collective Unconscious,* CW 9, i, pp. 79 f.)

". . . it seems to me probable that the real nature of the archetype is not capable of being made conscious, that it is transcendent, on which account I call it psychoid [*q.v.*]."

(*The Structure and Dynamics of the Psyche,* CW 8, p. 213)

Association. The linking of ideas, perceptions, etc. according to similarity, coexistence, opposition, and causal dependence. *Free association* in Freudian dream interpretation: spontaneous ideas occurring to the dreamer, which need not necessarily refer to the dream situation. *Directed or controlled association* in Jungian dream interpretation: spontaneous ideas which proceed from a given dream situation and constantly relate to it.

Association test. Methods for discovering complexes (*q.v.*) by measuring the reaction time and interpreting the answers to given stimulus words. *Complex-indicators:* prolonged reaction time, faults, or the idiosyncratic quality of the answers when the stimulus words touch on complexes which the subject wishes to hide cr of which he is not conscious.

Complex. c. g. jung: "Complexes are psychic fragments which have split off owing to traumatic influences or certain incompatible tendencies. As the association experiments prove, complexes interfere with the intentions of the will and disturb the conscious performance; they produce disturbances of memory and blockages in the flow of associations [*q.v.*]; they appear and disappear according to their own laws;

they can temporarily obsess consciousness, or influence speech and action in an unconscious way. In a word, complexes behave like independent beings, a fact especially evident in abnormal states of mind. In the voices heard by the insane they even take on a personal ego-character like that of the spirits who manifest themselves through automatic writing and similar techniques."

(*The Structure and Dynamics of the Psyche*, CW 8, p. 121)

Consciousness. C. G. JUNG: "When one reflects upon what consciousness really is, one is profoundly impressed by the extreme wonder of the fact that an event which takes place outside in the cosmos simultaneously produces an internal image, that it takes place, so to speak, inside as well, which is to say: becomes conscious."

(Basel Seminar, privately printed, 1934, p. 1)

"For indeed our consciousness does not create itself—it wells up from unknown depths. In childhood it awakens gradually, and all through life it wakes each morning out of the depths of sleep from an unconscious condition. It is like a child that is born daily out of the primordial womb of the unconscious."

(*Psychology and Religion: West and East*, CW 11, pp. 569 f.)

Dream. C. G. JUNG: "The dream is a little hidden door in the innermost and most secret recesses of the psyche, opening into that cosmic night which was psyche long before there was any ego-consciousness, and which will remain psyche no matter how far our ego-consciousness may extend . . . All consciousness separates; but in dreams we put on the likeness of that more universal, truer, more eternal man dwelling in the darkness of primordial night. There he is still the whole, and the whole is in him, indistinguishable from nature and bare of all egohood. Out of these all-uniting depths arises the dream, be it never so childish, grotesque, and immoral."

(*Civilization in Transition*, CW 10, pars. 304 f.)

Extraversion. Attitude-type characterized by concentration of interest on the external object. See *Introversion*.

God-image. A term derived from the Church Fathers, according to whom the *imago Dei* is imprinted on the human soul. When such an image is spontaneously produced in dreams, fantasies, visions, etc. it is, from the psychological point of view, a symbol of the self (*q.v.*), of psychic wholeness.

C. G. JUNG: "It is only through the psyche that we can establish that God acts upon us, but we are unable to distinguish whether these actions emanate from God or from the unconscious. We cannot tell whether God and the unconscious are two different entities. Both are border-line concepts for transcendental contents. But empirically it can be established, with a sufficient degree of probability, that there is in the unconscious an archetype of wholeness which manifests itself spontaneously in dreams, etc., and a tendency, independent of the conscious will, to relate other archetypes to this centre. Consequently, it does not seem improbable that the archetype produces a symbolism which has always characterized and expressed the Deity . . . The God-image does not coincide with the unconscious as such, but with a special content of it, namely the archetype of the self. It is this archetype from which we can no longer distinguish the God-image empirically."

(*Psychology and Religion: West and East,* CW 11, pp. 468 f.)

"One can, then, explain the God-image . . . as a reflection of the self, or, conversely, explain the self as an *imago Dei* in man."

(*Ibid.,* p. 190)

Hierosgamos. Sacred or spiritual marriage, union of archetypal figures in the rebirth mysteries of antiquity and also in alchemy. Typical examples are the representation of Christ and the Church as bridegroom and bride (*sponsus et sponsa*) and the alchemical conjunction of sun and moon.

Individuation. C. G. JUNG: "I use the term 'individuation' to denote the process by which a person becomes a psychological 'in-dividual,' that is, a separate, indivisible unity or 'whole.'"

(*The Archetypes and the Collective Unconscious,* CW 9, i, p. 275)

"Individuation means becoming a single, homogeneous being, and, in so far as 'individuality' embraces our innermost, last, and incomparable uniqueness, it also implies becoming one's own self. We could therefore translate individuation as 'coming to selfhood' or 'self-realization.'" (*Two Essays on Analytical Psychology,* CW 7, par. 266)

"But again and again I note that the individuation process is confused with the coming of the ego into consciousness and that the ego is in consequence identified with the self, which naturally produces a hopeless conceptual muddle. Individuation is then nothing but ego-centredness and autoeroticism. But the self comprises infinitely more than a mere ego . . . It is as much one's self, and all other selves, as the ego. Individuation does not shut one out from the world, but gathers the world to oneself."

(*The Structure and Dynamics of the Psyche*, CW 8, p. 226)

Inflation. Expansion of the personality beyond its proper limits by identification with the persona (*q.v.*) or with an archetype (*q.v.*), or in pathological cases with a historical or religious figure. It produces an exaggerated sense of one's self-importance and is usually compensated by feelings of inferiority.

Introversion. Attitude-type characterized by orientation in life through subjective psychic contents. See *Extraversion*.

Mana. Melanesian word for extraordinarily effective power emanating from a human being, object, action, or event, or from supernatural beings and spirits. Also health, prestige, power to work magic and to heal. A primitive concept of psychic energy.

Mandala (Sanskrit). Magic circle. In Jung, symbol of the center, the goal, or the self (*q.v.*) as psychic totality; self-representation of a psychic process of centering; production of a new center of personality. This is symbolically represented by the circle, the square, or the quaternity (*q.v.*), by symmetrical arrangements of the number four and its multiples. In Lamism and Tantric Yoga the mandala is an instrument of contemplation (*yantra*), seat and birthplace of the gods. *Disturbed mandala:* Any form that deviates from the circle, square, or equal-armed cross, or whose basic number is not four or its multiples.

C. G. JUNG: "Mandala means a circle, more especially a magic circle, and this form of symbol is not only to be found all through the East, but also among us; mandalas are amply represented in the Middle Ages. The specifically Christian ones come from the earlier Middle Ages. Most of them show Christ in the centre, with the four evangelists, or their symbols, at the cardinal points. This conception must be a very ancient one because Horus was represented with his four sons in the same way by the Egyptians . . . For the most part, the mandala form is that of a flower, cross, or wheel, with a distinct tendency toward four as the basis of the structure."

(Commentary to *Secret of the Golden Flower*, CW 13, par. 31, mod.)

"Mandalas . . . usually appear in situations of psychic confusion and perplexity. The archetype thereby constellated represents a pattern of order which, like a psychological 'view-finder' marked with a cross or circle divided into four, is superimposed on the psychic chaos so that each content falls into place and the weltering confusion is held together by the protective circle . . . At the same time they are *yantras,* instruments with whose help the order is brought into being." (*Civilization in Transition,* CW 10, par. 803)

Numinosum. Rudolf Otto's term (in his *Idea of the Holy*) for the inexpressible, mysterious, terrifying, directly experienced and pertaining only to the divinity.

Persona. Originally, the mask worn by an actor.
    c. g. jung: "The persona . . . is the individual's system of adaptation to, or the manner he assumes in dealing with, the world. Every calling or profession, for example, has its own characteristic persona. . . . Only, the danger is that [people] become identical with their personas—the professor with his text-book, the tenor with his voice. . . . One could say, with a little exaggeration, that the persona is that which in reality one is not, but which oneself as well as others think one is."
(*The Archetypes and the Collective Unconscious,* CW 9, i, pp. 122 f.)

Primordial image. (Jakob Burckhardt) Term originally used by Jung for *archetype* (*q.v.*).

Psychoid. "Soul-like" or "quasi-psychic."
    c. g. jung: ". . . the collective unconscious . . . represents a psyche that . . . cannot be directly perceived or 'represented,' in contrast to the perceptible psychic phenomena, and on account of its 'irrepresentable' nature I have called it 'psychoid.'"
(*The Structure and Dynamics of the Psyche,* CW 8, p. 436)

Quaternity. c. g. jung: "The quaternity is an archetype of almost universal occurrence. It forms the logical basis for any whole judgment. If one wishes to pass such a judgment, it must have this fourfold aspect. For instance, if you want to describe the horizon as a whole, you name the four quarters of heaven. . . . There are always four elements, four prime qualities, four colours, four castes, four ways of spiritual development, etc. So, too, there are four aspects of psychological orientation . . . In order to orient ourselves, we must have a function which ascertains that something is there (sensation); a second function which established *what* is is (thinking); a third function which states whether it suits us or not, whether we wish to accept it or not (feeling), and a fourth function which indicates where it came from and where it is going (intuition). When this has been done, there is nothing more to say. . . . The ideal of completeness is the circle or sphere, but its natural minimal division is a quaternity."

(*Psychology and Religion: West and East,* CW 11, p. 167)

A quaternity or quaternion often has a 3 + 1 structure, in that one of the terms composing it occupies an exceptional position or has a nature unlike that of the others. (For instance three of the symbols of the Evangelists are animals and that of the fourth, of St. Luke, is an angel.) This is the "Fourth," which, added to the other three, makes them "One," symbolizing totality. In analytical psychology often the "inferior" function (i.e., that function which is not at the conscious disposal of the subject) represents the "Fourth," and its integration into consciousness is one of the major tasks of the process of individuation (*q.v.*).

Self. The central archetype (*q.v.*); the archetype of order; the totality of the personality. Symbolized by circle, square, quaternity (*q.v.*), child, mandala (*q.v.*), etc.

C. G. JUNG: ". . . the self is a quantity that is supraordinate to the conscious ego. It embraces not only the conscious but also the unconscious psyche, and is therefore, so to speak, a personality which we *also* are. . . . There is little hope of our ever being able to reach even approximate consciousness of the self, since however much we may make conscious there will always exist an indeterminate and indeterminable amount of unconscious material which belongs to the totality of the self."

(*Two Essays on Analytical Psychology,* CW 7, par. 274)

"The self is not only the centre but also the whole circumference which embraces both conscious and unconscious; it is the centre of this totality, just as the ego is the centre of consciousness."

(*Psychology and Alchemy,* CW 12, par. 44)

". . . the self is our life's goal, for it is the completest expression of that fateful combination we call individuality . . ."

(*Two Essays on Analytical Psychology,* CW 7, par. 404)

Shadow. The inferior part of the personality; sum of all personal and collective psychic elements which, because of their incompatibility with the chosen conscious attitude, are denied expression in life and therefore coalesce into a relatively autonomous "splinter personality" with contrary tendencies in the unconscious. The shadow behaves compensatorily to consciousness; hence its effects can be positive as well as negative. In dreams, the shadow figure is always of the same sex as the dreamer.

C. G. JUNG: "The shadow personifies everything that the subject refuses to acknowledge about himself and yet is always thrusting itself upon him directly or indirectly—for instance, inferior traits of character and other incompatible tendencies."

(*The Archetypes and the Collective Unconscious,* CW 9, i, pp. 284 f.)

". . . the shadow [is] that hidden, repressed, for the most part inferior and guilt-laden personality whose ultimate ramifications reach back into the realm of our animal ancestors and so comprise the whole historical aspect of the unconscious. . . . If it has been believed hitherto that the human shadow was the source of all evil, it can now be ascertained on closer investigation that the unconscious man, that is, his shadow, does not consist only of morally reprehensible tendencies, but also displays a number of good qualities, such as normal instincts, appropriate reactions, realistic insights, creative impulses, etc."

(*Aion,* CW 9, ii, p. 266)

Soul. C. G. JUNG: "If the human [soul] is anything, it must be of unimaginable complexity and diversity, so that it cannot possibly be approached through a mere psychology of instinct. I can only gaze with wonder and awe at the depths and heights of our psychic nature. Its non-spatial universe conceals an untold abundance of images which have accumulated over millions of years of living development and become fixed in the organism. My consciousness is like an eye that penetrates to the most distant spaces, yet it is the psychic non-ego that fills them with nonspatial images. And these images are not pale shadows, but tremendously powerful psychic factors. . . . Beside this picture I would like to place the spectacle of the starry heavens at night, for the only equivalent of the universe within is the universe without; and just as I reach this world through the medium of the body, so I reach that world through the medium of the psyche."

(*Freud and Psychoanalysis,* CW 4, pp. 331 f.)

"It would be blasphemy to assert that God can manifest Himself everywhere save only in the human soul. Indeed the very intimacy of the relationship between God and the soul automatically precludes any devaluation of the latter. It would be going perhaps too far to speak of an affinity; but at all events the soul must contain in itself the faculty of relation to God, i.e. a correspondence, otherwise a connection could never come about. This correspondence is, in psychological terms, the archetype of the God-image [*q.v.*]."

(*Psychology and Alchemy,* CW 12, par. 11)

Synchronicity. A term coined by Jung to designate the meaningful coincidence or equivalence (*a*) of a psychic and a physical state or event which have no causal relationship to one another. Such synchronistic phenomena occur, for instance, when an inwardly perceived event (dream, vision, premonition, etc.) is seen to have a correspondence in external reality: the inner image of premonition has "come true"; (*b*) of similar or identical thoughts, dreams, etc. occurring at the same time in different places. Neither the one nor the other coincidence can be explained by causality, but seems to be connected primarily with activated archetypal processes in the unconscious.

C. G. JUNG: "My preoccupation with the psychology of unconscious processes long ago compelled me to look about for another principle of explanation, because the causality principle seemed to me inadequate to explain certain remarkable phenomena of the psychology of the unconscious. Thus I found that there are psychic parallelisms which cannot be related to each other causally, but which must be connected through another principle, namely the contingency of events. This connection of events seemed to me essentially given by the fact of their relative simultaneity, hence the term 'synchronistic.' It seems, indeed, as though time, far from being an abstraction, is a concrete continuum which contains qualities or basic conditions that manifest themselves simultaneously in different places through parallelisms that cannot be explained causally, as, for example, in cases of the simultaneous occurrence of identical thoughts, symbols, or psychic states." ("Richard Wilhelm: In Memoriam," CW 15, par. 81, mod.)

"I chose this term because the simultaneous occurrence of two meaningfully but not causally connected events seemed to me an essential criterion. I am therefore using the general concept of synchronicity in the special sense of a coincidence in time of two or more causally unrelated events which have the same or a similar meaning, in contrast to 'synchronism,' which simply means the simultaneous occurrence of two events."

(*The Structure and Dynamics of the Psyche,* CW 8, p. 441)

"Synchronicity is no more baffling or mysterious than the discontinuities of physics. It is only the ingrained belief in the sovereign power of causality that creates intellectual difficulties and makes it appear unthinkable that causeless events exist or could ever occur. . . . Meaningful coincidences are thinkable as pure chance. But the more they multiply and the greater and more exact the correspondence is, the more their probability sinks and their unthinkability increases, until they can no longer be regarded as pure chance but, for lack of a causal explanation, have to be thought of as meaningful arrangements. . . . Their 'inexplicability' is not due to the fact that the cause is unknown, but to the fact that a cause is not even thinkable in intellectual terms." *(Ibid.,* pp. 518 f.)

Unconscious, the. C. G. JUNG: "Theoretically, no limits can be set to the field of consciousness, since it is capable of indefinite extension. Empirically, however, it always finds its limit when it comes up against the *unknown.* This consists of everything we do not know, which, therefore, is not related to the ego as the centre of the field of consciousness. The unknown falls into two groups of objects: those which are outside and can be experienced by the senses, and those which are inside and are experienced immediately. The first group comprises the unknown in the outer world; the second the unknown in the inner world. We call this latter territory the *unconscious.*"

(Aion, CW 9, ii, p. 3)

". . . everything of which I know, but of which I am not at the moment thinking; everything of which I was once conscious but have now forgotten; everything perceived by my senses, but not noted by my conscious mind; everything which, involuntarily and without paying attention to it, I feel, think, remember, want, and do; all the future things that are taking shape in me and will sometime come to consciousness: all this is the content of the unconscious."

(The Structure and Dynamics of the Psyche, CW 8, p. 185)

"Besides these we must include all more or less intentional repressions of painful thoughts and feelings. I call the sum of all these contents the 'personal unconscious.' But, over and above that, we also find in the unconscious qualities that are not individually acquired but are inherited, e.g., instincts as impulses to carry out actions from necessity, without conscious motivation. In this 'deeper' stratum we also find the . . . archetypes . . . The instincts and archetypes together form the 'collective unconscious.' I call it 'collective' because, unlike the personal unconscious, it is not made up of individual and more or less unique contents but of those which are universal and of regular occurrence." (*Ibid.*, pp. 133 f.)

"The first group comprises contents which are integral components of the individual personality and therefore could just as well be conscious; the second group forms, as it were, an omnipresent, unchanging, and everywhere identical *quality or substrate of the psyche per se.*" (*Aion*, CW 9, ii, p. 7)

"The deeper 'layers' of the psyche lose their individual uniqueness as they retreat farther and farther into darkness. 'Lower down,' that is to say as they approach the autonomous functional systems, they become increasingly collective until they are universalized and extinguished in the body's materiality, i.e., in chemical substances. The body's carbon is simply carbon. Hence 'at bottom' the psyche is simply 'world.'"

(*The Archetypes and the Collective Unconscious*, CW 9, i, p. 173)

The Collected Works of C. G. Jung

The publication of the first complete collected edition, in English, of the works of C. G. Jung has been undertaken by Routledge and Kegan Paul, Ltd., in England and by Bollingen Foundation in the United States. Sir Herbert Read, Dr. Michael Fordham, Dr. Gerhard Adler, and William McGuire compose the Editorial Committee; the translator is R. F. C. Hull. Since 1967, Princeton University Press has been the American publisher.

In the following list, dates of original publication are given in parentheses (of original composition, in brackets). Multiple dates indicate revisions.

Dagger (†) denotes volumes in preparation.

1. PSYCHIATRIC STUDIES

On the Psychology and Pathology of So-Called Occult Phenomena (1902)
On Hysterical Misreading (1904)
Cryptomnesia (1905)
On Manic Mood Disorder (1903)
A Case of Hysterical Stupor in a Prisoner in Detention (1902)
On Simulated Insanity (1903)
A Medical Opinion on a Case of Simulated Insanity (1904)
A Third and Final Opinion on Two Contradictory Psychiatric Diagnoses (1906)
On the Psychological Diagnosis of Facts (1905)

2. EXPERIMENTAL RESEARCHES
TRANSLATED BY LEOPOLD STEIN
IN COLLABORATION WITH DIANA RIVIERE

Studies in Word Association (1904–7, 1910)
The Associations of Normal Subjects (by Jung and F. Riklin)
An Analysis of the Associations of an Epileptic

The Reaction-Time Ratio in the Association Experiment
Experimental Observations on the Faculty of Memory
Psychoanalysis and Association Experiments
The Psychological Diagnosis of Evidence
Association, Dream, and Hysterical Symptom
The Psychopathological Significance of the Association Experiment
Disturbances in Reproduction in the Association Experiment
The Association Method
The Family Constellation

Psychophysical Researches (1907–8)
On the Psychophysical Relations of the Association Experiment
Psychophysical Investigations with the Galvanometer and Pneumo-
    graph in Normal and Insane Individuals (by F. Peterson and
    Jung)
Further Investigations on the Galvanic Phenomenon and Respiration
    in Normal and Insane Individuals (by C. Ricksher and Jung)
Appendix: Statistical Details of Enlistment (1906); New Aspects of
    Criminal Psychology (1908); The Psychological Methods of
    Investigation Used in the Psychiatric Clinic of the University of
    Zurich (1910); On the Doctrine of Complexes ([1911] 1913); On
    the Psychological Diagnosis of Evidence (1937)

3. THE PSYCHOGENESIS OF MENTAL DISEASE

The Psychology of Dementia Praecox (1907)
The Content of the Psychoses (1908/1914)
On Psychological Understanding (1914)
A Criticism of Bleuler's Theory of Schizophrenic Negativism (1911)
On the Importance of the Unconscious in Psychopathology (1914)
On the Problem of Psychogenesis in Mental Disease (1919)
Mental Disease and the Psyche (1928)
On the Psychogenesis of Schizophrenia (1939)
Recent Thoughts on Schizophrenia (1957)
Schizophrenia (1958)

4. FREUD AND PSYCHOANALYSIS

Freud's Theory of Hysteria: A Reply to Aschaffenburg (1906)
The Freudian Theory of Hysteria (1908)
The Analysis of Dreams (1909)
A Contribution to the Psychology of Rumour (1910–11)

On the Significance of Number Dreams (1910–11)

Morton Prince, "Mechanism and Interpretation of Dreams": A Critical Review (1911)

On the Criticism of Psychoanalysis (1910)

Concerning Psychoanalysis (1912)

The Theory of Psychoanalysis (1913)

General Aspects of Psychoanalysis (1913)

Psychoanalysis and Neurosis (1916)

Some Crucial Points in Psychoanalysis: The Jung-Loÿ Correspondence (1914)

Prefaces to "Collected Papers on Analytical Psychology" (1916, 1917)

The Significance of the Father in the Destiny of the Individual (1909/1949)

Introduction to Kranefeldt's "Secret Ways of the Mind" (1930)

Freud and Jung: Contrasts (1929)

5. SYMBOLS OF TRANSFORMATION (1912/1952)

Original German version, *Wandlungen und Symbole der Libido*, 1912 (= *Psychology of the Unconscious*); present extensively revised version, 1952.

Appendix: The Miller Fantasies

6. PSYCHOLOGICAL TYPES (1921)

Appendix: Four Papers on Psychological Typology (1913, 1925, 1931, 1936)

7. TWO ESSAYS ON ANALYTICAL PSYCHOLOGY

On the Psychology of the Unconscious (1917/1926/1943)

The Relations between the Ego and the Unconscious (1928)

Appendices:

New Paths in Psychology (1912)

The Structure of the Unconscious (1916)

8. THE STRUCTURE AND DYNAMICS OF THE PSYCHE

On Psychic Energy (1928)

The Transcendent Function ([1916]/1957)

9. PART I
THE ARCHETYPES AND THE COLLECTIVE UNCONSCIOUS

9. PART II

AION: RESEARCHES INTO THE
PHENOMENOLOGY OF THE SELF (1951)

10. CIVILIZATION IN TRANSITION

The Role of the Unconscious (1918)
Mind and Earth (1927/1931)
Archaic Man (1931)
The Spiritual Problem of Modern Man (1928/1931)
The Love Problem of a Student (1928)
Woman in Europe (1927)
The Meaning of Psychology for Modern Man (1933/1934)
The State of Psychotherapy Today (1934)
Wotan (1936)
After the Catastrophe (1945)
The Fight with the Shadow (1946)
Epilogue to "Essays on Contemporary Events" (1946)
The Undiscovered Self (Present and Future) (1957)
Flying Saucers: A Modern Myth (1958)
A Psychological View of Conscience (1958)
Good and Evil in Analytical Psychology (1959)
Introduction to Wolff's "Studies in Jungian Psychology" (1959)
The Swiss Line in the European Spectrum (1928)
Reviews of Keyserling's "America Set Free" (1930) and "La Révolu-
    tion Mondiale" (1934)
Complications of American Psychology (1930)
The Dreamlike World of India (1939)
What India Can Teach Us (1939)

Appendix: Documents (1933–1938)

11. PSYCHOLOGY AND RELIGION:
WEST AND EAST

Western Religion
Psychology and Religion (The Terry Lectures) (1938/1940)
A Psychological Approach to the Dogma of the Trinity (1942/1948)
Transformation Symbolism in the Mass (1942/1954)

Forewords to White's "God and the Unconscious" and Werblowsky's
   "Lucifer and Prometheus" (1952)
Brother Klaus (1933)
Psychotherapists or the Clergy (1932)
Psychoanalysis and the Cure of Souls (1928)
Answer to Job (1952)

Eastern Religion
Psychological Commentaries on "The Tibetan Book of the Great
   Liberation" (1939) and "The Tibetan Book of the Dead" (1935/
   1953)
Yoga and the West (1936)
Foreword to Suzuki's "Introduction to Zen Buddhism" (1939)
The Psychology of Eastern Meditation (1943)
The Holy Men of India: Introduction to Zimmer's "Der Weg zum
   Selbst" (1944)
Foreword to the "I Ching" (1950)

12. PSYCHOLOGY AND ALCHEMY (1944)

Introduction to the Religious and Psychological Problems of Alchemy
Individual Dream Symbolism in Relation to Alchemy (1936)
Religious Ideas in Alchemy (1937)
Epilogue

13. ALCHEMICAL STUDIES

Commentary on "The Secret of the Golden Flower" (1929)
The Visions of Zosimos (1938/1954)
Paracelsus as a Spiritual Phenomenon (1942)
The Spirit Mercurius (1943/1948)
The Philosophical Tree (1945/1954)

14. MYSTERIUM CONIUNCTIONIS: AN INQUIRY INTO THE SEPARATION AND SYNTHESIS OF PSYCHIC OPPOSITES IN ALCHEMY (1955–56)

15. THE SPIRIT IN MAN, ART, AND LITERATURE

Paracelsus (1929)
Paracelsus the Physician (1941)
Sigmund Freud in His Historical Setting (1932)
In Memory of Sigmund Freud (1939)
Richard Wilhelm: In Memoriam (1930)
On the Relation of Analytical Psychology to Poetry (1922)
Psychology and Literature (1930/1950)
"Ulysses": A Monologue (1932)
Picasso (1932)

16. THE PRACTICE OF PSYCHOTHERAPY

General Problems of Psychotherapy
Principles of Practical Psychotherapy (1935)
What Is Psychotherapy? (1935)
Some Aspects of Modern Psychotherapy (1930)
The Aims of Psychotherapy (1931)
Problems of Modern Psychotherapy (1929)
Psychotherapy and a Philosophy of Life (1943)
Medicine and Psychotherapy (1945)
Psychotherapy Today (1945)
Fundamental Questions of Psychotherapy (1951)

Specific Problems of Psychotherapy
The Therapeutic Value of Abreaction (1921/1928)
The Practical Use of Dream-Analysis (1934)
Psychology of the Transference (1946)

Appendix: The Realities of Practical Psychotherapy [1937]

17. THE DEVELOPMENT OF PERSONALITY

Psychic Conflicts in a Child (1910/1946)
Introduction to Wickes's "Analyse der Kinderseele" (1927/1931)
Child Development and Education (1928)
Analytical Psychology and Education: Three Lectures (1926/1946)
The Gifted Child (1943)
The Significance of the Unconscious in Individual Education (1928)

The Development of Personality (1934)
Marriage as a Psychological Relationship (1925)

FINAL VOLUMES†

Posthumous and Other Miscellaneous Works
Bibliography of C. G. Jung's Writings
General Index to the Collected Works

Related Publications

C. G. JUNG: LETTERS, 1906–1950
Selected and edited by Gerhard Adler in collaboration with Aniela
Jaffé. 1972, Princeton University Press (*Bollingen Series* XCV).
(A second volume, 1951–1961, in preparation.)

C. G. JUNG: PSYCHOLOGICAL REFLECTIONS. A NEW ANTHOLOGY OF HIS
WRITINGS, 1905–1961
Selected and edited by Jolande Jacobi in collaboration with R. F. C.
Hull. 1970, Princeton University Press (*Bollingen Series* XXXI).

ANALYTICAL PSYCHOLOGY: ITS THEORY AND PRACTICE (THE TAVISTOCK
LECTURES)
By C. G. Jung. 1968, Pantheon Books; 1970, Vintage Books.

Index

411